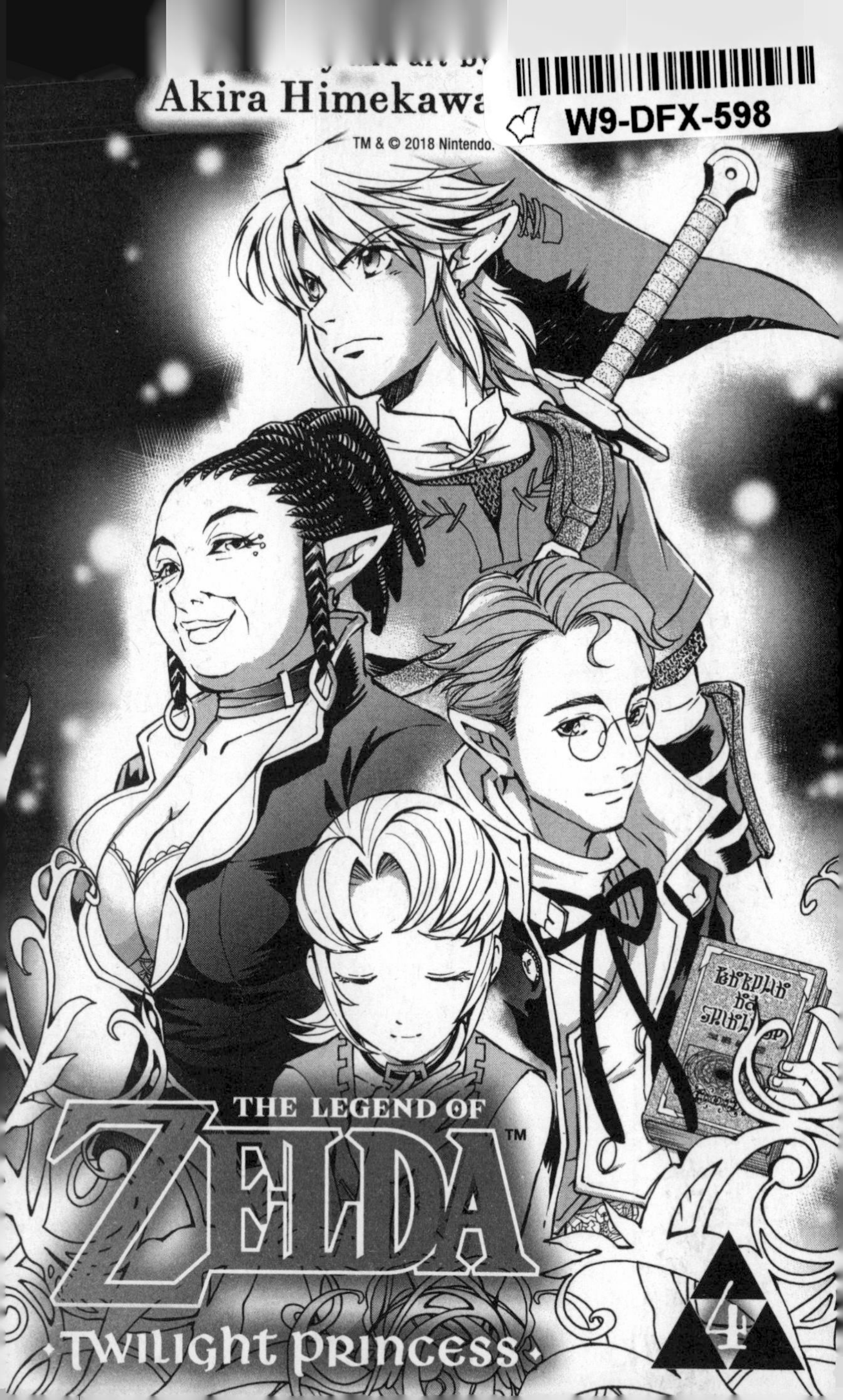
Akira Himekawa
TM & © 2018 Nintendo.
THE LEGEND OF
ZELDA™
·Twilight Princess·
4

THE LEGEND OF ZELDA

4

·TWILIGHT PRINCESS·

CONTENTS

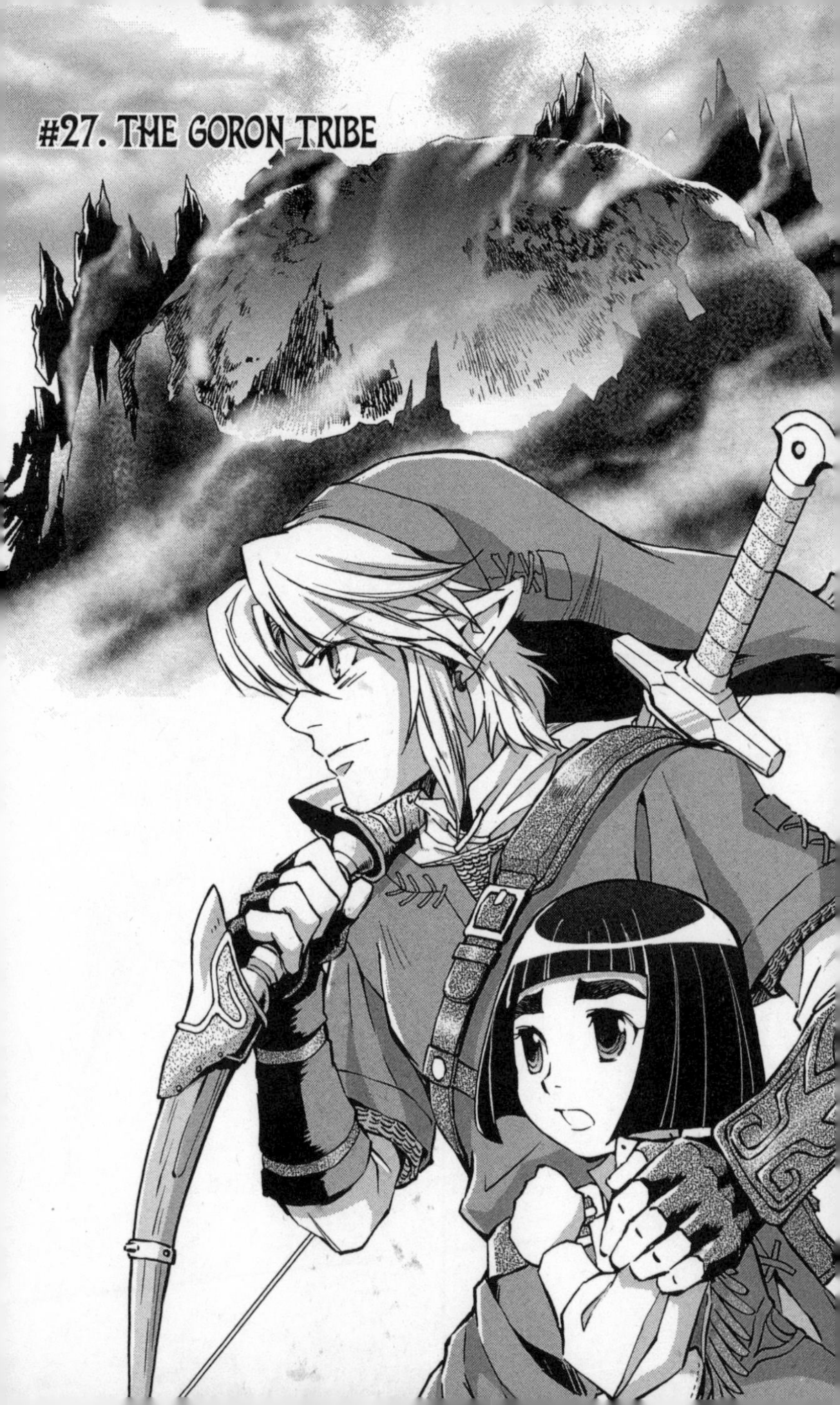
#27. THE GORON TRIBE

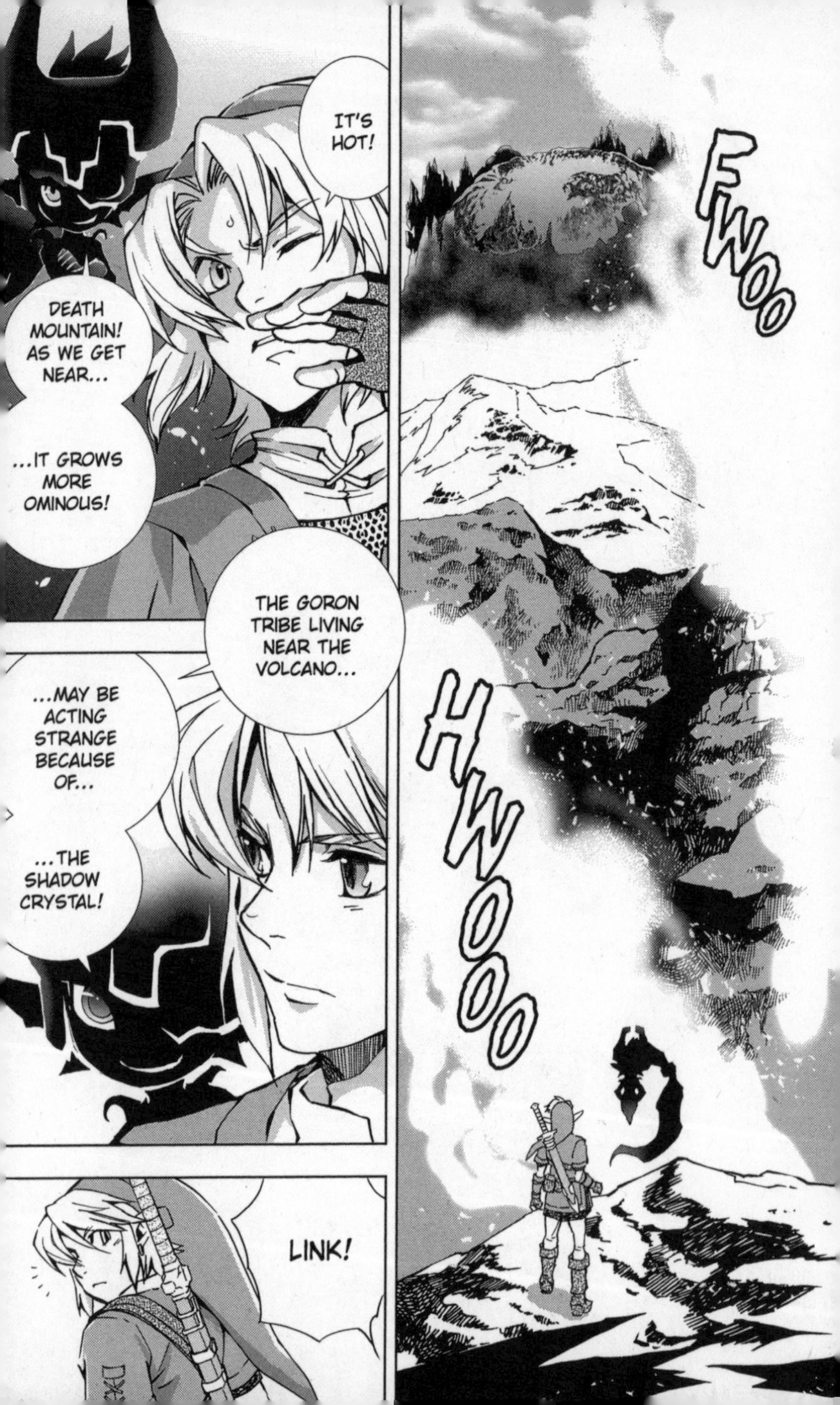
FWOO
HWOOO
IT'S HOT!
DEATH MOUNTAIN! AS WE GET NEAR...
...IT GROWS MORE OMINOUS!
THE GORON TRIBE LIVING NEAR THE VOLCANO...
...MAY BE ACTING STRANGE BECAUSE OF...
...THE SHADOW CRYSTAL!
LINK!

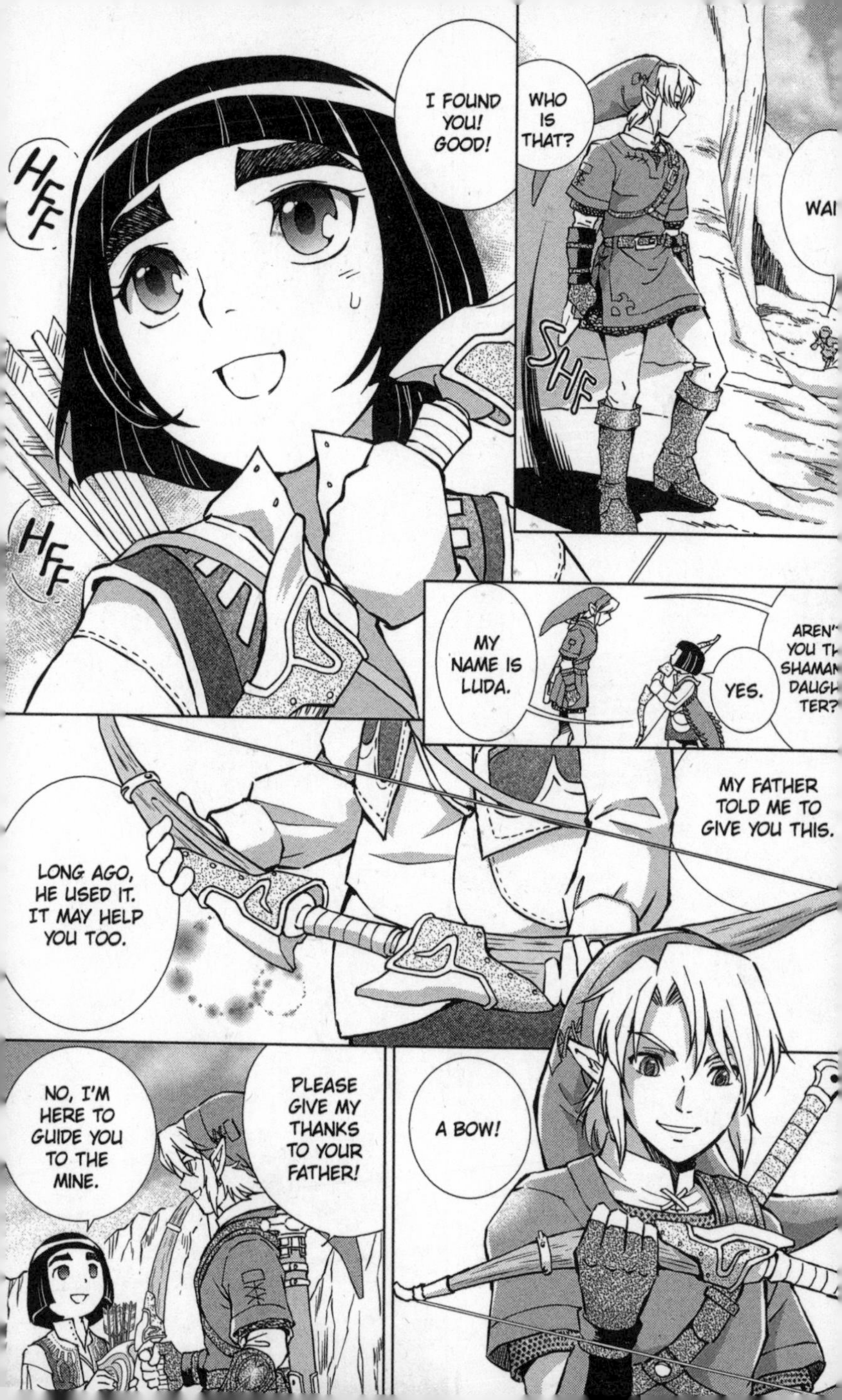
WAI
WHO IS THAT?
SHF
I FOUND YOU! GOOD!
HFF
HFF
AREN' YOU TH SHAMAN DAUGH TER?
YES.
MY NAME IS LUDA.
MY FATHER TOLD ME TO GIVE YOU THIS.
LONG AGO, HE USED IT. IT MAY HELP YOU TOO.
A BOW!
PLEASE GIVE MY THANKS TO YOUR FATHER!
NO, I'M HERE TO GUIDE YOU TO THE MINE.

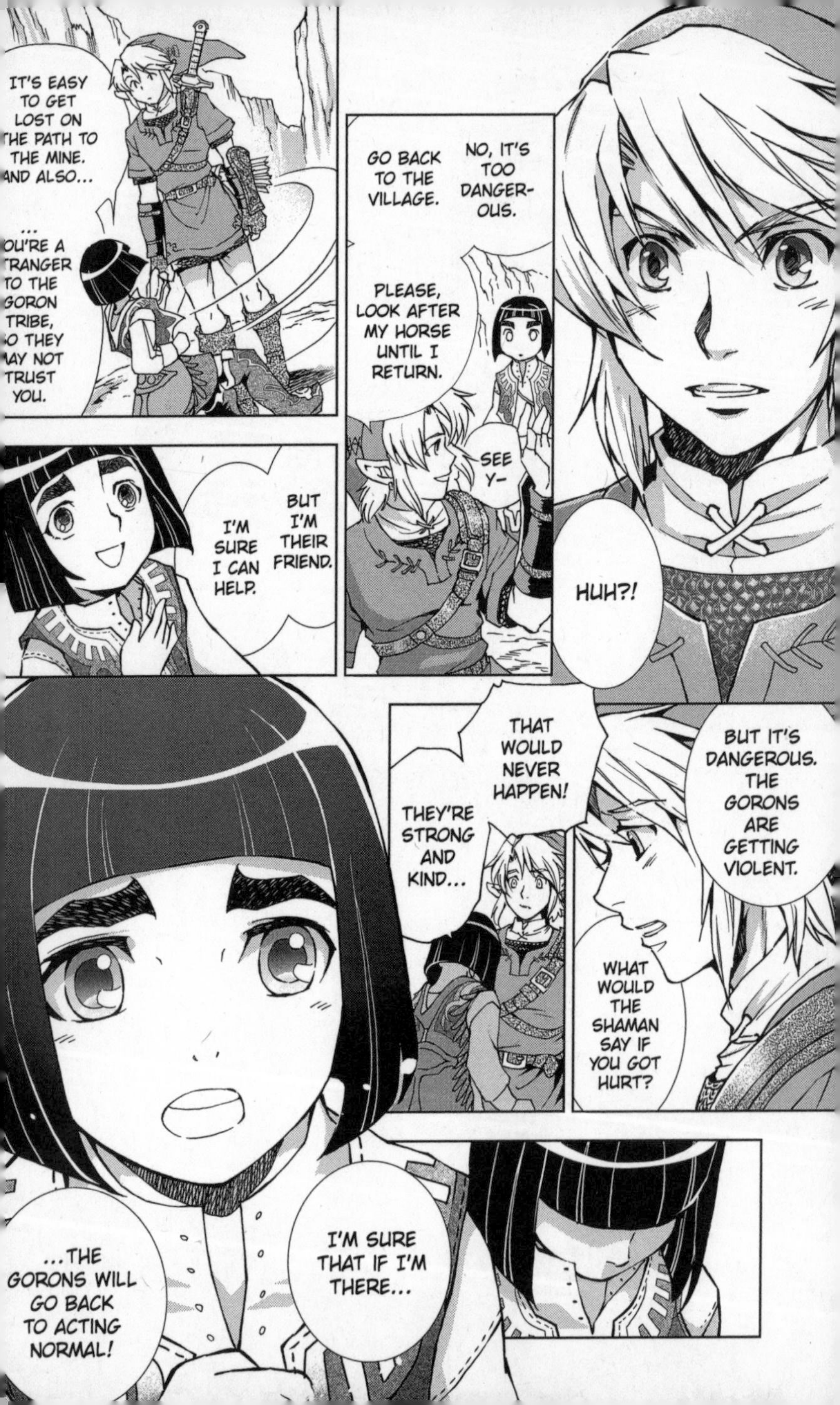
HUH?!
NO, IT'S TOO DANGER-OUS.
GO BACK TO THE VILLAGE.
PLEASE, LOOK AFTER MY HORSE UNTIL I RETURN.
SEE Y–
IT'S EASY TO GET LOST ON HE PATH TO THE MINE. ND ALSO...
... OU'RE A TRANGER TO THE ORON TRIBE, O THEY AY NOT TRUST YOU.
BUT I'M THEIR FRIEND.
I'M SURE I CAN HELP.
BUT IT'S DANGEROUS. THE GORONS ARE GETTING VIOLENT.
WHAT WOULD THE SHAMAN SAY IF YOU GOT HURT?
THAT WOULD NEVER HAPPEN!
THEY'RE STRONG AND KIND...
I'M SURE THAT IF I'M THERE...
...THE GORONS WILL GO BACK TO ACTING NORMAL!

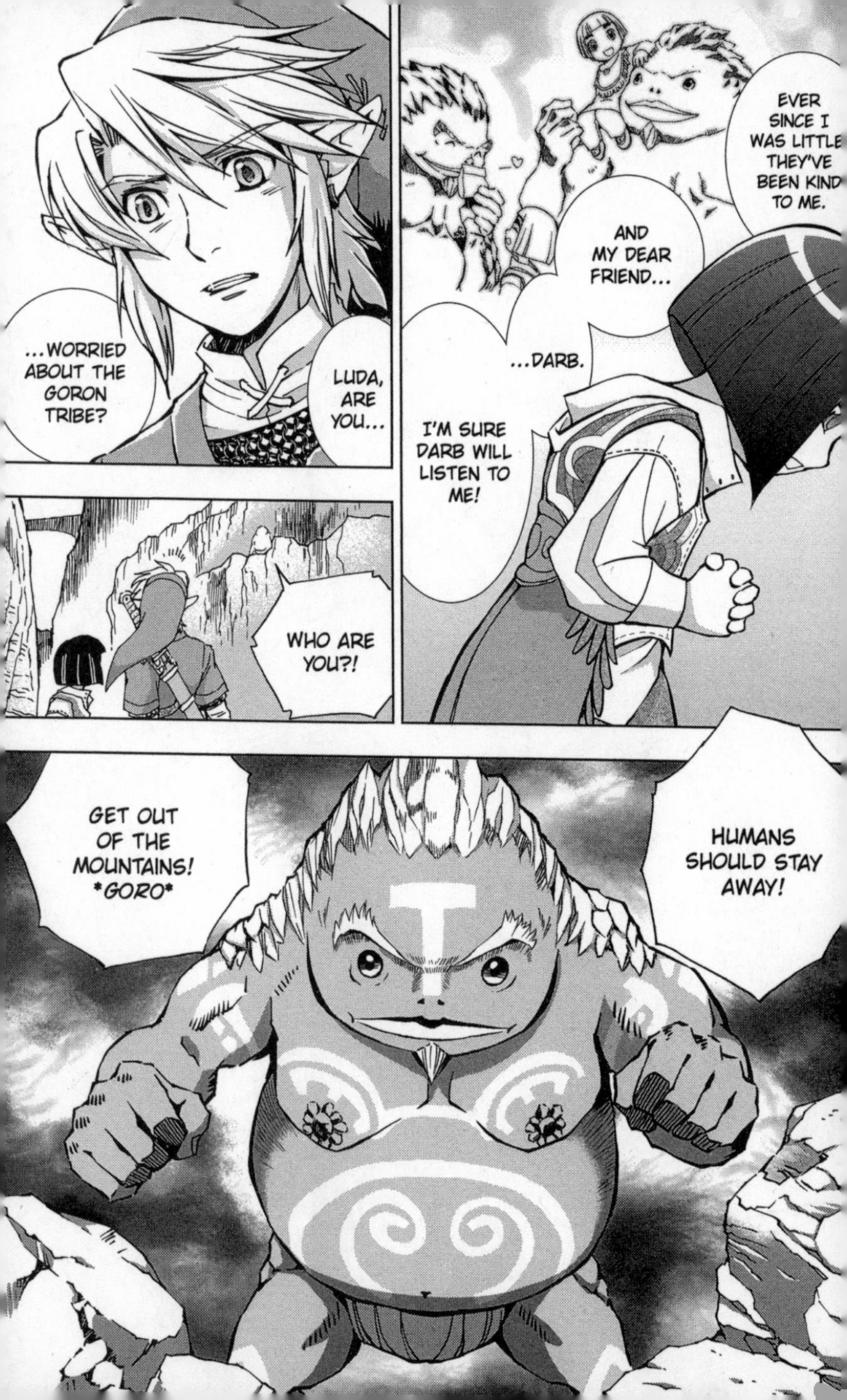
EVER SINCE I WAS LITTLE THEY'VE BEEN KIND TO ME.
AND MY DEAR FRIEND...
...DARB.
I'M SURE DARB WILL LISTEN TO ME!
LUDA, ARE YOU...
...WORRIED ABOUT THE GORON TRIBE?
WHO ARE YOU?!
HUMANS SHOULD STAY AWAY!
GET OUT OF THE MOUNTAINS! *GORO*

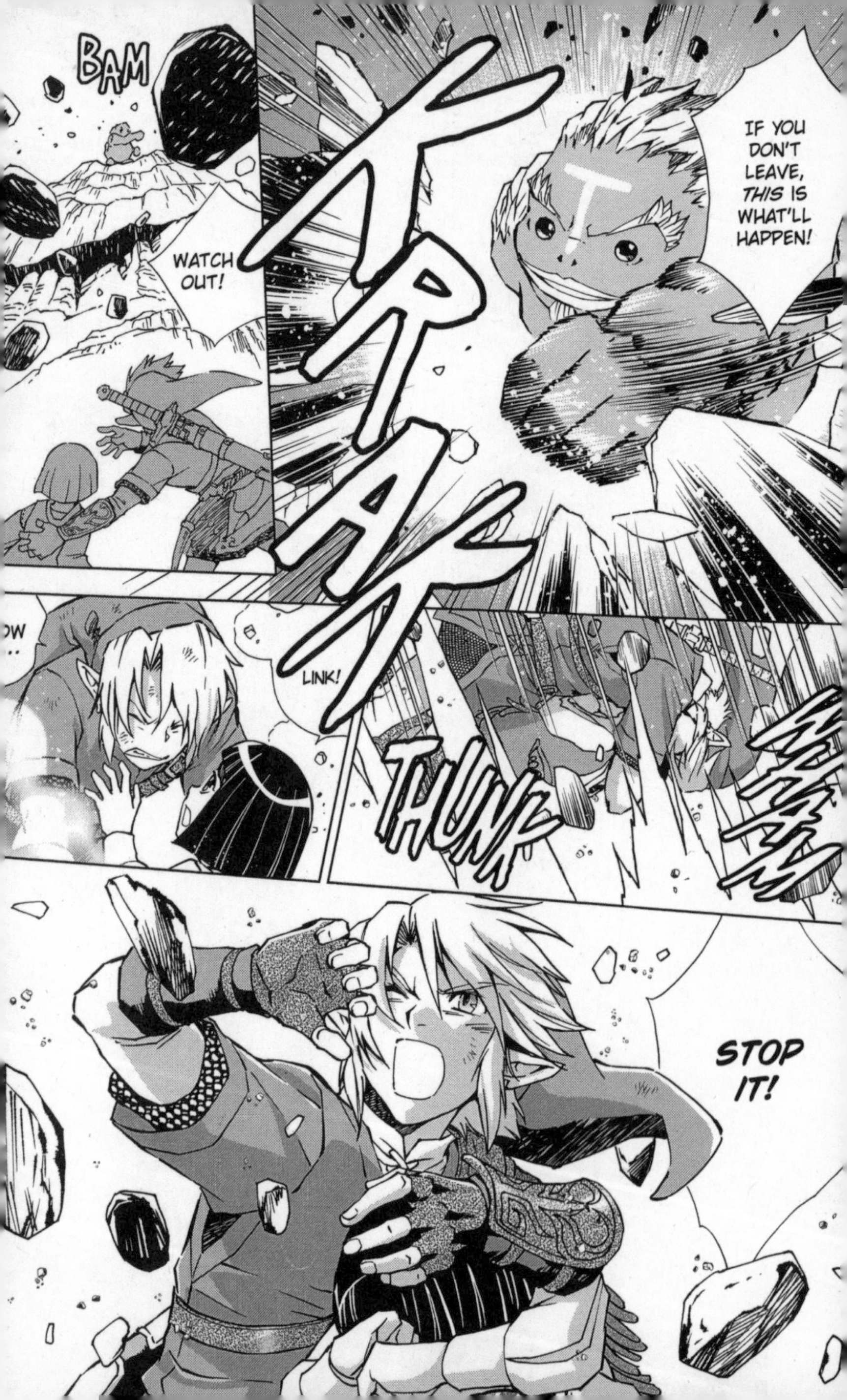
IF YOU DON'T LEAVE, *THIS* IS WHAT'LL HAPPEN!
KRAK
BAM
WATCH OUT!
WHAM
THUNK
LINK!
STOP IT!

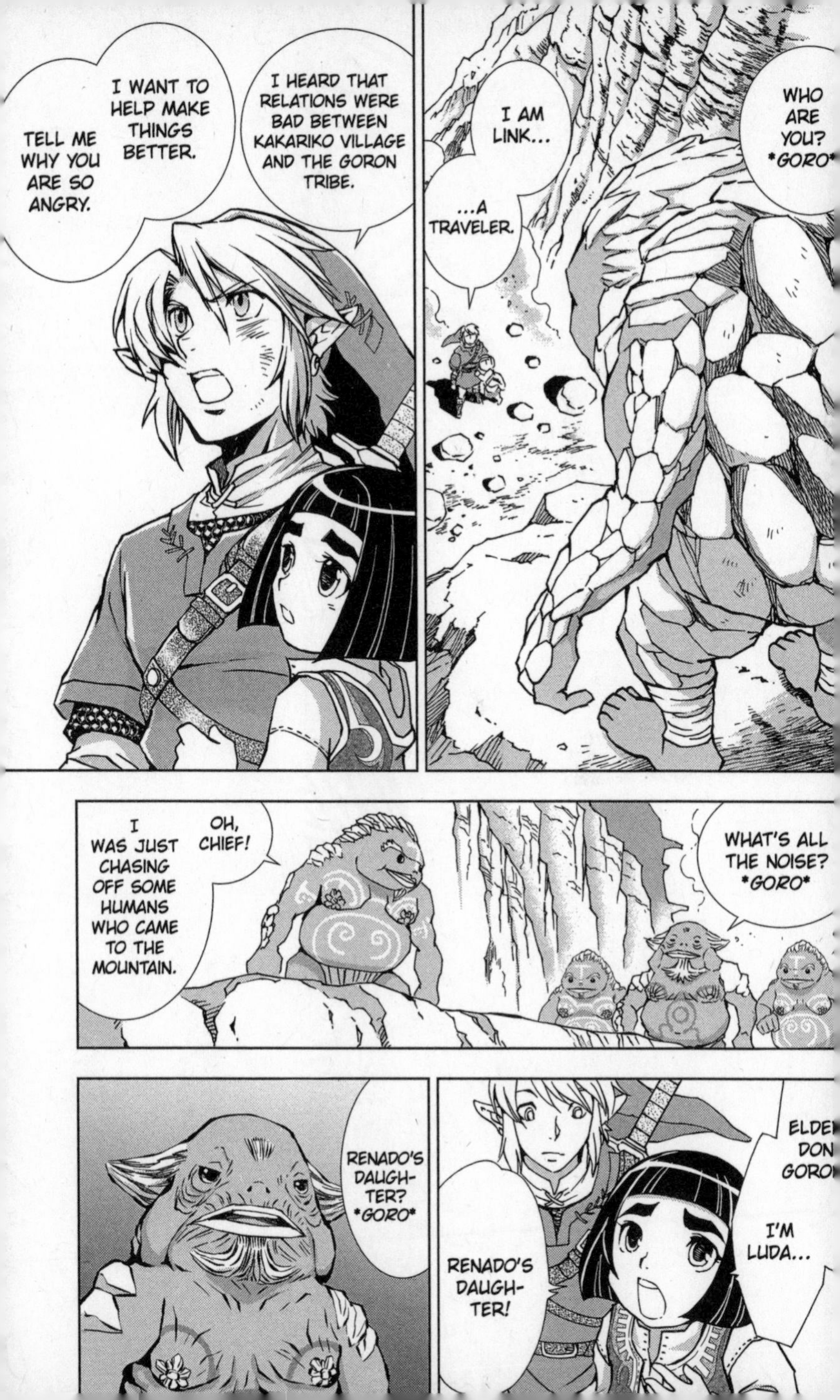
WHO ARE YOU? *GORO*
I AM LINK...
...A TRAVELER.
I HEARD THAT RELATIONS WERE BAD BETWEEN KAKARIKO VILLAGE AND THE GORON TRIBE.
I WANT TO HELP MAKE THINGS BETTER.
TELL ME WHY YOU ARE SO ANGRY.
WHAT'S ALL THE NOISE? *GORO*
OH, CHIEF!
I WAS JUST CHASING OFF SOME HUMANS WHO CAME TO THE MOUNTAIN.
ELDE DON GORO
I'M LUDA...
RENADO'S DAUGHTER!
RENADO'S DAUGHTER? *GORO*

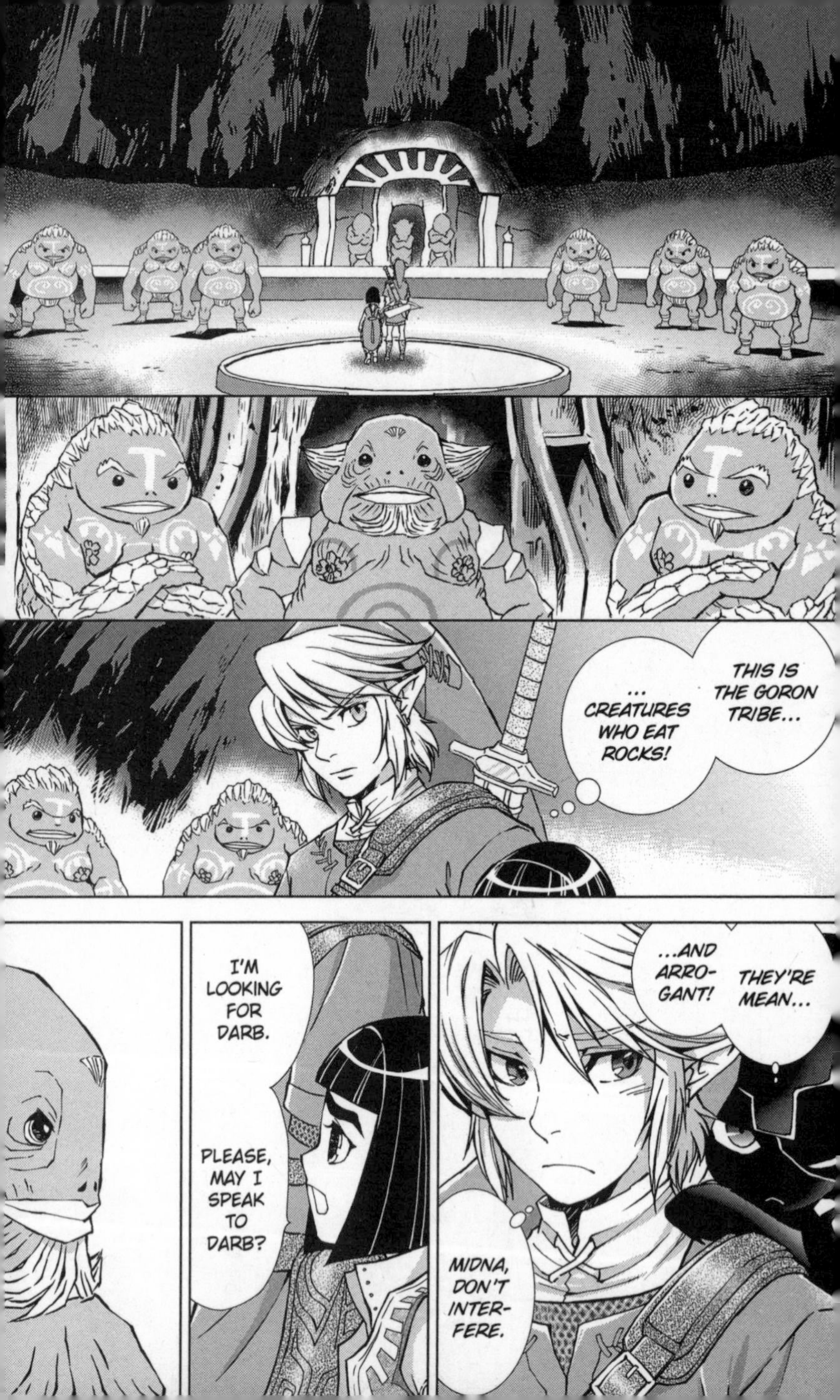

THIS IS THE GORON TRIBE...
...CREATURES WHO EAT ROCKS!
THEY'RE MEAN...
...AND ARRO-GANT!
MIDNA, DON'T INTER-FERE.
I'M LOOKING FOR DARB.
PLEASE, MAY I SPEAK TO DARB?

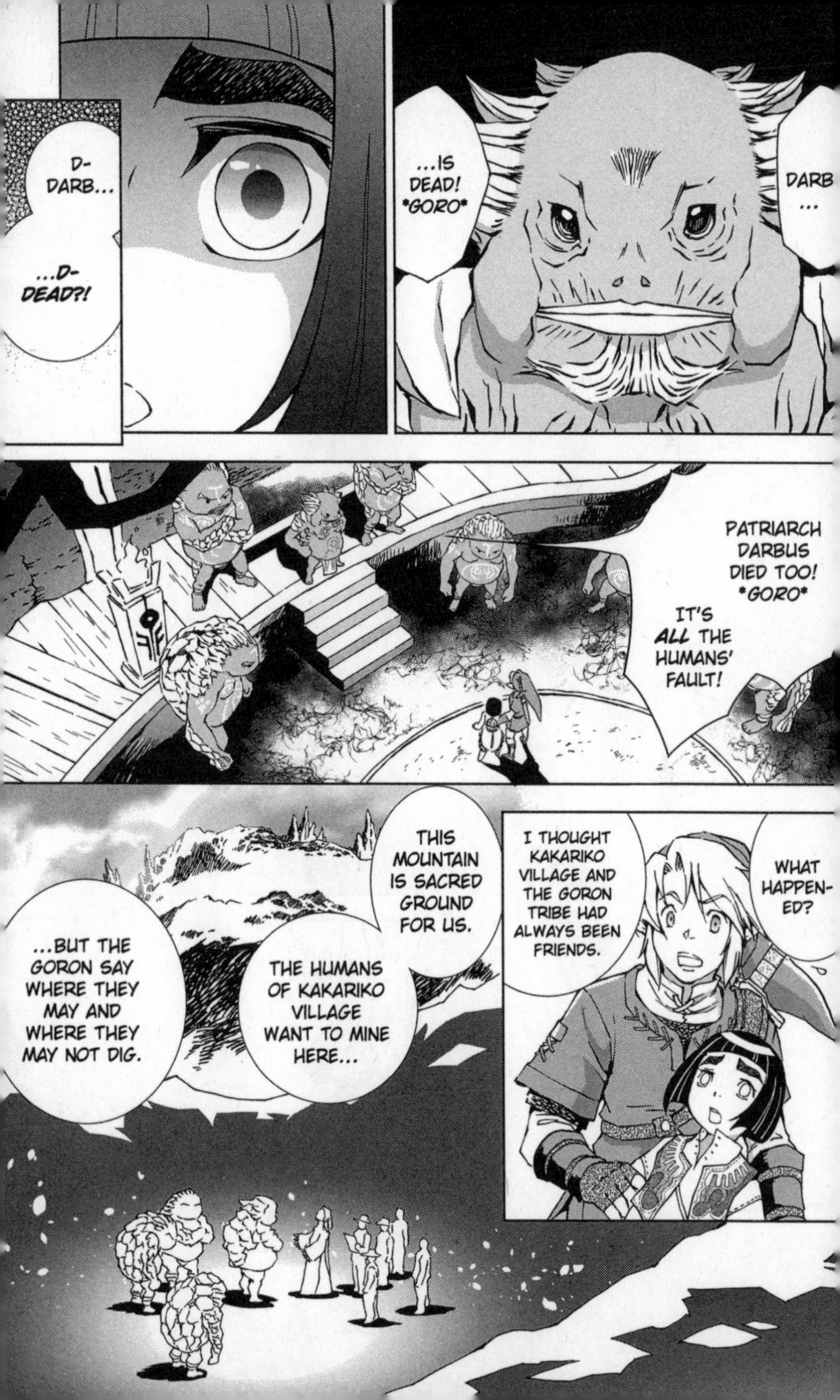
DARB ...
...IS DEAD! *GORO*
D-DARB...
...D-DEAD?!
PATRIARCH DARBUS DIED TOO! *GORO*
IT'S ALL THE HUMANS' FAULT!
WHAT HAPPEN-ED?
I THOUGHT KAKARIKO VILLAGE AND THE GORON TRIBE HAD ALWAYS BEEN FRIENDS.
THIS MOUNTAIN IS SACRED GROUND FOR US.
THE HUMANS OF KAKARIKO VILLAGE WANT TO MINE HERE...
...BUT THE GORON SAY WHERE THEY MAY AND WHERE THEY MAY NOT DIG.

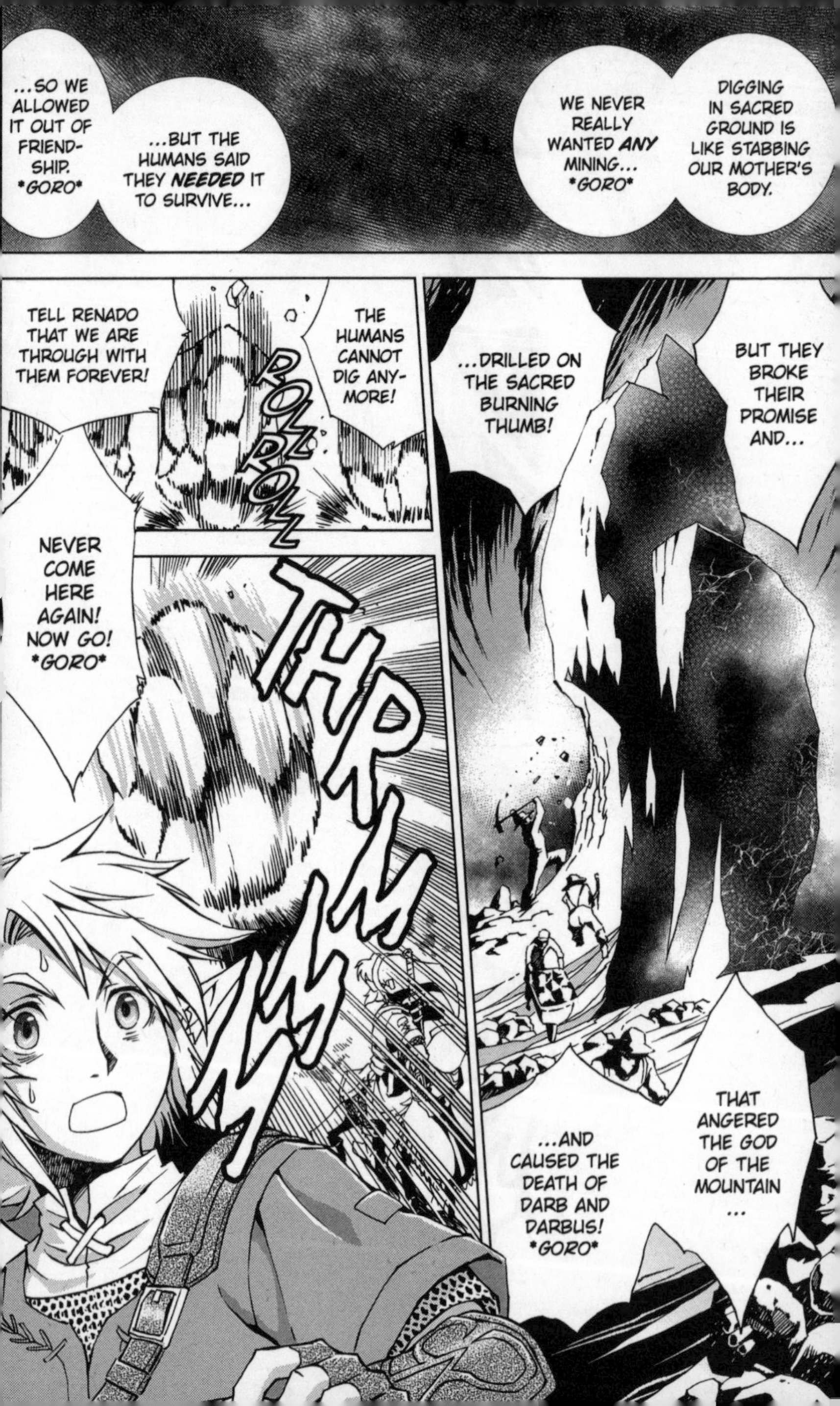
DIGGING IN SACRED GROUND IS LIKE STABBING OUR MOTHER'S BODY.
WE NEVER REALLY WANTED ANY MINING... *GORO*
...BUT THE HUMANS SAID THEY NEEDED IT TO SURVIVE...
...SO WE ALLOWED IT OUT OF FRIENDSHIP. *GORO*
BUT THEY BROKE THEIR PROMISE AND...
...DRILLED ON THE SACRED BURNING THUMB!
THAT ANGERED THE GOD OF THE MOUNTAIN...
...AND CAUSED THE DEATH OF DARB AND DARBUS! *GORO*
THE HUMANS CANNOT DIG ANYMORE!
TELL RENADO THAT WE ARE THROUGH WITH THEM FOREVER!
ROLL ROLL
NEVER COME HERE AGAIN! NOW GO! *GORO*
THRUMMM

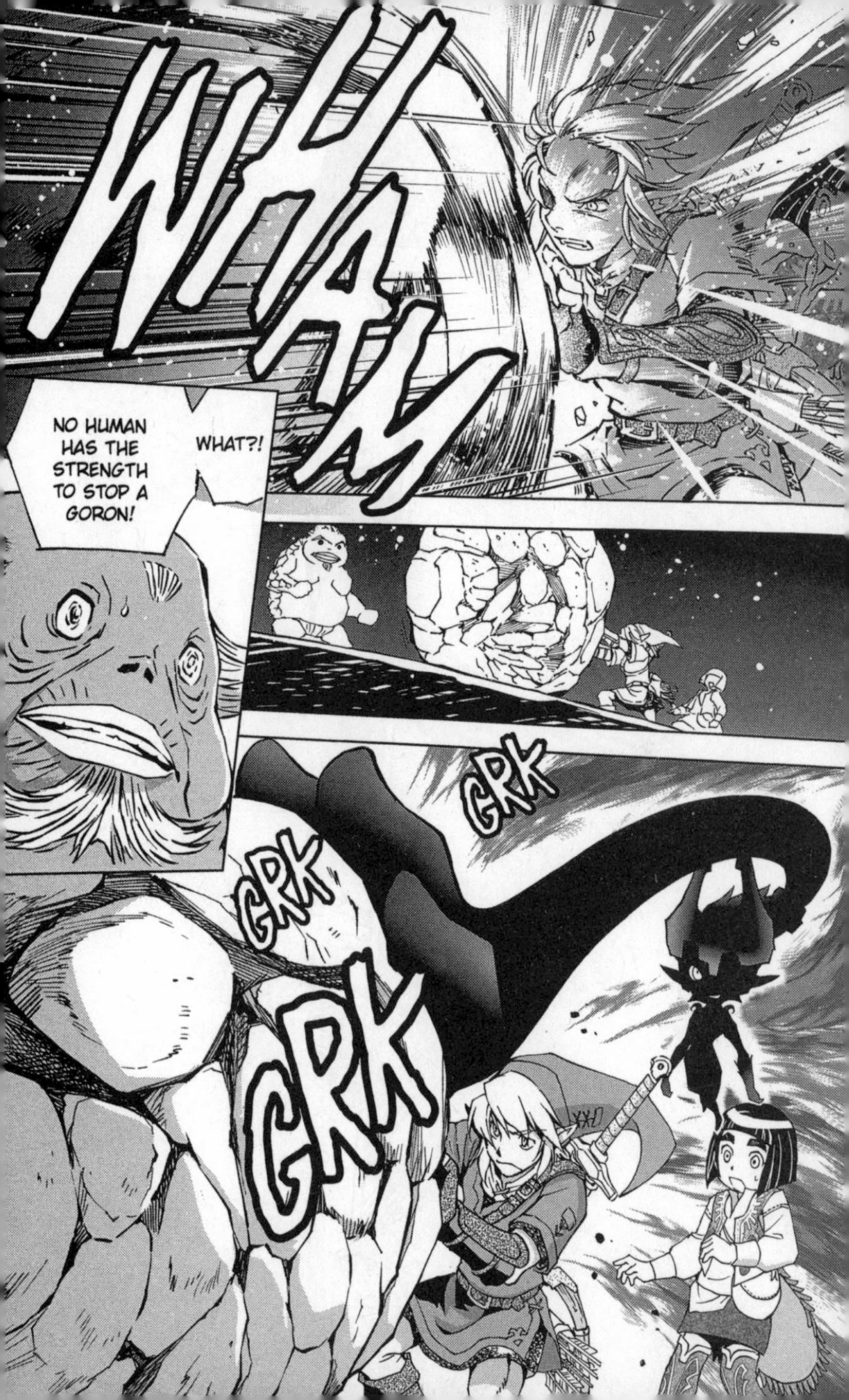
WHAM
WHAT?!
NO HUMAN HAS THE STRENGTH TO STOP A GORON!
GRK
GRK
GRK
GRK

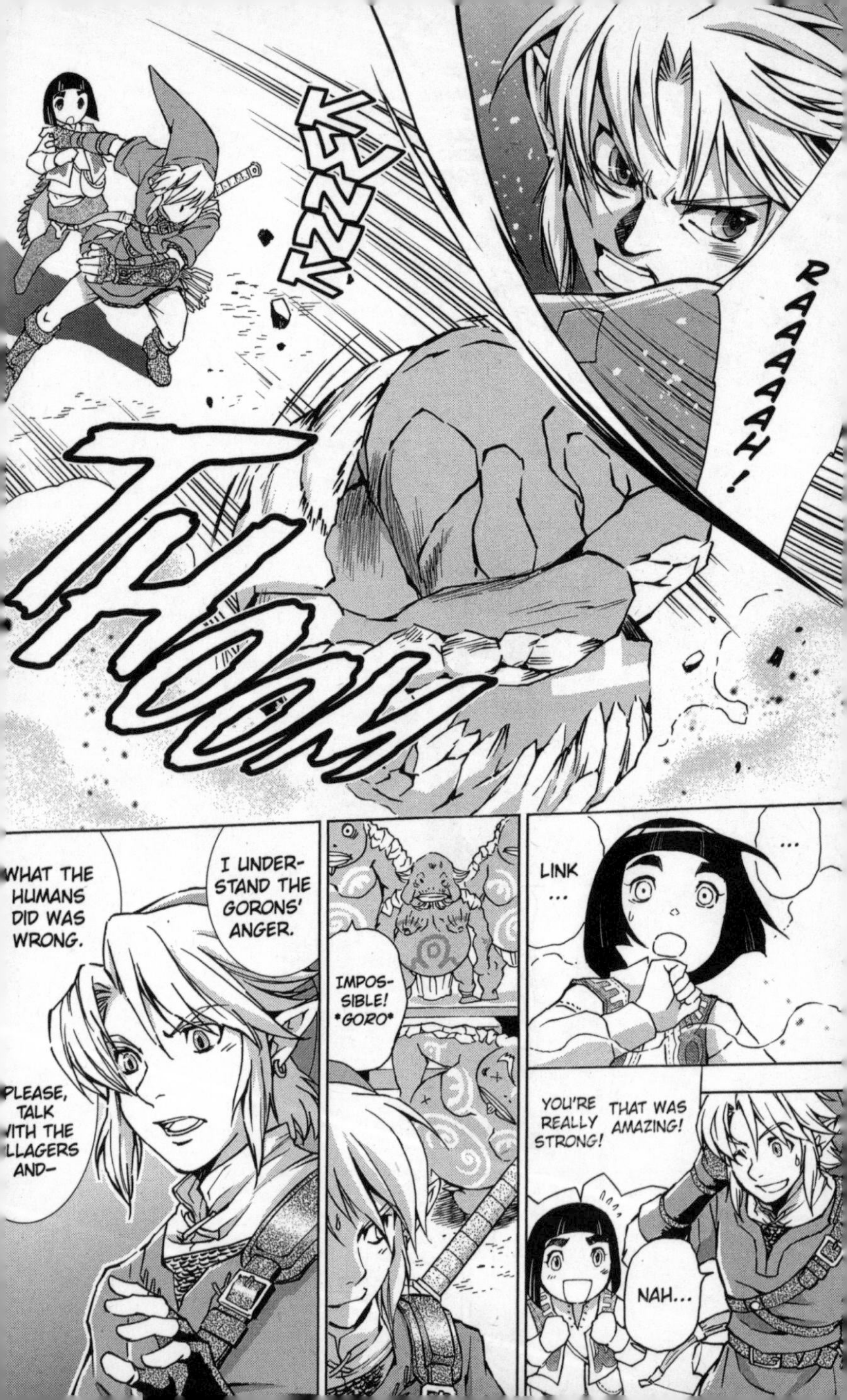
RAAAAAAH!
KZZZZK
THOOM
...
LINK ...
THAT WAS AMAZING!
YOU'RE REALLY STRONG!
NAH...
I UNDER-STAND THE GORONS' ANGER.
IMPOS-SIBLE! *GORO*
WHAT THE HUMANS DID WAS WRONG.
PLEASE, TALK ITH THE LLAGERS AND–

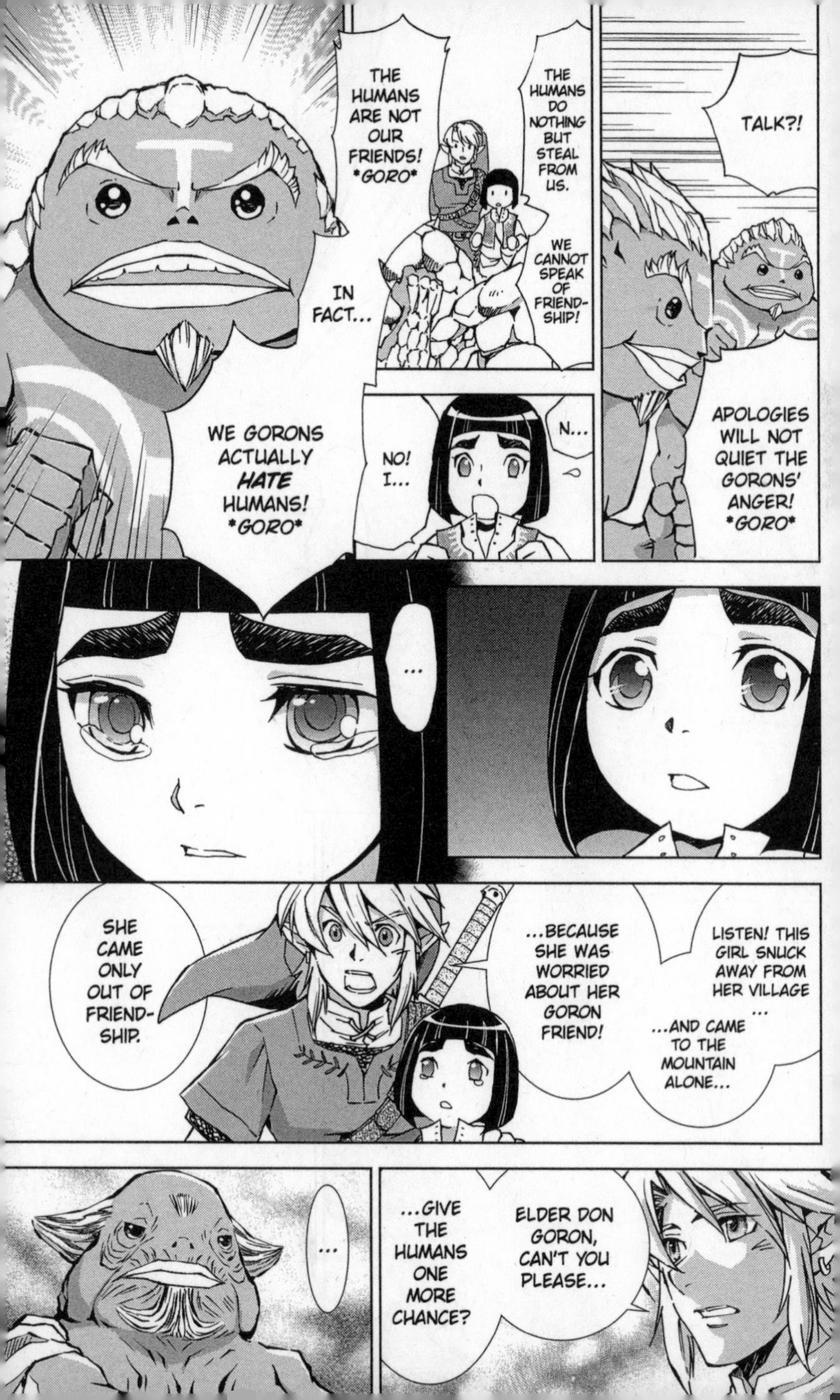
TALK?!
APOLOGIES WILL NOT QUIET THE GORONS' ANGER! *GORO*
THE HUMANS DO NOTHING BUT STEAL FROM US.
THE HUMANS ARE NOT OUR FRIENDS! *GORO*
WE CANNOT SPEAK OF FRIEND-SHIP!
IN FACT...
N...
NO! I...
WE GORONS ACTUALLY **HATE** HUMANS! *GORO*
...
LISTEN! THIS GIRL SNUCK AWAY FROM HER VILLAGE...
...AND CAME TO THE MOUNTAIN ALONE...
...BECAUSE SHE WAS WORRIED ABOUT HER GORON FRIEND!
SHE CAME ONLY OUT OF FRIEND-SHIP.
ELDER DON GORON, CAN'T YOU PLEASE...
...GIVE THE HUMANS ONE MORE CHANCE?
...

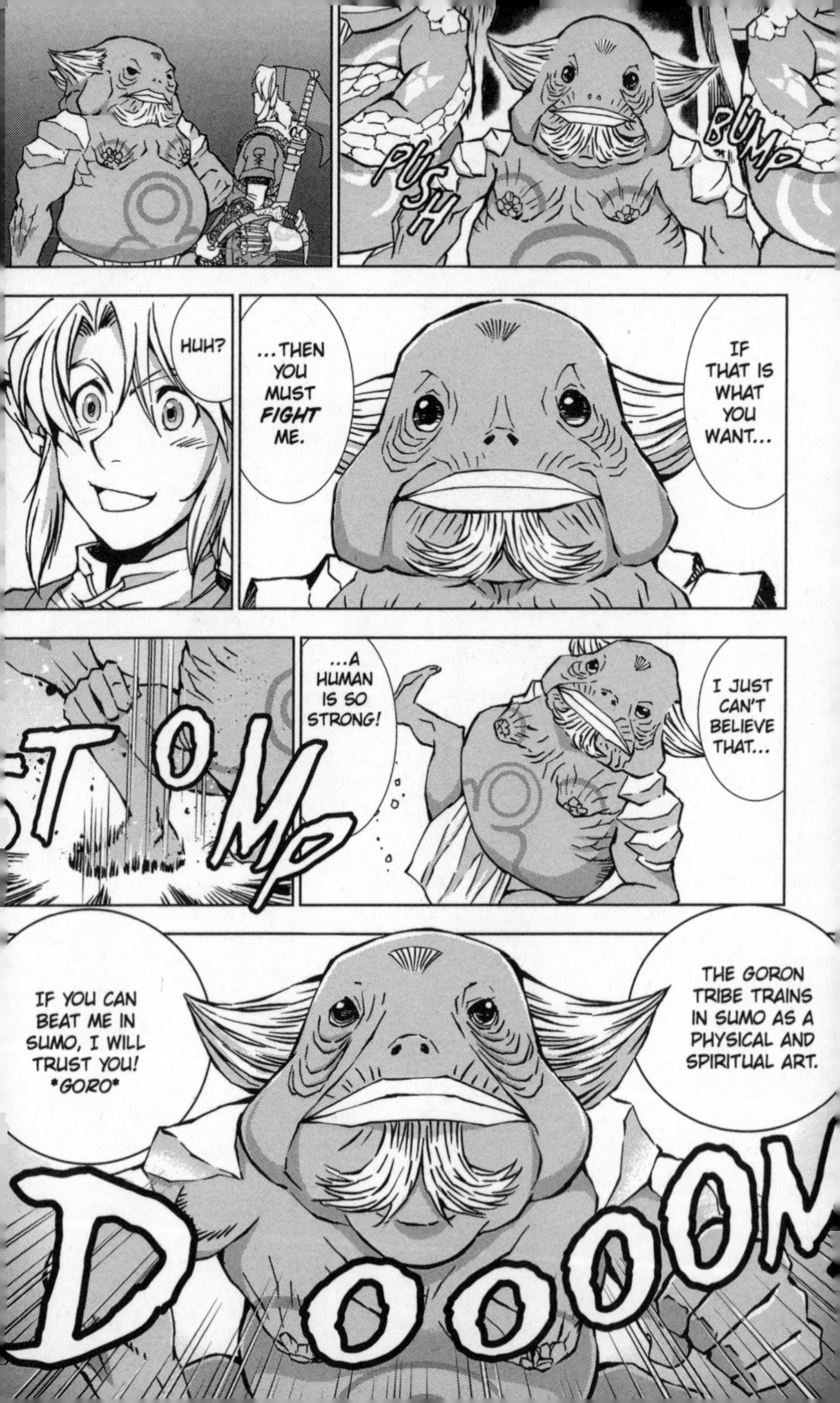
BUMP
PUSH
IF THAT IS WHAT YOU WANT...
...THEN YOU MUST FIGHT ME.
HUH?
I JUST CAN'T BELIEVE THAT...
...A HUMAN IS SO STRONG!
TOMP
THE GORON TRIBE TRAINS IN SUMO AS A PHYSICAL AND SPIRITUAL ART.
IF YOU CAN BEAT ME IN SUMO, I WILL TRUST YOU! *GORO*
DOOOOON

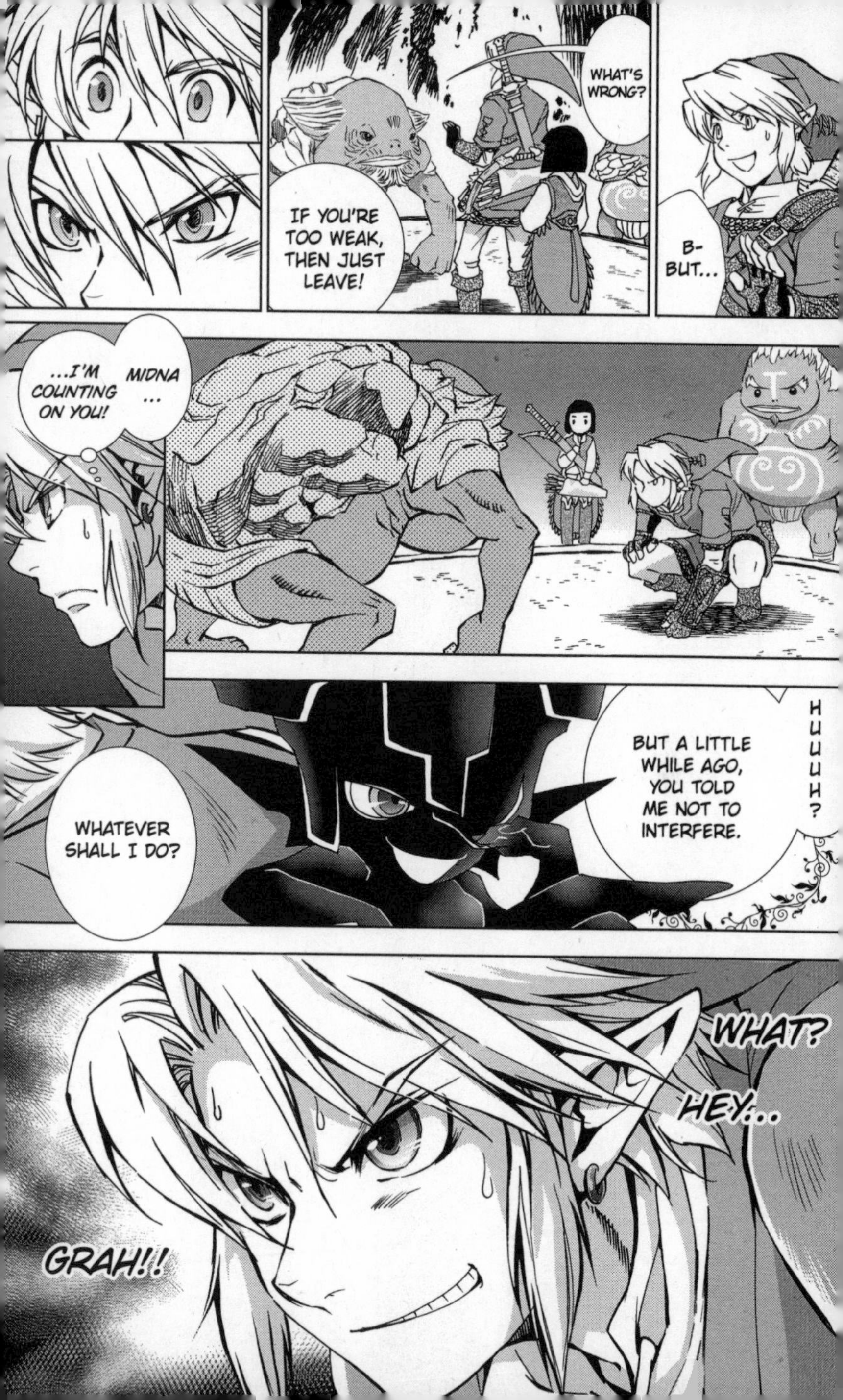
B-BUT...
WHAT'S WRONG?
IF YOU'RE TOO WEAK, THEN JUST LEAVE!
MIDNA ...
...I'M COUNTING ON YOU!
HUUUH?
BUT A LITTLE WHILE AGO, YOU TOLD ME NOT TO INTERFERE.
WHATEVER SHALL I DO?
WHAT?
HEY...
GRAH!!

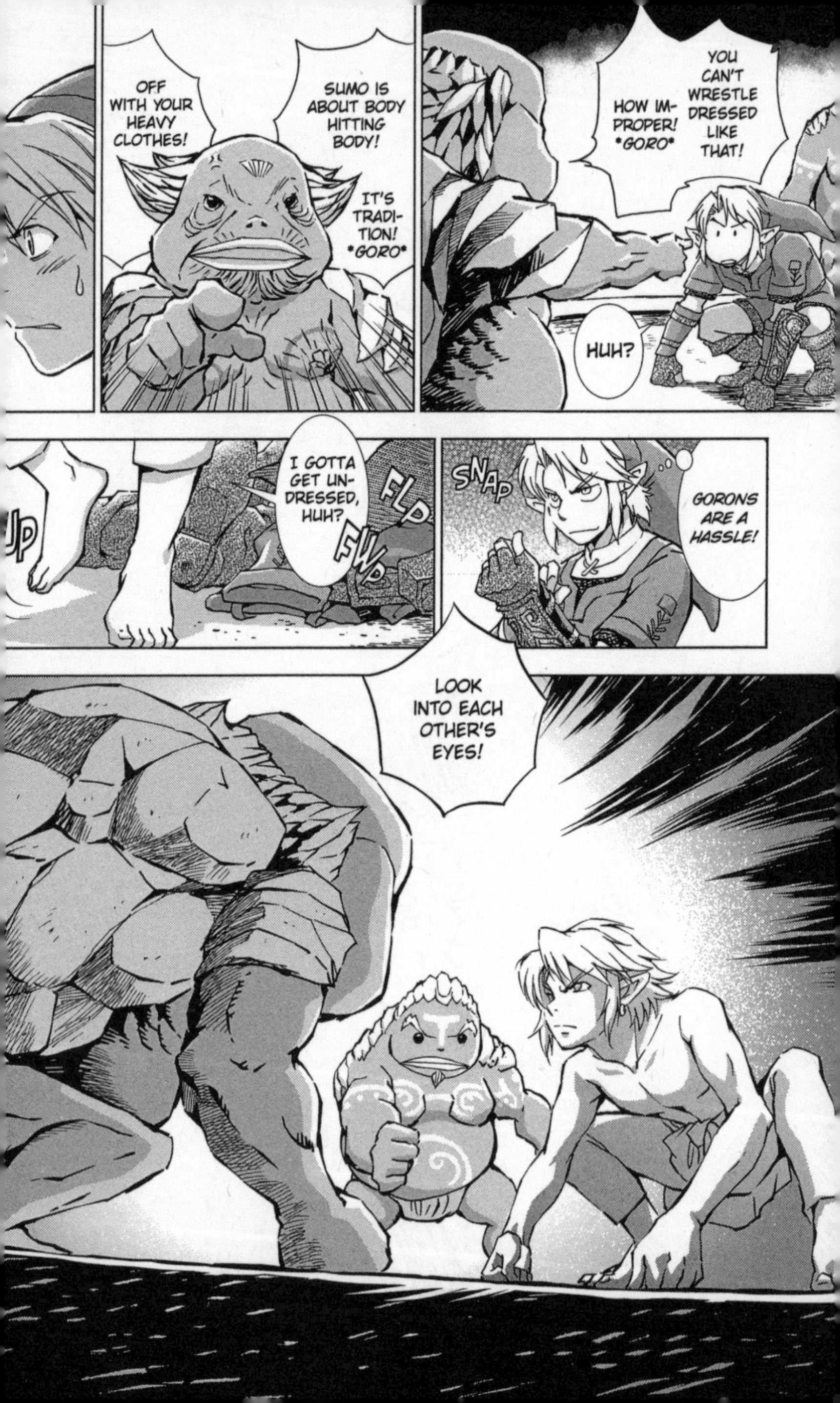
YOU CAN'T WRESTLE DRESSED LIKE THAT!
HOW IM-PROPER! *GORO*
HUH?
SUMO IS ABOUT BODY HITTING BODY!
OFF WITH YOUR HEAVY CLOTHES!
IT'S TRADI-TION! *GORO*
GORONS ARE A HASSLE!
SNAP
I GOTTA GET UN-DRESSED, HUH?
FLP
FWP
LOOK INTO EACH OTHER'S EYES!

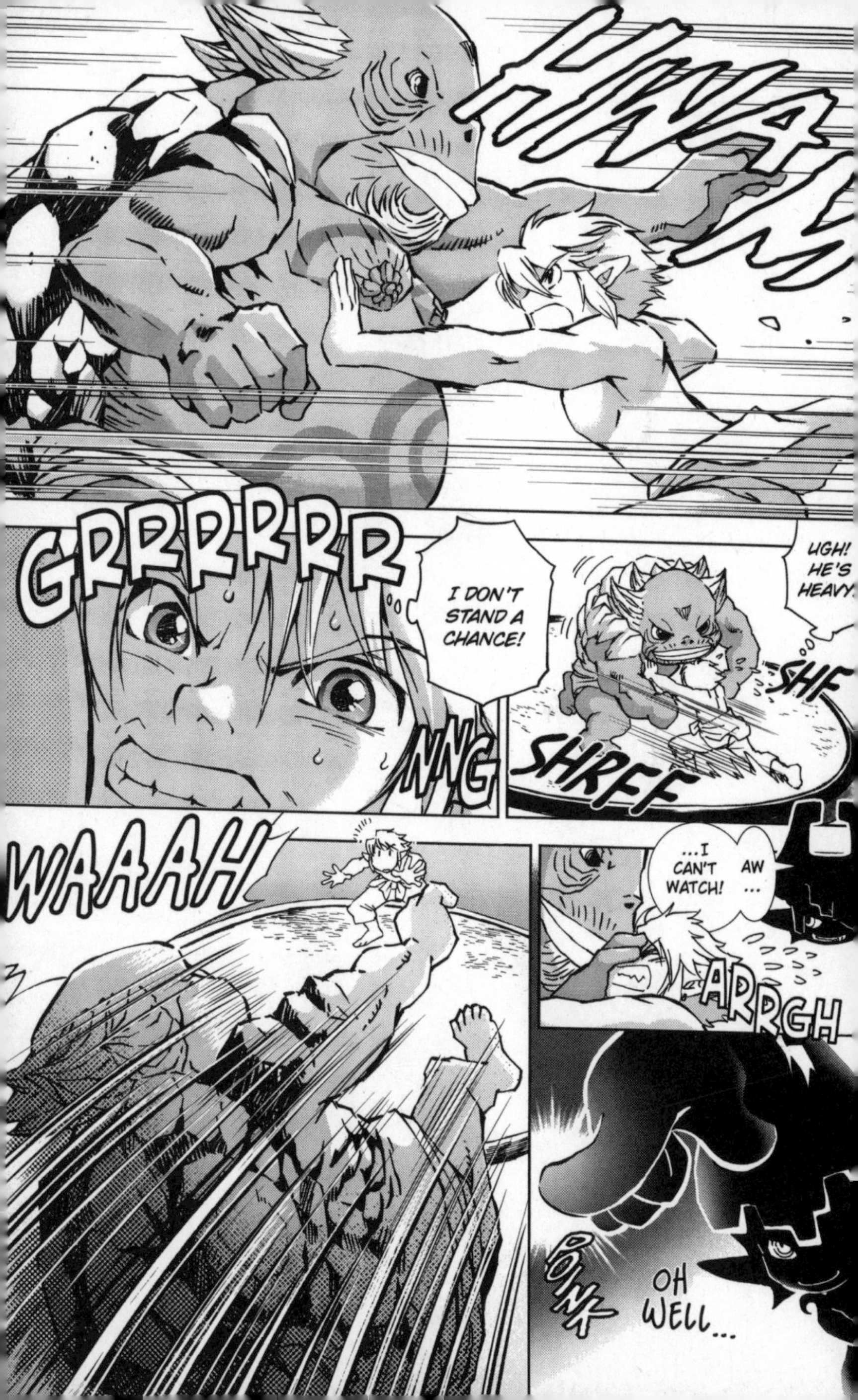
UGH! HE'S HEAVY!
SHF
SHRFF
GRRRRRR
I DON'T STAND A CHANCE!
NNG
AW...
...I CAN'T WATCH!
ARRGH
BONK
OH WELL...
WAAAAH

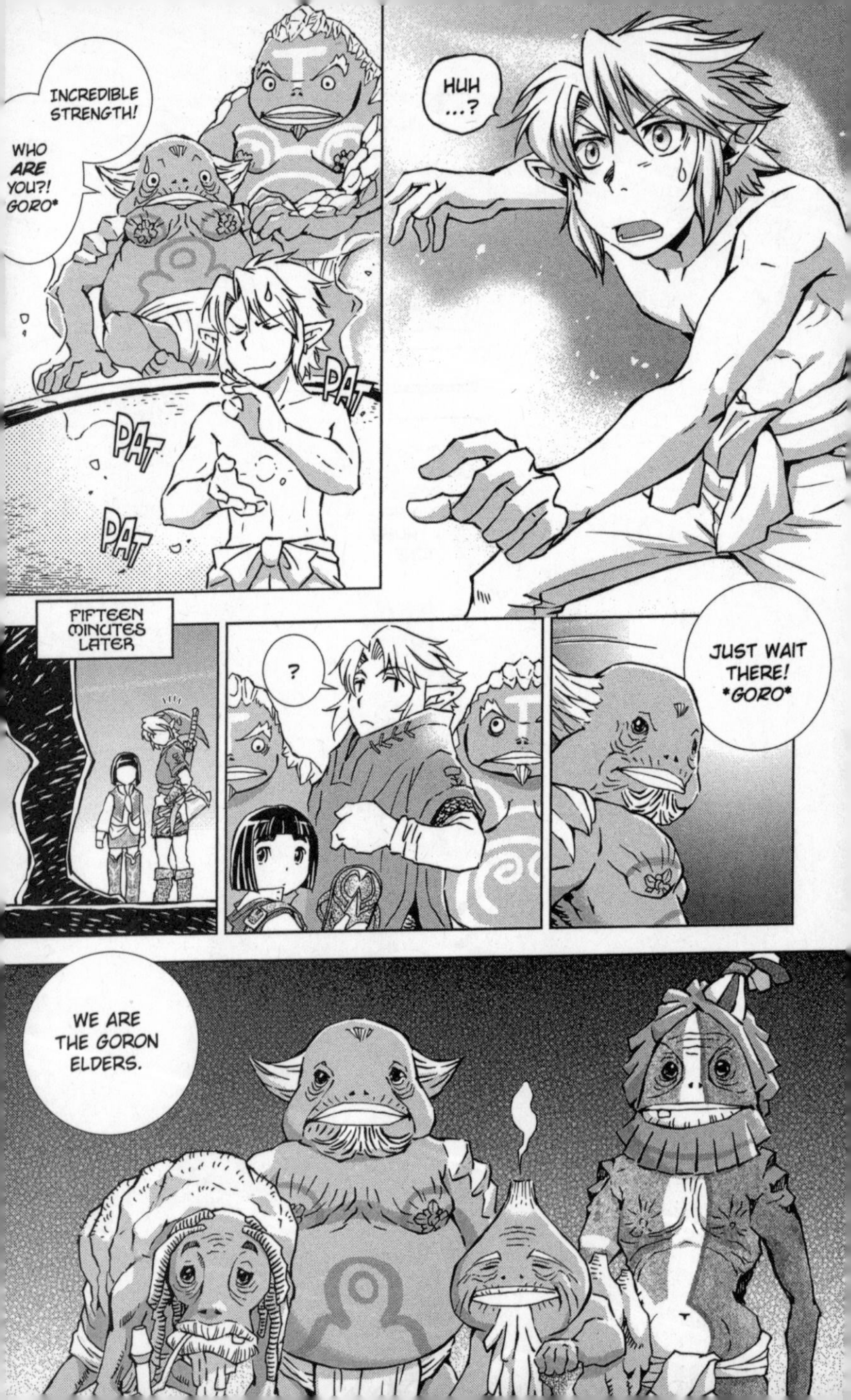
HUH ...?
INCREDIBLE STRENGTH!
WHO **ARE** YOU?! GORO*
PAT
PAT
PAT
JUST WAIT THERE! *GORO*
?
FIFTEEN MINUTES LATER
WE ARE THE GORON ELDERS.

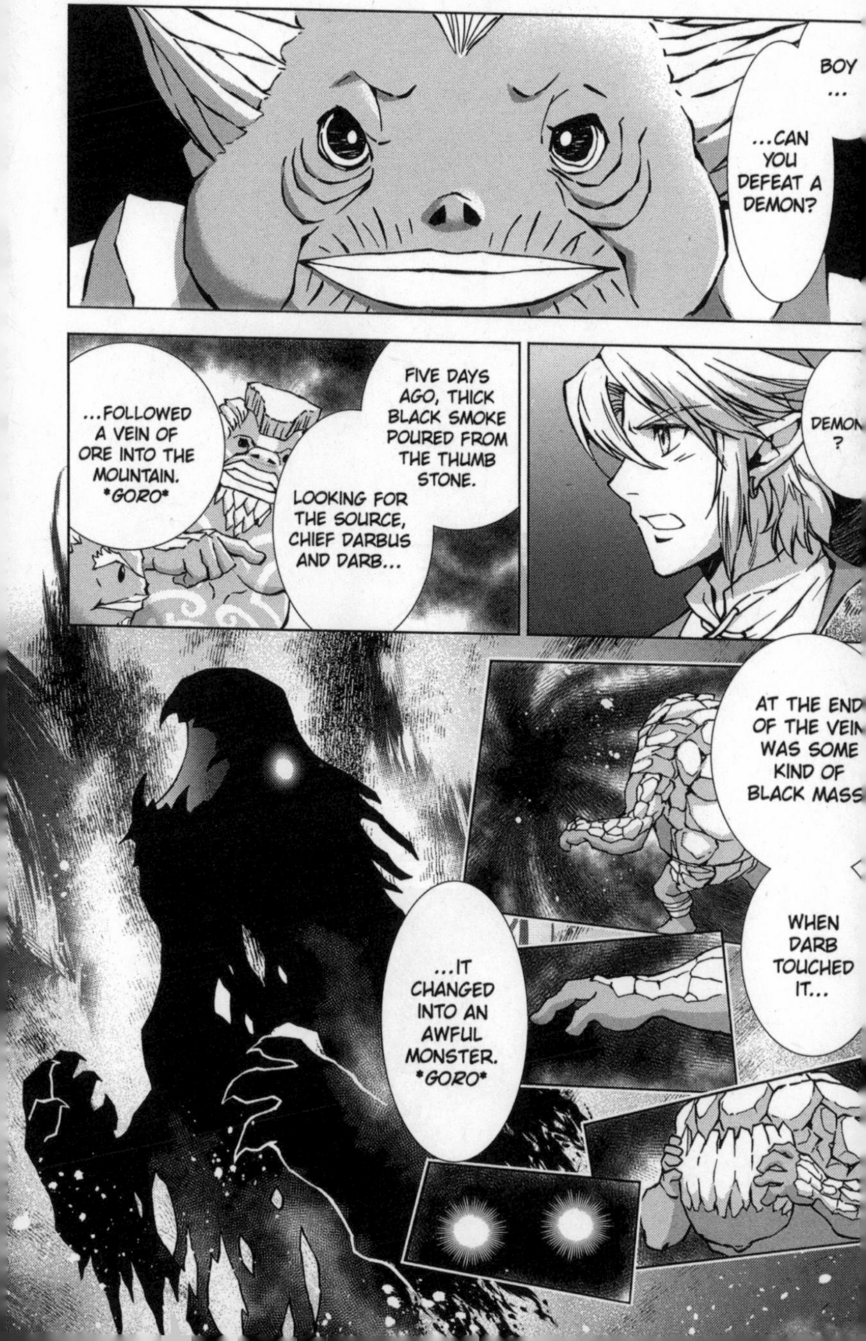
BOY ...
...CAN YOU DEFEAT A DEMON?
DEMON ?
FIVE DAYS AGO, THICK BLACK SMOKE POURED FROM THE THUMB STONE.
LOOKING FOR THE SOURCE, CHIEF DARBUS AND DARB...
...FOLLOWED A VEIN OF ORE INTO THE MOUNTAIN. *GORO*
AT THE END OF THE VEIN WAS SOME KIND OF BLACK MASS
WHEN DARB TOUCHED IT...
...IT CHANGED INTO AN AWFUL MONSTER. *GORO*

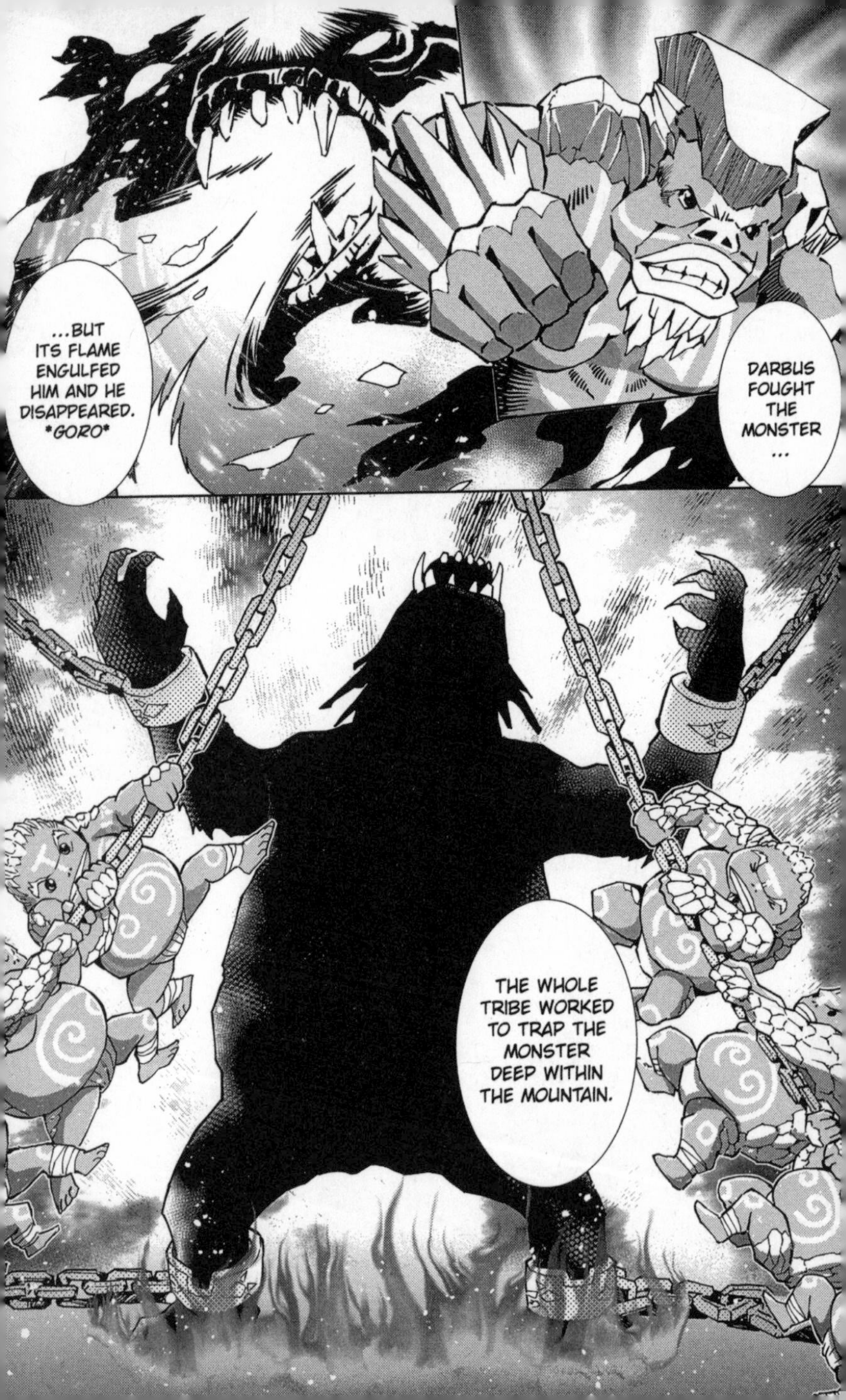
DARBUS FOUGHT THE MONSTER ...
...BUT ITS FLAME ENGULFED HIM AND HE DISAPPEARED. *GORO*
THE WHOLE TRIBE WORKED TO TRAP THE MONSTER DEEP WITHIN THE MOUNTAIN.

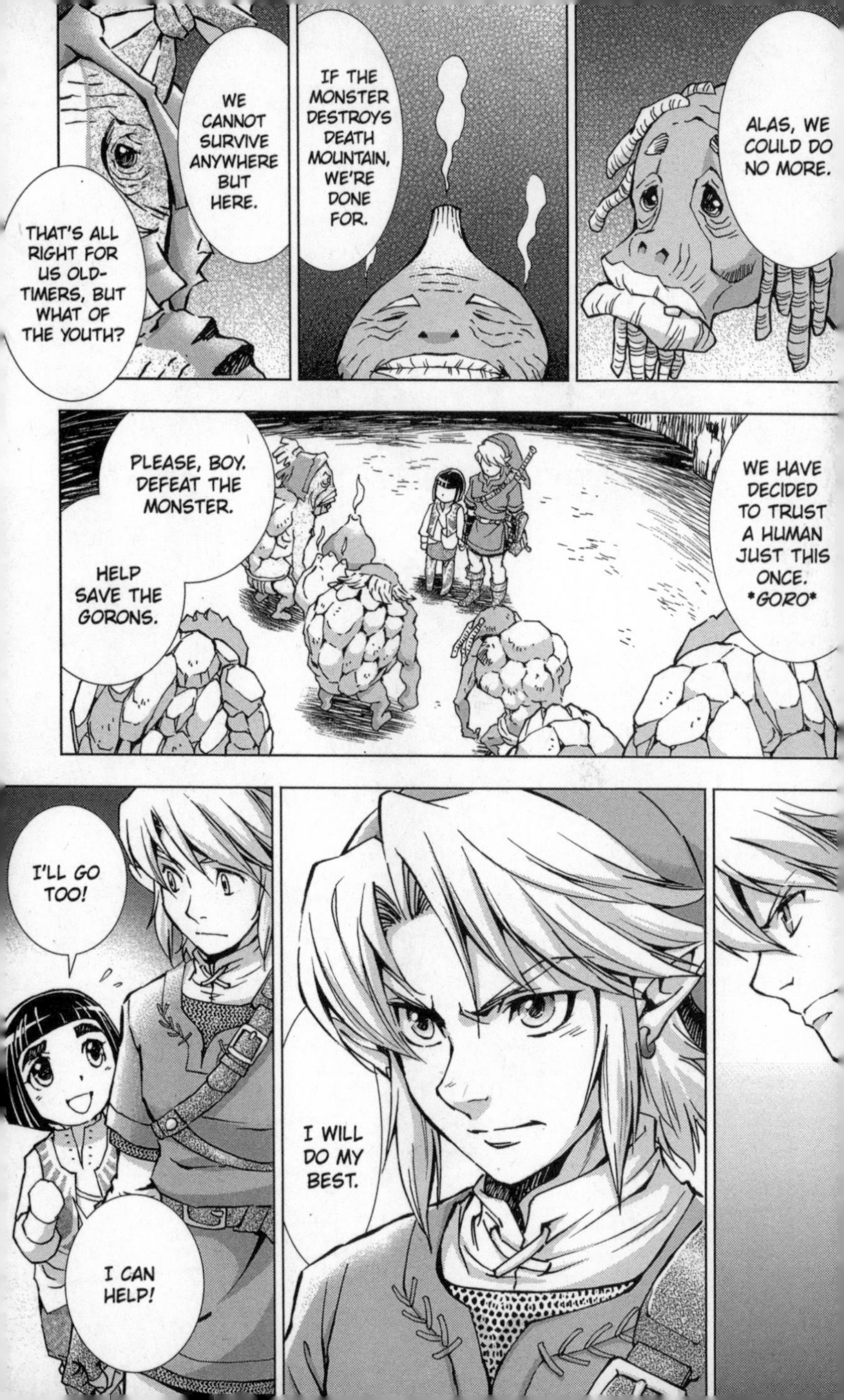
ALAS, WE COULD DO NO MORE.
IF THE MONSTER DESTROYS DEATH MOUNTAIN, WE'RE DONE FOR.
WE CANNOT SURVIVE ANYWHERE BUT HERE.
THAT'S ALL RIGHT FOR US OLD-TIMERS, BUT WHAT OF THE YOUTH?
WE HAVE DECIDED TO TRUST A HUMAN JUST THIS ONCE. *GORO*
PLEASE, BOY. DEFEAT THE MONSTER.
HELP SAVE THE GORONS.
I WILL DO MY BEST.
I'LL GO TOO!
I CAN HELP!

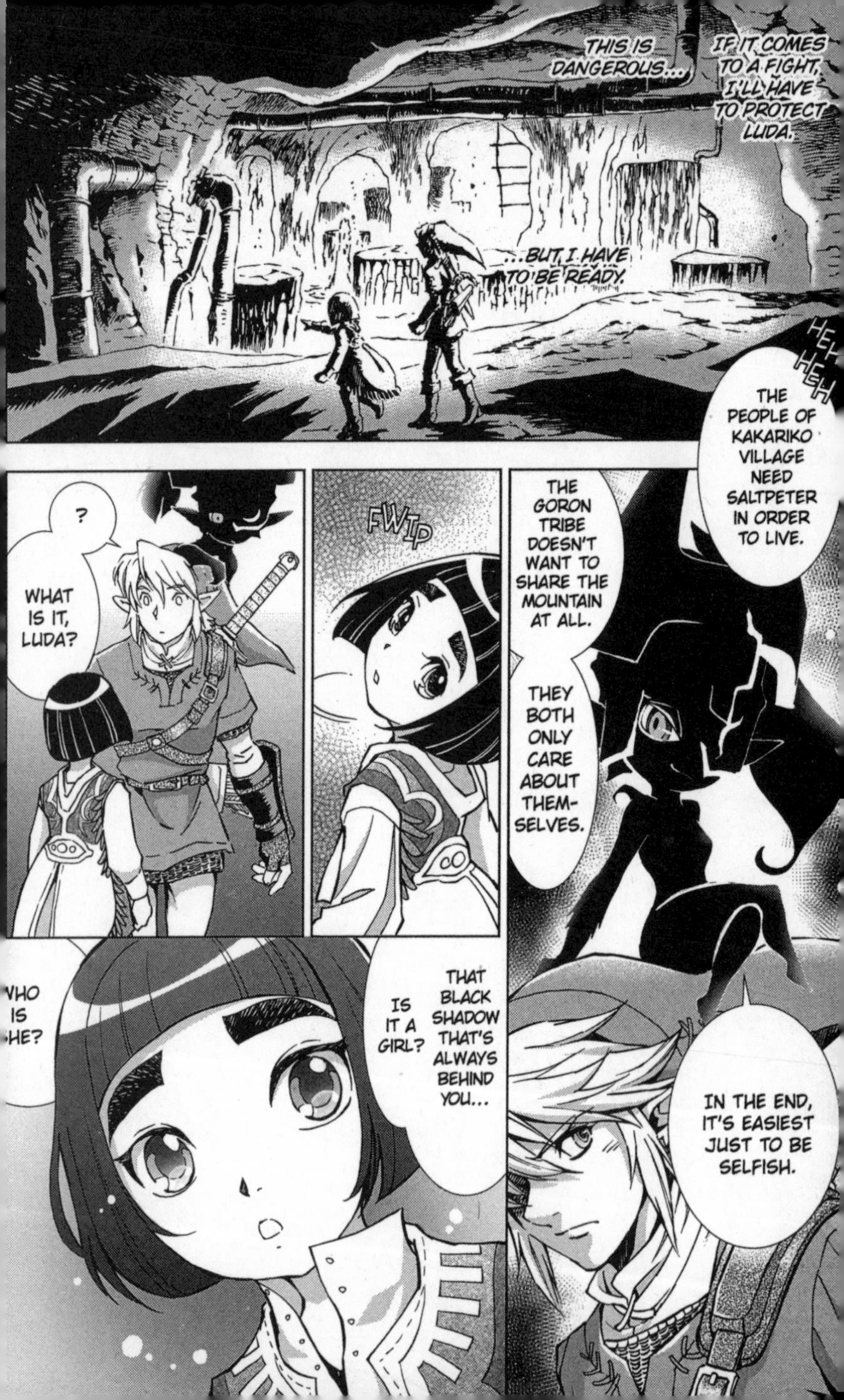
IF IT COMES TO A FIGHT, I'LL HAVE TO PROTECT LUDA.
THIS IS DANGEROUS...
...BUT I HAVE TO BE READY.
HEH HEH
THE PEOPLE OF KAKARIKO VILLAGE NEED SALTPETER IN ORDER TO LIVE.
THE GORON TRIBE DOESN'T WANT TO SHARE THE MOUNTAIN AT ALL.
THEY BOTH ONLY CARE ABOUT THEM-SELVES.
FWIP
?
WHAT IS IT, LUDA?
IN THE END, IT'S EASIEST JUST TO BE SELFISH.
THAT BLACK SHADOW THAT'S ALWAYS BEHIND YOU...
IS IT A GIRL?

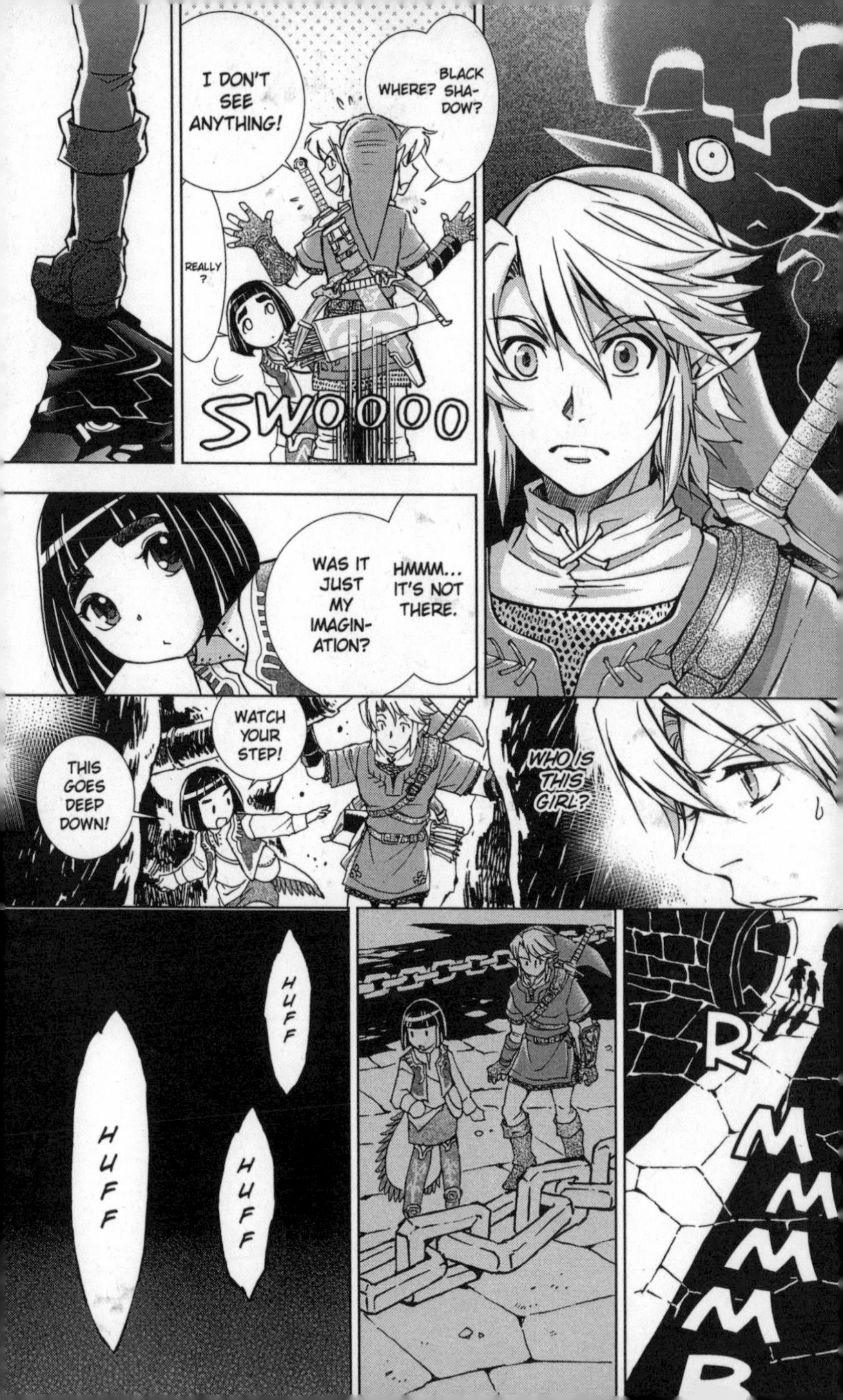
BLACK SHADOW?
WHERE?
I DON'T SEE ANYTHING!
REALLY?
SWOOOO
HMMM... IT'S NOT THERE.
WAS IT JUST MY IMAGINATION?
WHO IS THIS GIRL?
WATCH YOUR STEP!
THIS GOES DEEP DOWN!
RMMMMR
HUFF
HUFF
HUFF

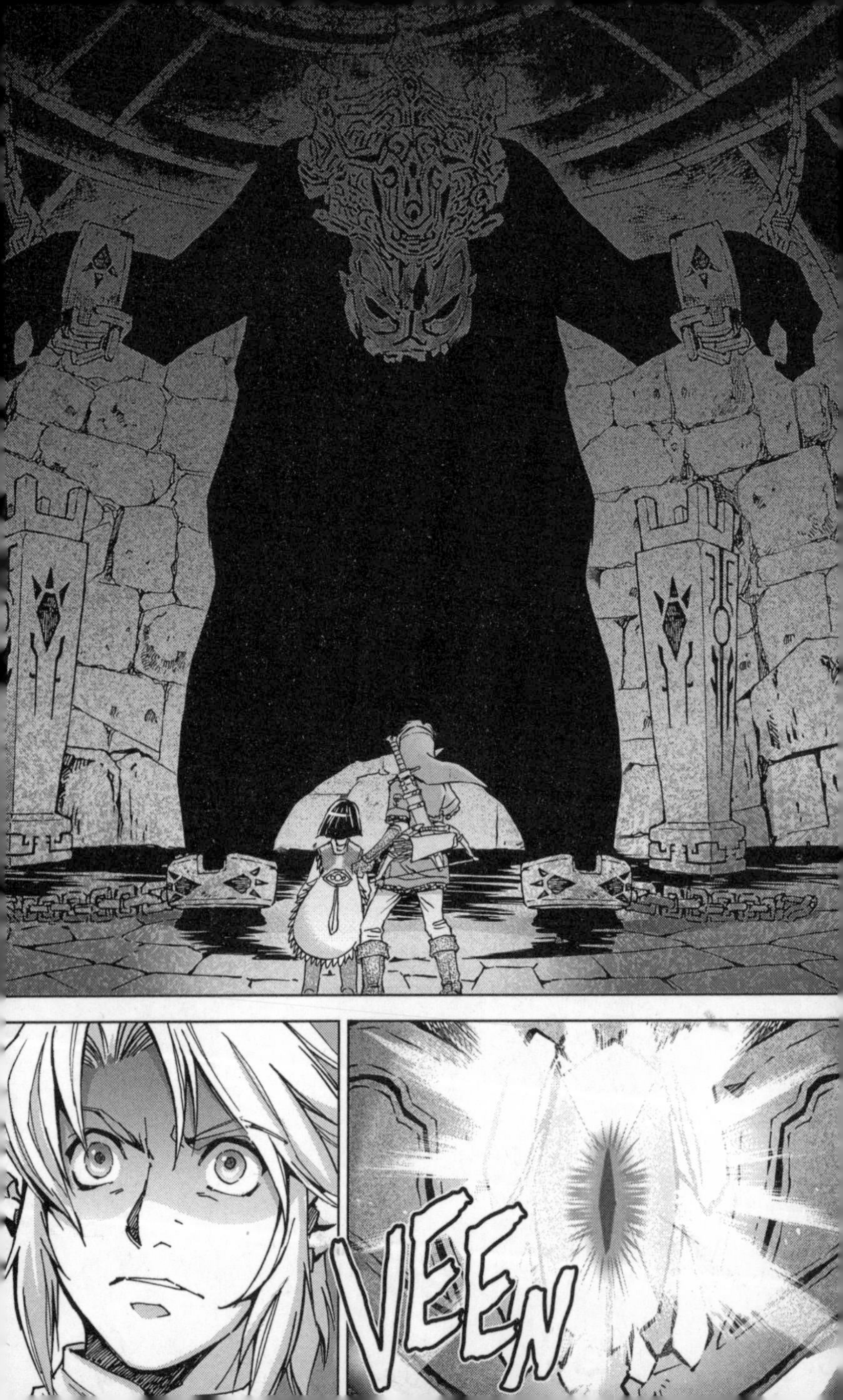
VEEN

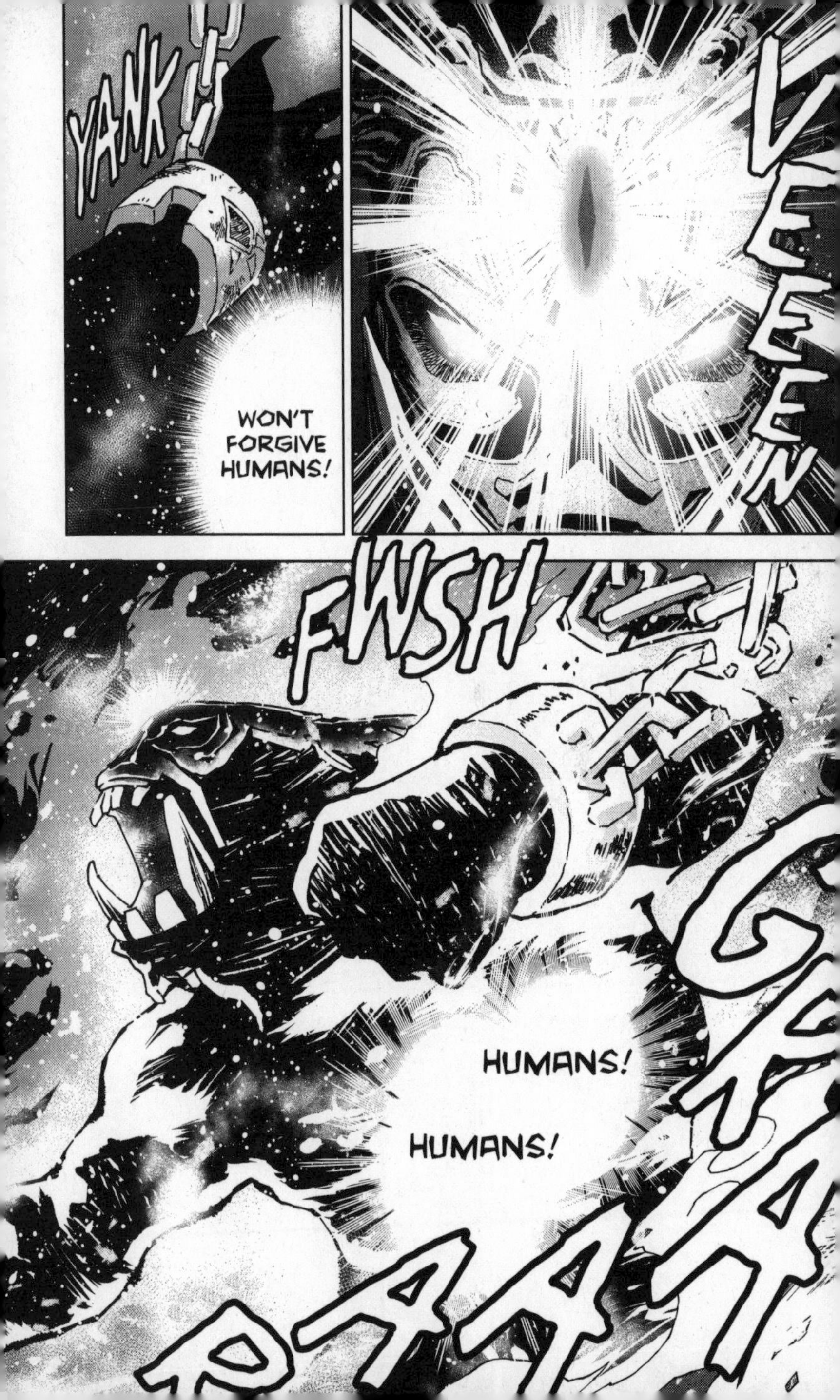
VEEEN
YANK
WON'T FORGIVE HUMANS!
FWSH
HUMANS!
HUMANS!

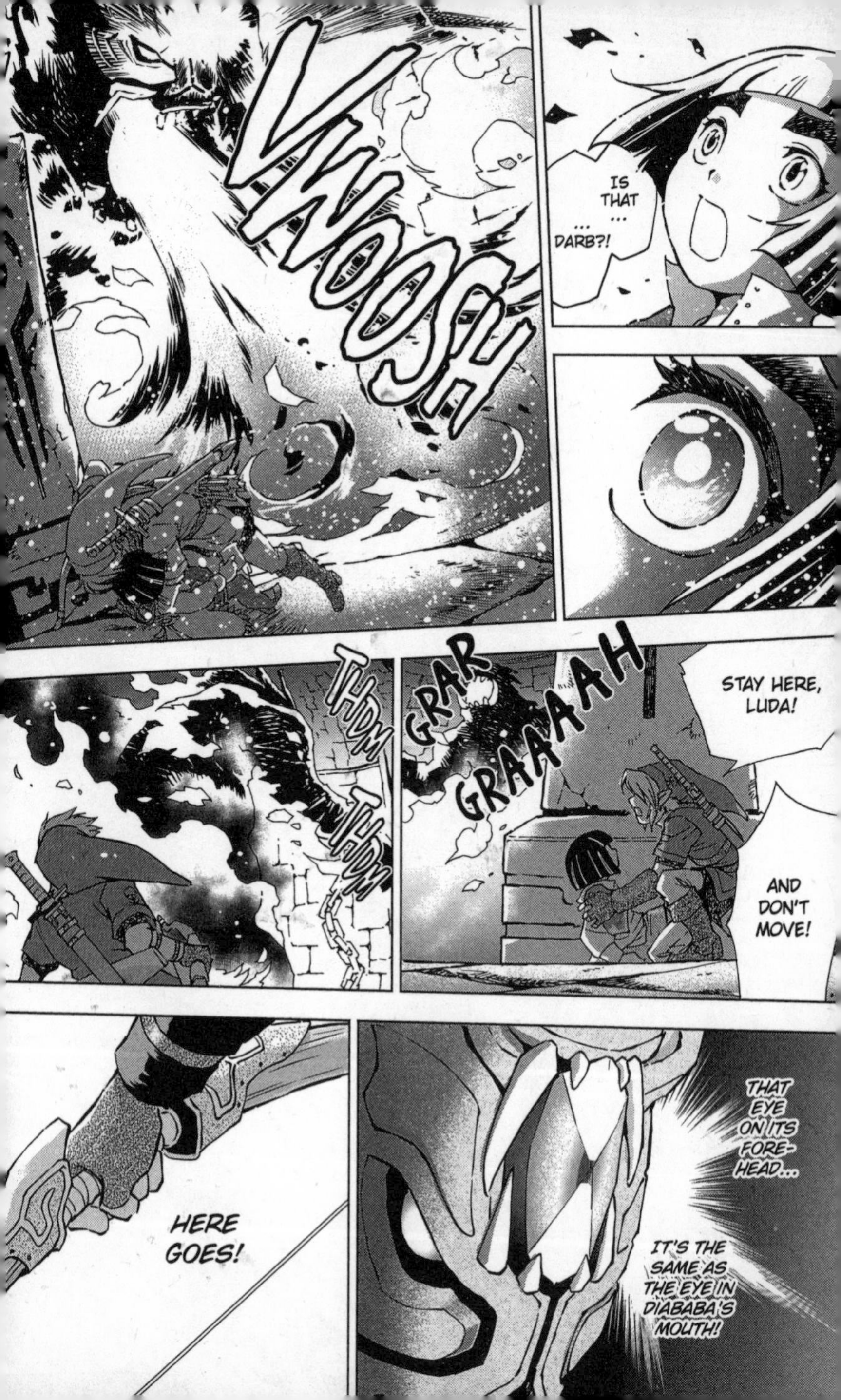

IS THAT ... DARB?!
VWOOSH
GRAR
GRAAAAH
STAY HERE, LUDA!
AND DON'T MOVE!
THUM
THUM
THAT EYE ON ITS FORE-HEAD...
IT'S THE SAME AS THE EYE IN DIABABA'S MOUTH!
HERE GOES!

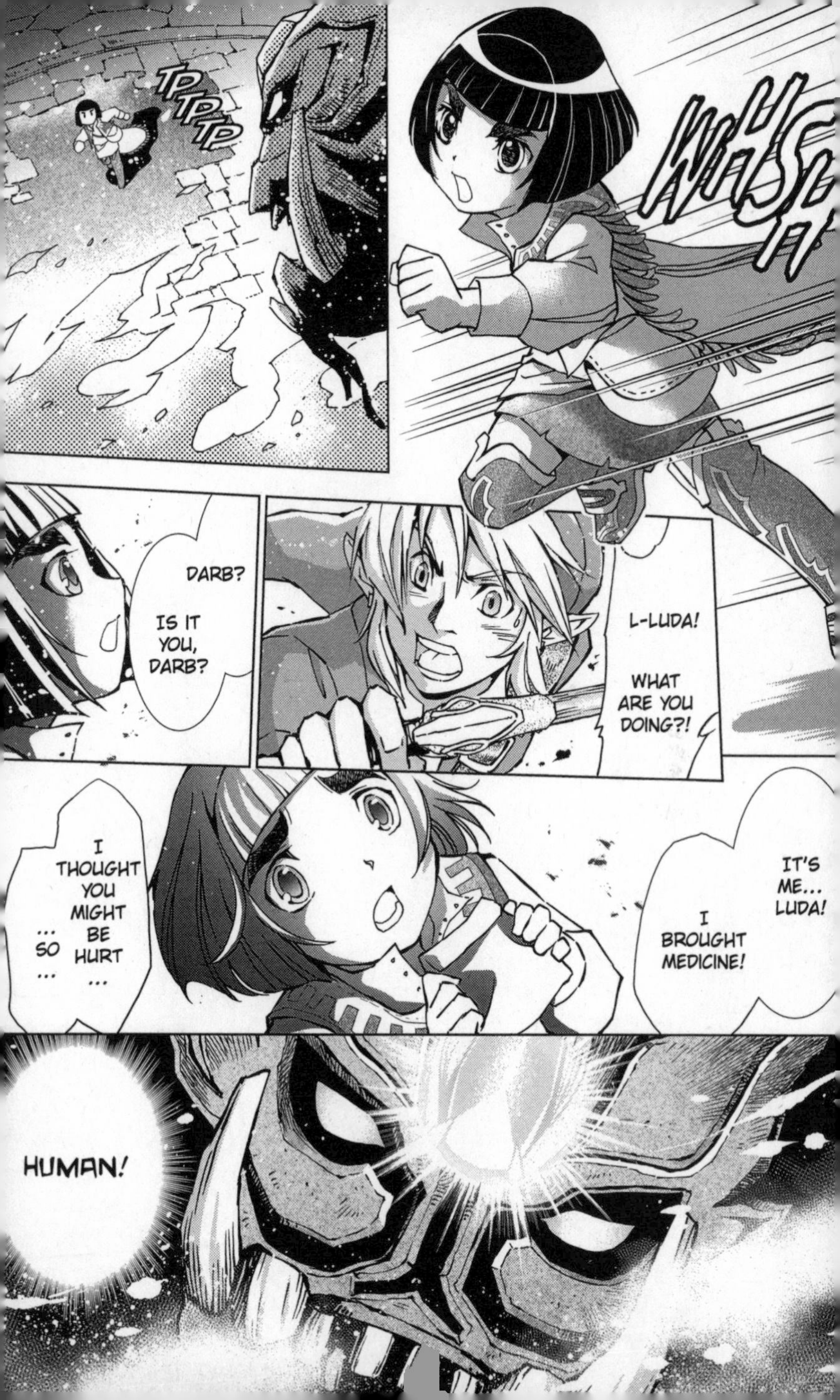
TPTPTP
L-LUDA!
WHAT ARE YOU DOING?!
DARB?
IS IT YOU, DARB?
IT'S ME... LUDA!
I BROUGHT MEDICINE!
I THOUGHT YOU MIGHT BE HURT...
...SO...
HUMAN!

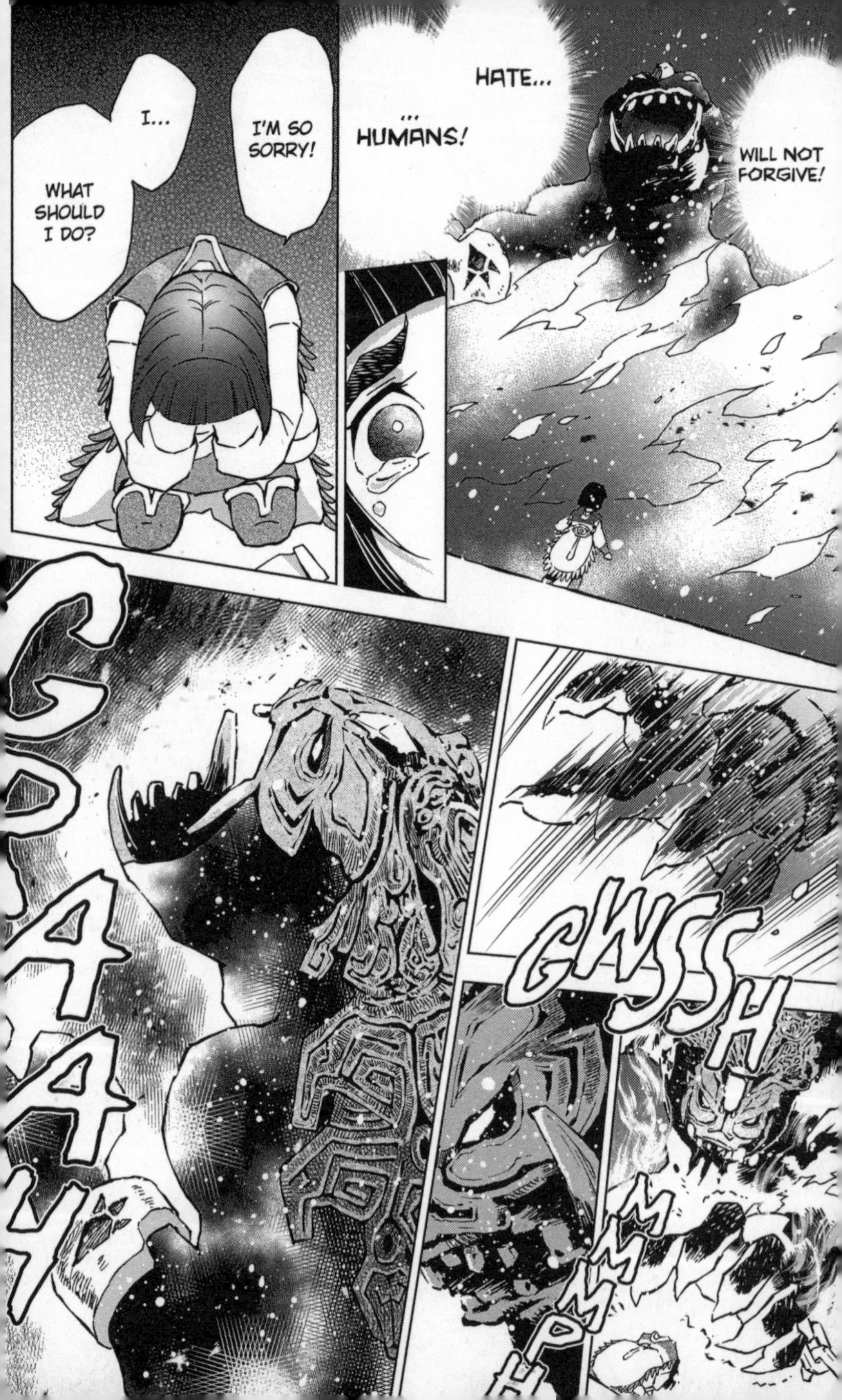
HATE...
...HUMANS!
WILL NOT FORGIVE!
I'M SO SORRY!
I...
WHAT SHOULD I DO?
GWSSH
MMMPH
GOAAH

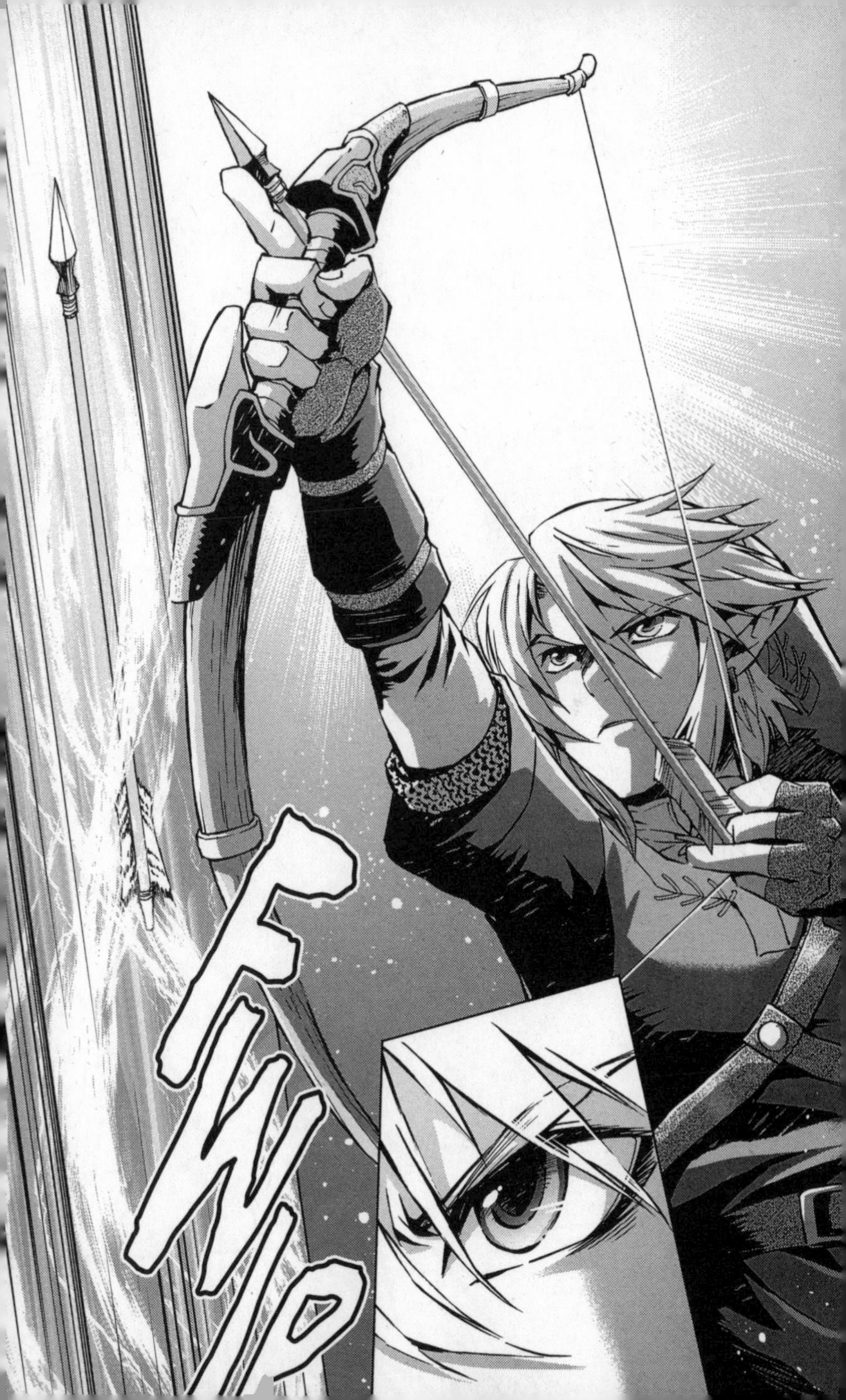
FWIP

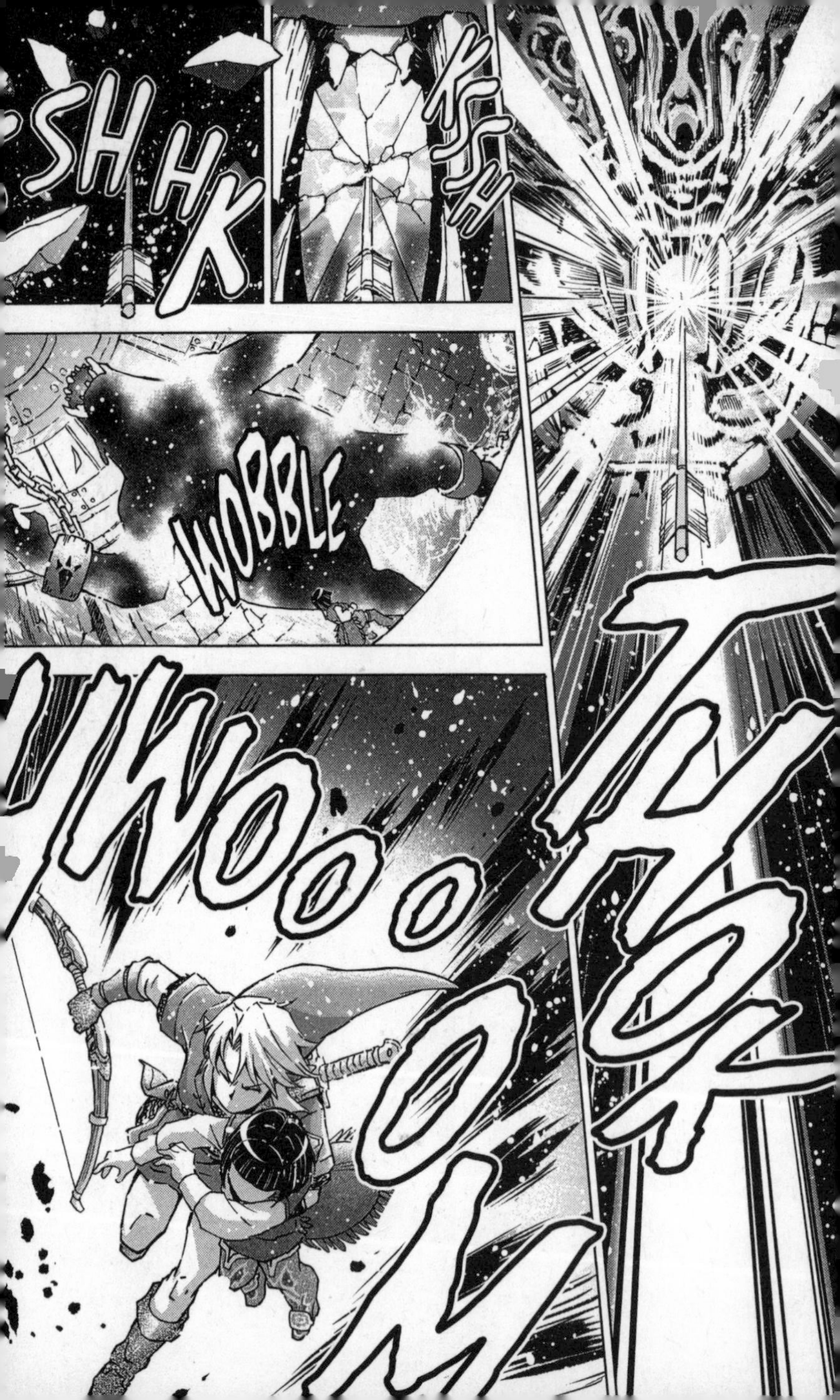
KSSH
SHHK
WOBBLE
WOOOOOOM

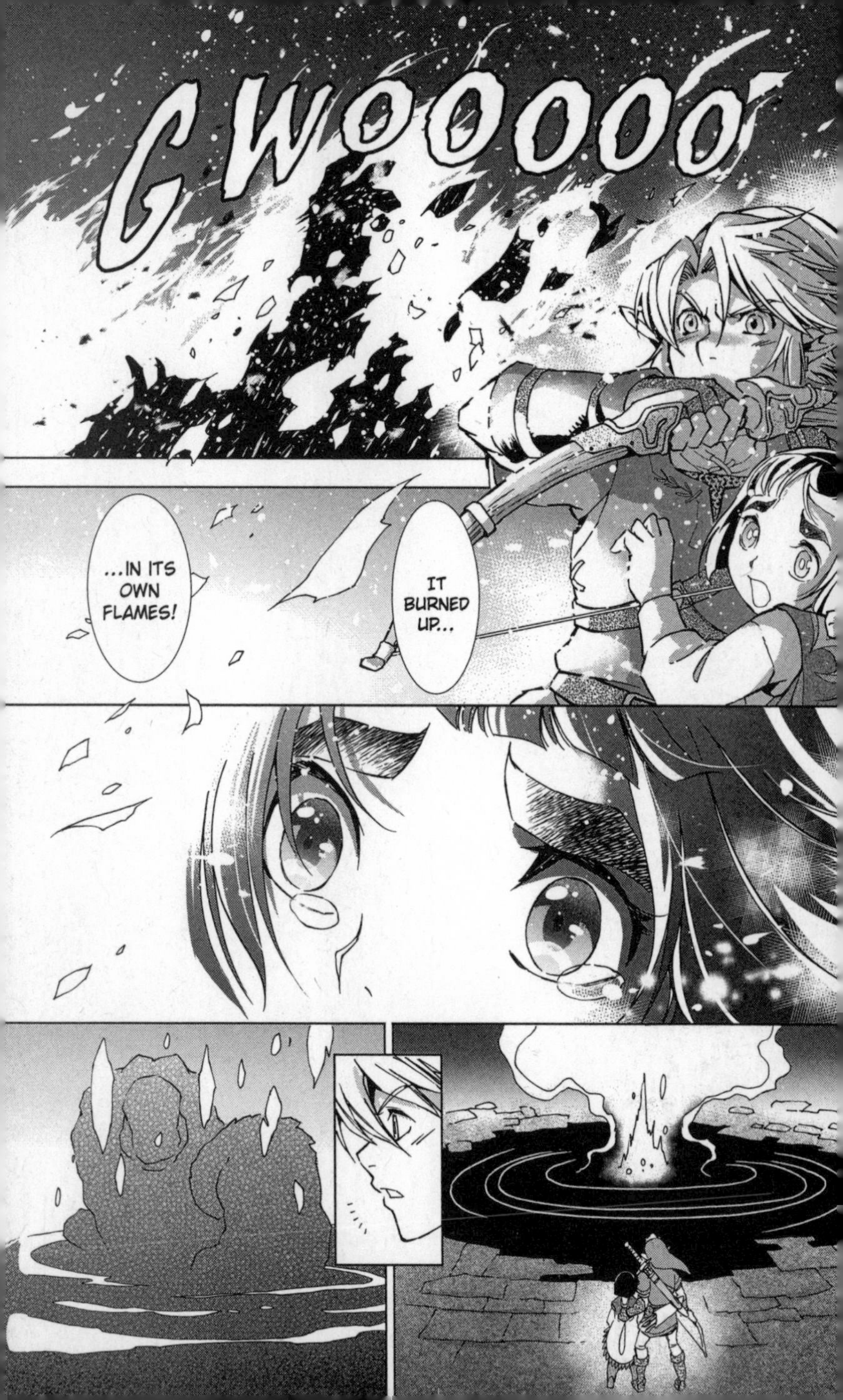
GWOOOOO
IT BURNED UP...
...IN ITS OWN FLAMES!

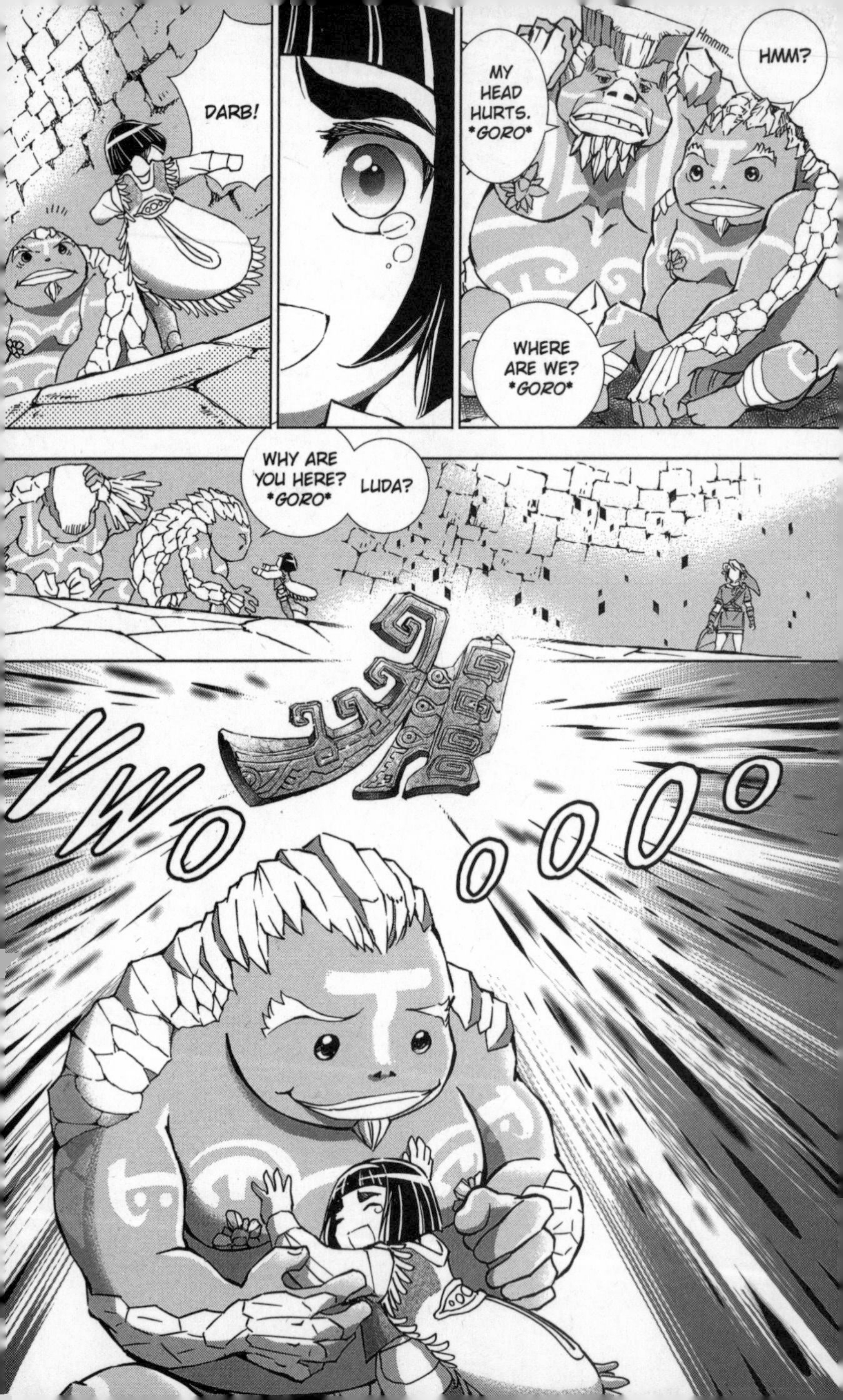
HMM?
Hmmm...
MY HEAD HURTS. *GORO*
WHERE ARE WE? *GORO*
DARB!
LUDA?
WHY ARE YOU HERE? *GORO*
VWOOOOOO

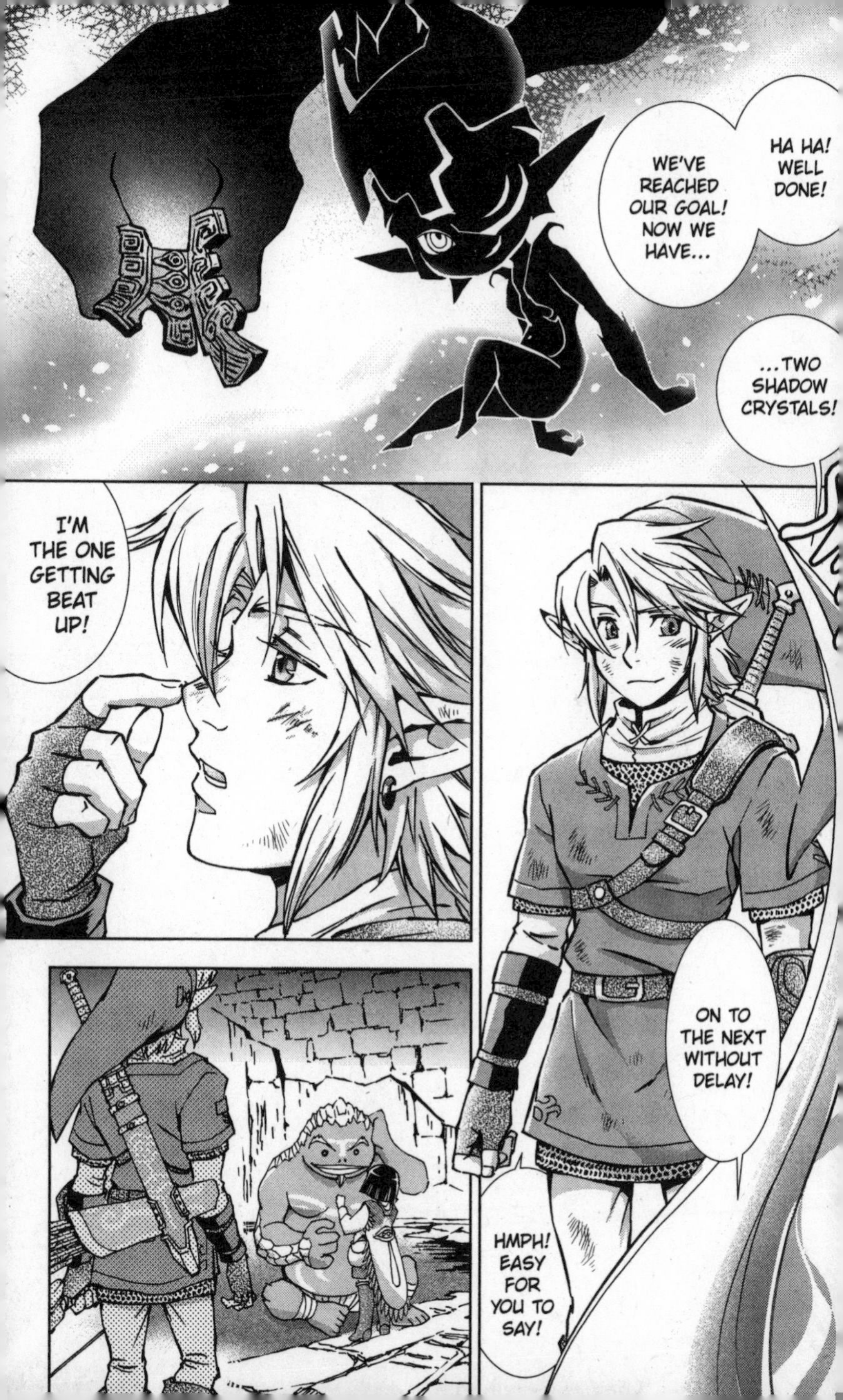
HA HA! WELL DONE!
WE'VE REACHED OUR GOAL! NOW WE HAVE...
...TWO SHADOW CRYSTALS!
ON TO THE NEXT WITHOUT DELAY!
HMPH! EASY FOR YOU TO SAY!
I'M THE ONE GETTING BEAT UP!

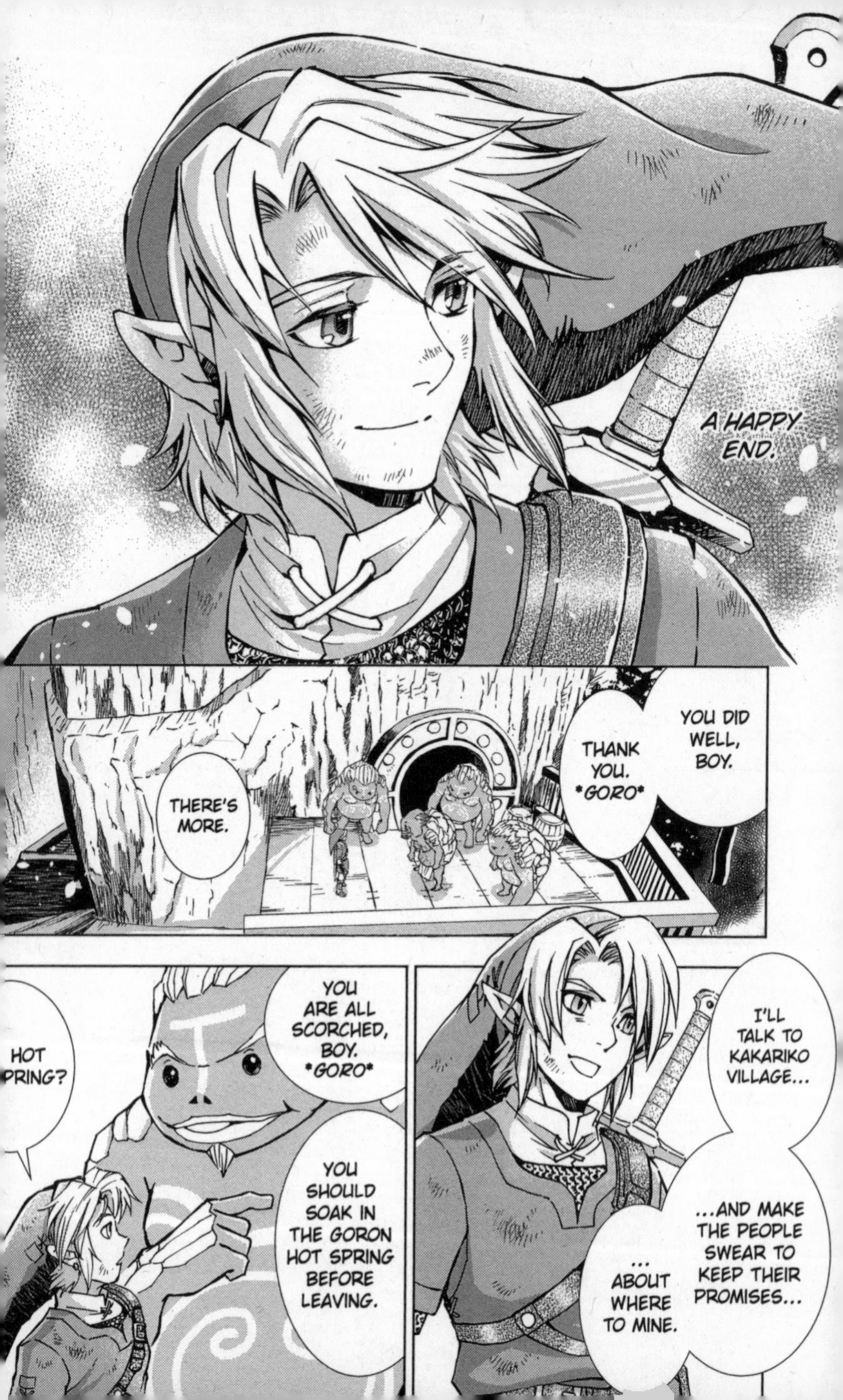
A HAPPY END.
YOU DID WELL, BOY.
THANK YOU. *GORO*
THERE'S MORE.
I'LL TALK TO KAKARIKO VILLAGE...
...AND MAKE THE PEOPLE SWEAR TO KEEP THEIR PROMISES...
... ABOUT WHERE TO MINE.
YOU ARE ALL SCORCHED, BOY. *GORO*
YOU SHOULD SOAK IN THE GORON HOT SPRING BEFORE LEAVING.
HOT PRING?

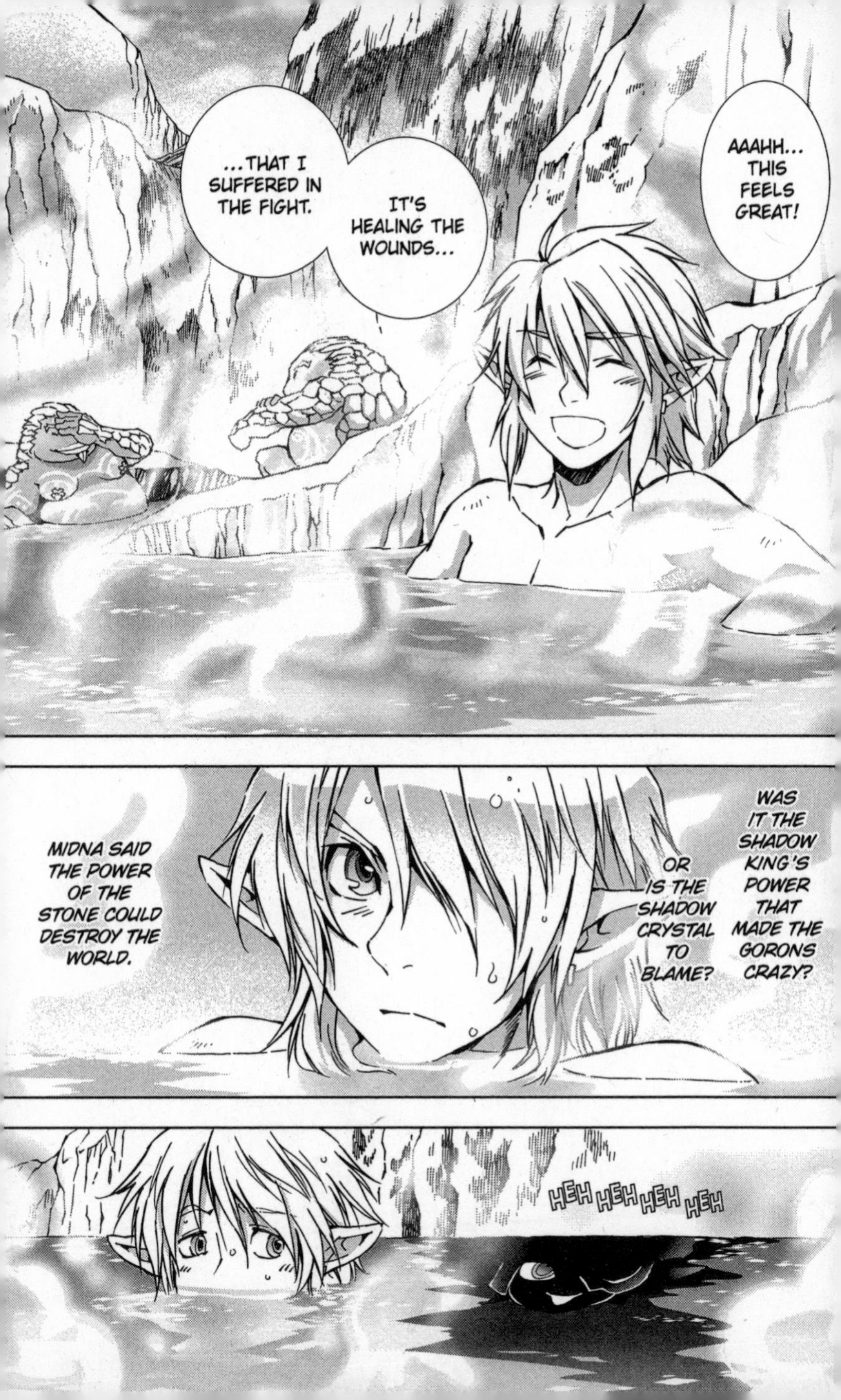
AAAHH... THIS FEELS GREAT!
IT'S HEALING THE WOUNDS...
...THAT I SUFFERED IN THE FIGHT.
WAS IT THE SHADOW KING'S POWER THAT MADE THE GORONS CRAZY?
OR IS THE SHADOW CRYSTAL TO BLAME?
MIDNA SAID THE POWER OF THE STONE COULD DESTROY THE WORLD.
HEH HEH HEH HEH

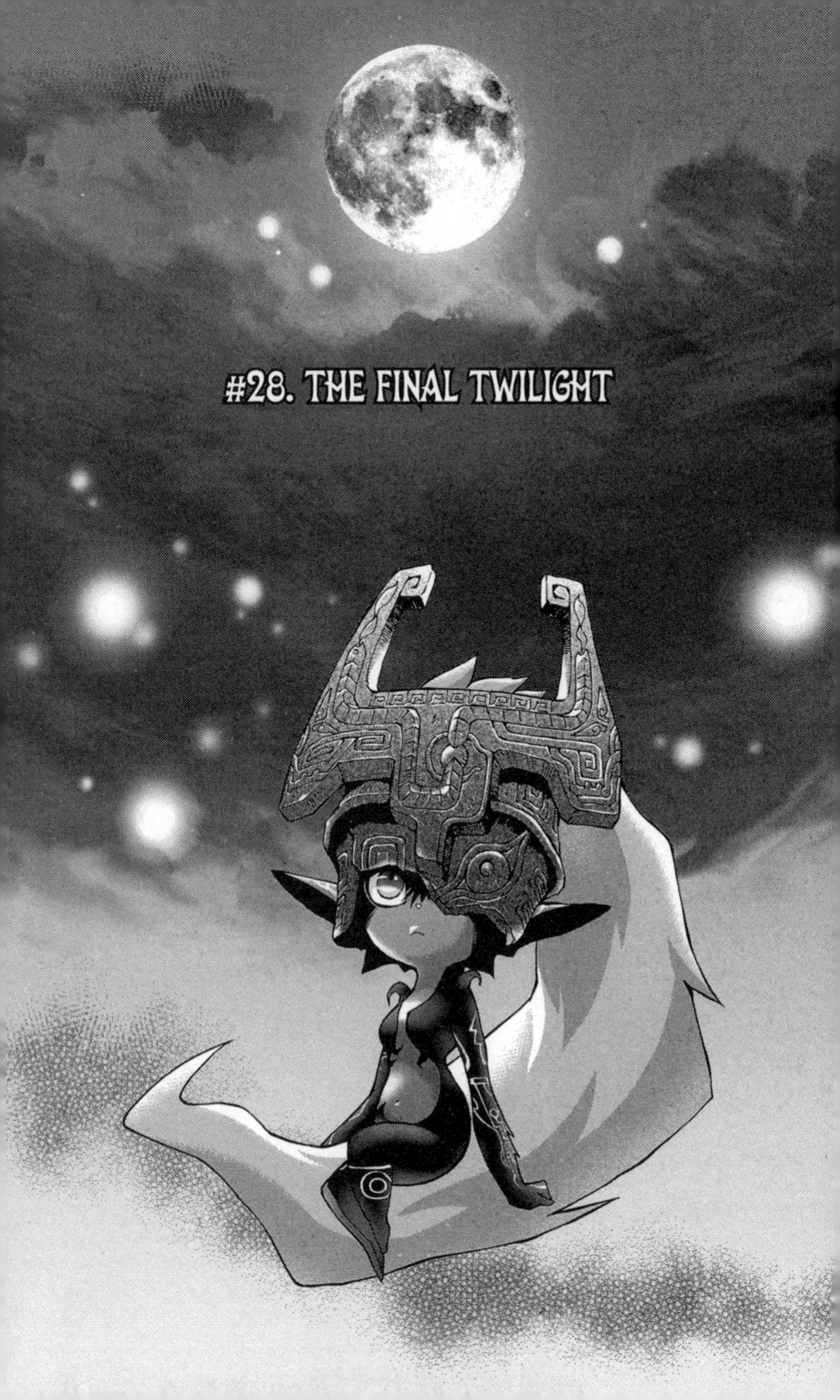
#28. THE FINAL TWILIGHT

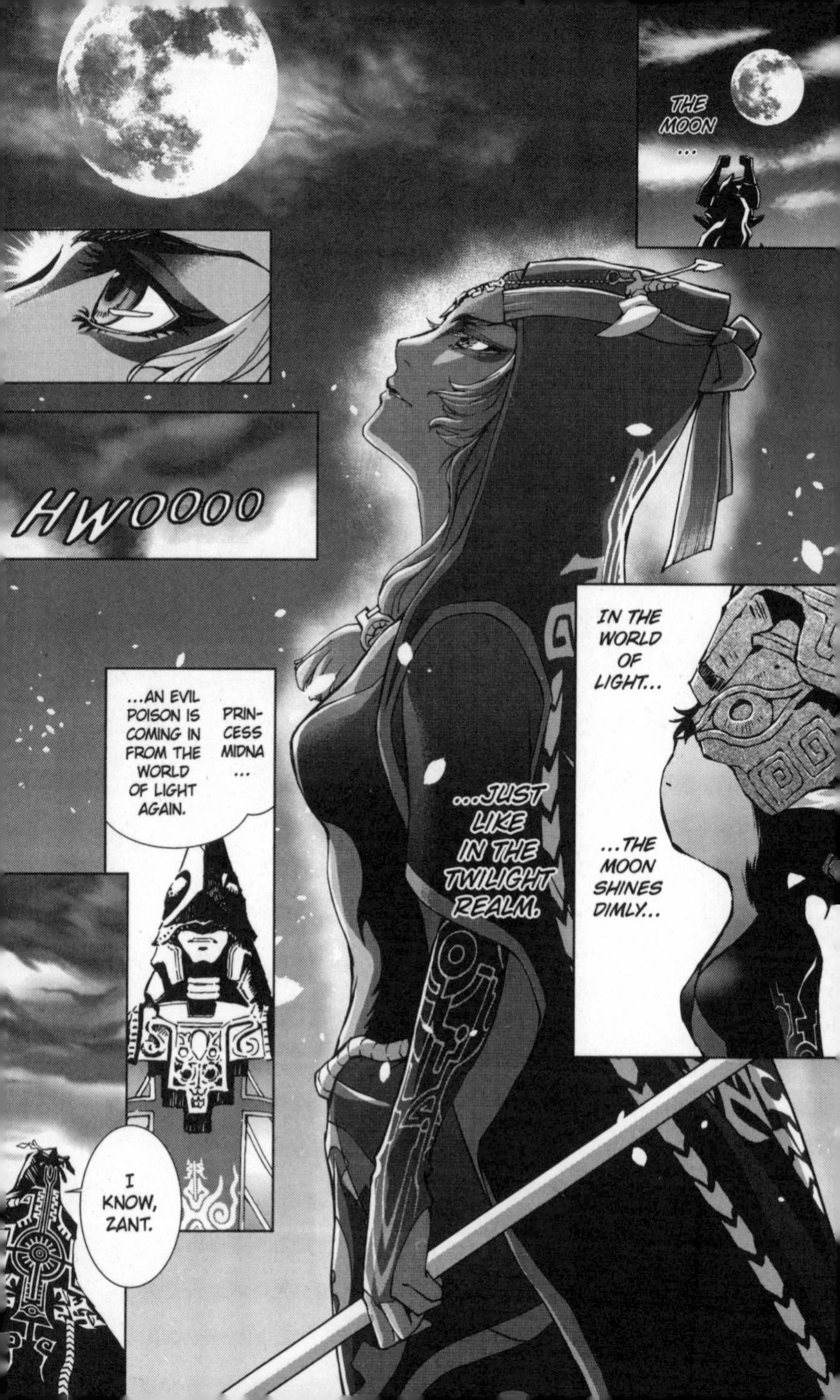
THE MOON ...
HWOOOO
IN THE WORLD OF LIGHT...
...THE MOON SHINES DIMLY...
...JUST LIKE IN THE TWILIGHT REALM.
PRIN-CESS MIDNA ...
...AN EVIL POISON IS COMING IN FROM THE WORLD OF LIGHT AGAIN.
I KNOW, ZANT.

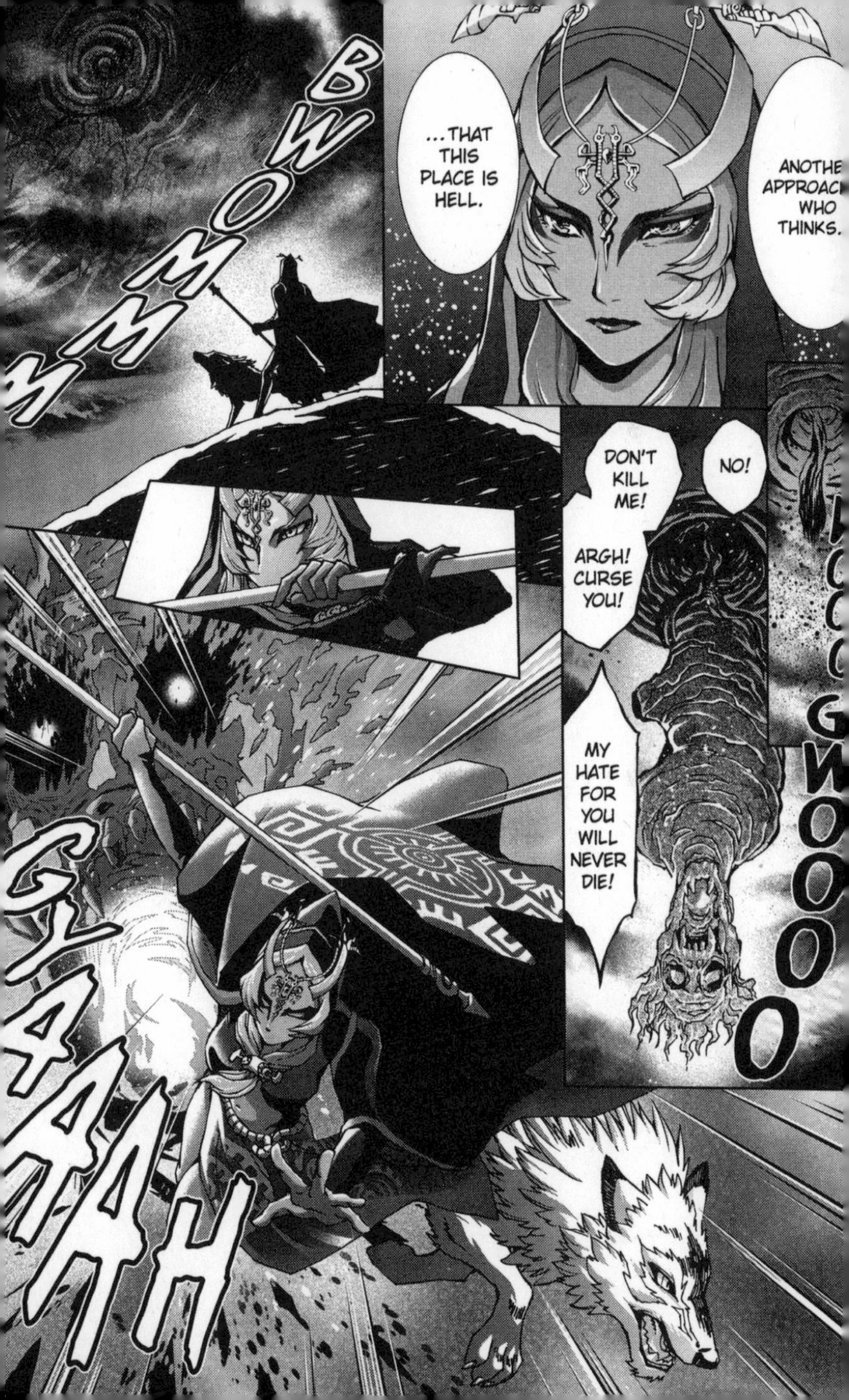
ANOTHE APPROAC WHO THINKS.
...THAT THIS PLACE IS HELL.
BWOMMM
NO!
DON'T KILL ME!
ARGH! CURSE YOU!
MY HATE FOR YOU WILL NEVER DIE!
GWOOOO
GYAAAHH

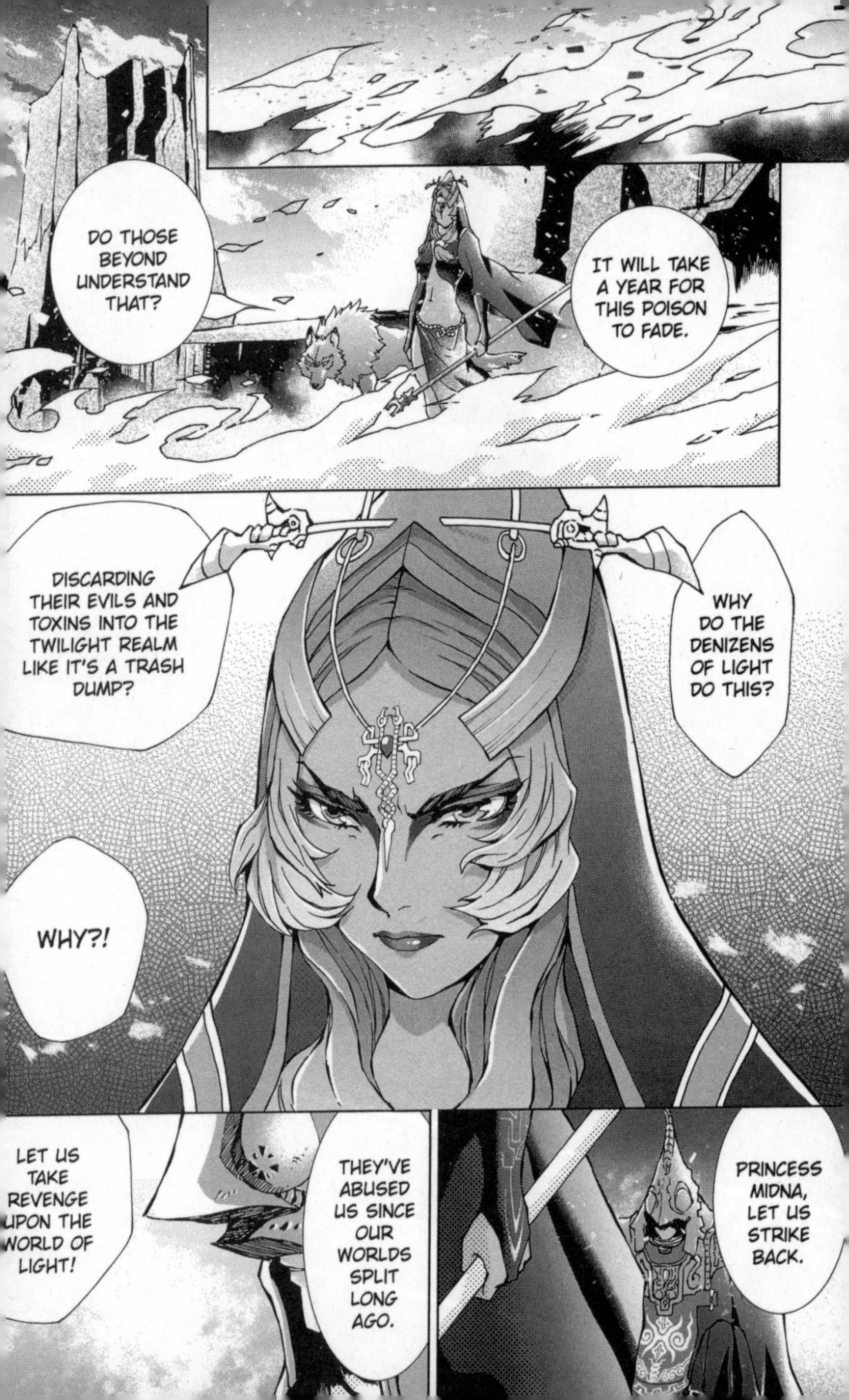
IT WILL TAKE A YEAR FOR THIS POISON TO FADE.
DO THOSE BEYOND UNDERSTAND THAT?
WHY DO THE DENIZENS OF LIGHT DO THIS?
DISCARDING THEIR EVILS AND TOXINS INTO THE TWILIGHT REALM LIKE IT'S A TRASH DUMP?
WHY?!
PRINCESS MIDNA, LET US STRIKE BACK.
THEY'VE ABUSED US SINCE OUR WORLDS SPLIT LONG AGO.
LET US TAKE REVENGE UPON THE WORLD OF LIGHT!

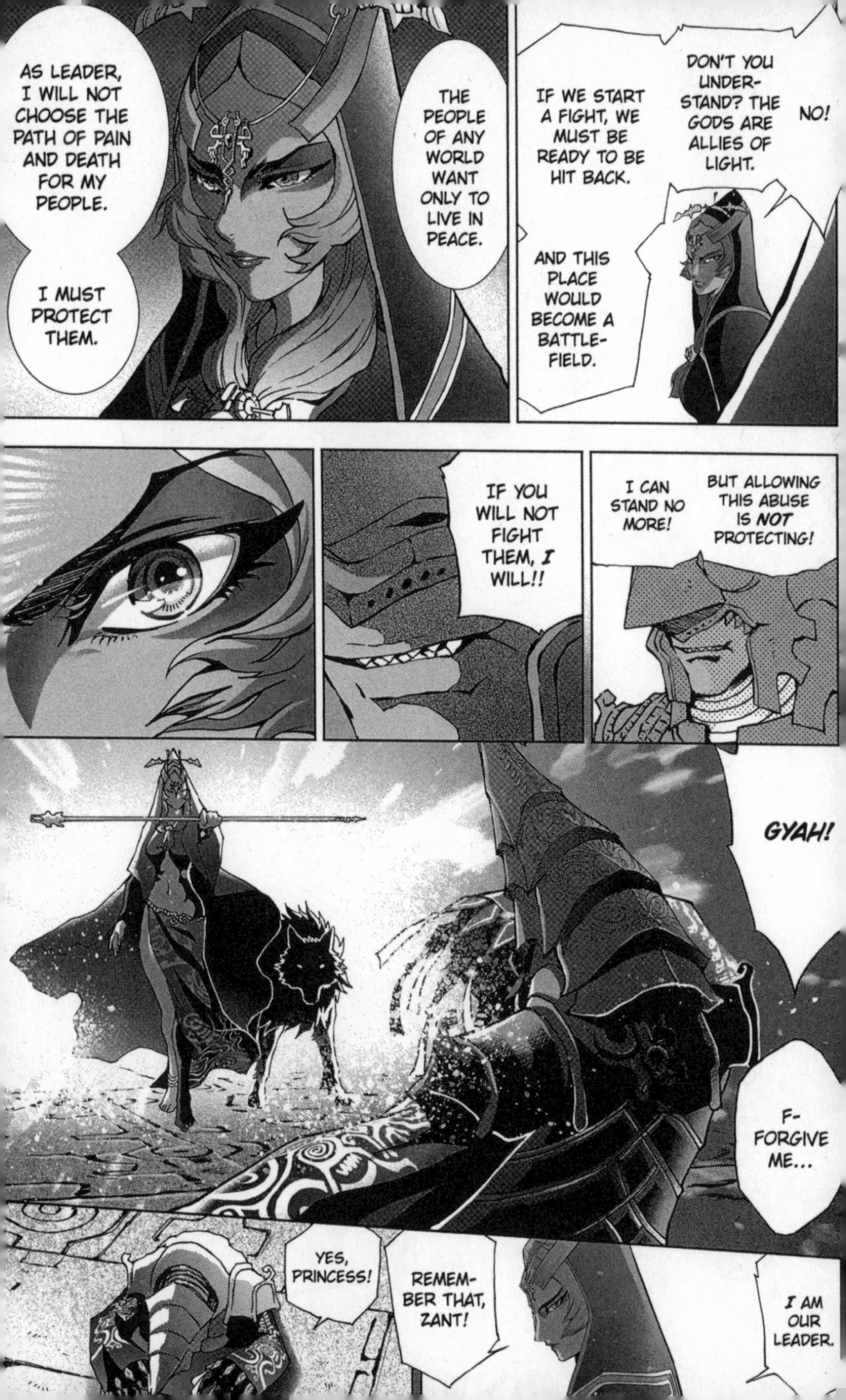
NO!
DON'T YOU UNDERSTAND? THE GODS ARE ALLIES OF LIGHT.
IF WE START A FIGHT, WE MUST BE READY TO BE HIT BACK.
AND THIS PLACE WOULD BECOME A BATTLEFIELD.
THE PEOPLE OF ANY WORLD WANT ONLY TO LIVE IN PEACE.
AS LEADER, I WILL NOT CHOOSE THE PATH OF PAIN AND DEATH FOR MY PEOPLE.
I MUST PROTECT THEM.
BUT ALLOWING THIS ABUSE IS *NOT* PROTECTING!
I CAN STAND NO MORE!
IF YOU WILL NOT FIGHT THEM, *I* WILL!!
GYAH!
F-FORGIVE ME...
I AM OUR LEADER.
REMEMBER THAT, ZANT!
YES, PRINCESS!

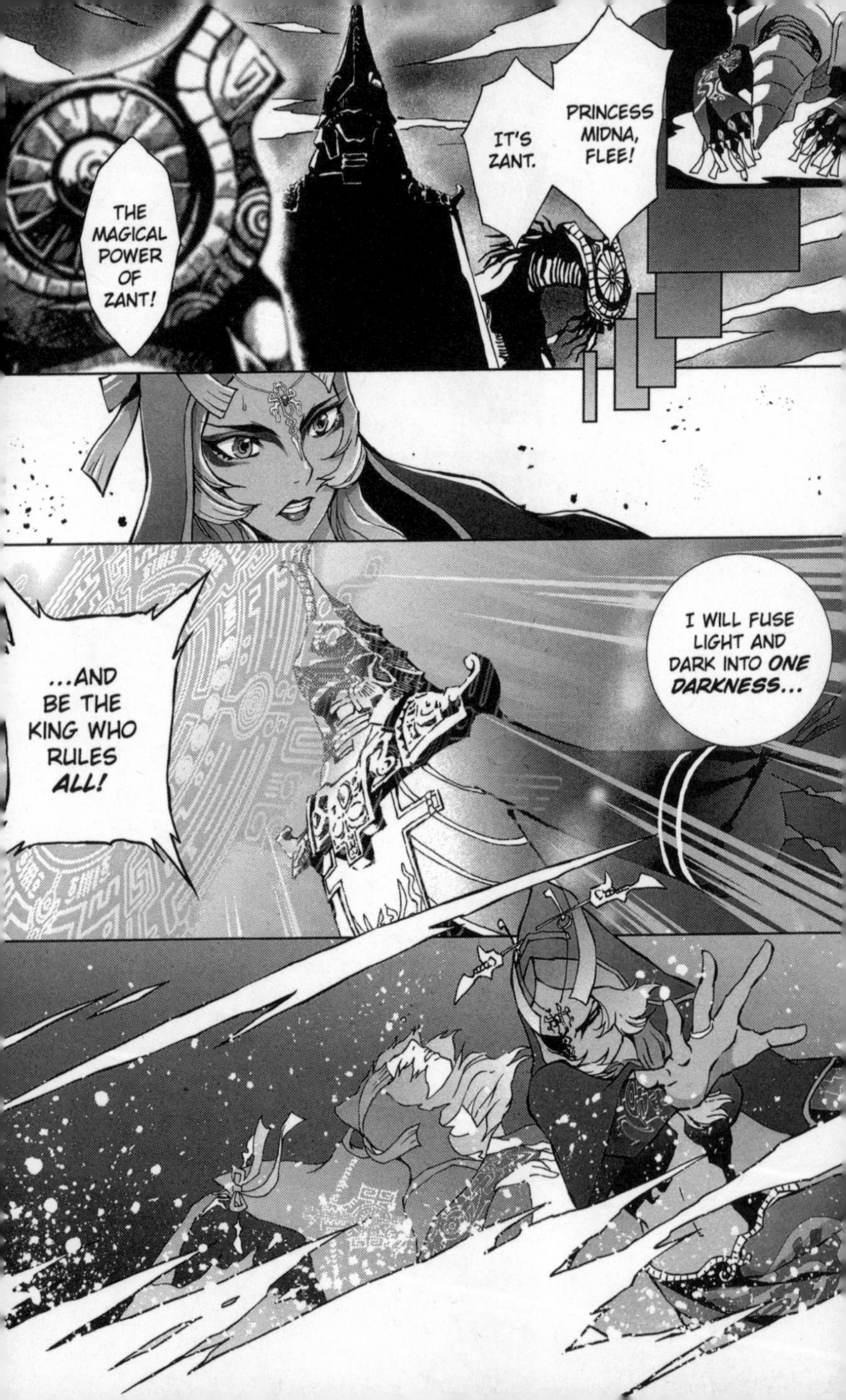
PRINCESS MIDNA, FLEE!
IT'S ZANT.
THE MAGICAL POWER OF ZANT!
I WILL FUSE LIGHT AND DARK INTO *ONE DARKNESS...*
...AND BE THE KING WHO RULES *ALL!*

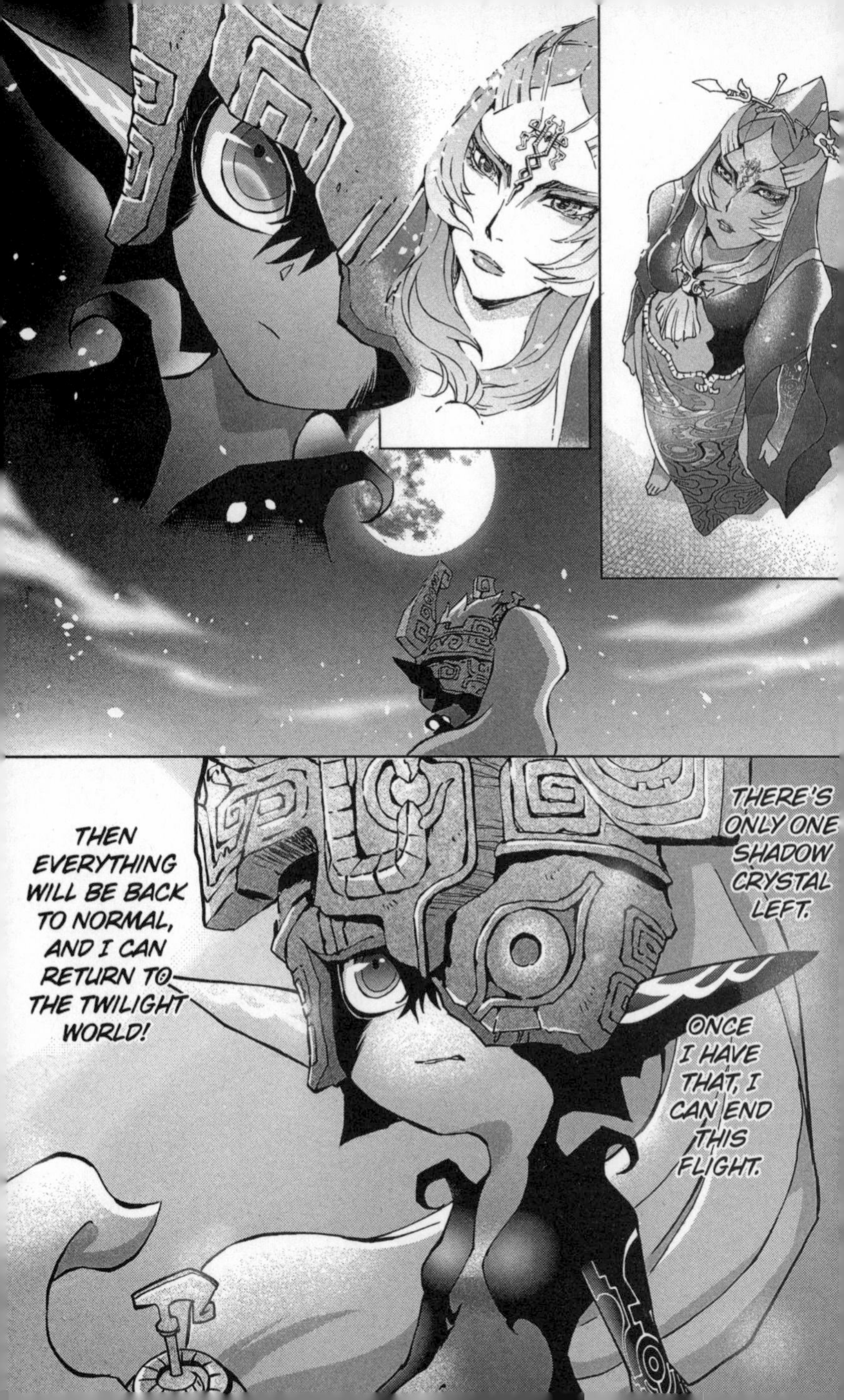
THERE'S ONLY ONE SHADOW CRYSTAL LEFT.
ONCE I HAVE THAT, I CAN END THIS FLIGHT.
THEN EVERYTHING WILL BE BACK TO NORMAL, AND I CAN RETURN TO THE TWILIGHT WORLD!

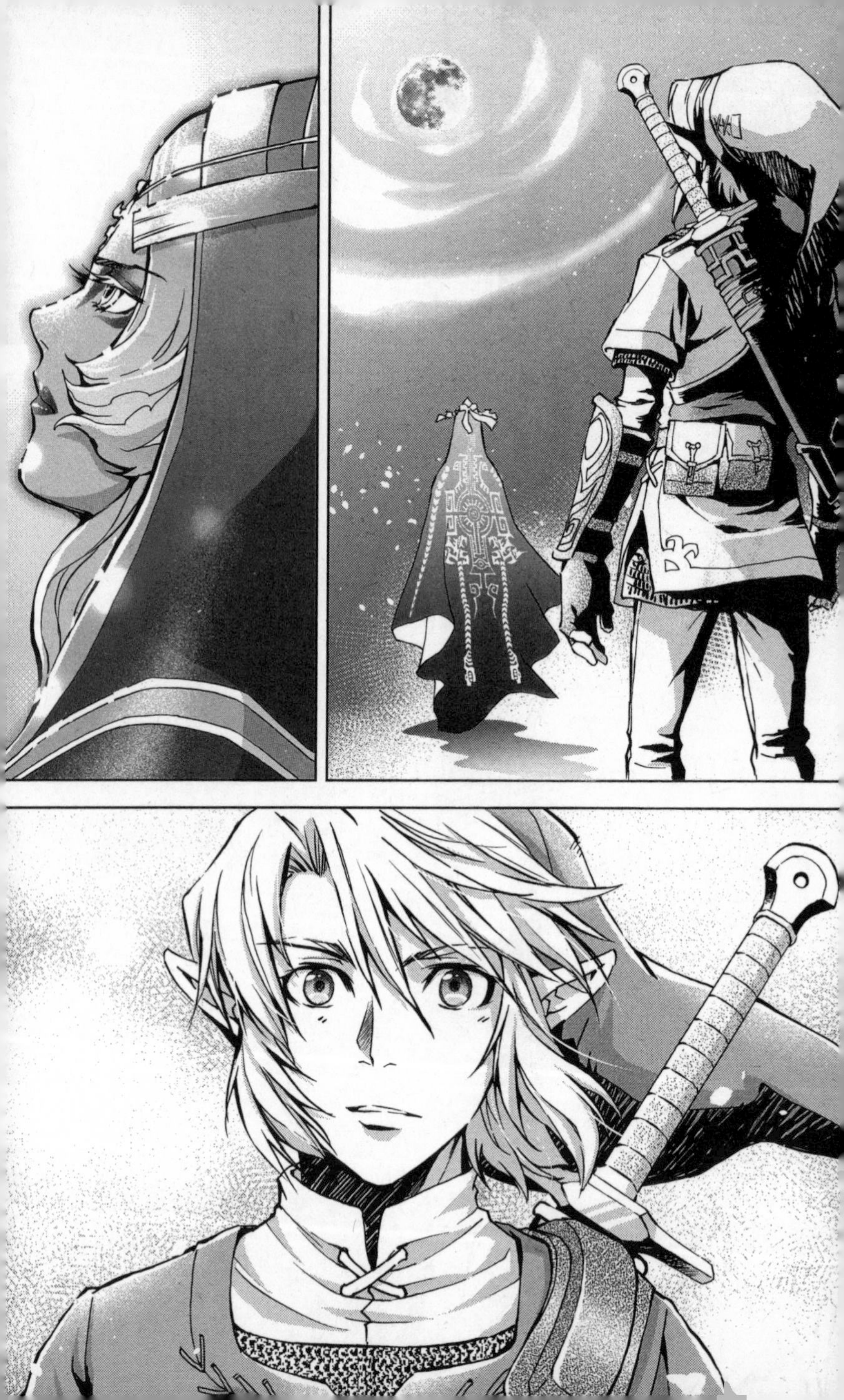

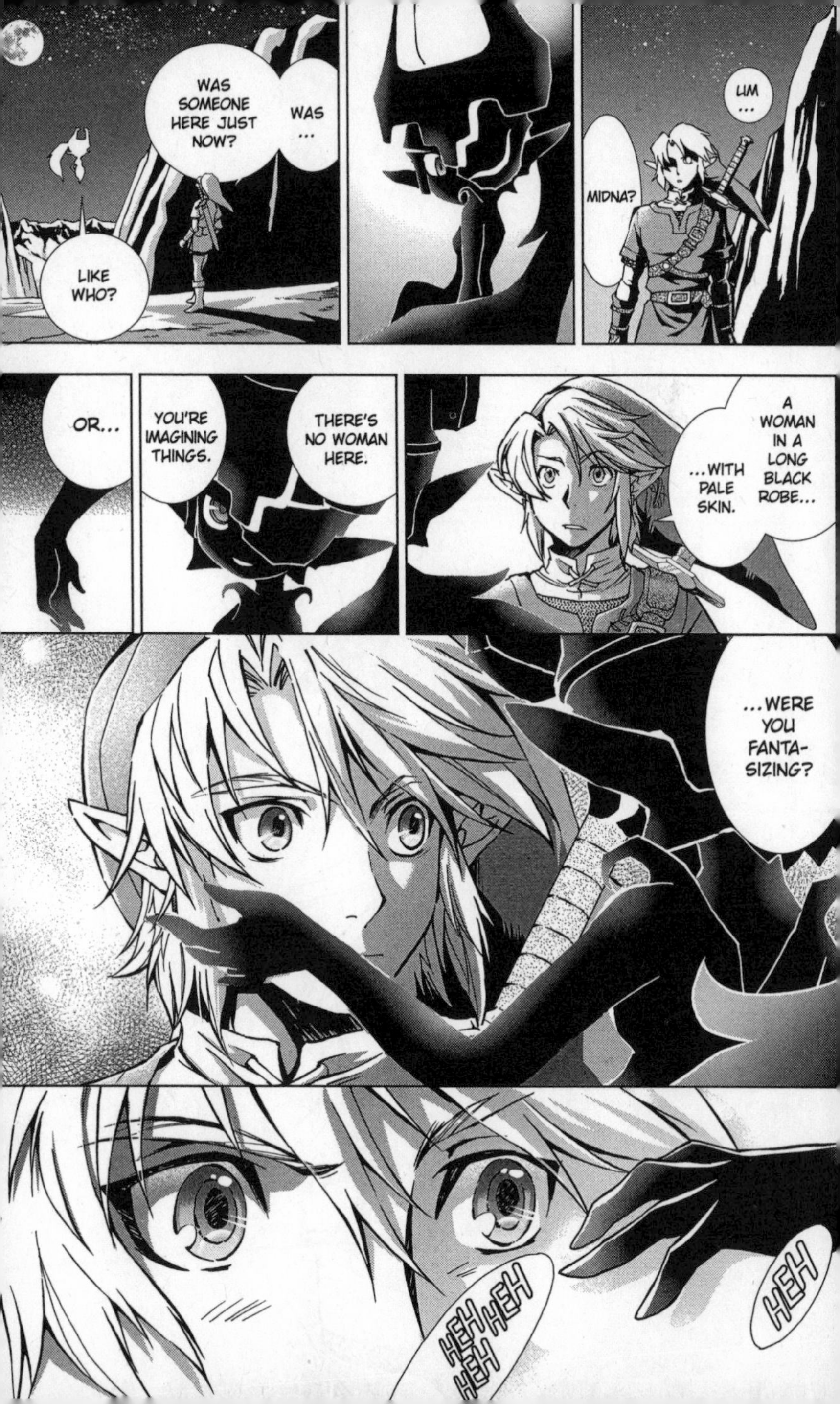
UM ...
MIDNA?
WAS ...
WAS SOMEONE HERE JUST NOW?
LIKE WHO?
A WOMAN IN A LONG BLACK ROBE...
...WITH PALE SKIN.
THERE'S NO WOMAN HERE.
YOU'RE IMAGINING THINGS.
OR...
...WERE YOU FANTA-SIZING?
HEH
HEH HEH HEH HEH

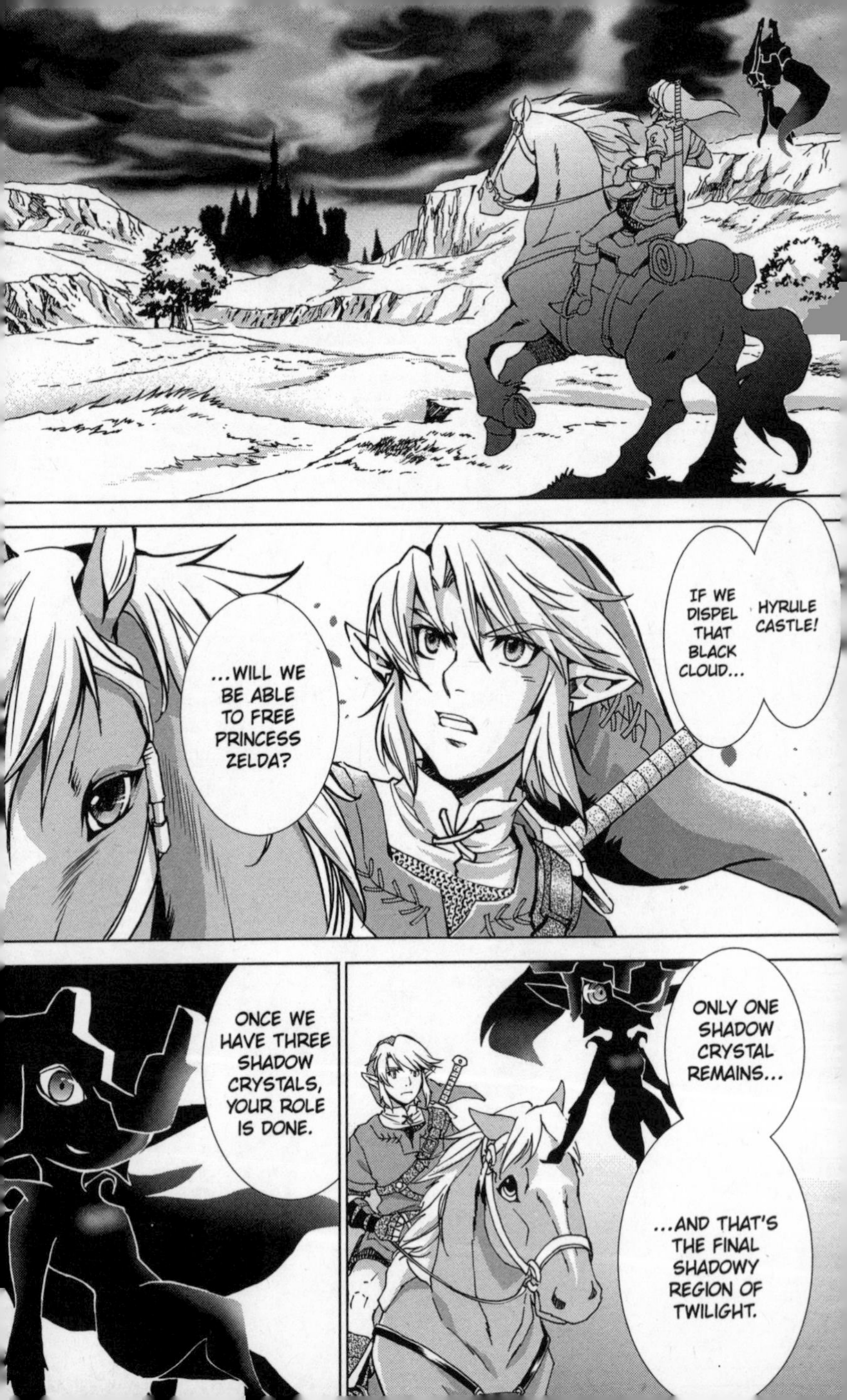
HYRULE CASTLE!
IF WE DISPEL THAT BLACK CLOUD...
...WILL WE BE ABLE TO FREE PRINCESS ZELDA?
ONLY ONE SHADOW CRYSTAL REMAINS...
...AND THAT'S THE FINAL SHADOWY REGION OF TWILIGHT.
ONCE WE HAVE THREE SHADOW CRYSTALS, YOUR ROLE IS DONE.

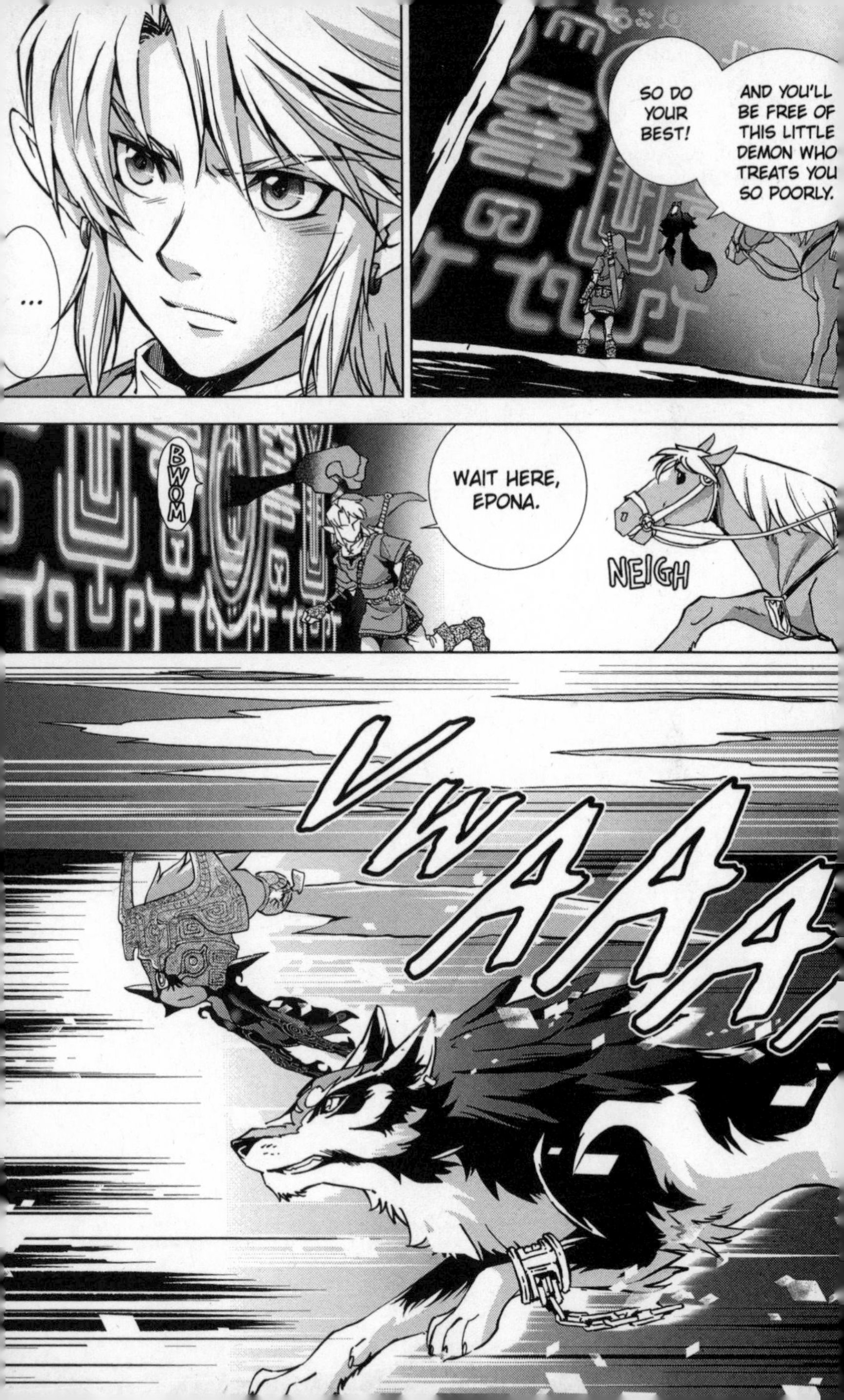
AND YOU'LL BE FREE OF THIS LITTLE DEMON WHO TREATS YOU SO POORLY.
SO DO YOUR BEST!
...
NEIGH
WAIT HERE, EPONA.
BWOM
VWAA

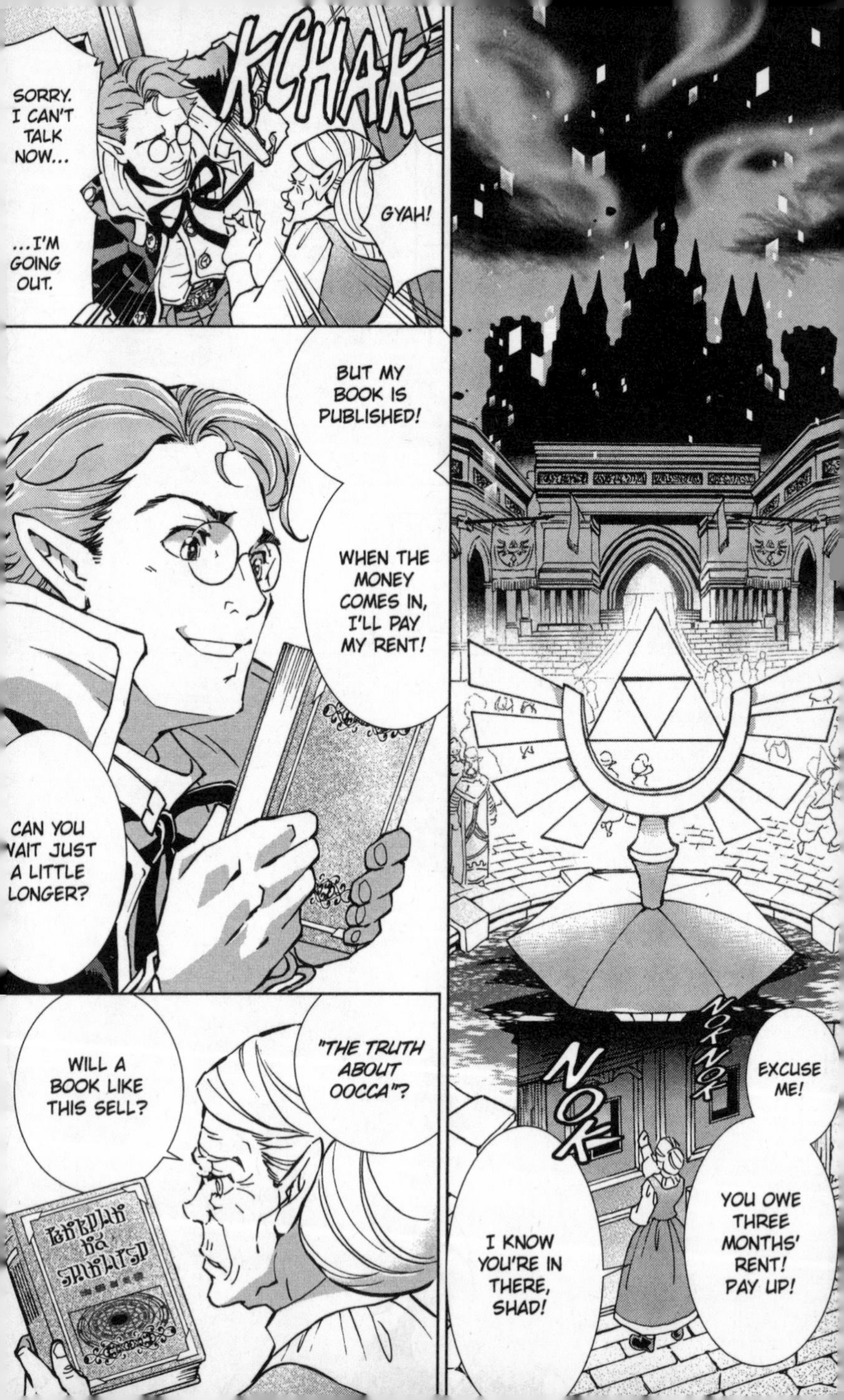
EXCUSE ME!
NOK NOK
NOK
YOU OWE THREE MONTHS' RENT! PAY UP!
I KNOW YOU'RE IN THERE, SHAD!
KCHAK
GYAH!
SORRY. I CAN'T TALK NOW...
...I'M GOING OUT.
BUT MY BOOK IS PUBLISHED!
WHEN THE MONEY COMES IN, I'LL PAY MY RENT!
CAN YOU WAIT JUST A LITTLE LONGER?
"THE TRUTH ABOUT OOCCA"?
WILL A BOOK LIKE THIS SELL?

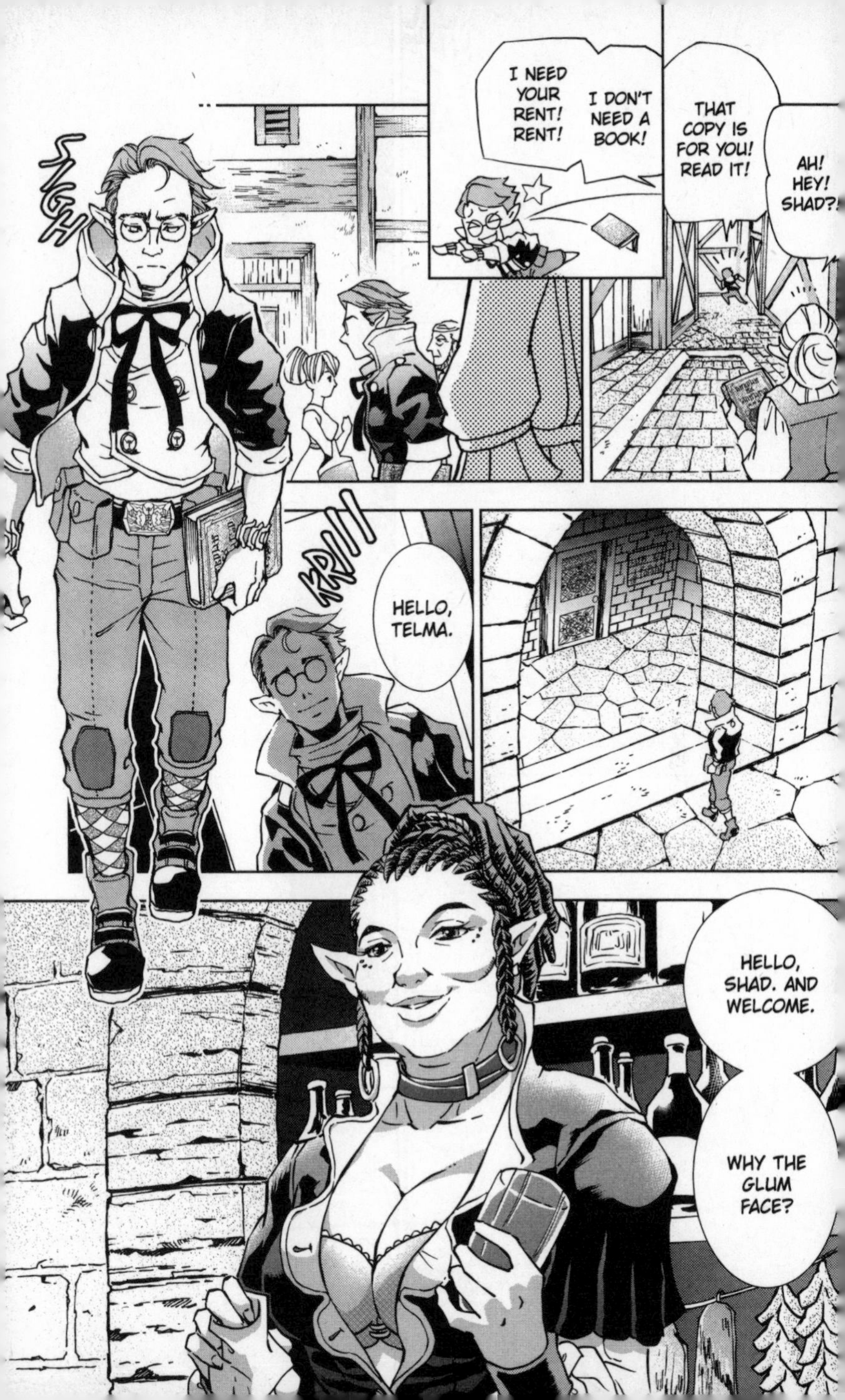
I NEED YOUR RENT! RENT!
I DON'T NEED A BOOK!
THAT COPY IS FOR YOU! READ IT!
AH! HEY! SHAD?!
SIGH
KRII
HELLO, TELMA.
HELLO, SHAD. AND WELCOME.
WHY THE GLUM FACE?

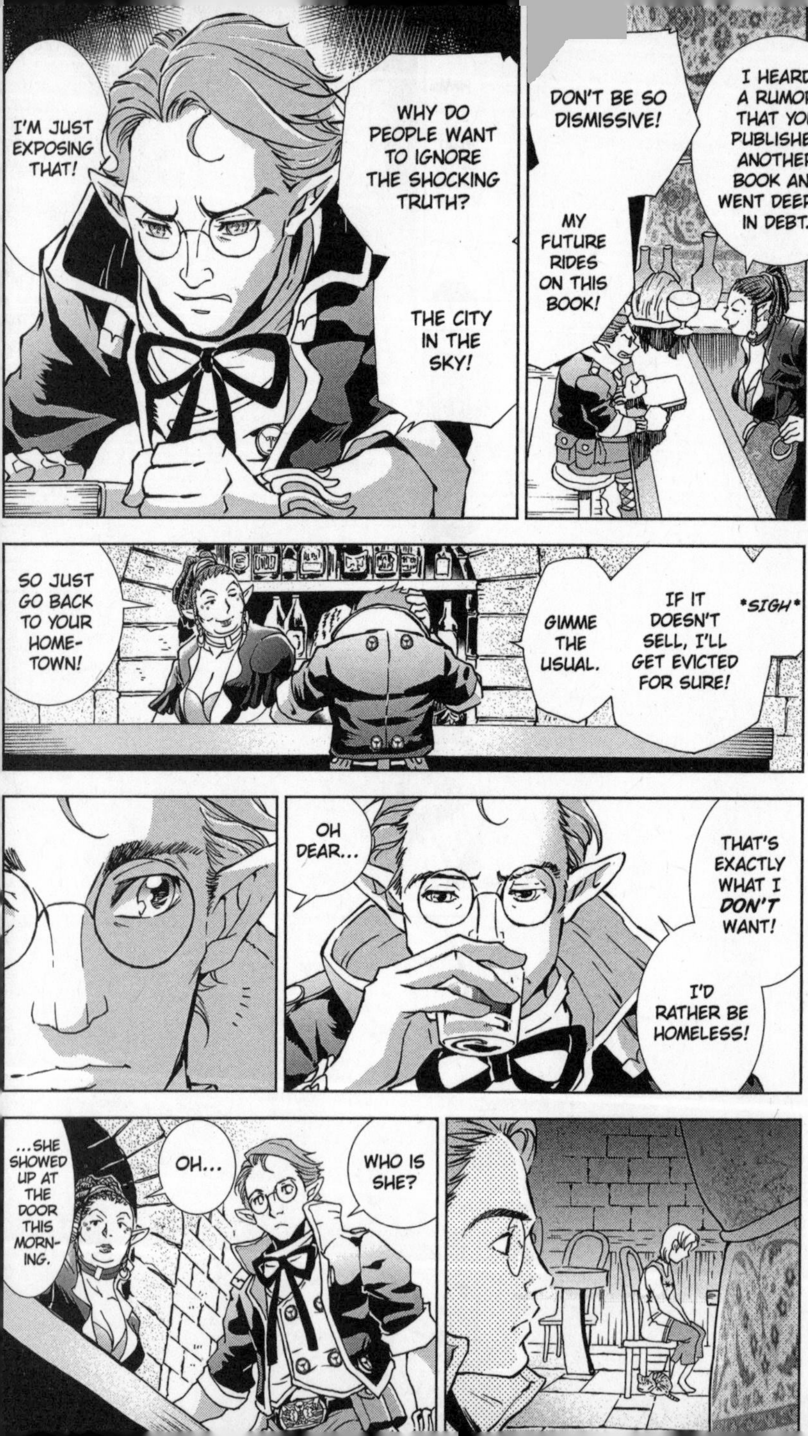
I HEARD A RUMOR THAT YOU PUBLISHED ANOTHER BOOK AND WENT DEEPER IN DEBT.
DON'T BE SO DISMISSIVE!
MY FUTURE RIDES ON THIS BOOK!
WHY DO PEOPLE WANT TO IGNORE THE SHOCKING TRUTH?
THE CITY IN THE SKY!
I'M JUST EXPOSING THAT!
SIGH
IF IT DOESN'T SELL, I'LL GET EVICTED FOR SURE!
GIMME THE USUAL.
SO JUST GO BACK TO YOUR HOME-TOWN!
THAT'S EXACTLY WHAT I ***DON'T*** WANT!
I'D RATHER BE HOMELESS!
OH DEAR...
WHO IS SHE?
OH...
...SHE SHOWED UP AT THE DOOR THIS MORNING.

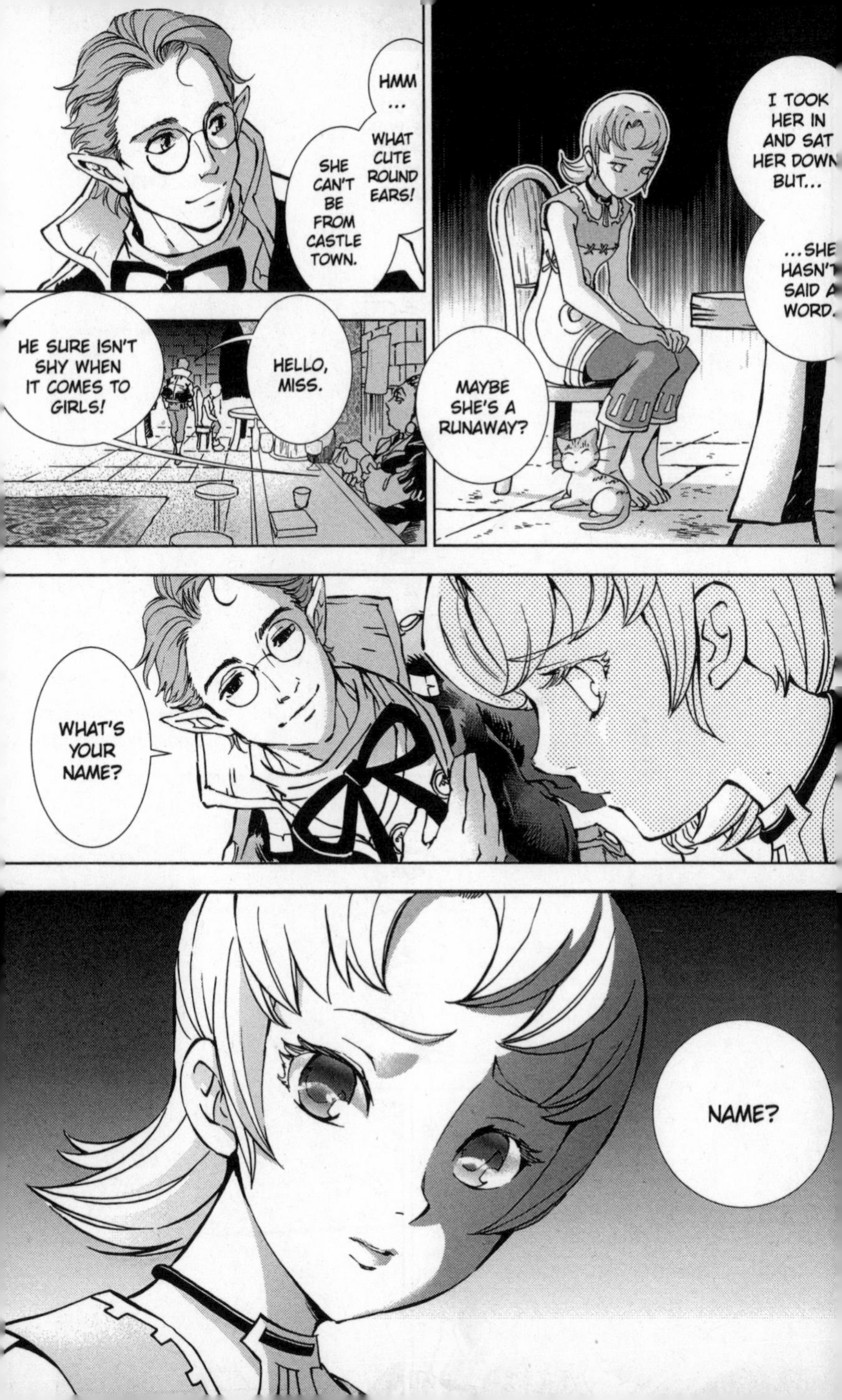
I TOOK HER IN AND SAT HER DOWN BUT...
...SHE HASN'T SAID A WORD.
MAYBE SHE'S A RUNAWAY?
HMM ... WHAT CUTE ROUND EARS!
SHE CAN'T BE FROM CASTLE TOWN.
HELLO, MISS.
HE SURE ISN'T SHY WHEN IT COMES TO GIRLS!
WHAT'S YOUR NAME?
NAME?

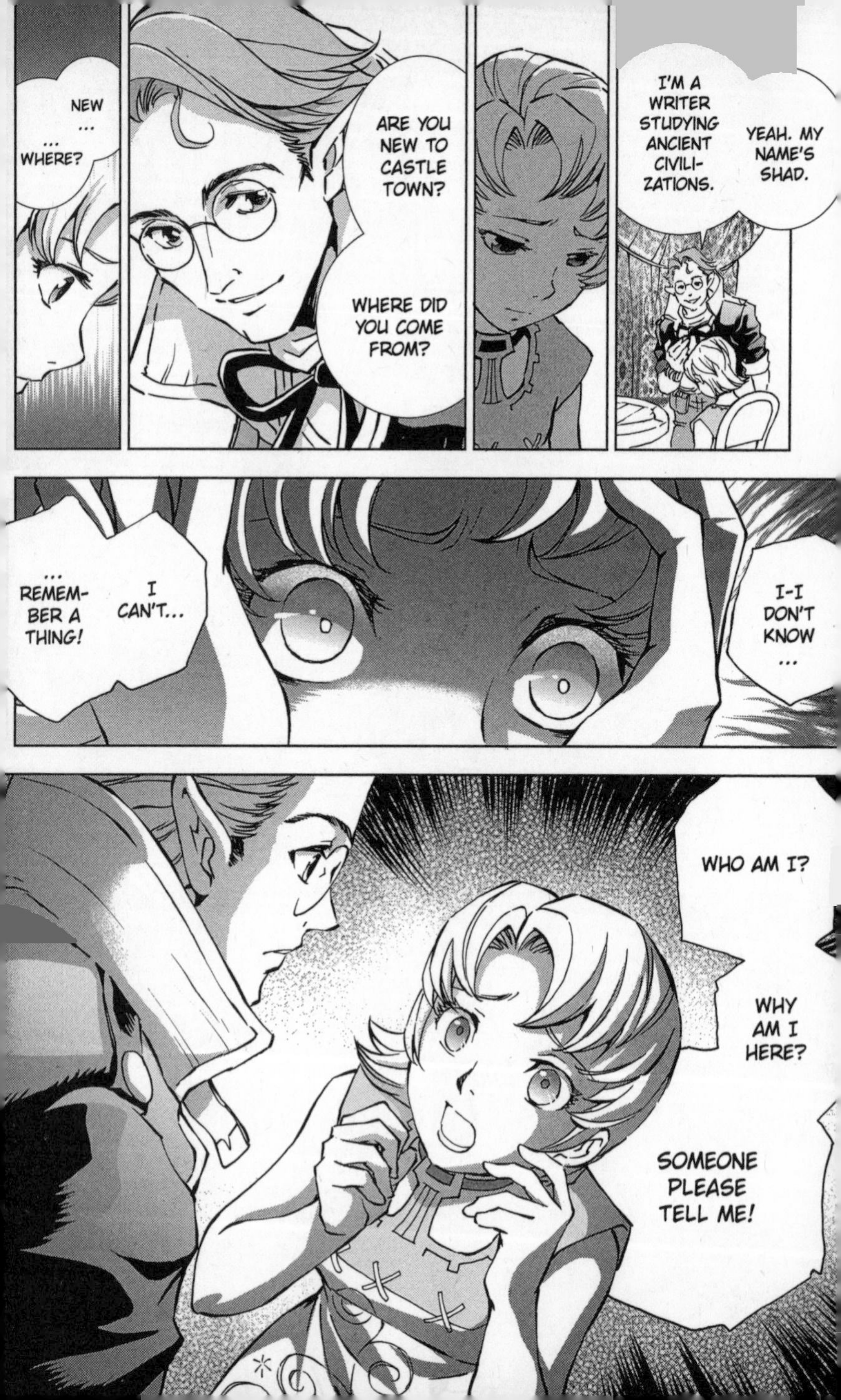
YEAH. MY NAME'S SHAD.
I'M A WRITER STUDYING ANCIENT CIVILI-ZATIONS.
ARE YOU NEW TO CASTLE TOWN?
WHERE DID YOU COME FROM?
NEW ...
... WHERE?
I-I DON'T KNOW ...
I CAN'T...
... REMEM-BER A THING!
WHO AM I?
WHY AM I HERE?
SOMEONE PLEASE TELL ME!

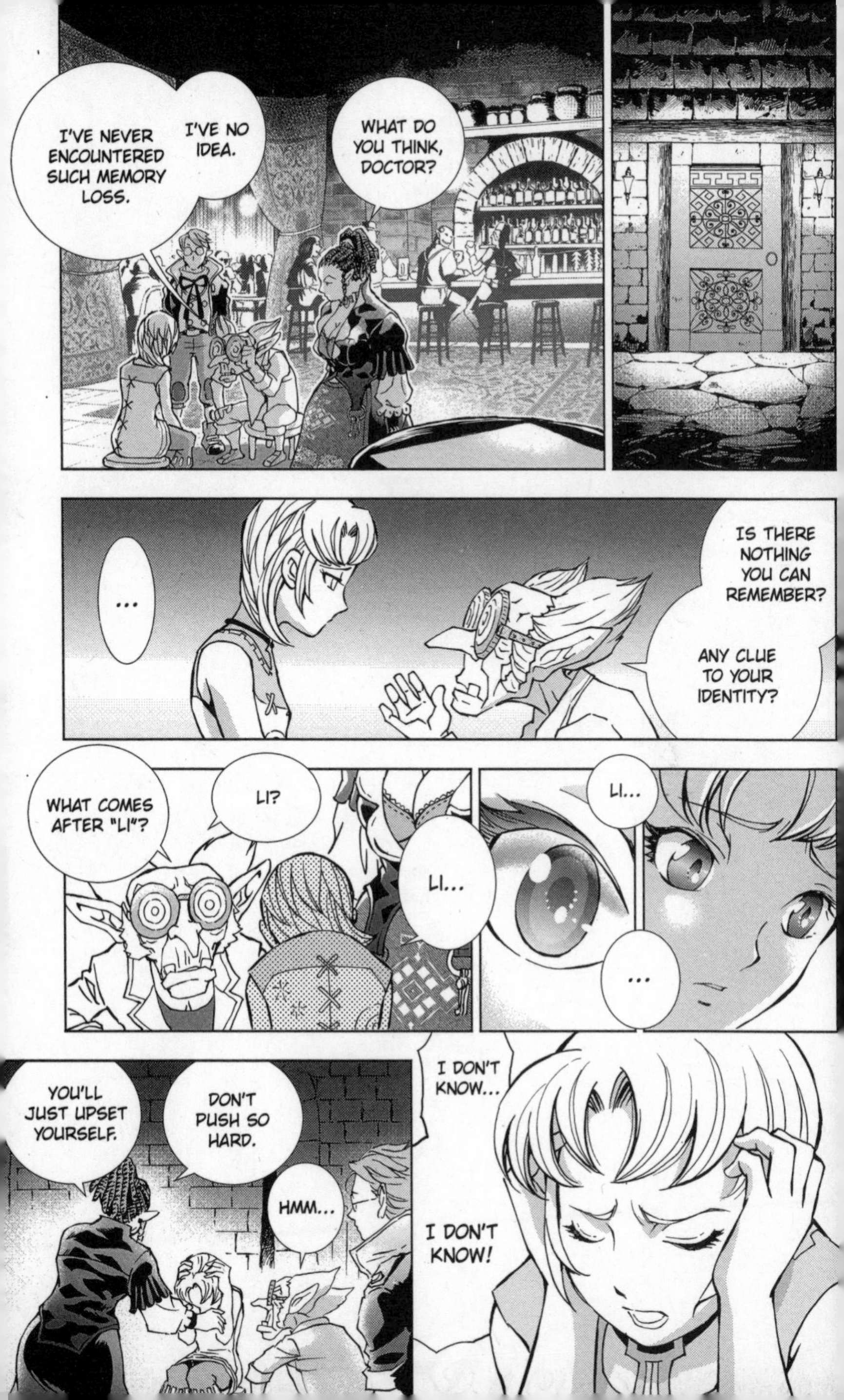
WHAT DO YOU THINK, DOCTOR?
I'VE NO IDEA.
I'VE NEVER ENCOUNTERED SUCH MEMORY LOSS.
IS THERE NOTHING YOU CAN REMEMBER?
ANY CLUE TO YOUR IDENTITY?
...
LI...
...
LI...
LI?
WHAT COMES AFTER "LI"?
I DON'T KNOW...
I DON'T KNOW!
DON'T PUSH SO HARD.
YOU'LL JUST UPSET YOURSELF.
HMM...

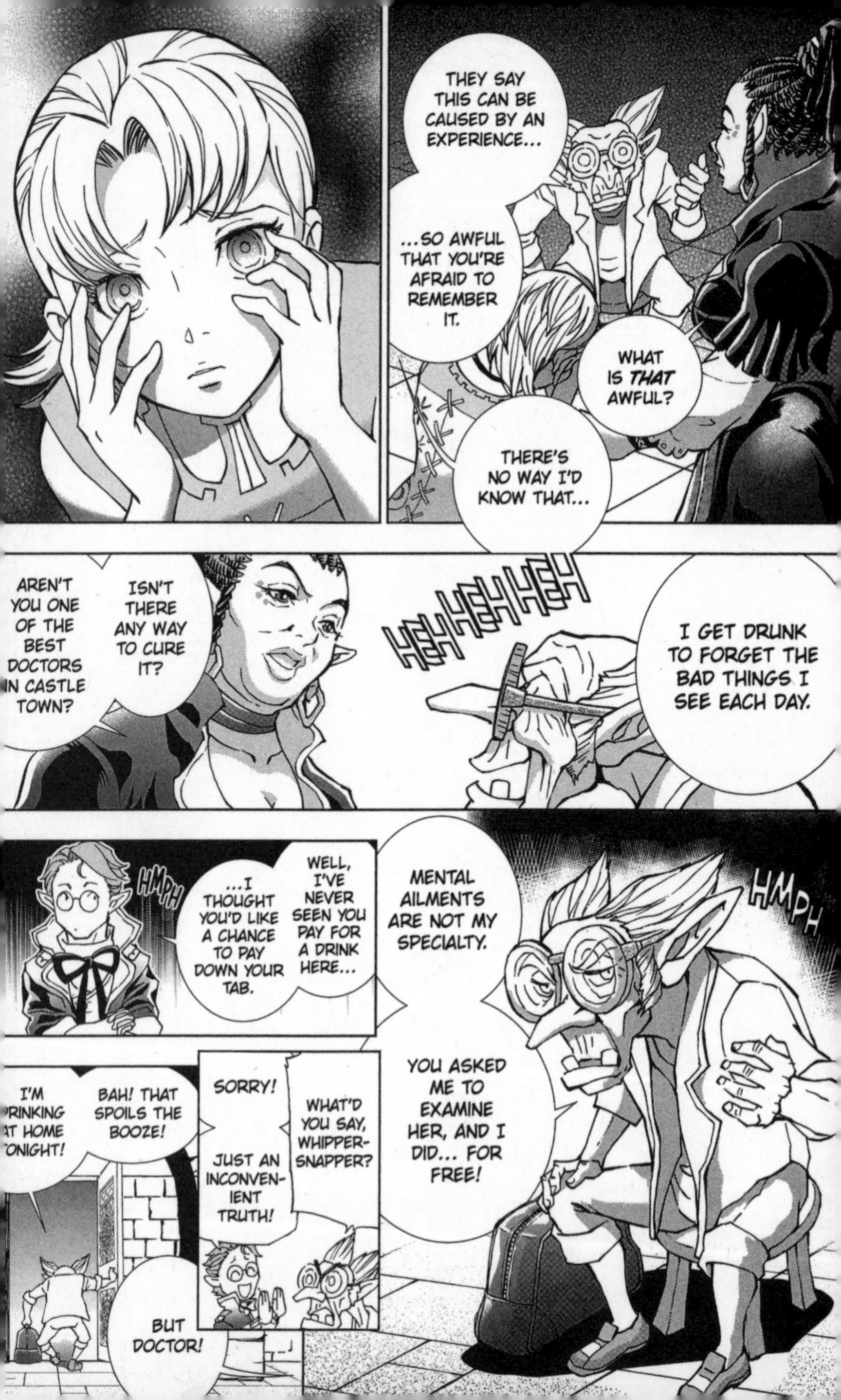

THEY SAY THIS CAN BE CAUSED BY AN EXPERIENCE...
...SO AWFUL THAT YOU'RE AFRAID TO REMEMBER IT.
WHAT IS *THAT* AWFUL?
THERE'S NO WAY I'D KNOW THAT...
I GET DRUNK TO FORGET THE BAD THINGS I SEE EACH DAY.
HEH HEH HEH HEH
ISN'T THERE ANY WAY TO CURE IT?
AREN'T YOU ONE OF THE BEST DOCTORS IN CASTLE TOWN?
HMPH
MENTAL AILMENTS ARE NOT MY SPECIALTY.
YOU ASKED ME TO EXAMINE HER, AND I DID... FOR FREE!
WELL, I'VE NEVER SEEN YOU PAY FOR A DRINK HERE...
...I THOUGHT YOU'D LIKE A CHANCE TO PAY DOWN YOUR TAB.
HMPH
WHAT'D YOU SAY, WHIPPER-SNAPPER?
SORRY!
JUST AN INCONVEN-IENT TRUTH!
BAH! THAT SPOILS THE BOOZE!
I'M DRINKING AT HOME TONIGHT!
BUT DOCTOR!

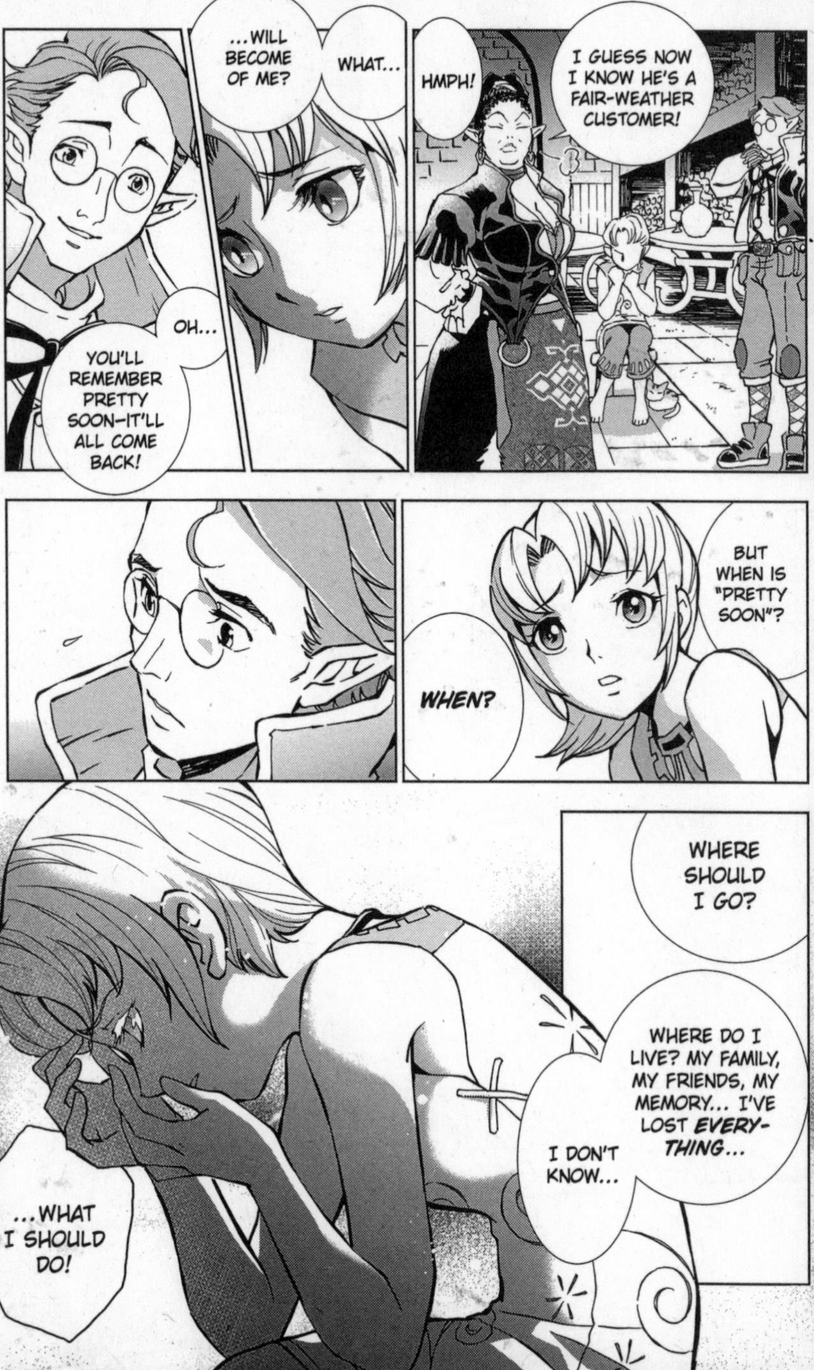
I GUESS NOW I KNOW HE'S A FAIR-WEATHER CUSTOMER!
HMPH!
WHAT...
...WILL BECOME OF ME?
OH...
YOU'LL REMEMBER PRETTY SOON—IT'LL ALL COME BACK!
BUT WHEN IS "PRETTY SOON"?
WHEN?
WHERE SHOULD I GO?
WHERE DO I LIVE? MY FAMILY, MY FRIENDS, MY MEMORY... I'VE LOST *EVERY-THING*...
I DON'T KNOW...
...WHAT I SHOULD DO!

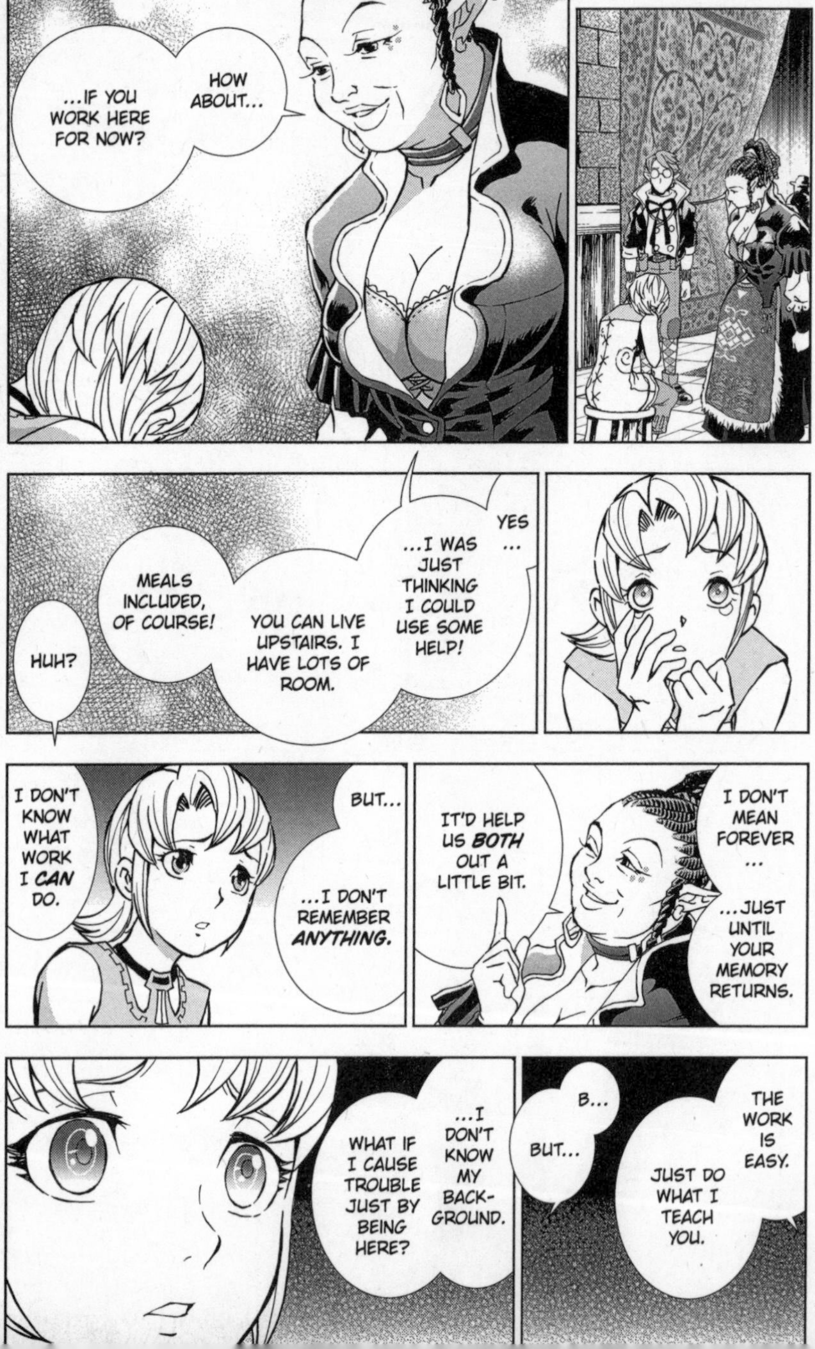
HOW ABOUT...
...IF YOU WORK HERE FOR NOW?
YES ...
...I WAS JUST THINKING I COULD USE SOME HELP!
YOU CAN LIVE UPSTAIRS. I HAVE LOTS OF ROOM.
MEALS INCLUDED, OF COURSE!
HUH?
I DON'T MEAN FOREVER ...
...JUST UNTIL YOUR MEMORY RETURNS.
IT'D HELP US *BOTH* OUT A LITTLE BIT.
BUT...
...I DON'T REMEMBER *ANYTHING.*
I DON'T KNOW WHAT WORK I *CAN* DO.
THE WORK IS EASY.
JUST DO WHAT I TEACH YOU.
B...
BUT...
...I DON'T KNOW MY BACK-GROUND.
WHAT IF I CAUSE TROUBLE JUST BY BEING HERE?

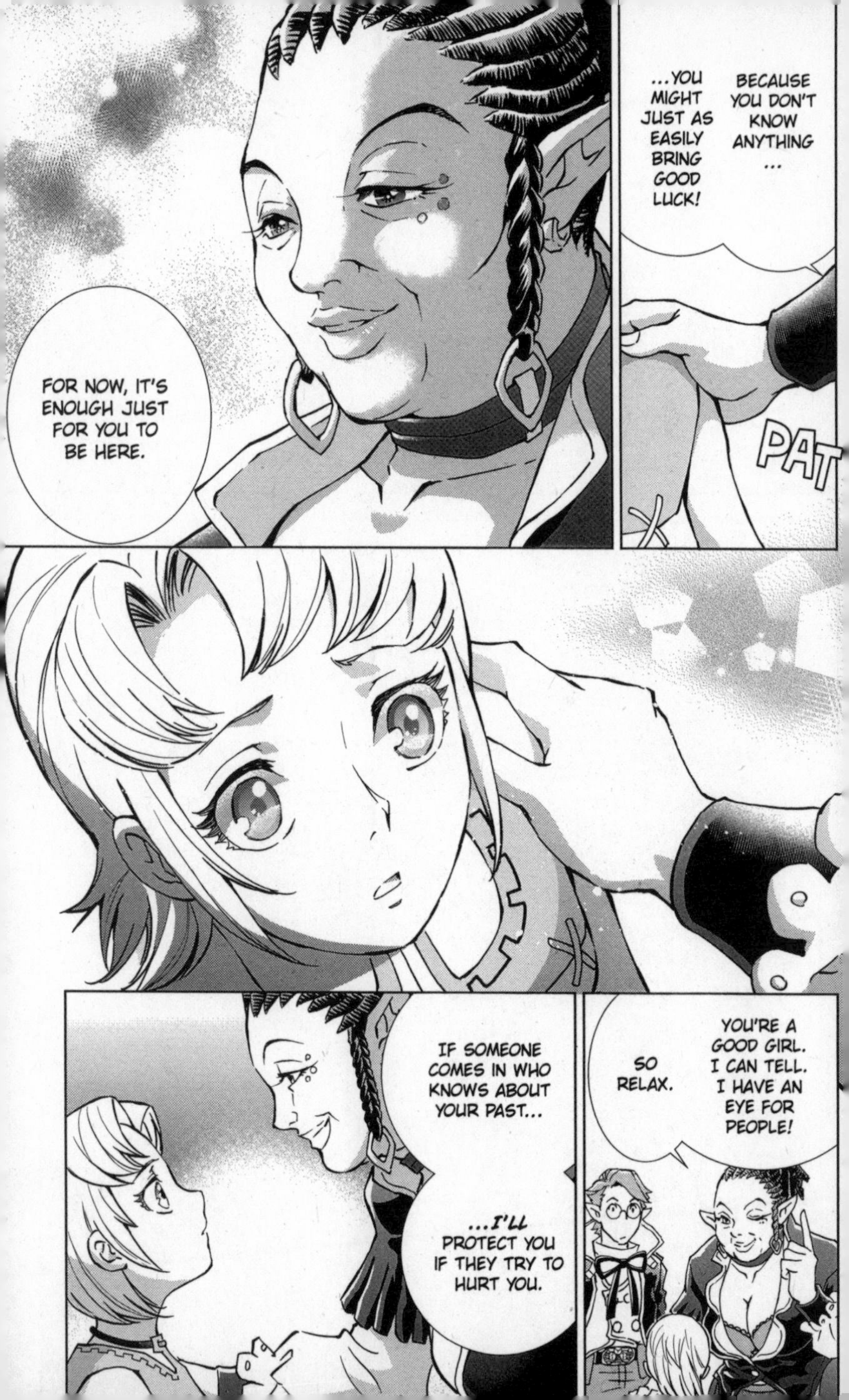
BECAUSE YOU DON'T KNOW ANYTHING...
...YOU MIGHT JUST AS EASILY BRING GOOD LUCK!
PAT
FOR NOW, IT'S ENOUGH JUST FOR YOU TO BE HERE.
YOU'RE A GOOD GIRL. I CAN TELL. I HAVE AN EYE FOR PEOPLE!
SO RELAX.
IF SOMEONE COMES IN WHO KNOWS ABOUT YOUR PAST...
...I'LL PROTECT YOU IF THEY TRY TO HURT YOU.

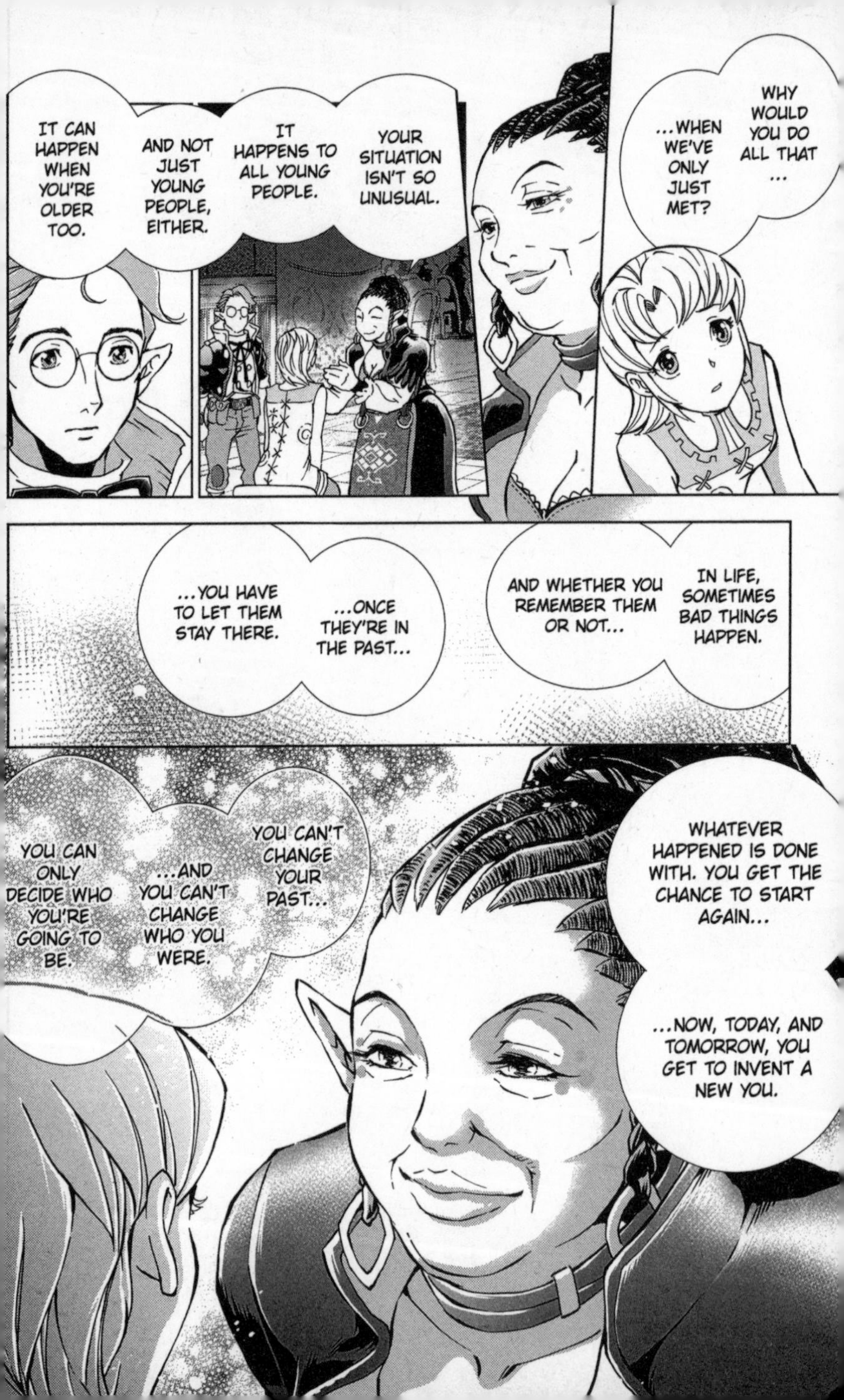
WHY WOULD YOU DO ALL THAT...
...WHEN WE'VE ONLY JUST MET?
YOUR SITUATION ISN'T SO UNUSUAL.
IT HAPPENS TO ALL YOUNG PEOPLE.
AND NOT JUST YOUNG PEOPLE, EITHER.
IT CAN HAPPEN WHEN YOU'RE OLDER TOO.
IN LIFE, SOMETIMES BAD THINGS HAPPEN.
AND WHETHER YOU REMEMBER THEM OR NOT...
...ONCE THEY'RE IN THE PAST...
...YOU HAVE TO LET THEM STAY THERE.
WHATEVER HAPPENED IS DONE WITH. YOU GET THE CHANCE TO START AGAIN...
...NOW, TODAY, AND TOMORROW, YOU GET TO INVENT A NEW YOU.
YOU CAN'T CHANGE YOUR PAST...
...AND YOU CAN'T CHANGE WHO YOU WERE.
YOU CAN ONLY DECIDE WHO YOU'RE GOING TO BE.

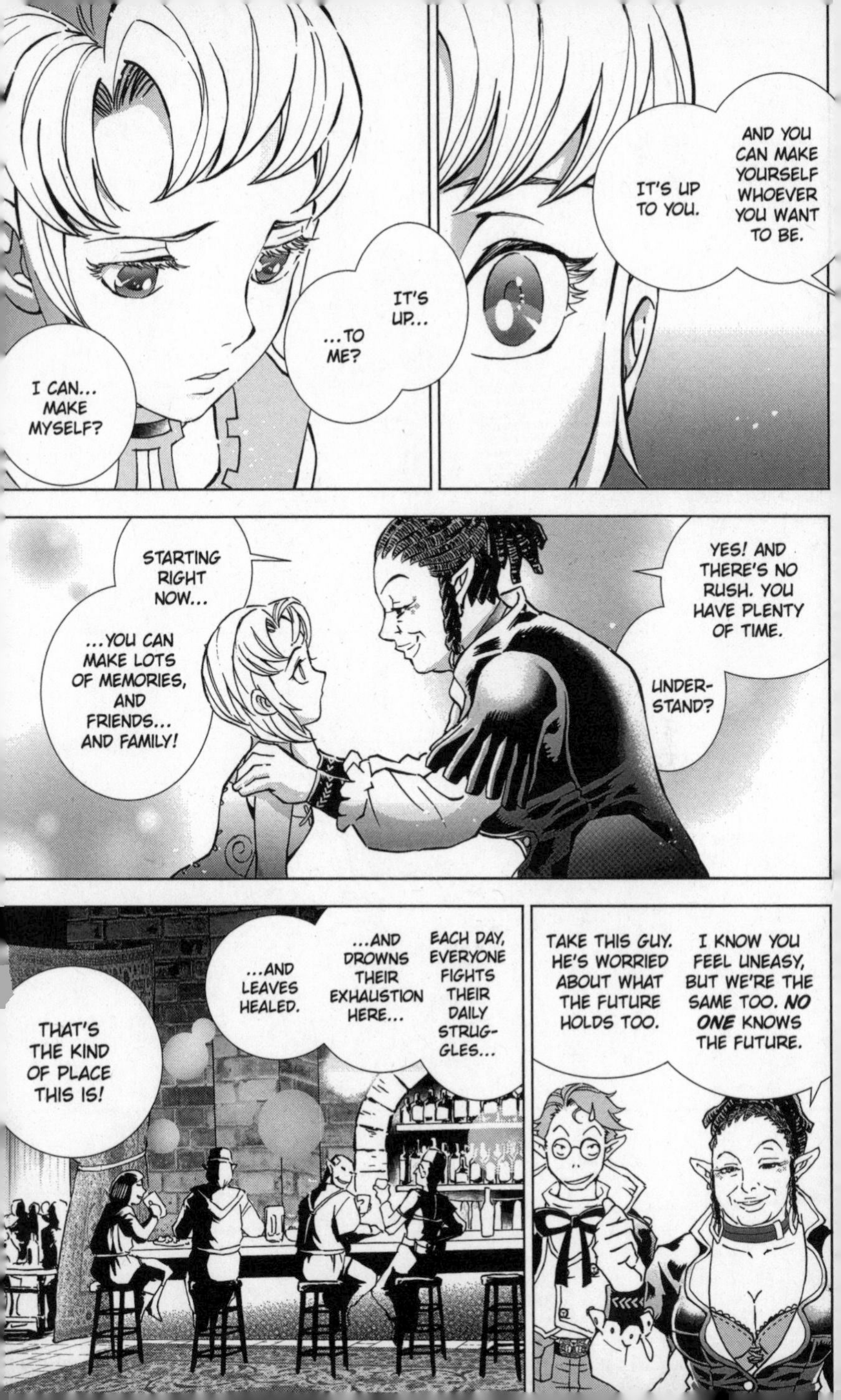
IT'S UP TO YOU.
AND YOU CAN MAKE YOURSELF WHOEVER YOU WANT TO BE.
IT'S UP...
...TO ME?
I CAN... MAKE MYSELF?
YES! AND THERE'S NO RUSH. YOU HAVE PLENTY OF TIME.
UNDER-STAND?
STARTING RIGHT NOW...
...YOU CAN MAKE LOTS OF MEMORIES, AND FRIENDS... AND FAMILY!
I KNOW YOU FEEL UNEASY, BUT WE'RE THE SAME TOO. *NO ONE* KNOWS THE FUTURE.
TAKE THIS GUY. HE'S WORRIED ABOUT WHAT THE FUTURE HOLDS TOO.
EACH DAY, EVERYONE FIGHTS THEIR DAILY STRUG-GLES...
...AND DROWNS THEIR EXHAUSTION HERE...
...AND LEAVES HEALED.
THAT'S THE KIND OF PLACE THIS IS!

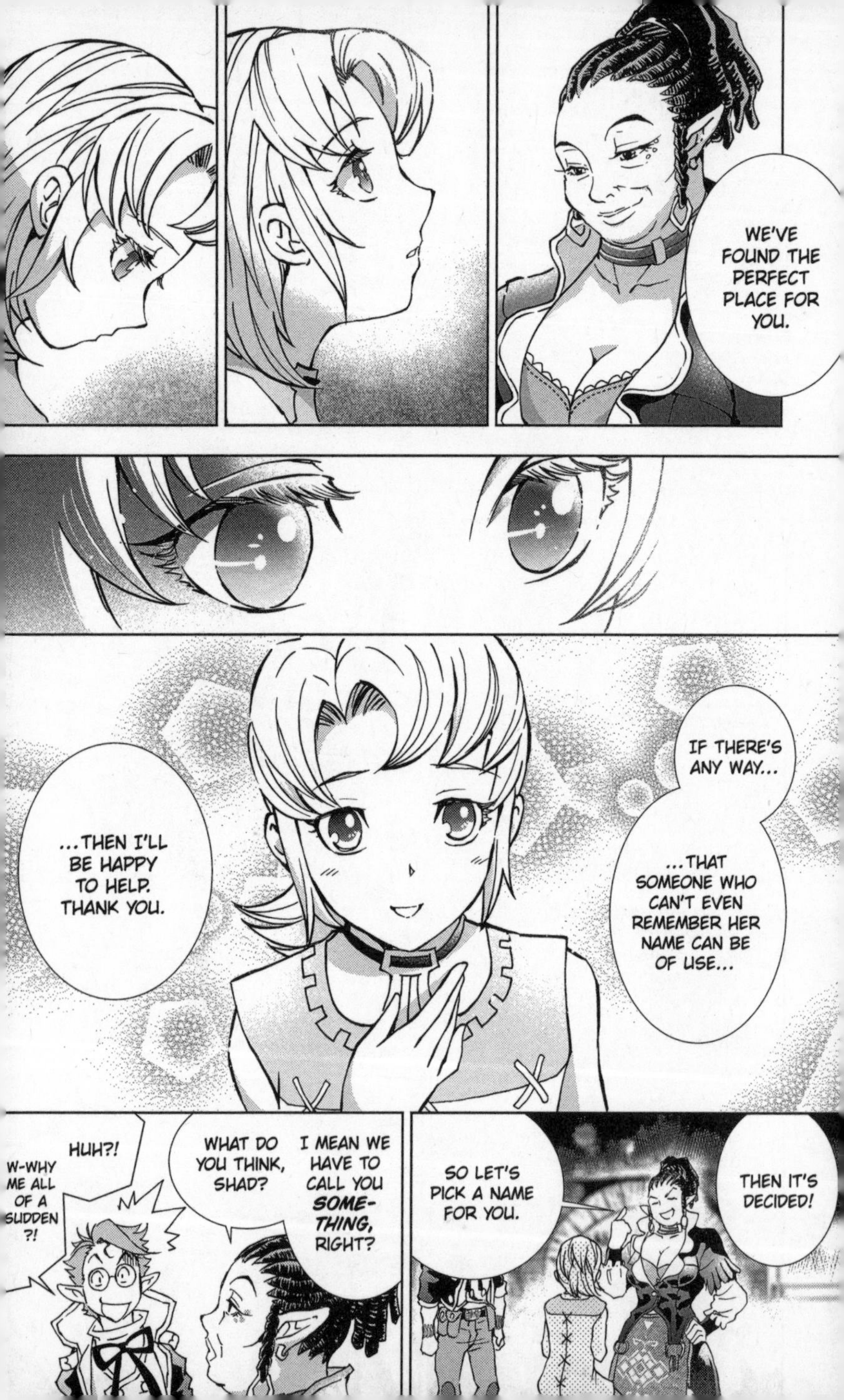
WE'VE FOUND THE PERFECT PLACE FOR YOU.
IF THERE'S ANY WAY...
...THAT SOMEONE WHO CAN'T EVEN REMEMBER HER NAME CAN BE OF USE...
...THEN I'LL BE HAPPY TO HELP. THANK YOU.
THEN IT'S DECIDED!
SO LET'S PICK A NAME FOR YOU.
I MEAN WE HAVE TO CALL YOU *SOMETHING*, RIGHT?
WHAT DO YOU THINK, SHAD?
HUH?!
W-WHY ME ALL OF A SUDDEN?!

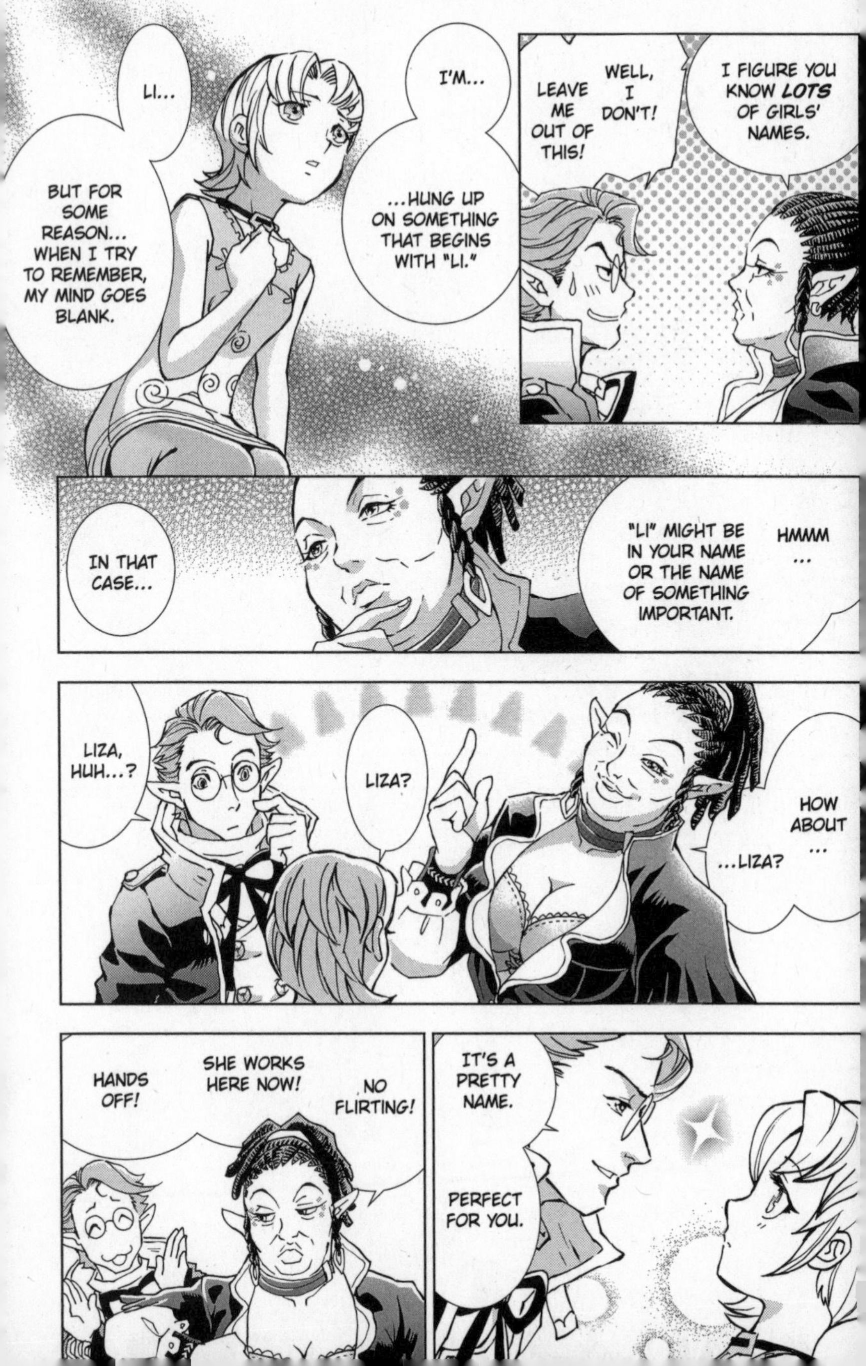
I FIGURE YOU KNOW **LOTS** OF GIRLS' NAMES.
WELL, I DON'T!
LEAVE ME OUT OF THIS!
I'M...
...HUNG UP ON SOMETHING THAT BEGINS WITH "LI."
LI...
BUT FOR SOME REASON... WHEN I TRY TO REMEMBER, MY MIND GOES BLANK.
HMMM ...
"LI" MIGHT BE IN YOUR NAME OR THE NAME OF SOMETHING IMPORTANT.
IN THAT CASE...
HOW ABOUT ...
...LIZA?
LIZA?
LIZA, HUH...?
IT'S A PRETTY NAME.
PERFECT FOR YOU.
NO FLIRTING!
SHE WORKS HERE NOW!
HANDS OFF!

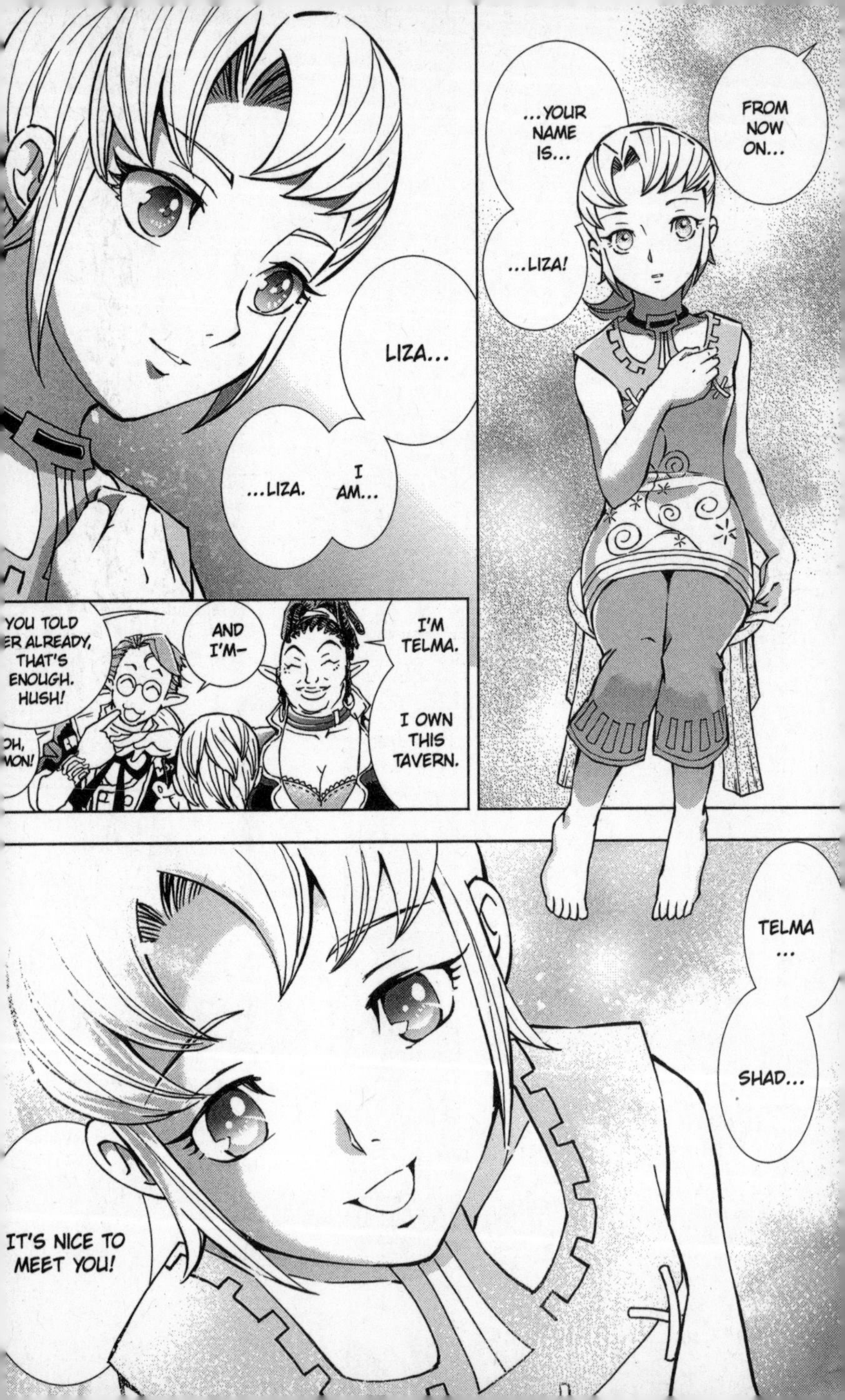
FROM NOW ON...
...YOUR NAME IS...
...LIZA!
LIZA...
I AM...
...LIZA.
I'M TELMA.
I OWN THIS TAVERN.
AND I'M-
YOU TOLD ER ALREADY, THAT'S ENOUGH. HUSH!
OH, MON!
TELMA...
SHAD...
IT'S NICE TO MEET YOU!

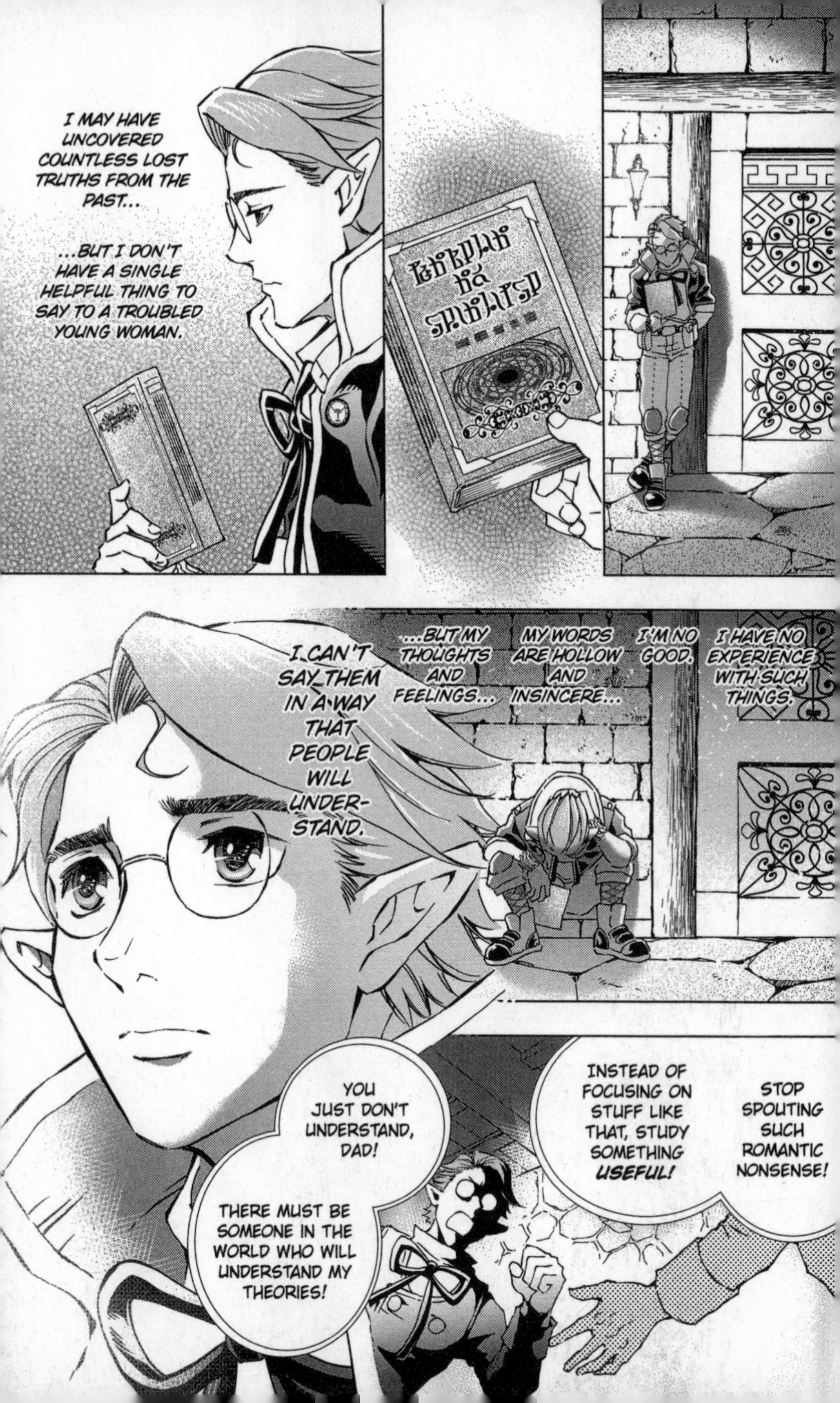

I MAY HAVE UNCOVERED COUNTLESS LOST TRUTHS FROM THE PAST...
...BUT I DON'T HAVE A SINGLE HELPFUL THING TO SAY TO A TROUBLED YOUNG WOMAN.
I HAVE NO EXPERIENCE WITH SUCH THINGS.
I'M NO GOOD.
MY WORDS ARE HOLLOW AND INSINCERE...
...BUT MY THOUGHTS AND FEELINGS...
I CAN'T SAY THEM IN A WAY THAT PEOPLE WILL UNDER-STAND.
STOP SPOUTING SUCH ROMANTIC NONSENSE!
INSTEAD OF FOCUSING ON STUFF LIKE THAT, STUDY SOMETHING **USEFUL!**
YOU JUST DON'T UNDERSTAND, DAD!
THERE MUST BE SOMEONE IN THE WORLD WHO WILL UNDERSTAND MY THEORIES!

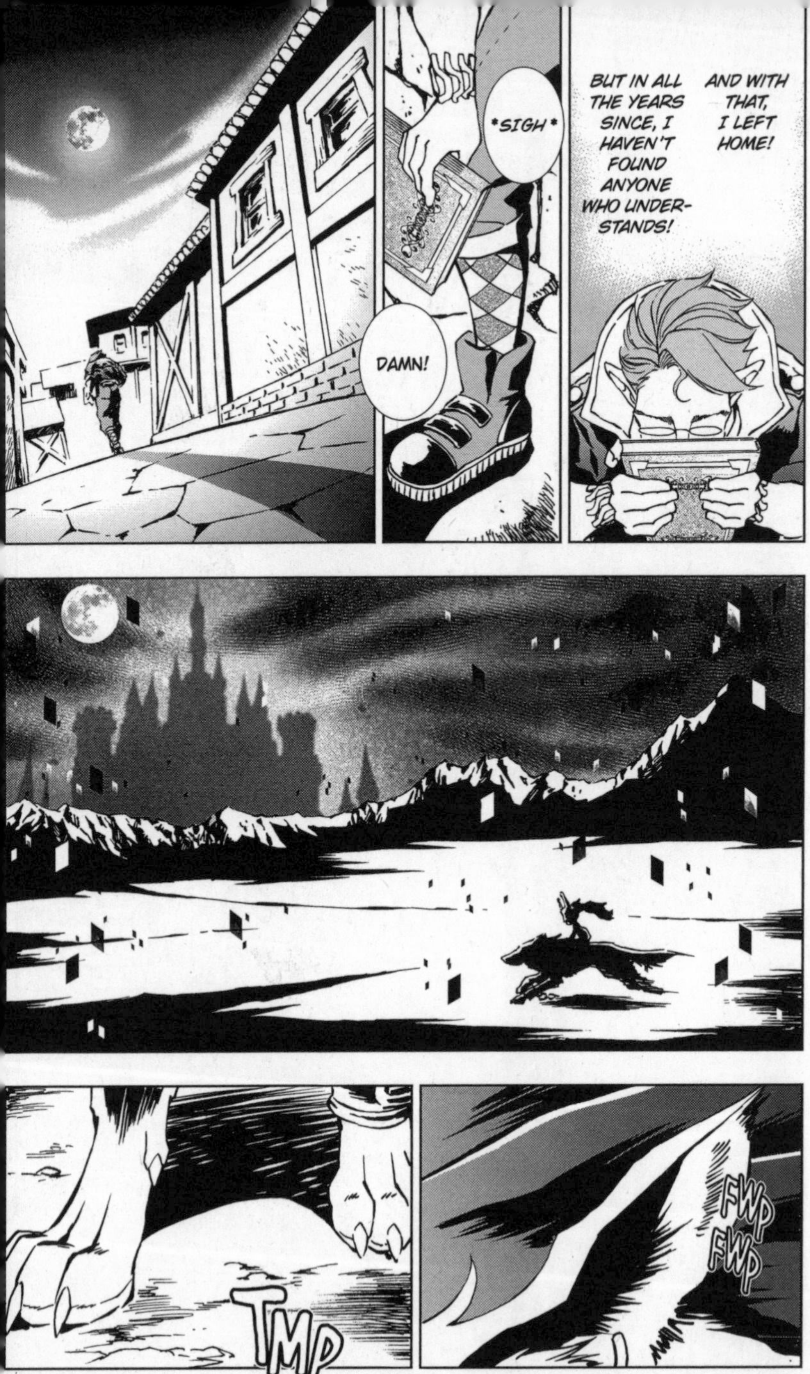
AND WITH THAT, I LEFT HOME!
BUT IN ALL THE YEARS SINCE, I HAVEN'T FOUND ANYONE WHO UNDER-STANDS!
SIGH
DAMN!
FWP FWP
TMP

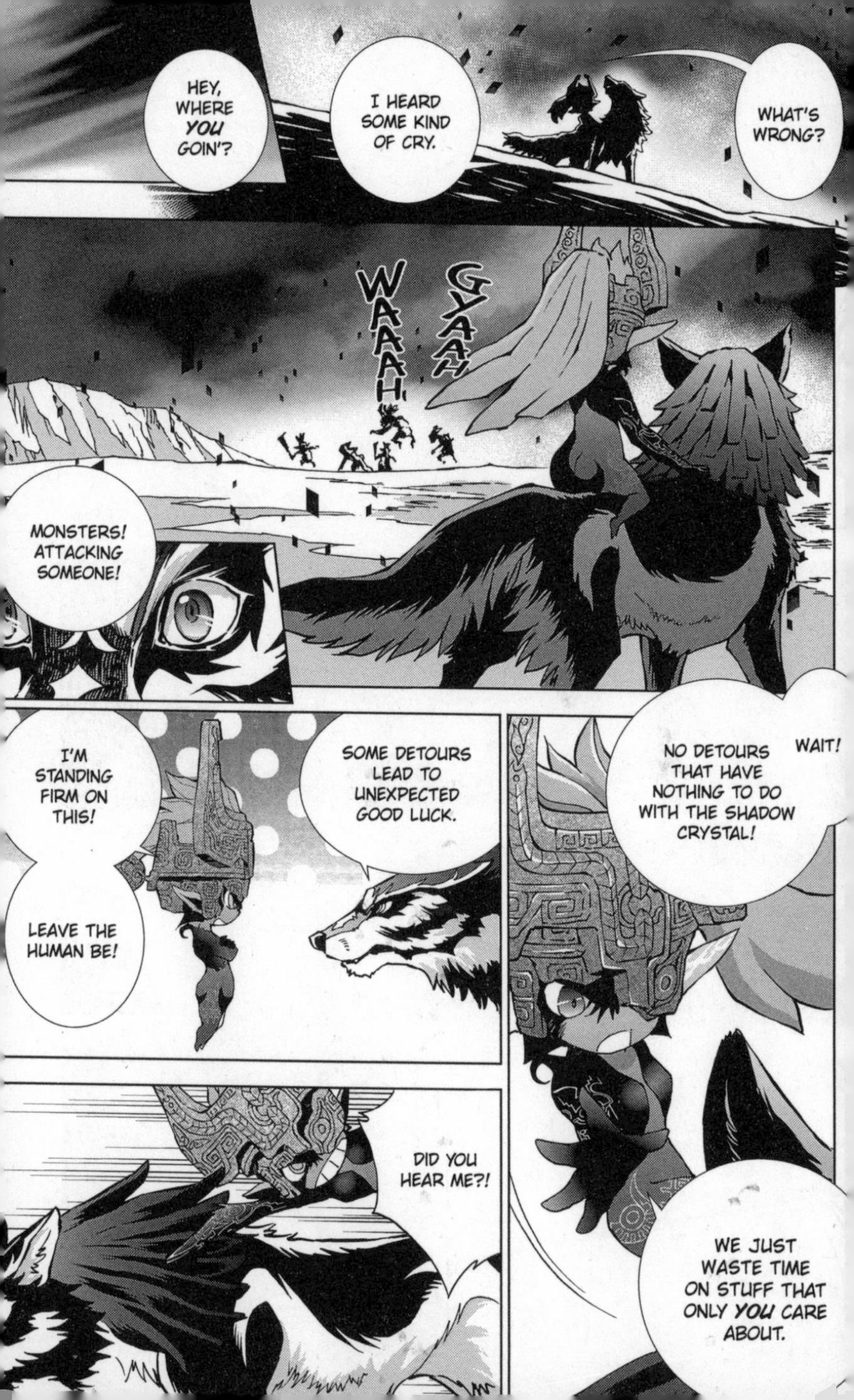
WHAT'S WRONG?
I HEARD SOME KIND OF CRY.
HEY, WHERE *YOU* GOIN'?
GYAAAH
WAAAAH
MONSTERS! ATTACKING SOMEONE!
WAIT!
NO DETOURS THAT HAVE NOTHING TO DO WITH THE SHADOW CRYSTAL!
WE JUST WASTE TIME ON STUFF THAT ONLY *YOU* CARE ABOUT.
SOME DETOURS LEAD TO UNEXPECTED GOOD LUCK.
I'M STANDING FIRM ON THIS!
LEAVE THE HUMAN BE!
DID YOU HEAR ME?!

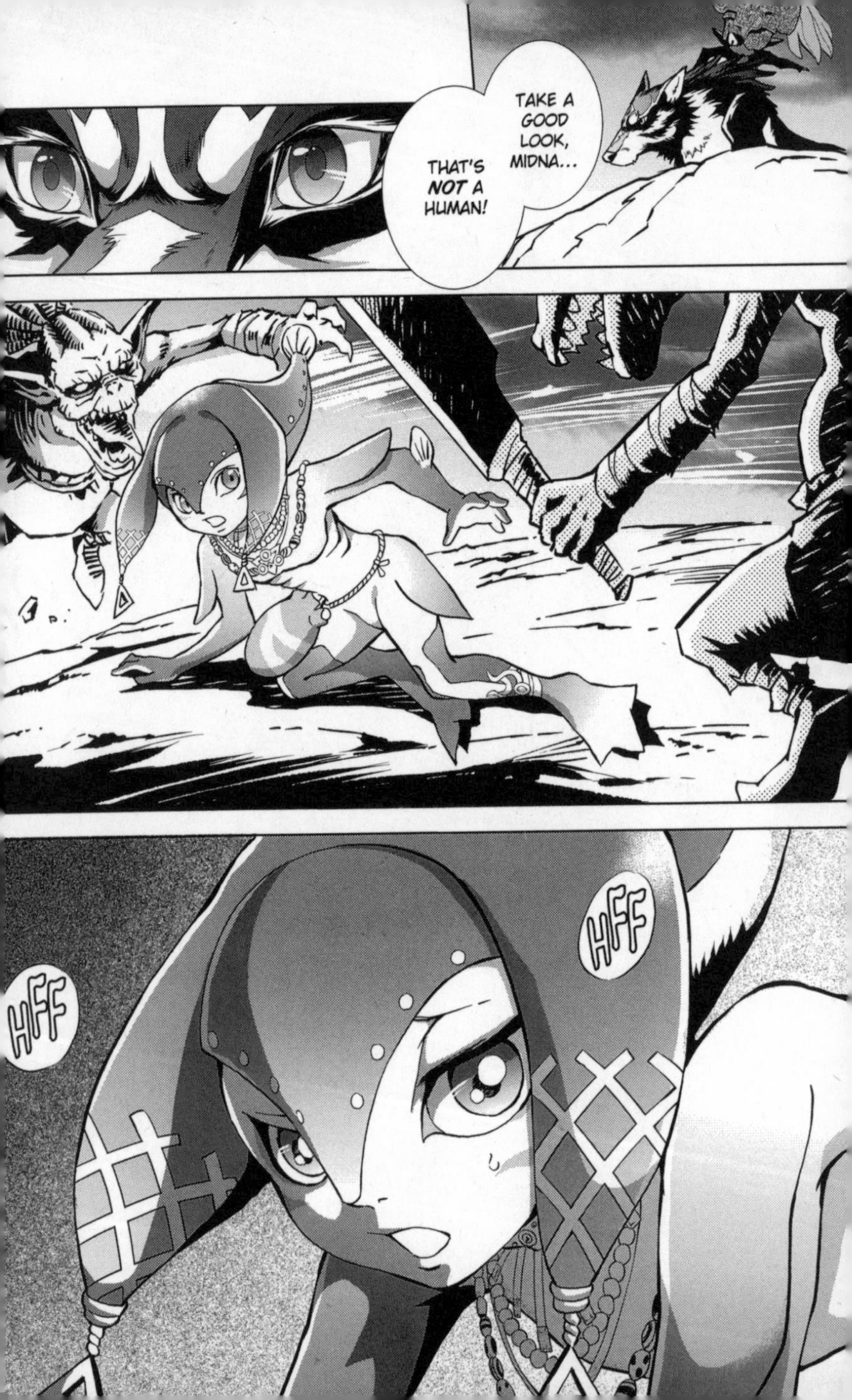
TAKE A GOOD LOOK, MIDNA...
THAT'S *NOT* A HUMAN!
HFF
HFF

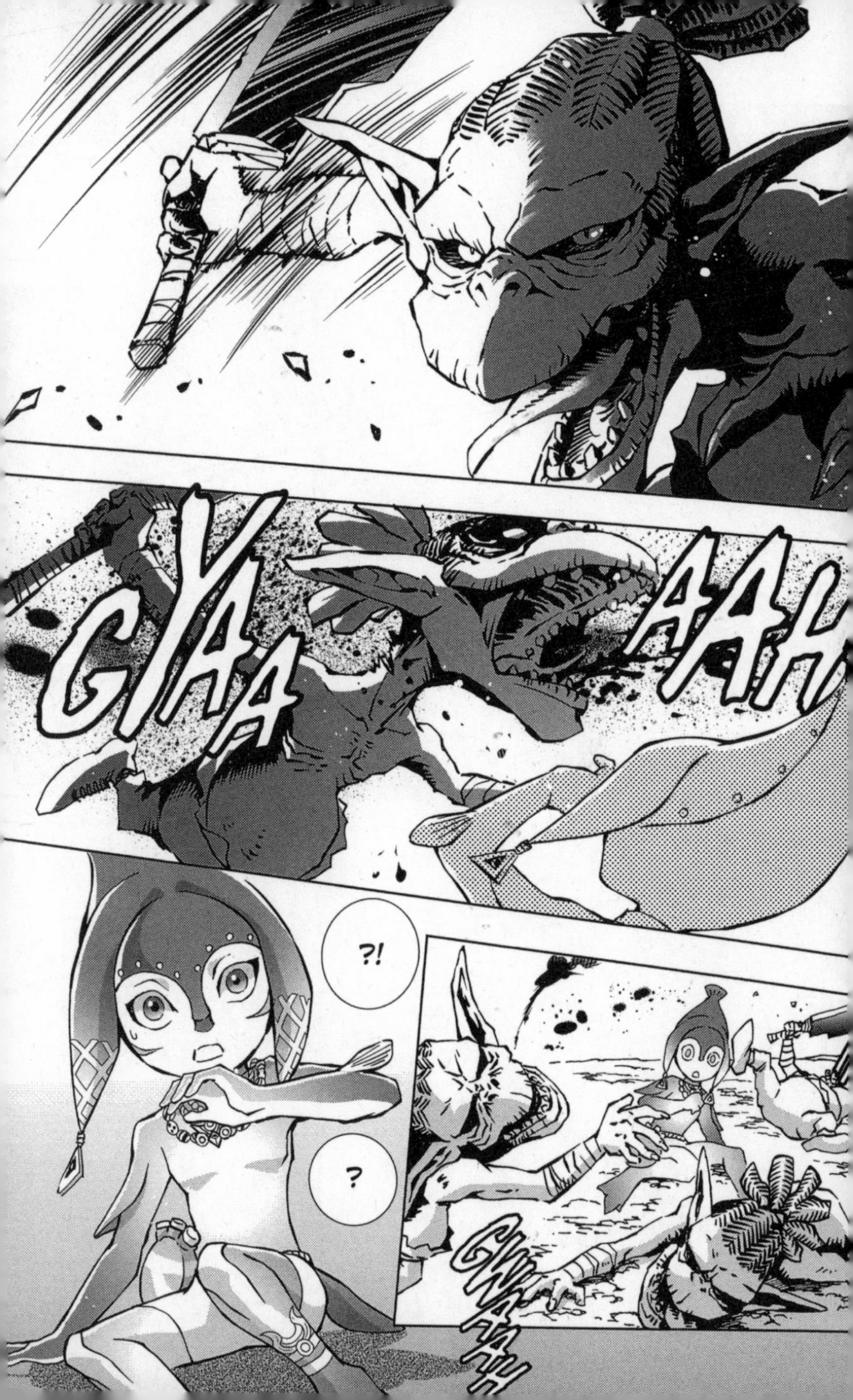
GYAAAH
?!
?
GWAAAH

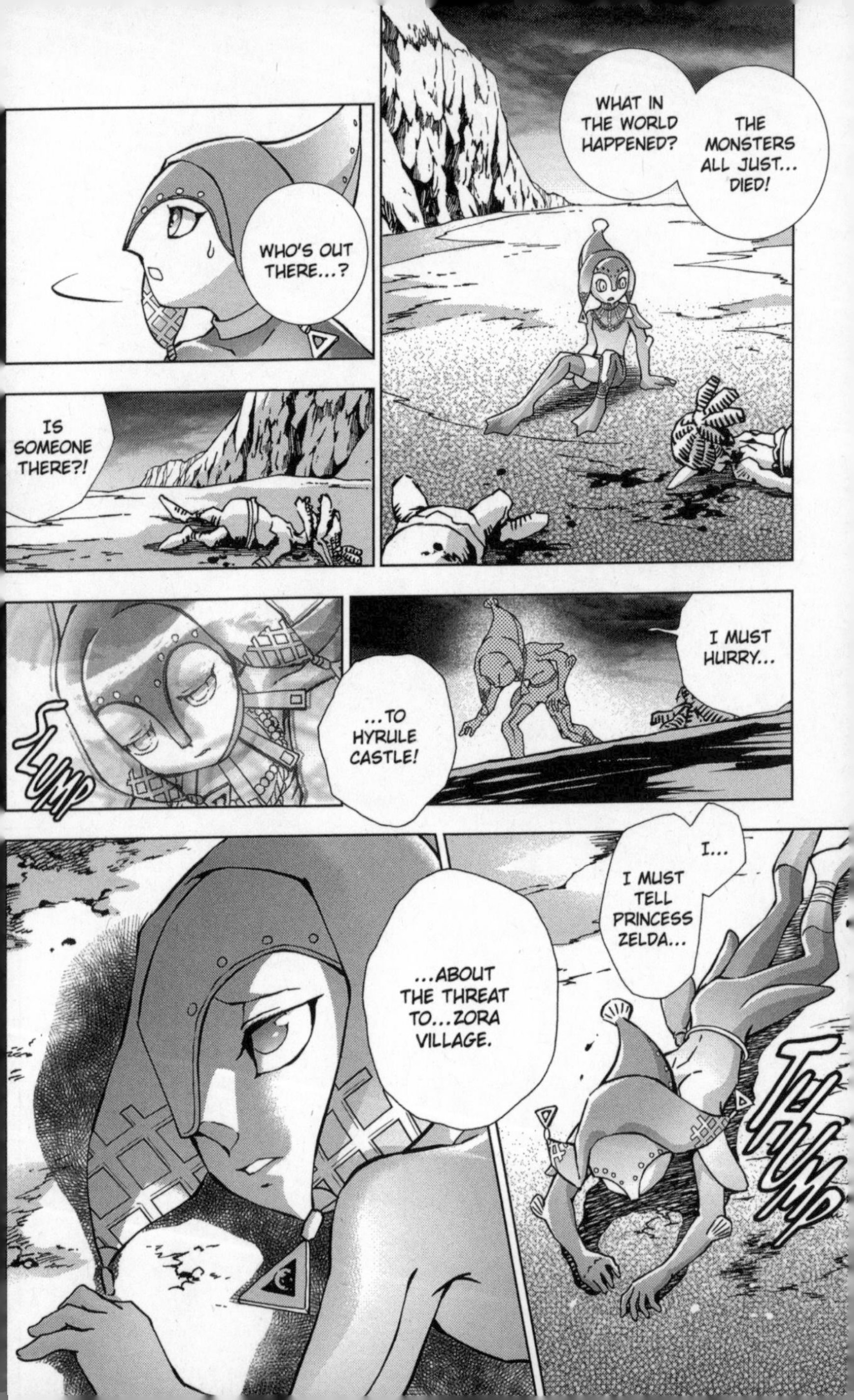
WHAT IN THE WORLD HAPPENED?
THE MONSTERS ALL JUST... DIED!
WHO'S OUT THERE...?
IS SOMEONE THERE?!
I MUST HURRY...
...TO HYRULE CASTLE!
SLUMP
I... I MUST TELL PRINCESS ZELDA...
THUMP
...ABOUT THE THREAT TO...ZORA VILLAGE.

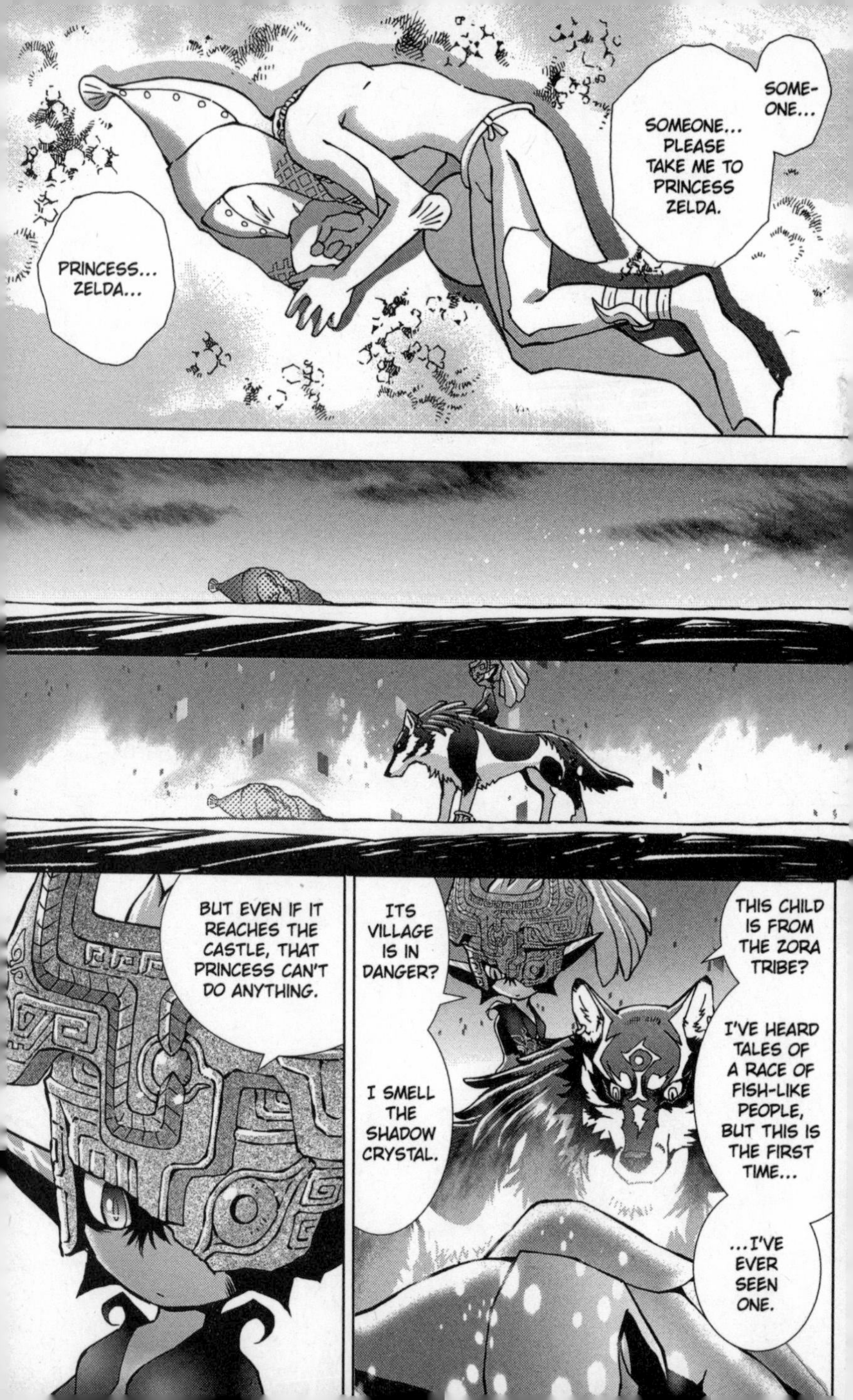
SOME-ONE...
SOMEONE... PLEASE TAKE ME TO PRINCESS ZELDA.
PRINCESS... ZELDA...
THIS CHILD IS FROM THE ZORA TRIBE?
I'VE HEARD TALES OF A RACE OF FISH-LIKE PEOPLE, BUT THIS IS THE FIRST TIME...
...I'VE EVER SEEN ONE.
ITS VILLAGE IS IN DANGER?
I SMELL THE SHADOW CRYSTAL.
BUT EVEN IF IT REACHES THE CASTLE, THAT PRINCESS CAN'T DO ANYTHING.

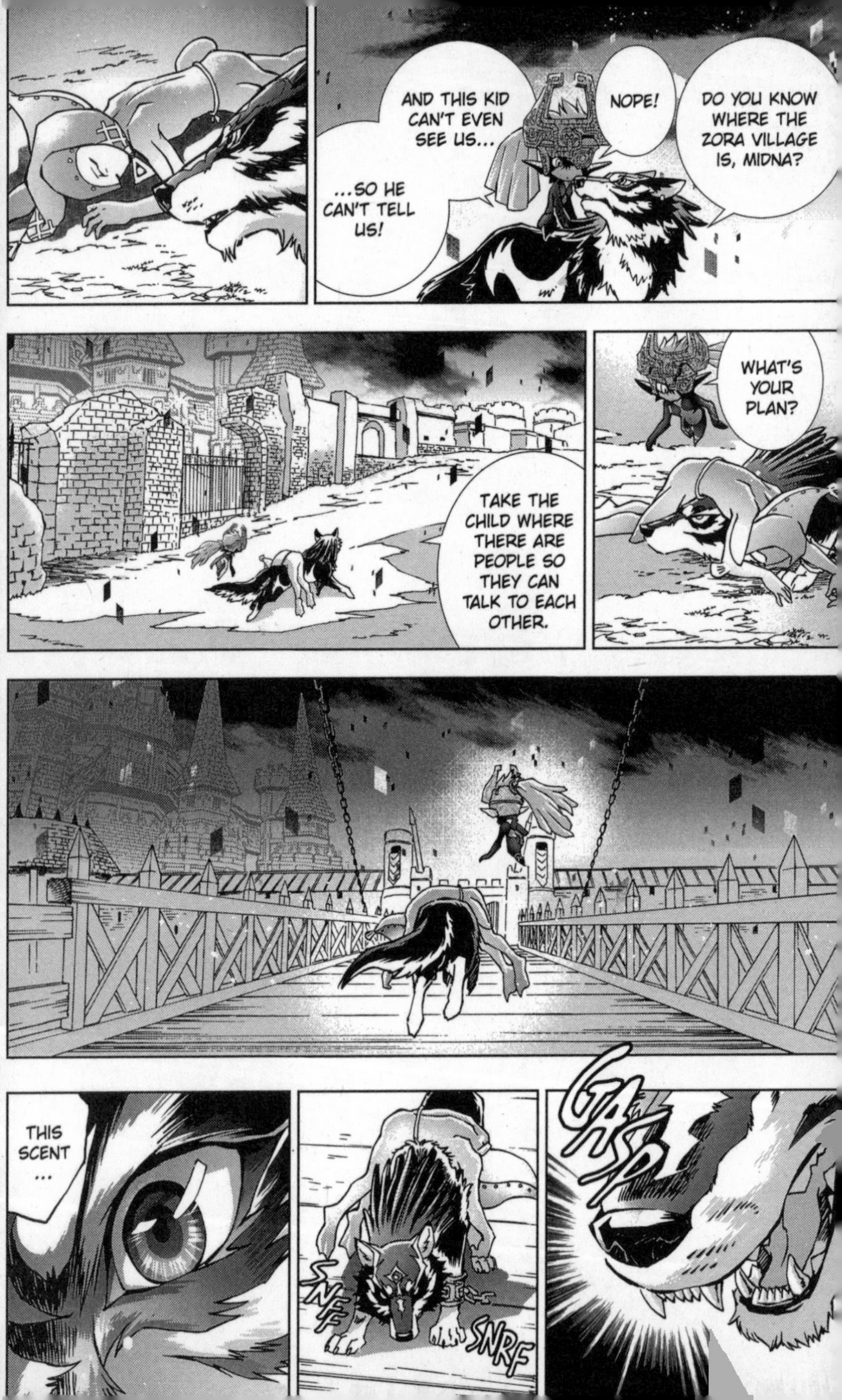
DO YOU KNOW WHERE THE ZORA VILLAGE IS, MIDNA?
NOPE!
AND THIS KID CAN'T EVEN SEE US...
...SO HE CAN'T TELL US!
WHAT'S YOUR PLAN?
TAKE THE CHILD WHERE THERE ARE PEOPLE SO THEY CAN TALK TO EACH OTHER.
GASP
SNF
SNRF
THIS SCENT ...

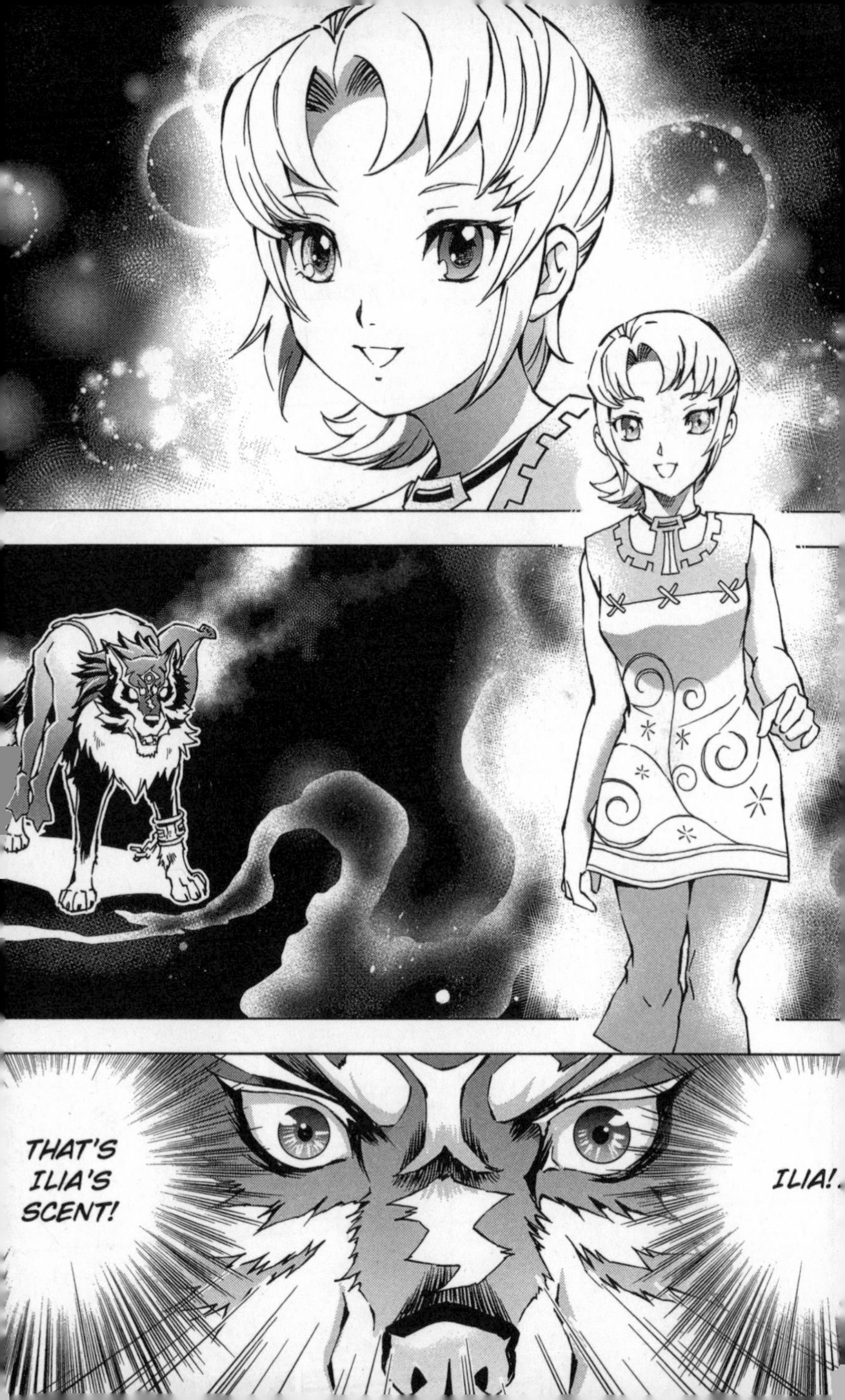
ILIA!.
THAT'S ILIA'S SCENT!

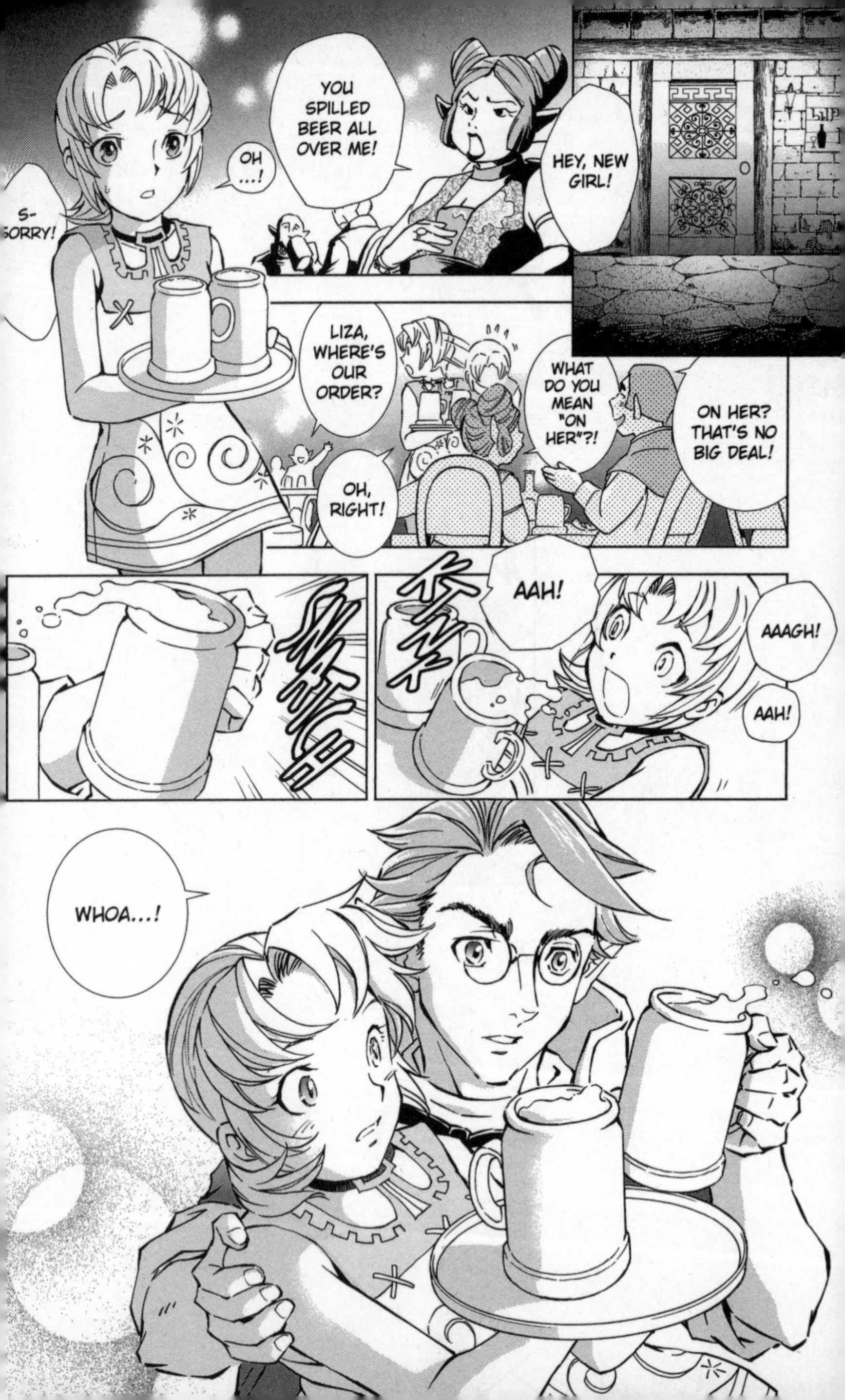
HEY, NEW GIRL!
YOU SPILLED BEER ALL OVER ME!
OH ...!
S-SORRY!
ON HER? THAT'S NO BIG DEAL!
WHAT DO YOU MEAN "ON HER"?!
LIZA, WHERE'S OUR ORDER?
OH, RIGHT!
AAH!
AAAGH!
AAH!
SNATCH
WHOA...!

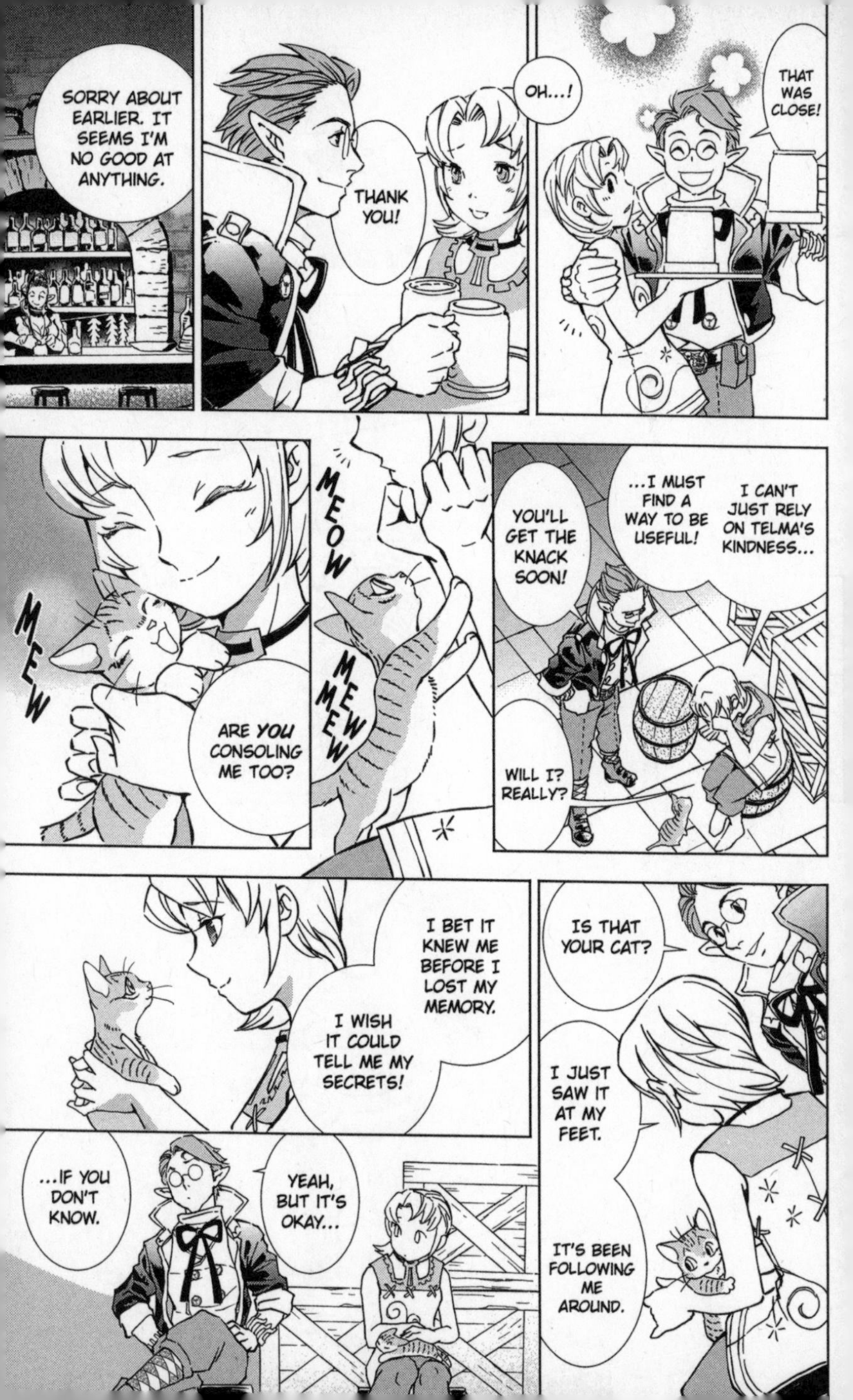
THAT WAS CLOSE!
OH...!
THANK YOU!
SORRY ABOUT EARLIER. IT SEEMS I'M NO GOOD AT ANYTHING.
I CAN'T JUST RELY ON TELMA'S KINDNESS...
...I MUST FIND A WAY TO BE USEFUL!
YOU'LL GET THE KNACK SOON!
WILL I? REALLY?
MEOW
MEW MEW
ARE YOU CONSOLING ME TOO?
MEW
IS THAT YOUR CAT?
I JUST SAW IT AT MY FEET.
IT'S BEEN FOLLOWING ME AROUND.
I BET IT KNEW ME BEFORE I LOST MY MEMORY.
I WISH IT COULD TELL ME MY SECRETS!
YEAH, BUT IT'S OKAY...
...IF YOU DON'T KNOW.

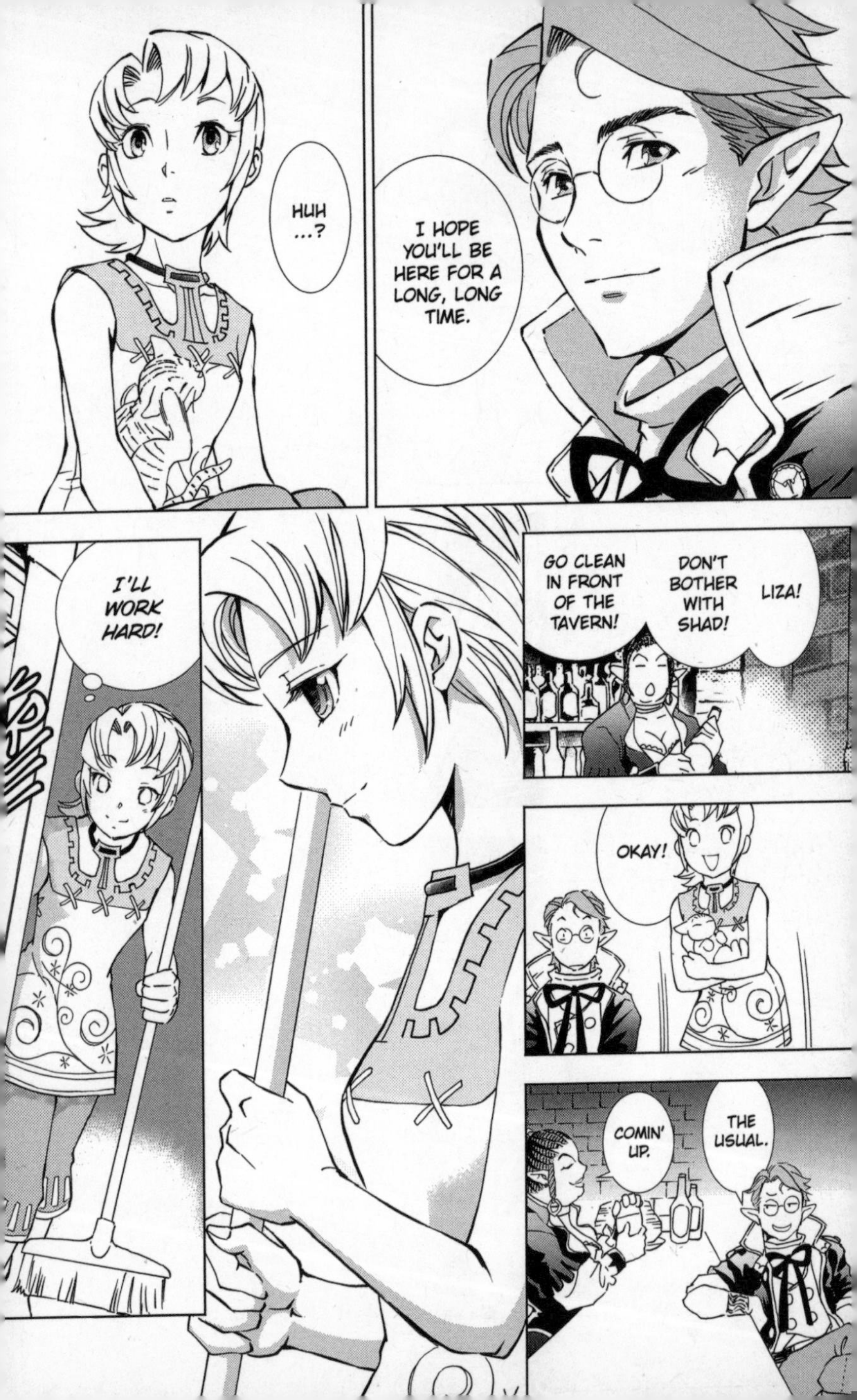
I HOPE YOU'LL BE HERE FOR A LONG, LONG TIME.
HUH ...?
LIZA!
DON'T BOTHER WITH SHAD!
GO CLEAN IN FRONT OF THE TAVERN!
OKAY!
THE USUAL.
COMIN' UP.
I'LL WORK HARD!

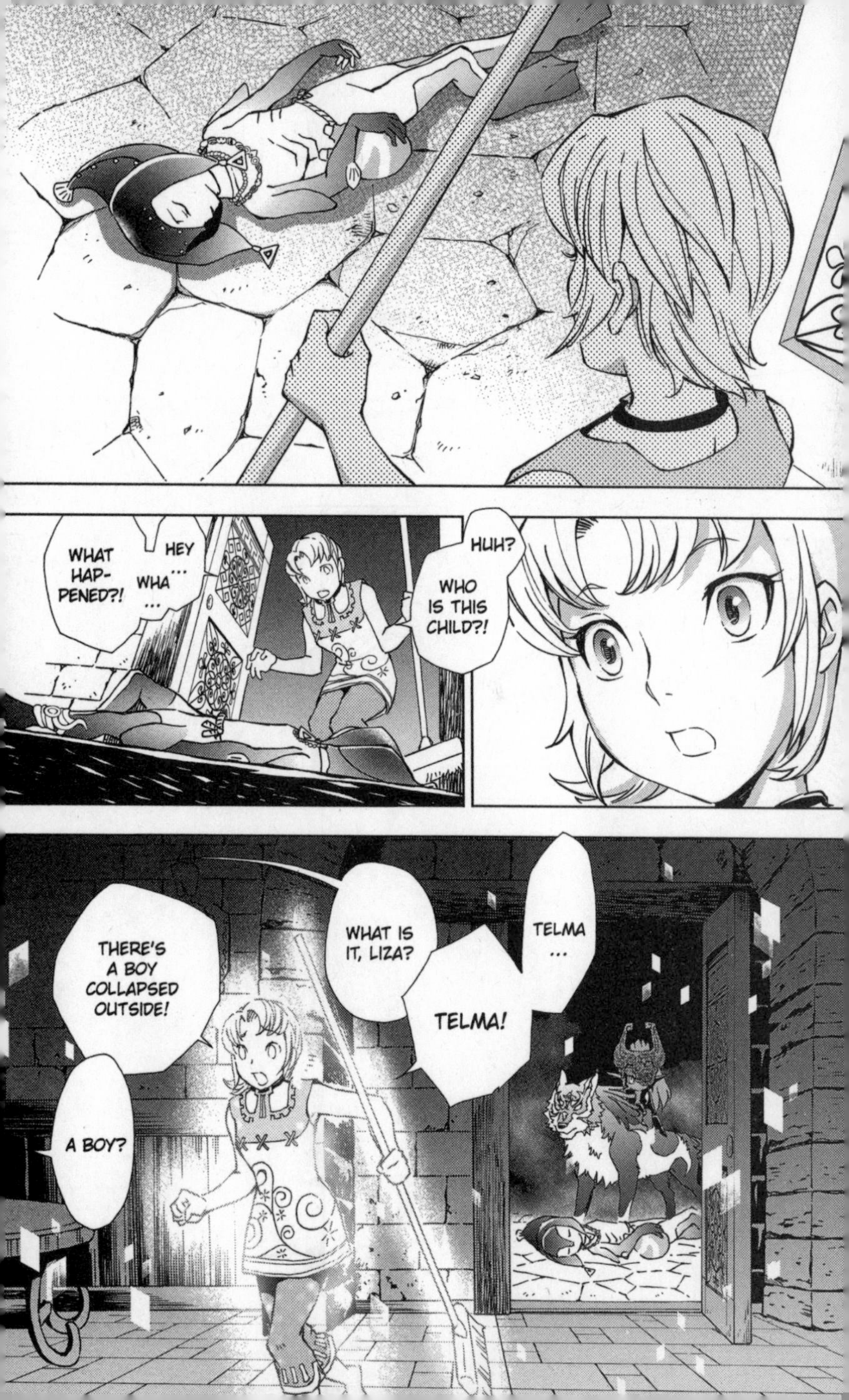
HUH?
WHO IS THIS CHILD?!
HEY ... WHA ...
WHAT HAP-PENED?!
TELMA ...
TELMA!
WHAT IS IT, LIZA?
THERE'S A BOY COLLAPSED OUTSIDE!
A BOY?

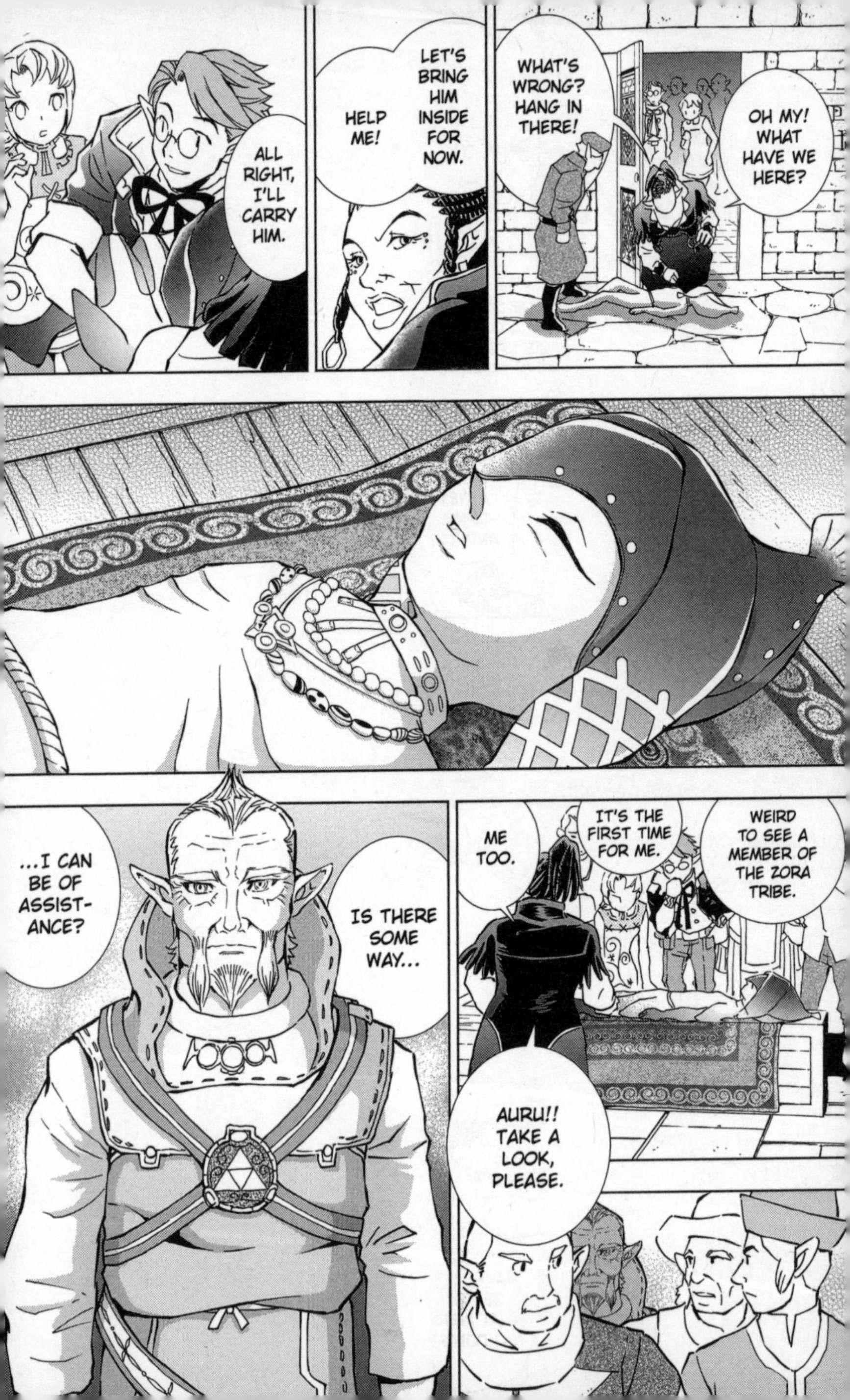
OH MY! WHAT HAVE WE HERE?
WHAT'S WRONG? HANG IN THERE!
LET'S BRING HIM INSIDE FOR NOW.
HELP ME!
ALL RIGHT, I'LL CARRY HIM.
WEIRD TO SEE A MEMBER OF THE ZORA TRIBE.
IT'S THE FIRST TIME FOR ME.
ME TOO.
AURU!! TAKE A LOOK, PLEASE.
IS THERE SOME WAY...
...I CAN BE OF ASSIST-ANCE?

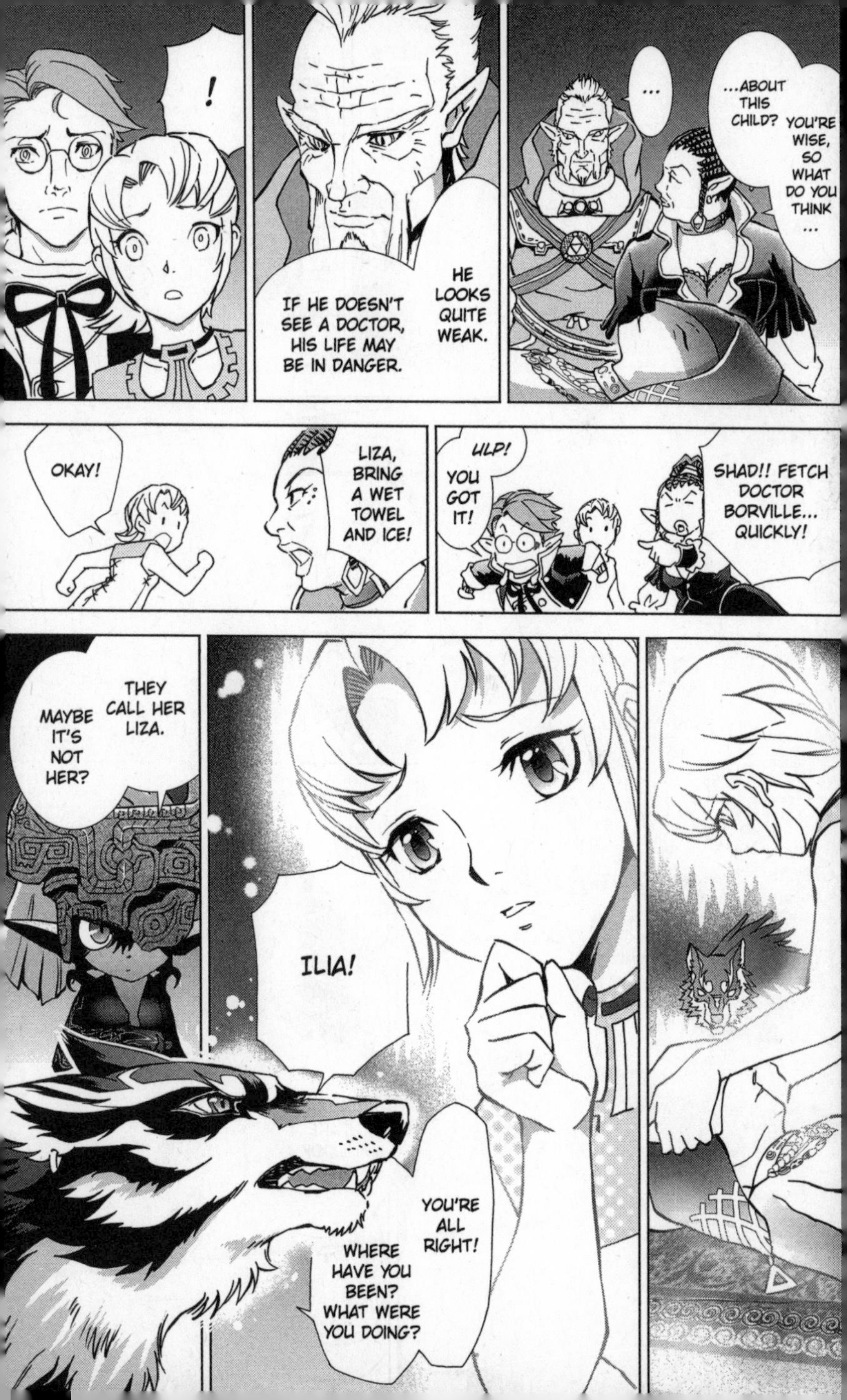
YOU'RE WISE, SO WHAT DO YOU THINK ...
...ABOUT THIS CHILD?
...
HE LOOKS QUITE WEAK.
IF HE DOESN'T SEE A DOCTOR, HIS LIFE MAY BE IN DANGER.
!
SHAD!! FETCH DOCTOR BORVILLE... QUICKLY!
ULP!
YOU GOT IT!
LIZA, BRING A WET TOWEL AND ICE!
OKAY!
ILIA!
YOU'RE ALL RIGHT!
WHERE HAVE YOU BEEN? WHAT WERE YOU DOING?
THEY CALL HER LIZA.
MAYBE IT'S NOT HER?

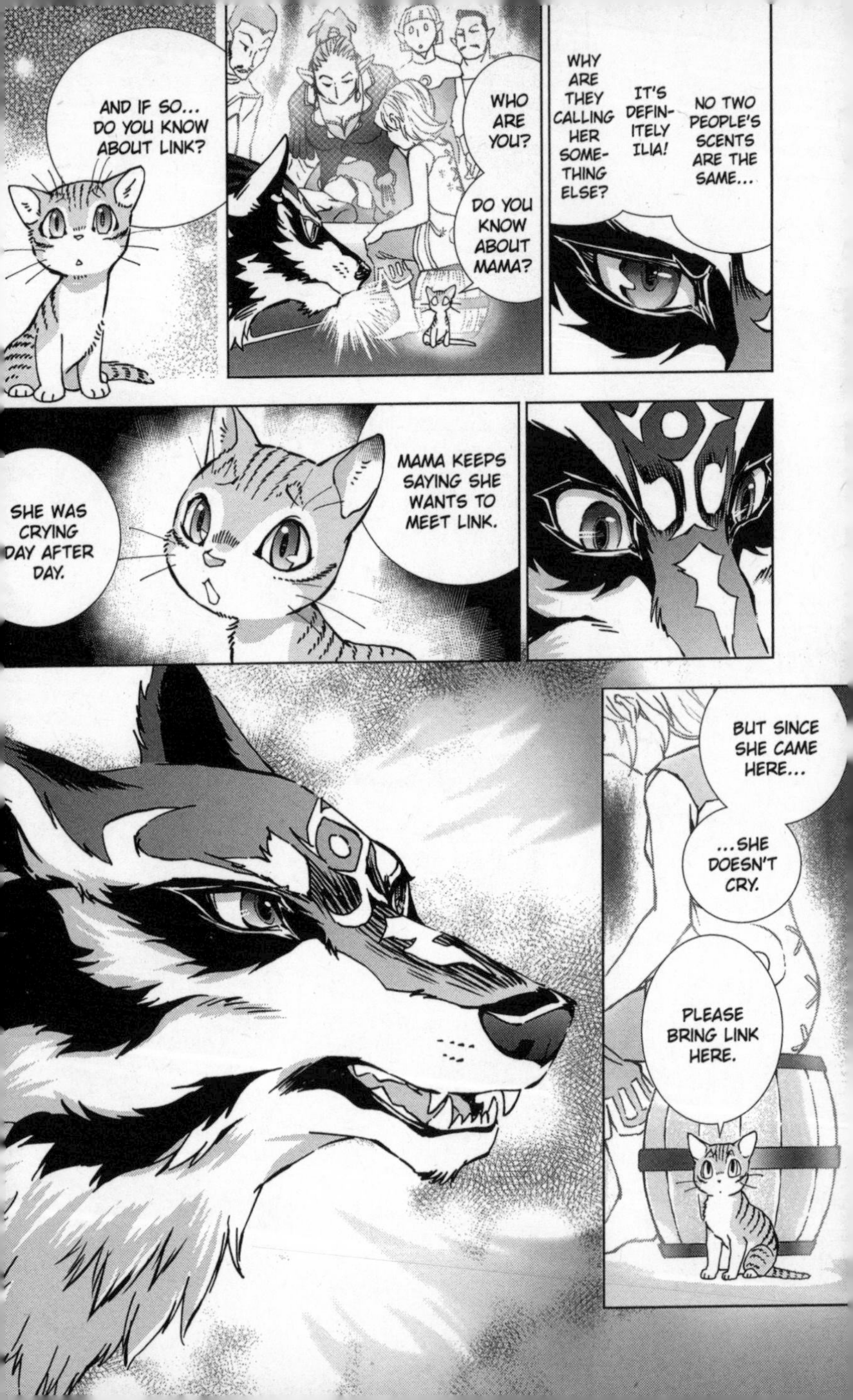
NO TWO PEOPLE'S SCENTS ARE THE SAME...
IT'S DEFINITELY ILIA!
WHY ARE THEY CALLING HER SOMETHING ELSE?
WHO ARE YOU?
DO YOU KNOW ABOUT MAMA?
AND IF SO... DO YOU KNOW ABOUT LINK?
MAMA KEEPS SAYING SHE WANTS TO MEET LINK.
SHE WAS CRYING DAY AFTER DAY.
BUT SINCE SHE CAME HERE...
...SHE DOESN'T CRY.
PLEASE BRING LINK HERE.

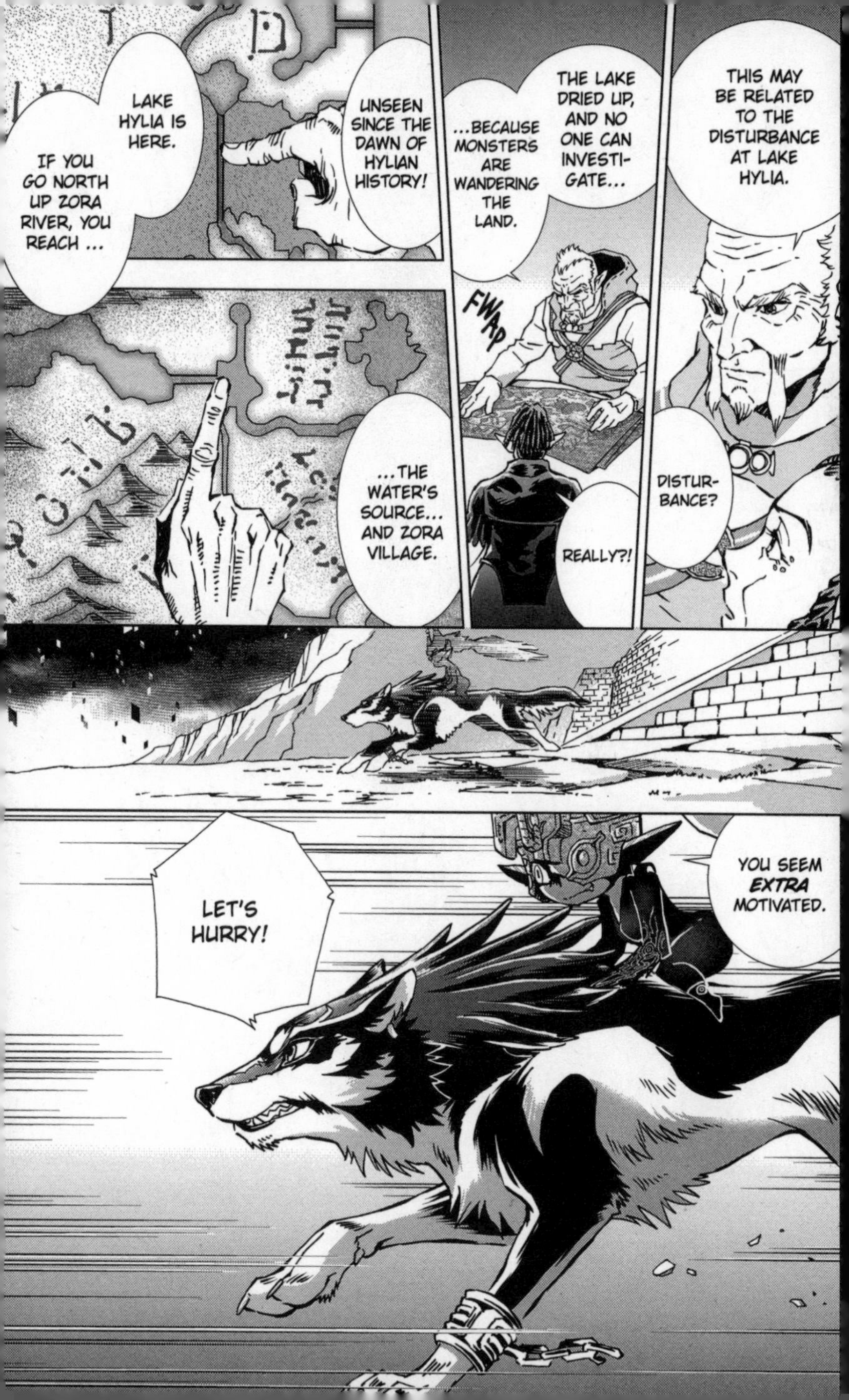
THIS MAY BE RELATED TO THE DISTURBANCE AT LAKE HYLIA.
DISTUR-BANCE?
THE LAKE DRIED UP, AND NO ONE CAN INVESTI-GATE...
...BECAUSE MONSTERS ARE WANDERING THE LAND.
FWAP
REALLY?!
UNSEEN SINCE THE DAWN OF HYLIAN HISTORY!
LAKE HYLIA IS HERE.
IF YOU GO NORTH UP ZORA RIVER, YOU REACH ...
...THE WATER'S SOURCE... AND ZORA VILLAGE.
YOU SEEM *EXTRA* MOTIVATED.
LET'S HURRY!

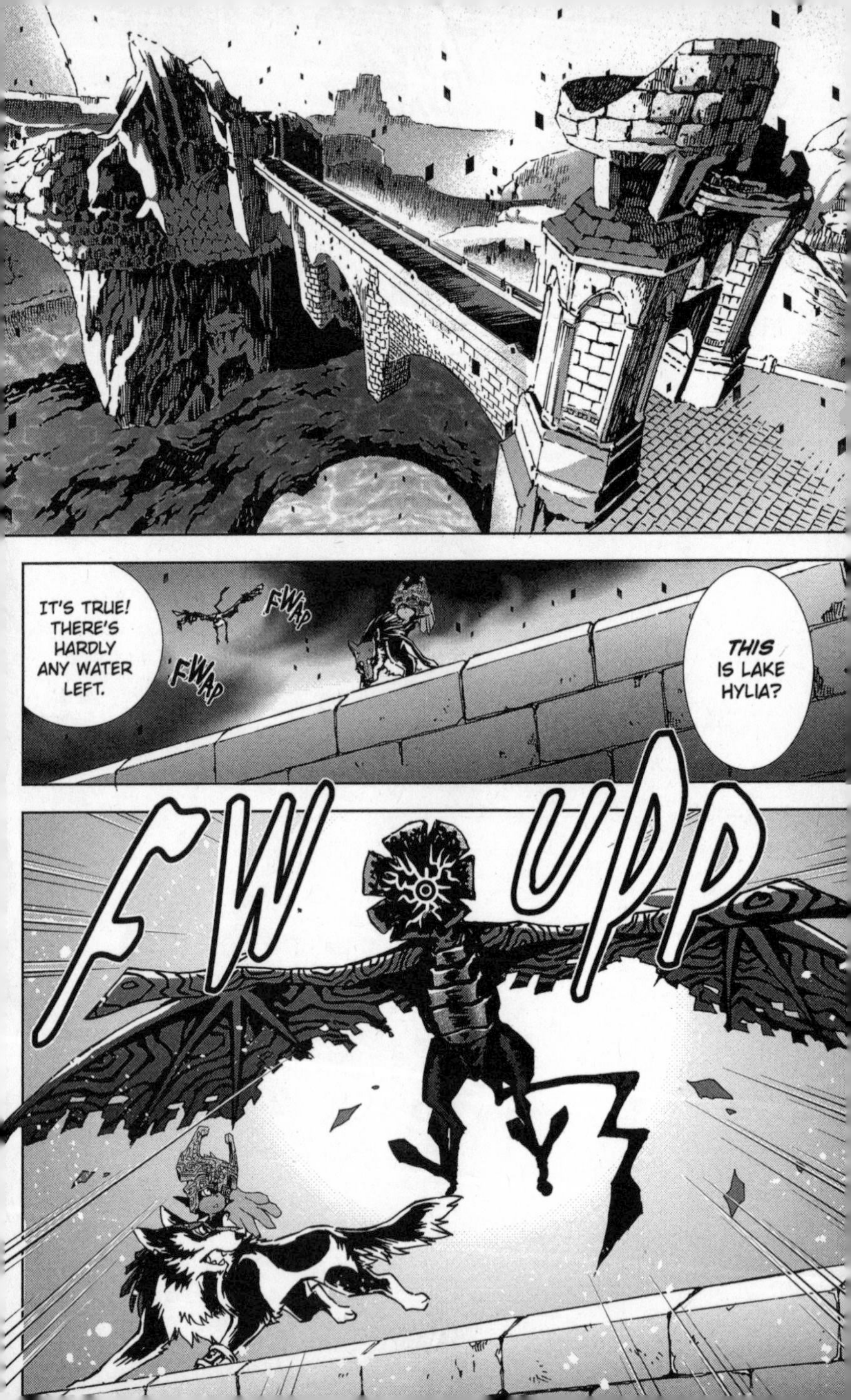
THIS IS LAKE HYLIA?
FWAP
FWAP
IT'S TRUE! THERE'S HARDLY ANY WATER LEFT.
FWUPP

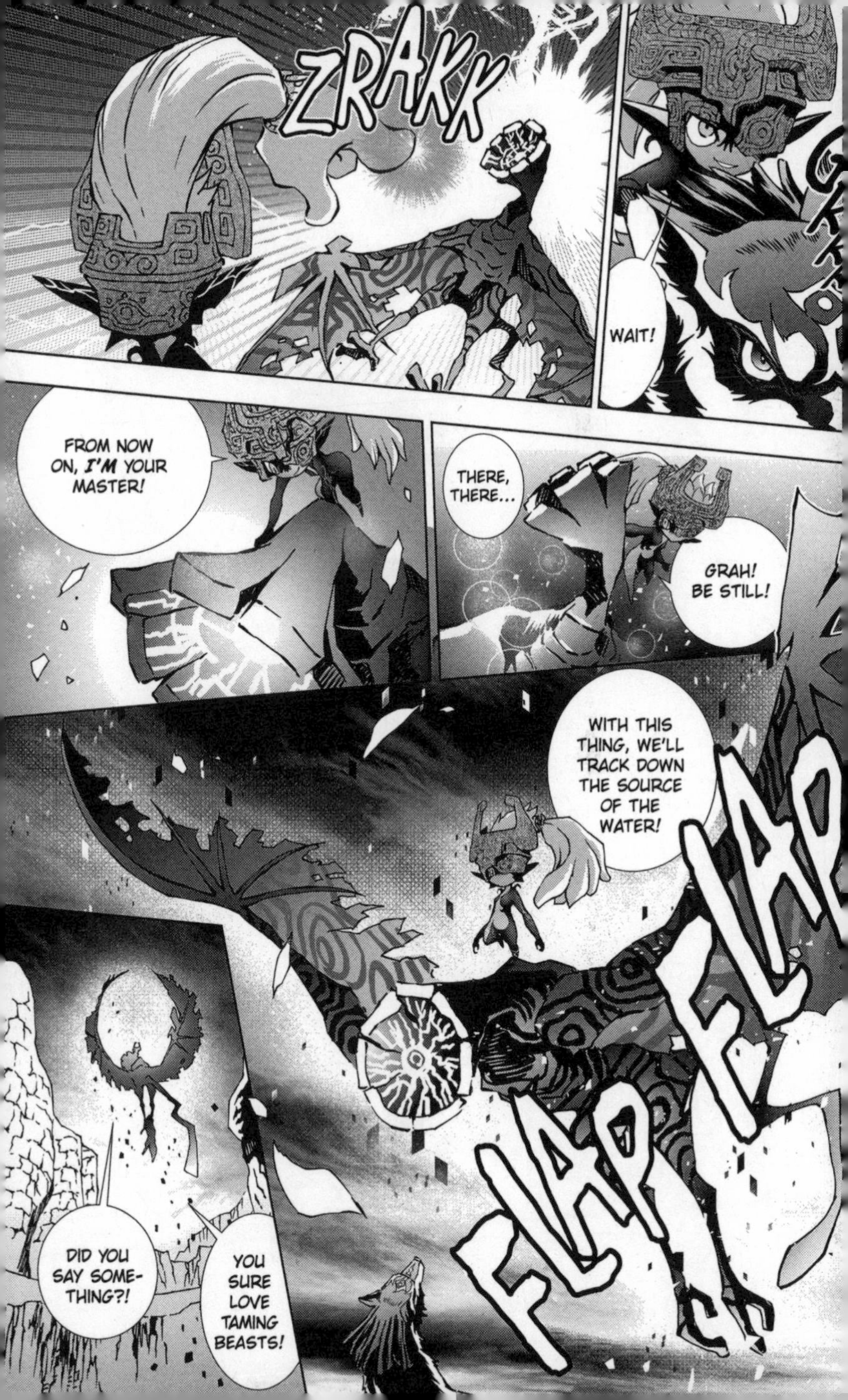
WAIT!
ZRAKK
GRAH! BE STILL!
THERE, THERE...
FROM NOW ON, *I'M* YOUR MASTER!
WITH THIS THING, WE'LL TRACK DOWN THE SOURCE OF THE WATER!
FLAP FLAP
YOU SURE LOVE TAMING BEASTS!
DID YOU SAY SOME-THING?!

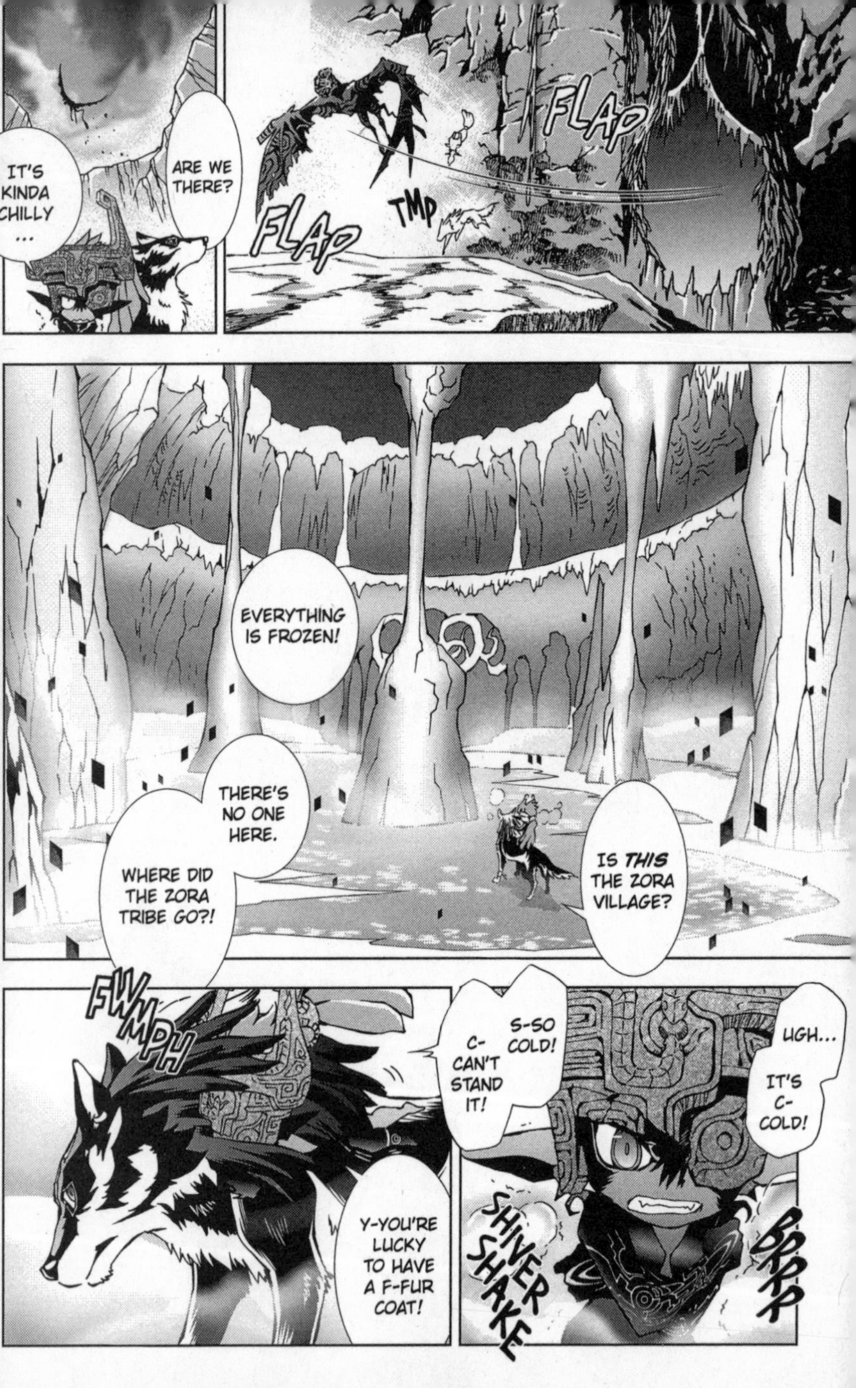
FLAP
TMP
FLAP
ARE WE THERE?
IT'S KINDA CHILLY ...
EVERYTHING IS FROZEN!
IS *THIS* THE ZORA VILLAGE?
THERE'S NO ONE HERE.
WHERE DID THE ZORA TRIBE GO?!
UGH... IT'S C-COLD!
S-SO COLD!
C-CAN'T STAND IT!
BRRR
SHIVER SHAKE
FWMPH
Y-YOU'RE LUCKY TO HAVE A F-FUR COAT!

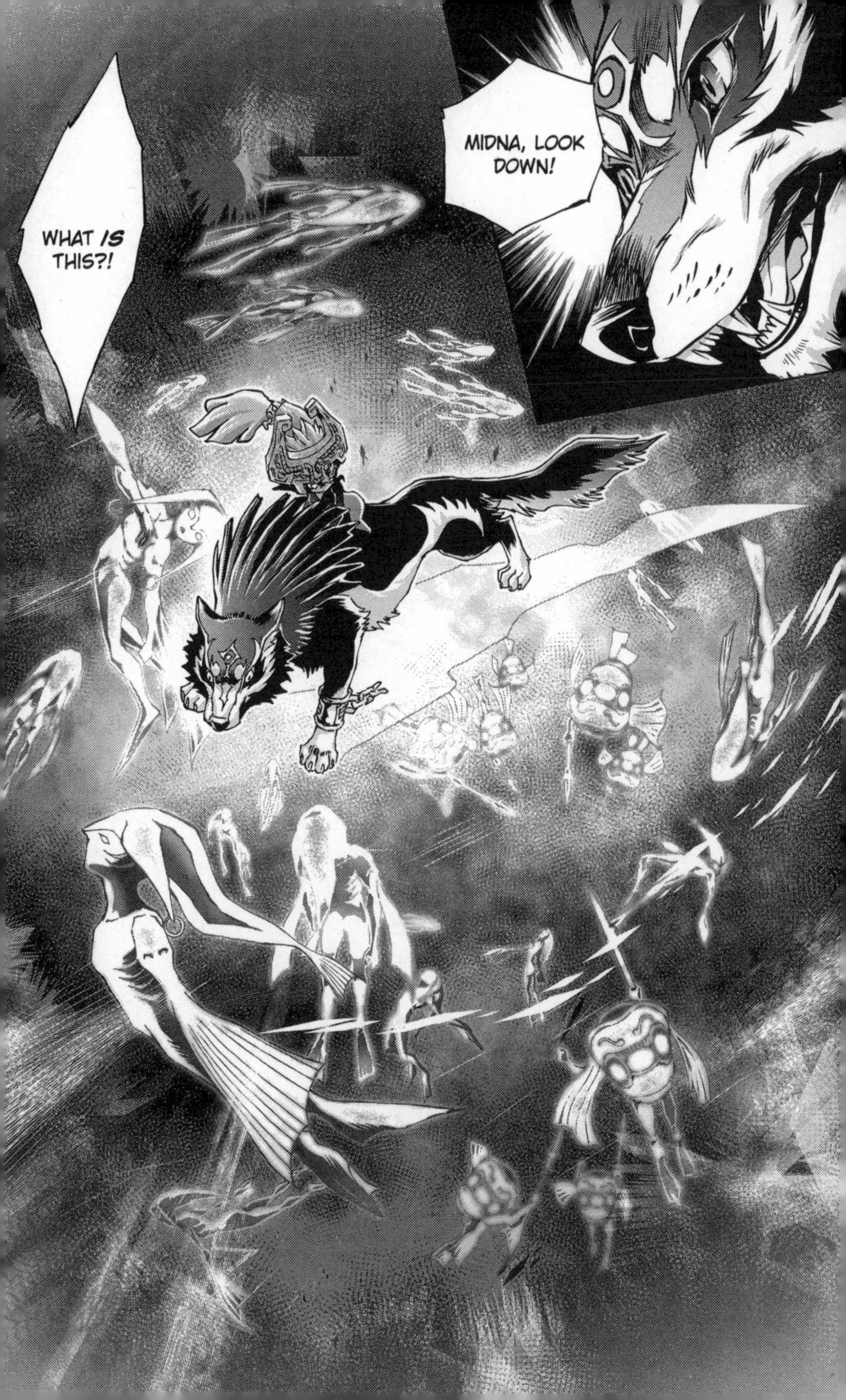
MIDNA, LOOK DOWN!
WHAT IS THIS?!

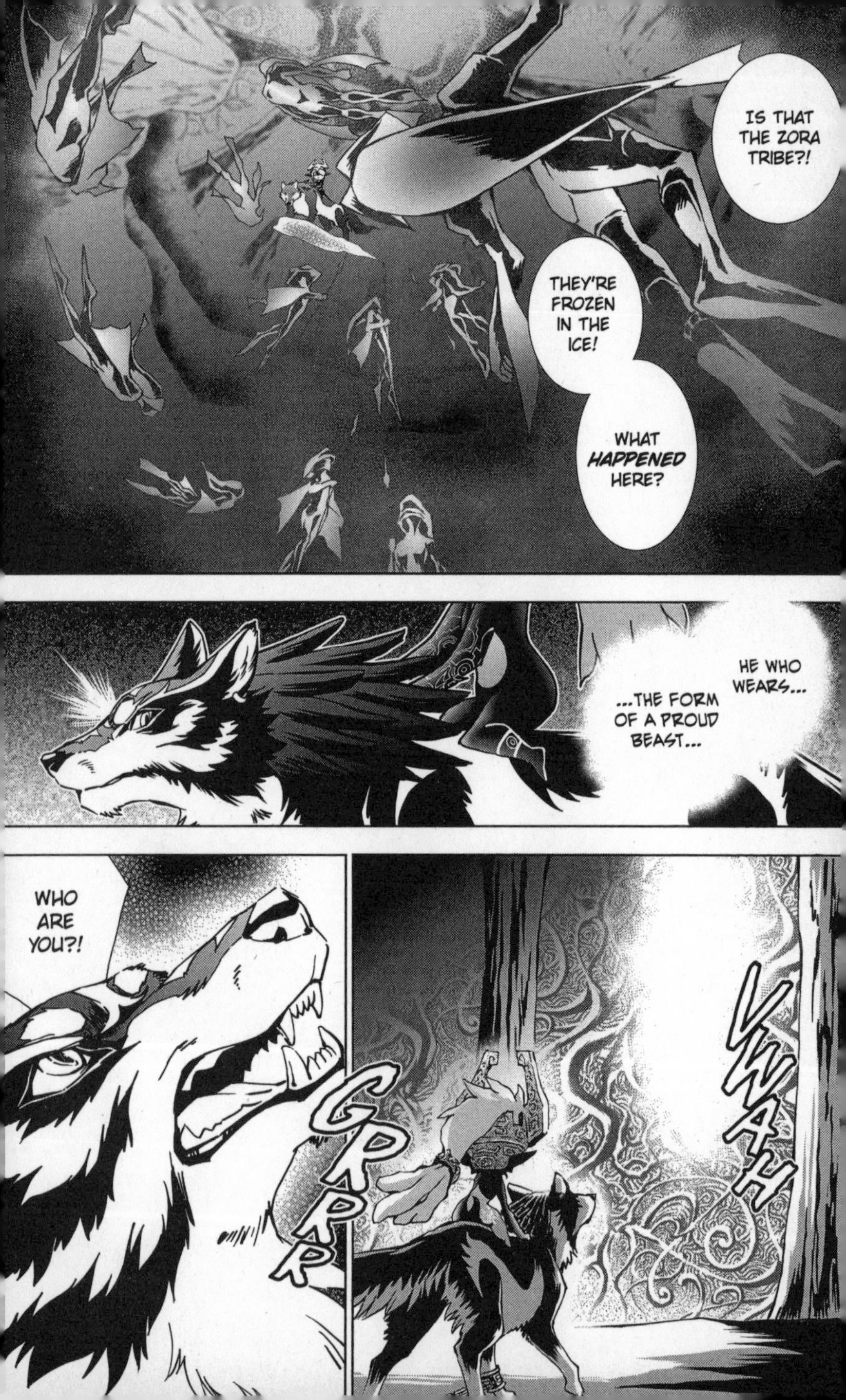
IS THAT THE ZORA TRIBE?!
THEY'RE FROZEN IN THE ICE!
WHAT *HAPPENED* HERE?
HE WHO WEARS...
...THE FORM OF A PROUD BEAST...
VWAH
WHO ARE YOU?!
GRRRR

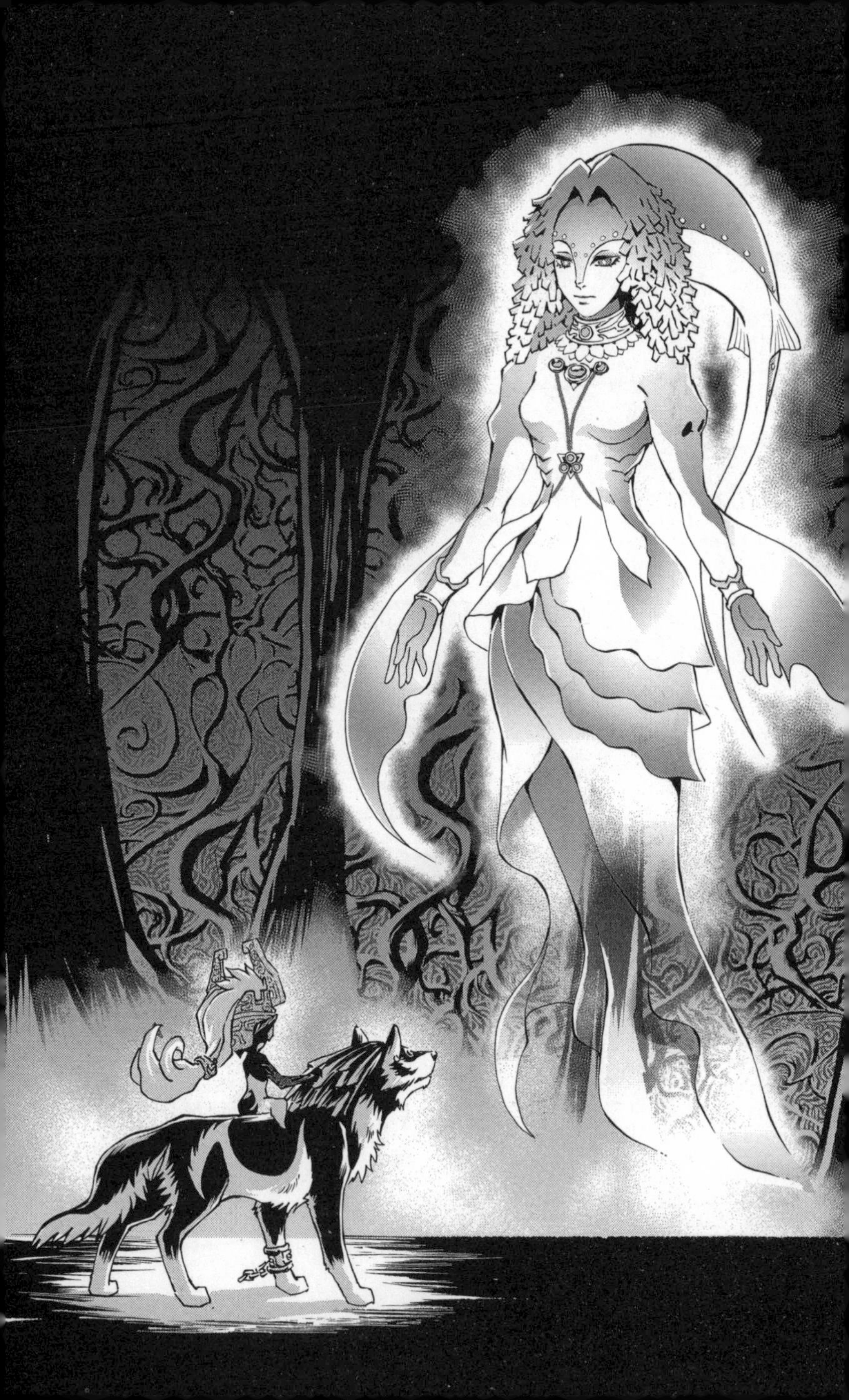

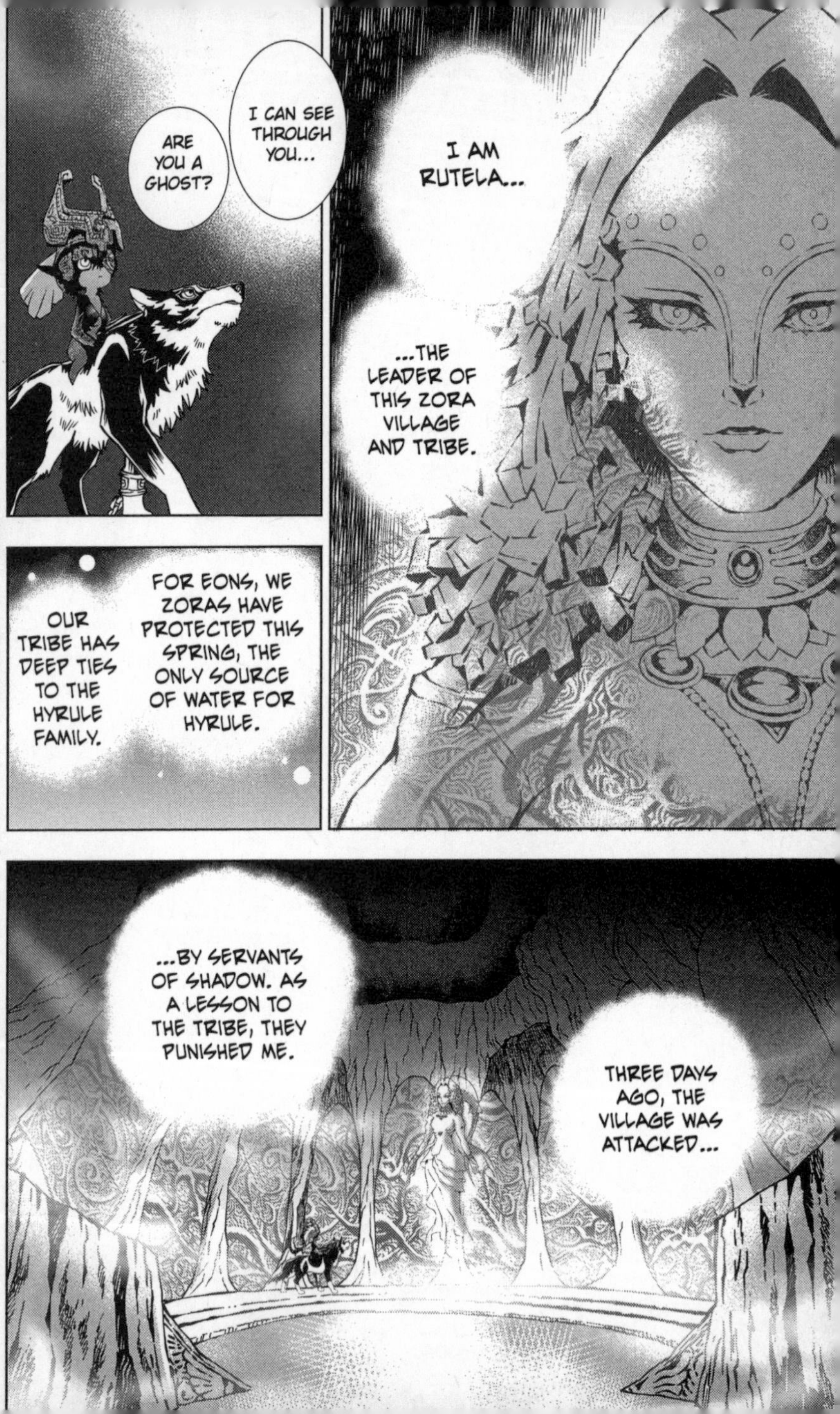
I AM RUTELA...
...THE LEADER OF THIS ZORA VILLAGE AND TRIBE.
I CAN SEE THROUGH YOU...
ARE YOU A GHOST?
FOR EONS, WE ZORAS HAVE PROTECTED THIS SPRING, THE ONLY SOURCE OF WATER FOR HYRULE.
OUR TRIBE HAS DEEP TIES TO THE HYRULE FAMILY.
THREE DAYS AGO, THE VILLAGE WAS ATTACKED...
...BY SERVANTS OF SHADOW. AS A LESSON TO THE TRIBE, THEY PUNISHED ME.

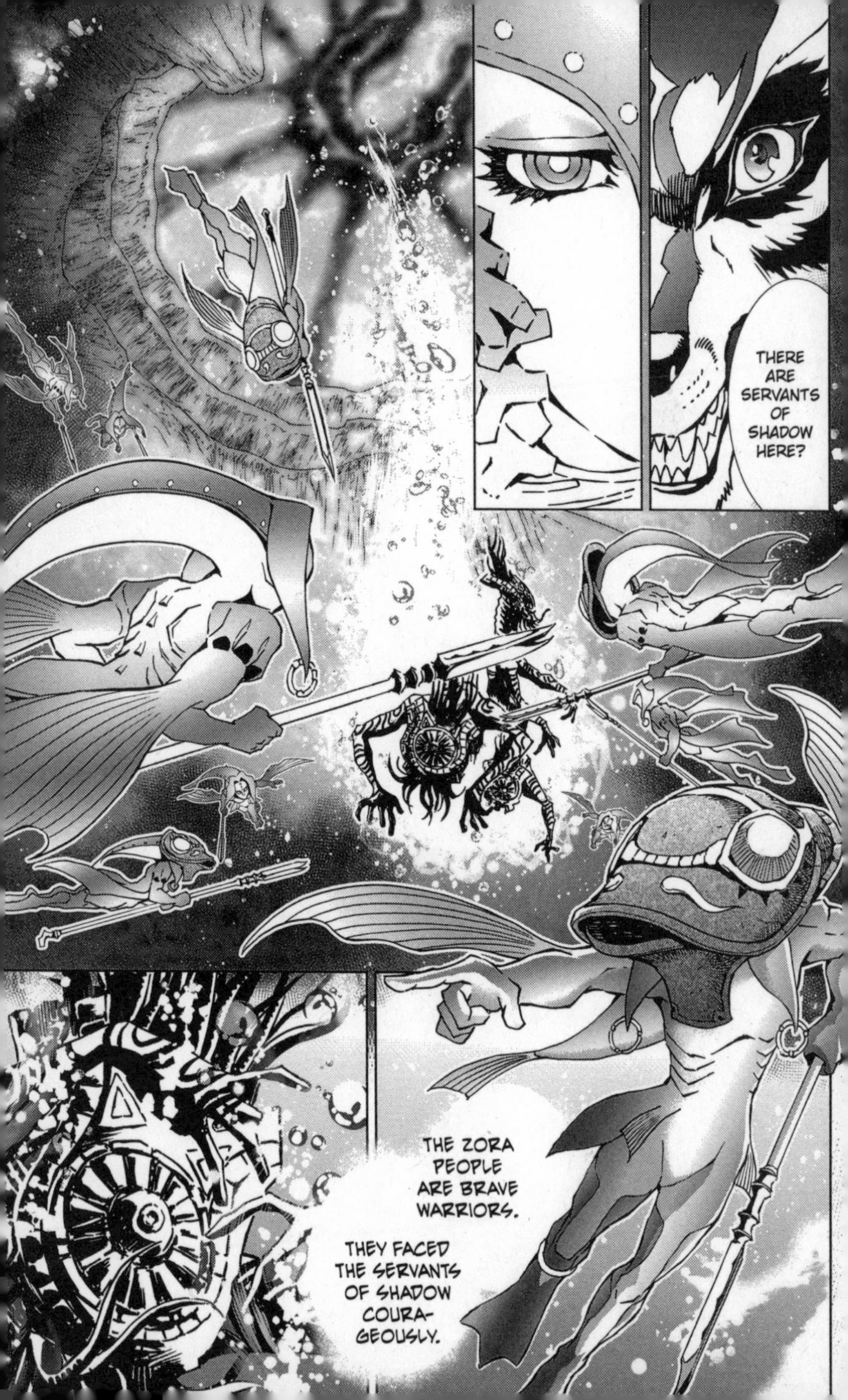
THERE ARE SERVANTS OF SHADOW HERE?
THE ZORA PEOPLE ARE BRAVE WARRIORS.
THEY FACED THE SERVANTS OF SHADOW COURA-GEOUSLY.

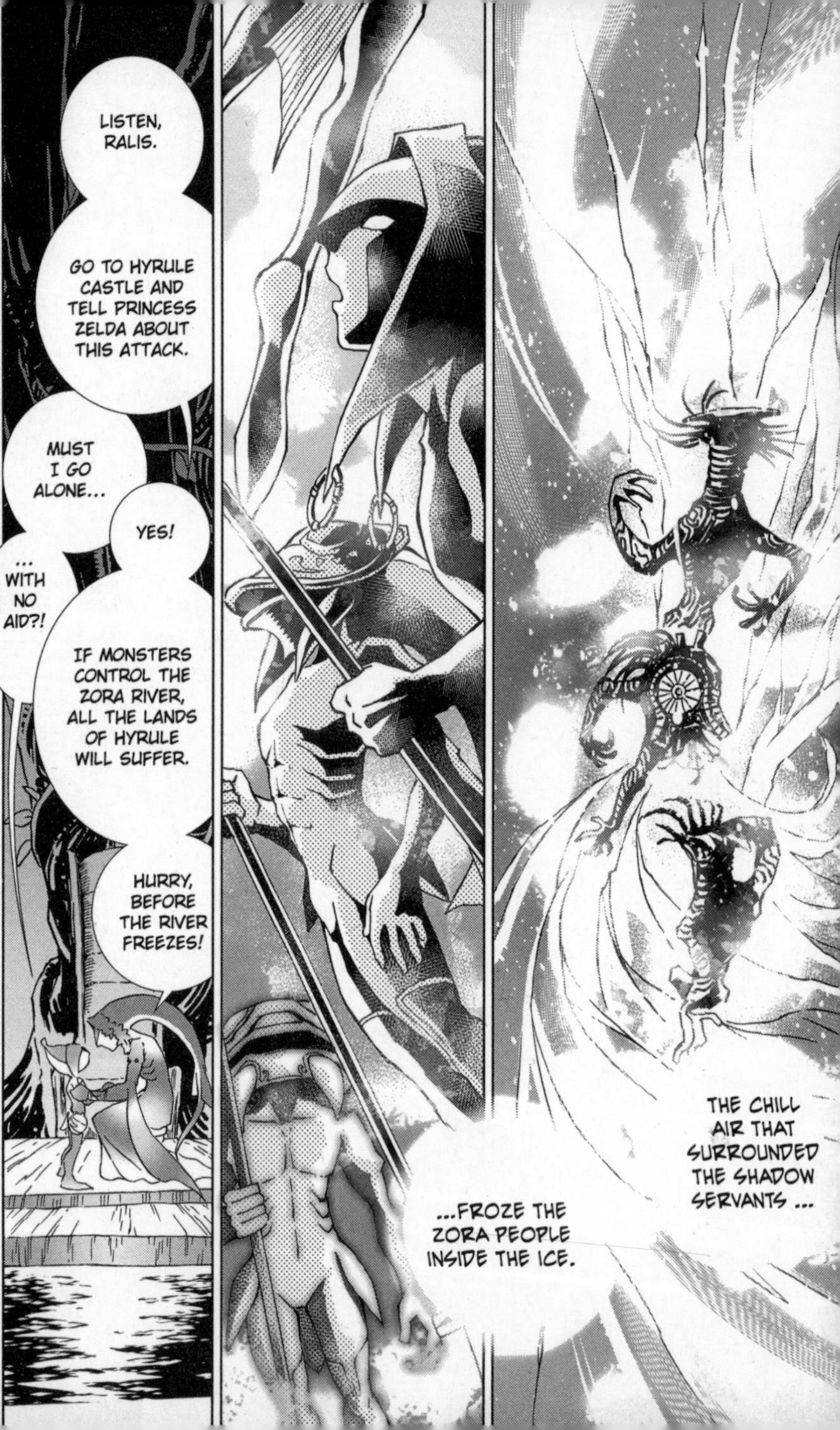
THE CHILL AIR THAT SURROUNDED THE SHADOW SERVANTS ...
...FROZE THE ZORA PEOPLE INSIDE THE ICE.
LISTEN, RALIS.
GO TO HYRULE CASTLE AND TELL PRINCESS ZELDA ABOUT THIS ATTACK.
MUST I GO ALONE...
YES!
...WITH NO AID?!
IF MONSTERS CONTROL THE ZORA RIVER, ALL THE LANDS OF HYRULE WILL SUFFER.
HURRY, BEFORE THE RIVER FREEZES!

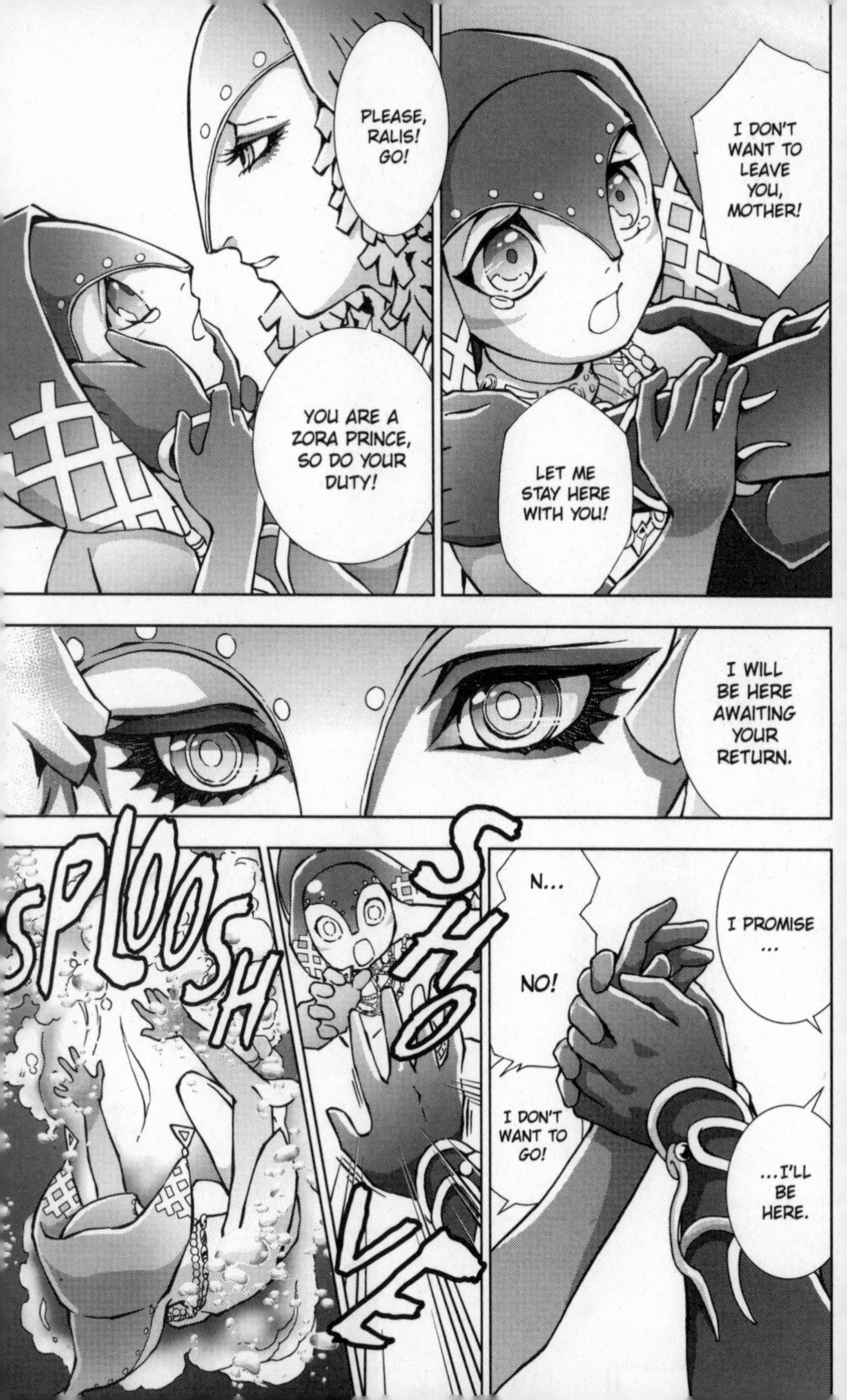
I DON'T WANT TO LEAVE YOU, MOTHER!
LET ME STAY HERE WITH YOU!
PLEASE, RALIS! GO!
YOU ARE A ZORA PRINCE, SO DO YOUR DUTY!
I WILL BE HERE AWAITING YOUR RETURN.
I PROMISE...
N...
NO!
...I'LL BE HERE.
I DON'T WANT TO GO!
SPLOOSH

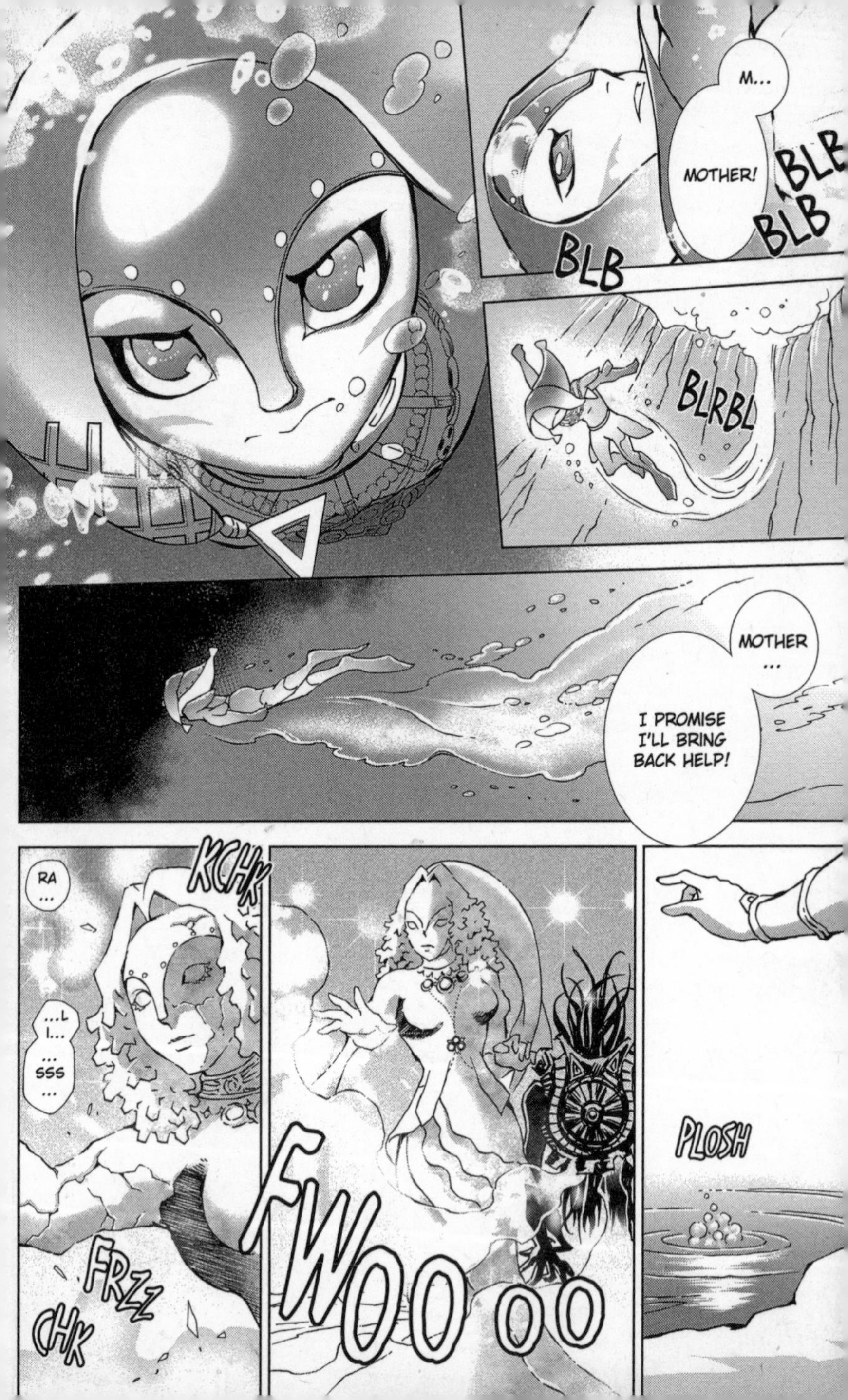
M...
MOTHER!
BLB
BLB
BLB
BLRBL
MOTHER
...
I PROMISE I'LL BRING BACK HELP!
PLOSH
FWOO OO
KCHK
RA
...
...L
I...
...
SSS
...
FRZZ
CHK

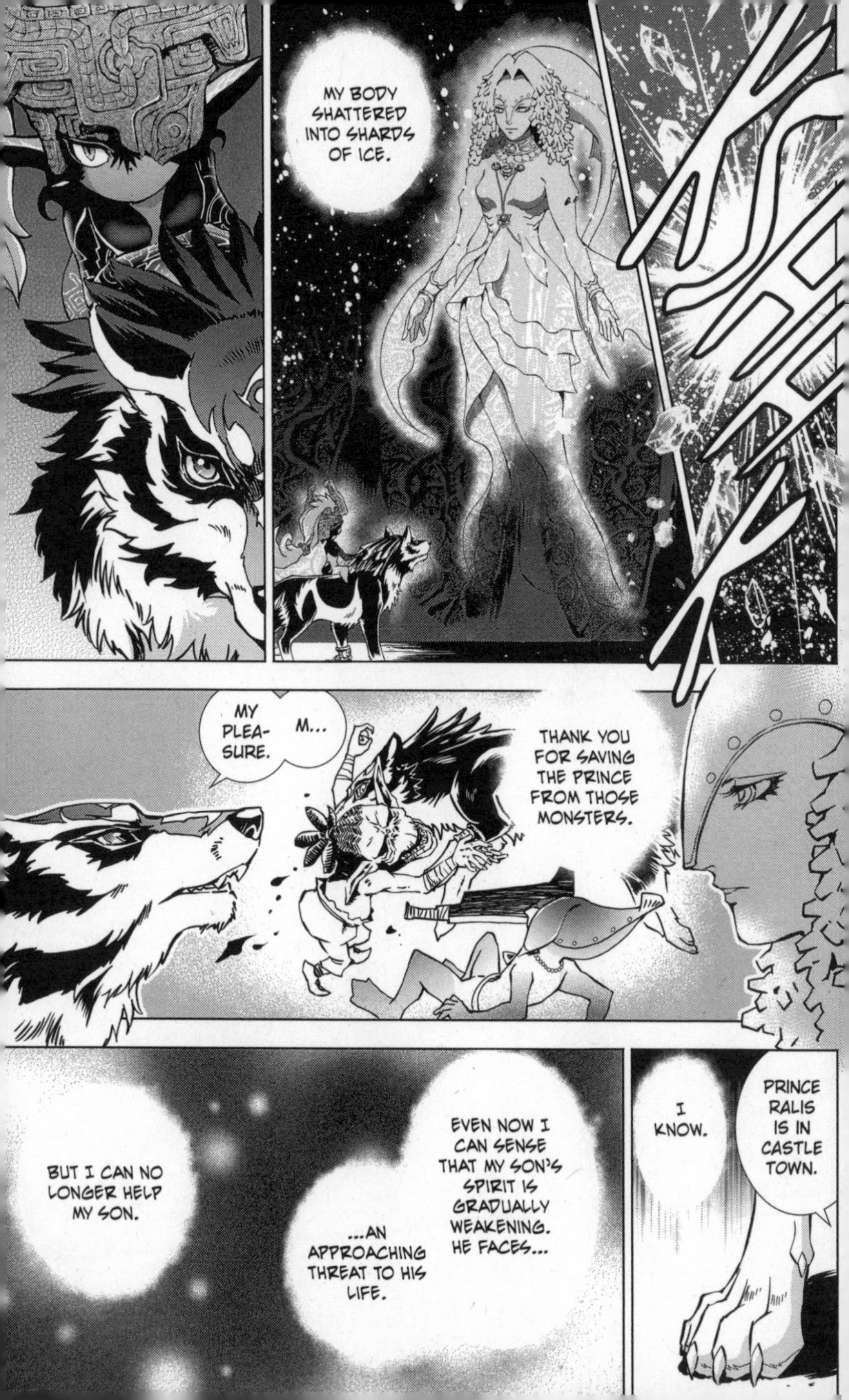
MY BODY SHATTERED INTO SHARDS OF ICE.
THANK YOU FOR SAVING THE PRINCE FROM THOSE MONSTERS.
M...
MY PLEA-SURE.
PRINCE RALIS IS IN CASTLE TOWN.
I KNOW.
EVEN NOW I CAN SENSE THAT MY SON'S SPIRIT IS GRADUALLY WEAKENING. HE FACES...
...AN APPROACHING THREAT TO HIS LIFE.
BUT I CAN NO LONGER HELP MY SON.

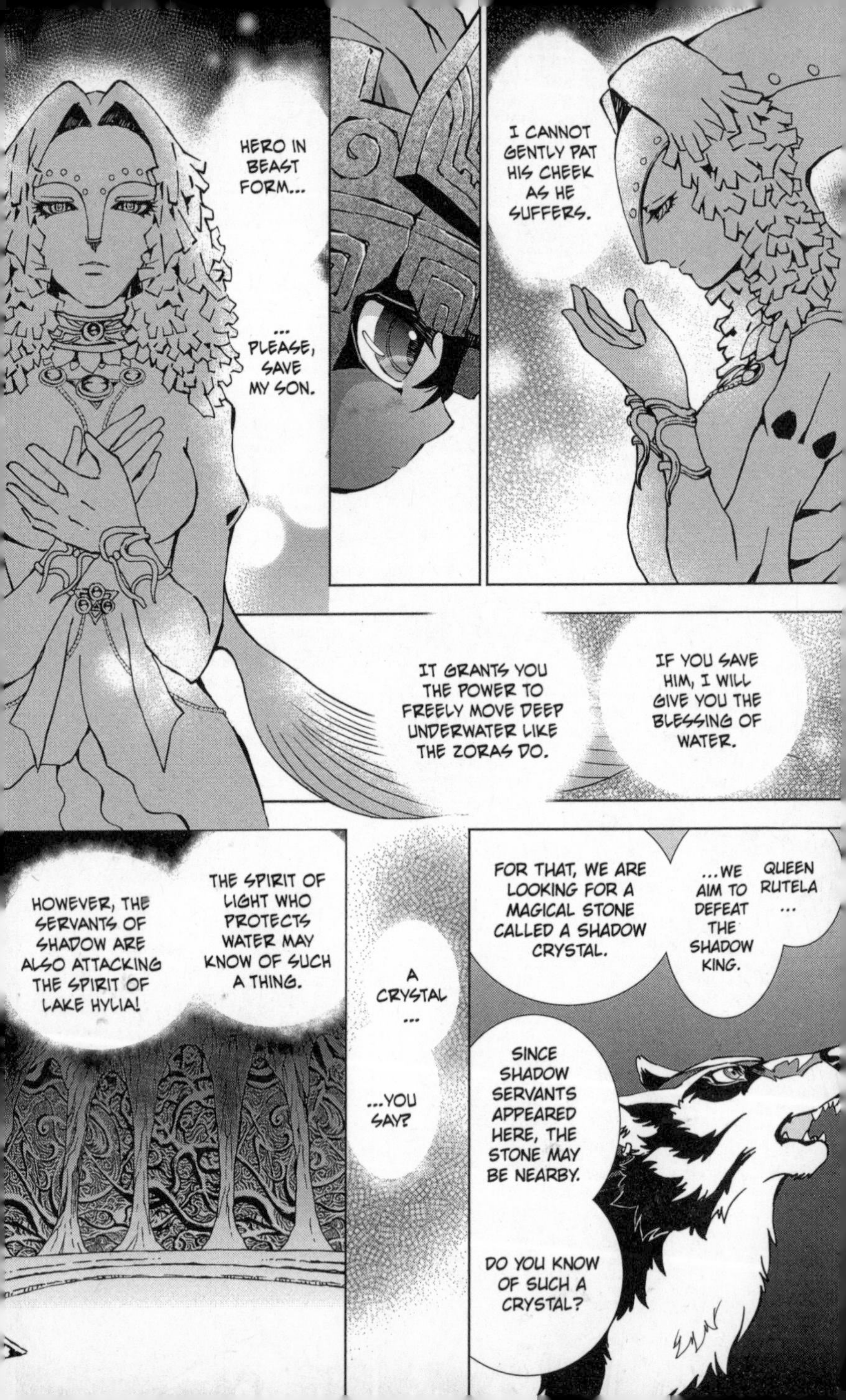
I CANNOT GENTLY PAT HIS CHEEK AS HE SUFFERS.
IF YOU SAVE HIM, I WILL GIVE YOU THE BLESSING OF WATER.
IT GRANTS YOU THE POWER TO FREELY MOVE DEEP UNDERWATER LIKE THE ZORAS DO.
HERO IN BEAST FORM...
...PLEASE, SAVE MY SON.
QUEEN RUTELA...
...WE AIM TO DEFEAT THE SHADOW KING.
FOR THAT, WE ARE LOOKING FOR A MAGICAL STONE CALLED A SHADOW CRYSTAL.
SINCE SHADOW SERVANTS APPEARED HERE, THE STONE MAY BE NEARBY.
DO YOU KNOW OF SUCH A CRYSTAL?
A CRYSTAL...
...YOU SAY?
THE SPIRIT OF LIGHT WHO PROTECTS WATER MAY KNOW OF SUCH A THING.
HOWEVER, THE SERVANTS OF SHADOW ARE ALSO ATTACKING THE SPIRIT OF LAKE HYLIA!

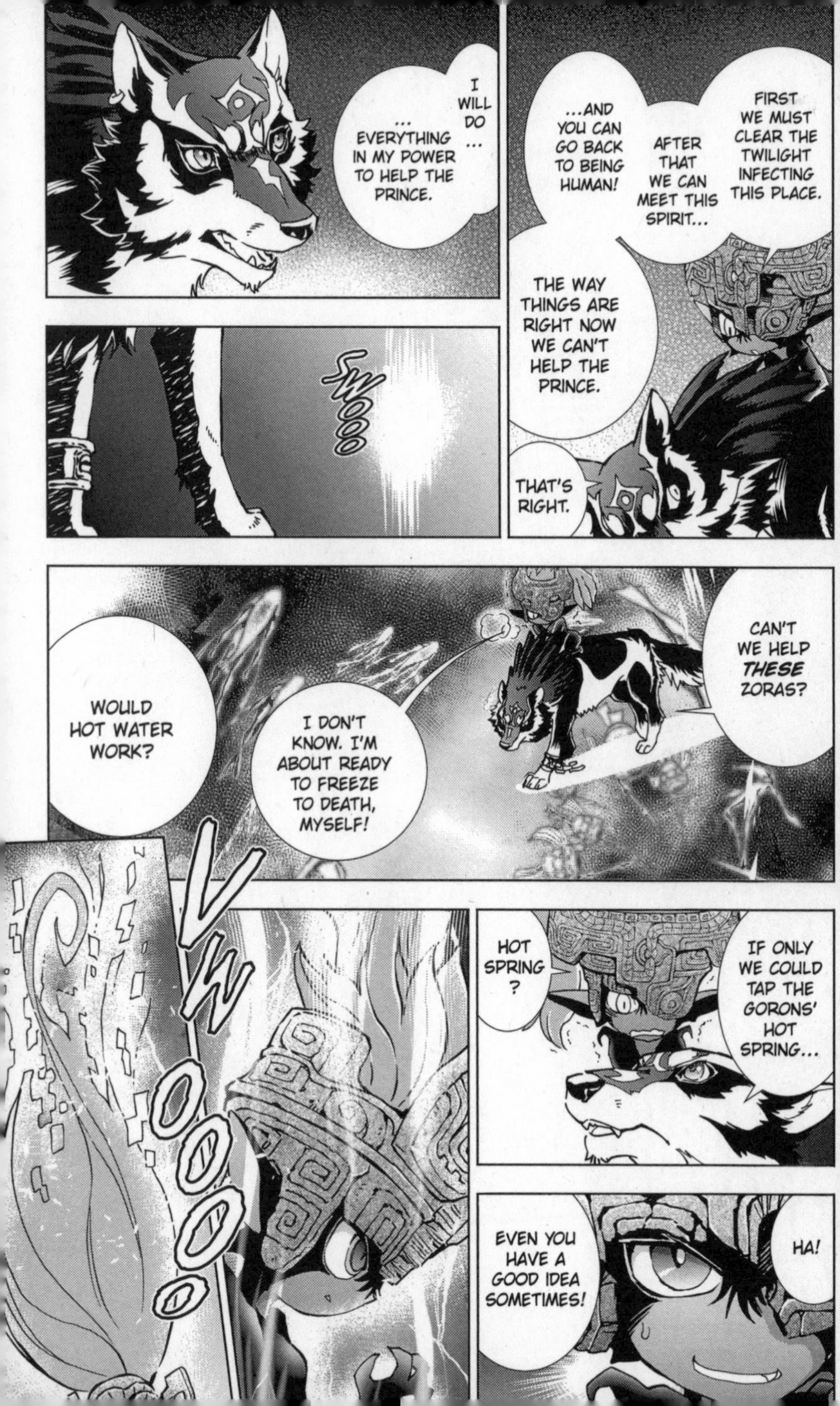

FIRST WE MUST CLEAR THE TWILIGHT INFECTING THIS PLACE.
AFTER THAT WE CAN MEET THIS SPIRIT...
...AND YOU CAN GO BACK TO BEING HUMAN!
THE WAY THINGS ARE RIGHT NOW WE CAN'T HELP THE PRINCE.
THAT'S RIGHT.
I WILL DO ...
... EVERYTHING IN MY POWER TO HELP THE PRINCE.
SWOOO
CAN'T WE HELP *THESE* ZORAS?
I DON'T KNOW. I'M ABOUT READY TO FREEZE TO DEATH, MYSELF!
WOULD HOT WATER WORK?
IF ONLY WE COULD TAP THE GORONS' HOT SPRING...
HOT SPRING?
HA!
EVEN YOU HAVE A GOOD IDEA SOMETIMES!
VWOOOOOO

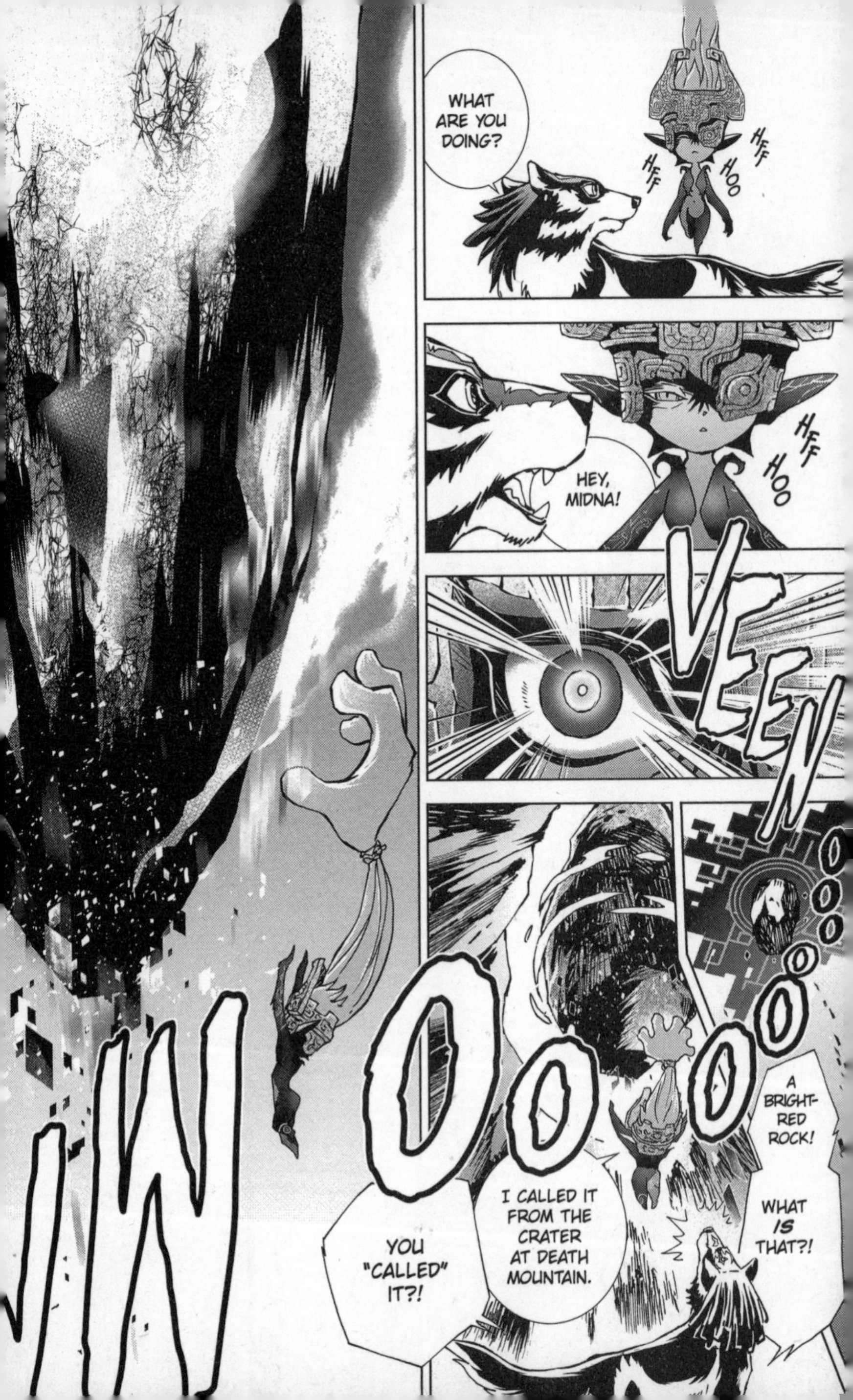
HFF HFF
HOO
WHAT ARE YOU DOING?
HFF
HOO
HEY, MIDNA!
VEEN
A BRIGHT-RED ROCK!
WHAT IS THAT?!
I CALLED IT FROM THE CRATER AT DEATH MOUNTAIN.
YOU "CALLED" IT?!
WOOOOOOOOO

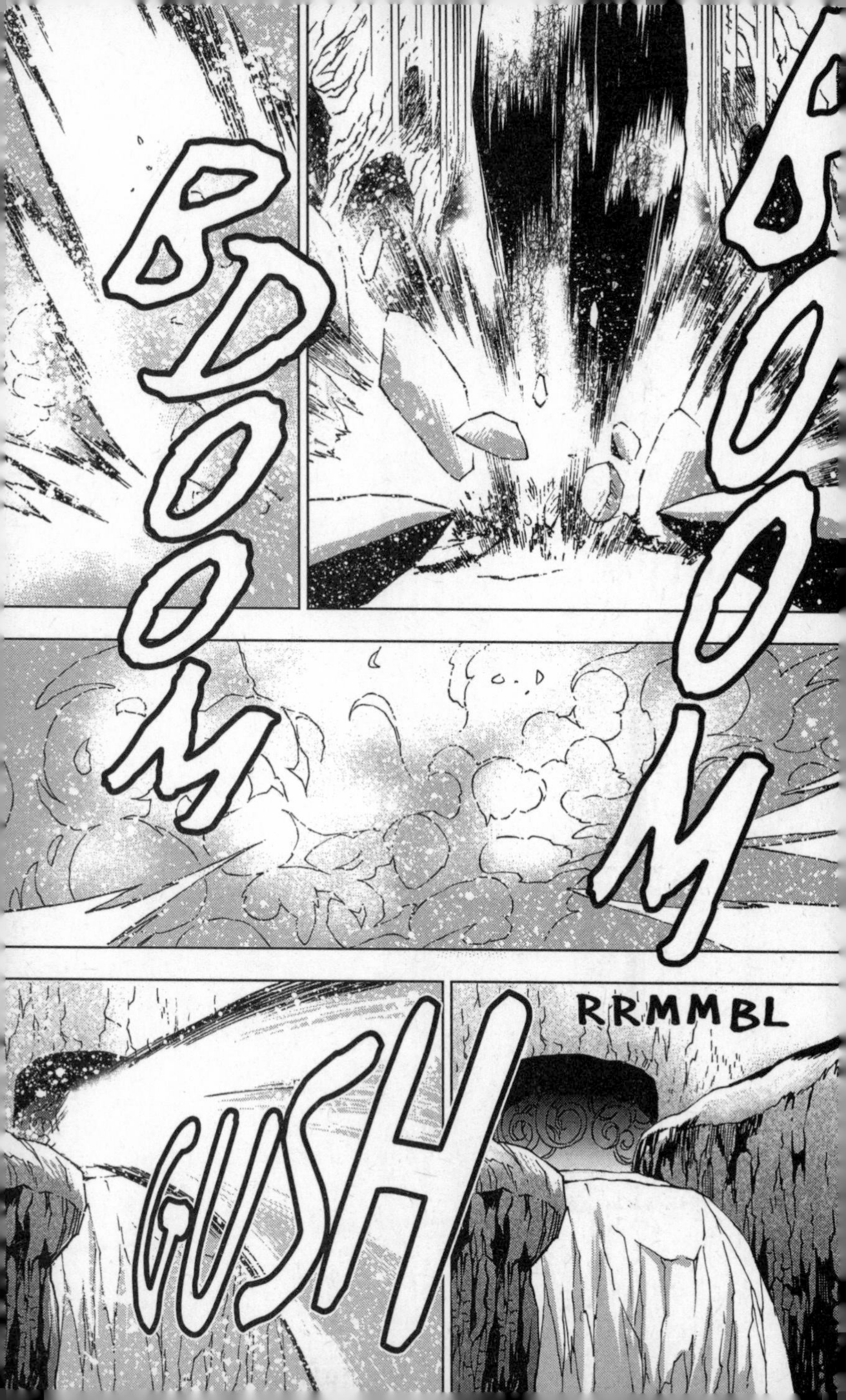
BOOM
BOOM
RRMMBL
GUSH

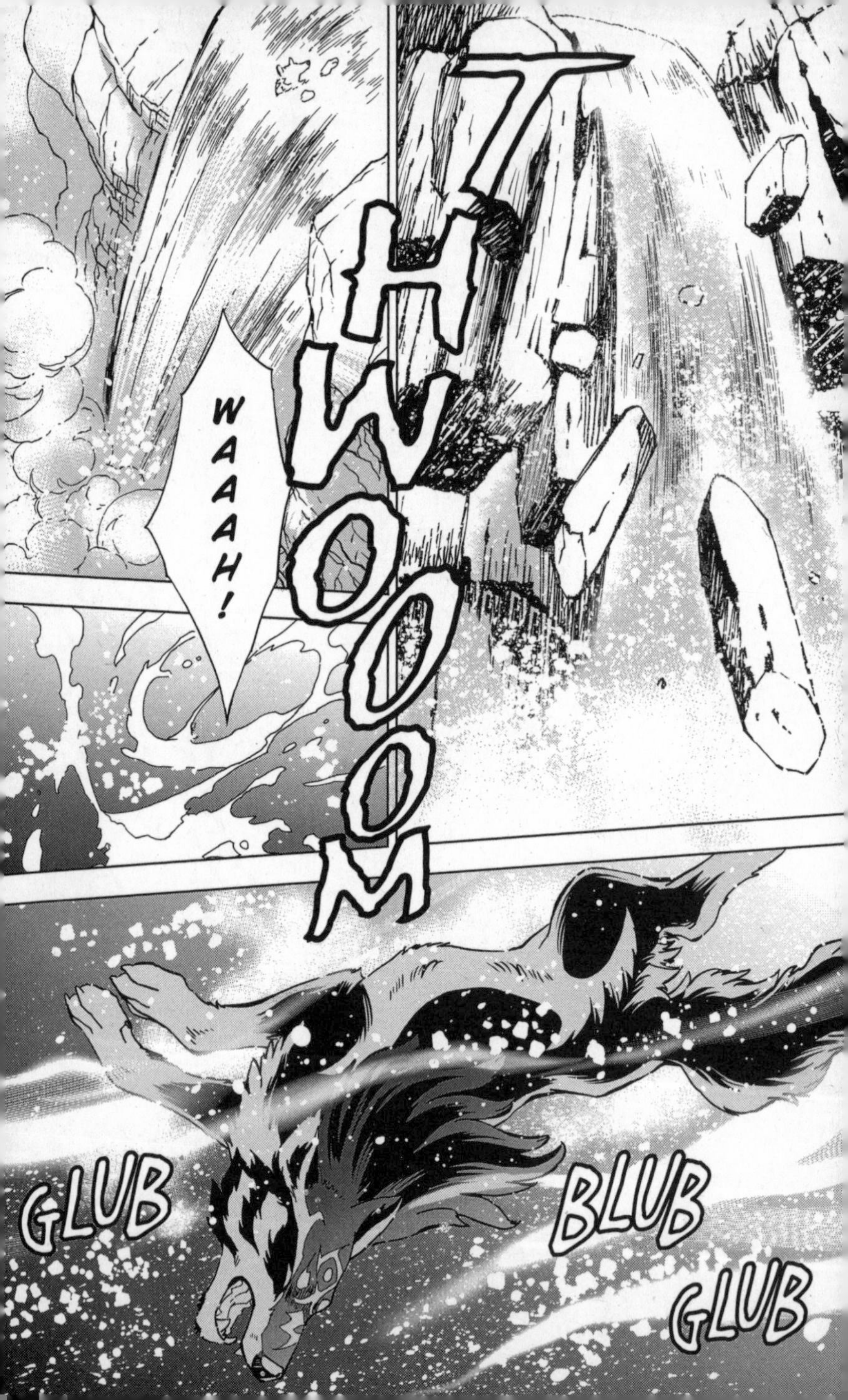
THWOOOM
WAAAAH!
BLUB
GLUB
GLUB

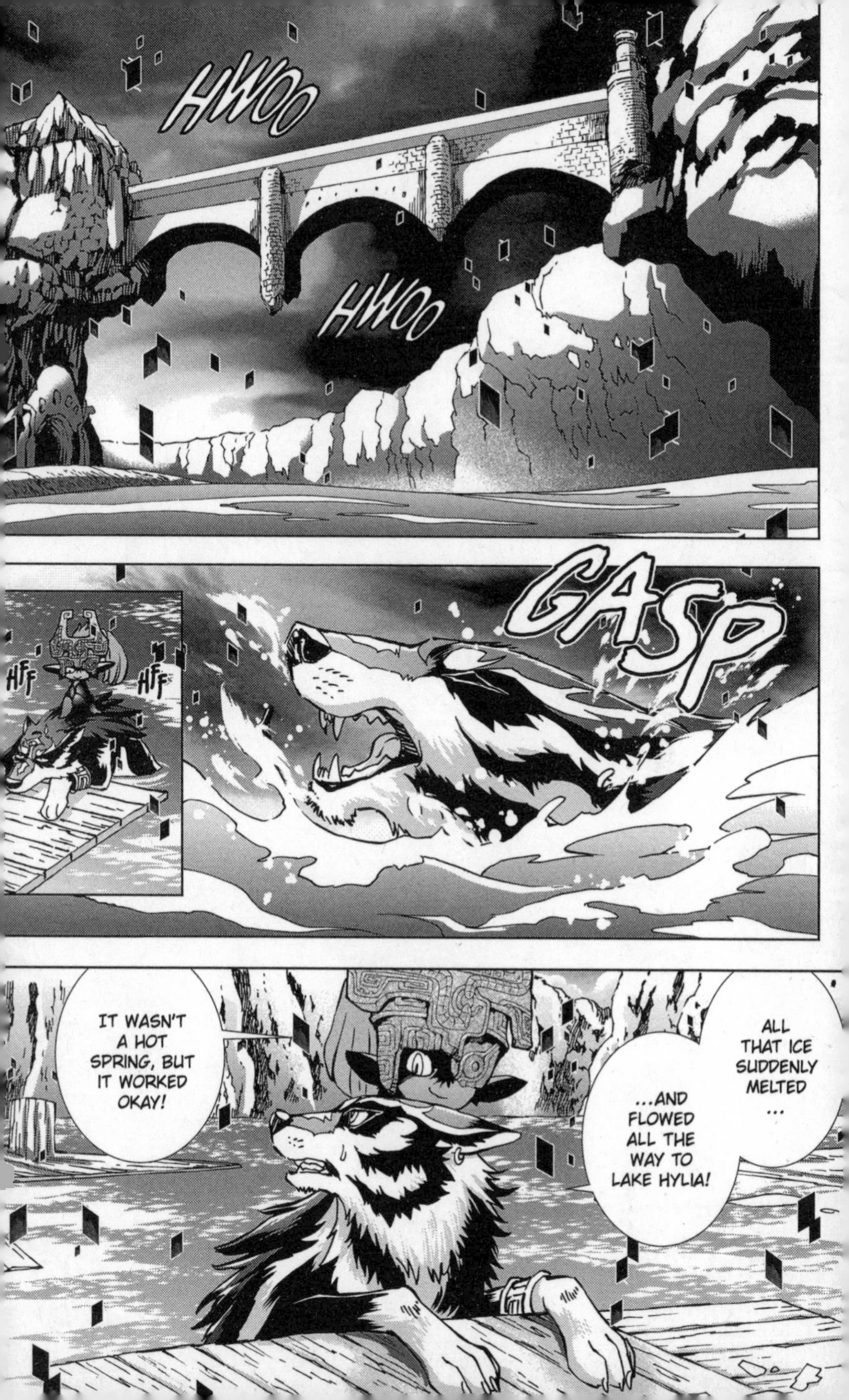
HWOO
HWOO
GASP
HFF
HFF
ALL THAT ICE SUDDENLY MELTED ...
...AND FLOWED ALL THE WAY TO LAKE HYLIA!
IT WASN'T A HOT SPRING, BUT IT WORKED OKAY!

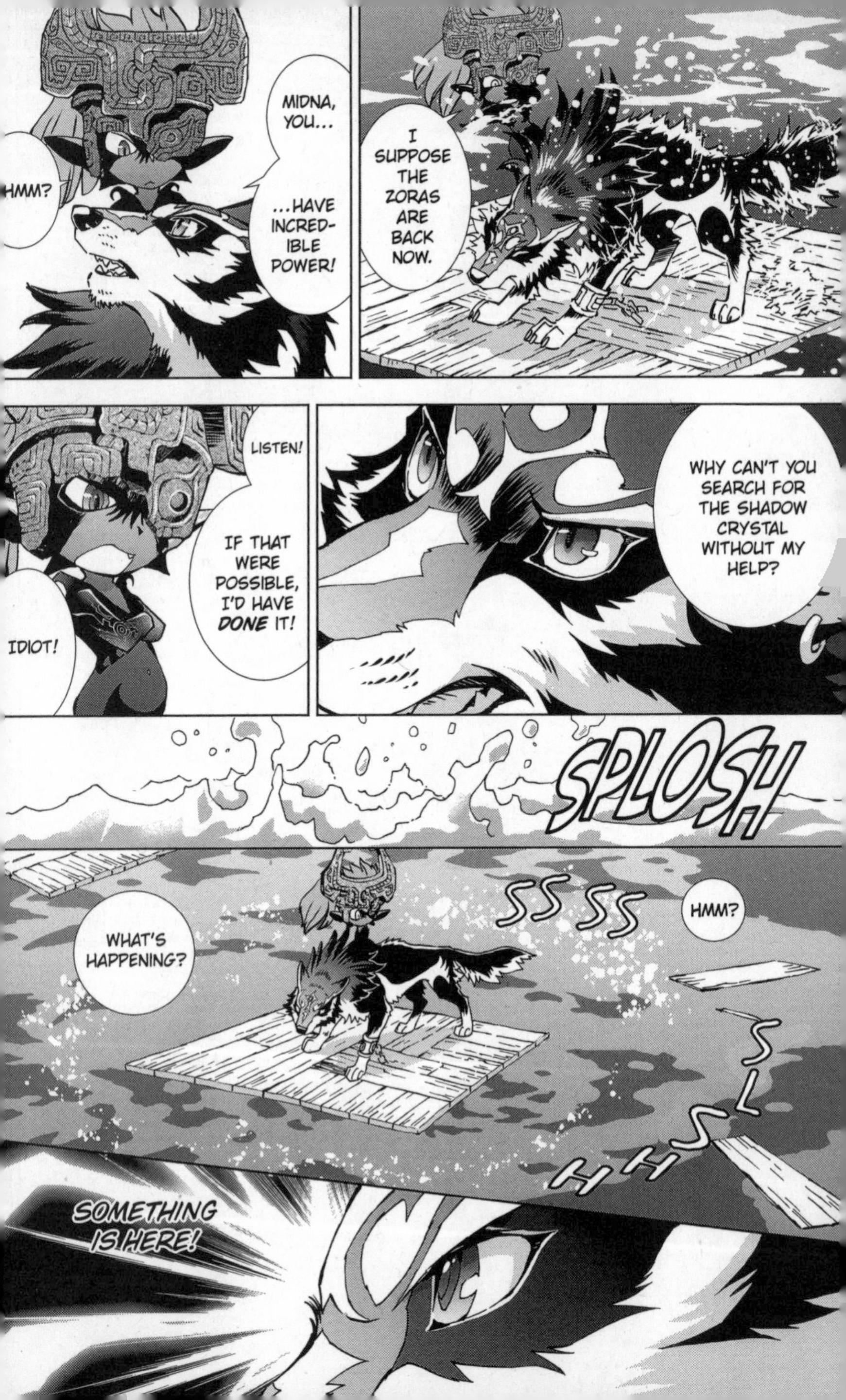
I SUPPOSE THE ZORAS ARE BACK NOW.
MIDNA, YOU...
...HAVE INCREDIBLE POWER!
HMM?
WHY CAN'T YOU SEARCH FOR THE SHADOW CRYSTAL WITHOUT MY HELP?
LISTEN!
IF THAT WERE POSSIBLE, I'D HAVE DONE IT!
IDIOT!
SPLOSH
HMM?
SSSSS
WHAT'S HAPPENING?
SSSHHH
SOMETHING IS HERE!

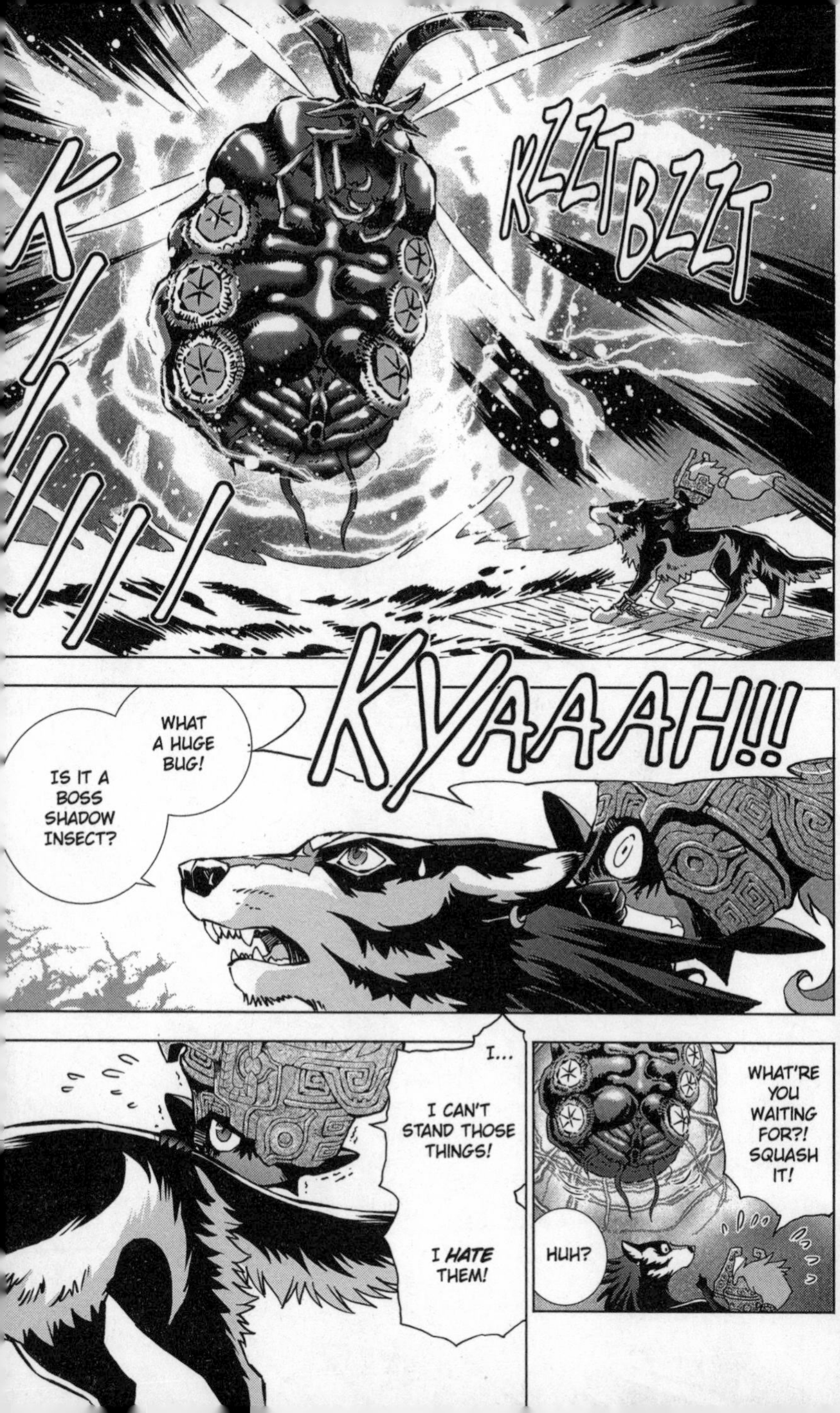

KZZZT BZZZT
K
KYAAAH!!
WHAT A HUGE BUG!
IS IT A BOSS SHADOW INSECT?
WHAT'RE YOU WAITING FOR?! SQUASH IT!
HUH?
I...
I CAN'T STAND THOSE THINGS!
I *HATE* THEM!

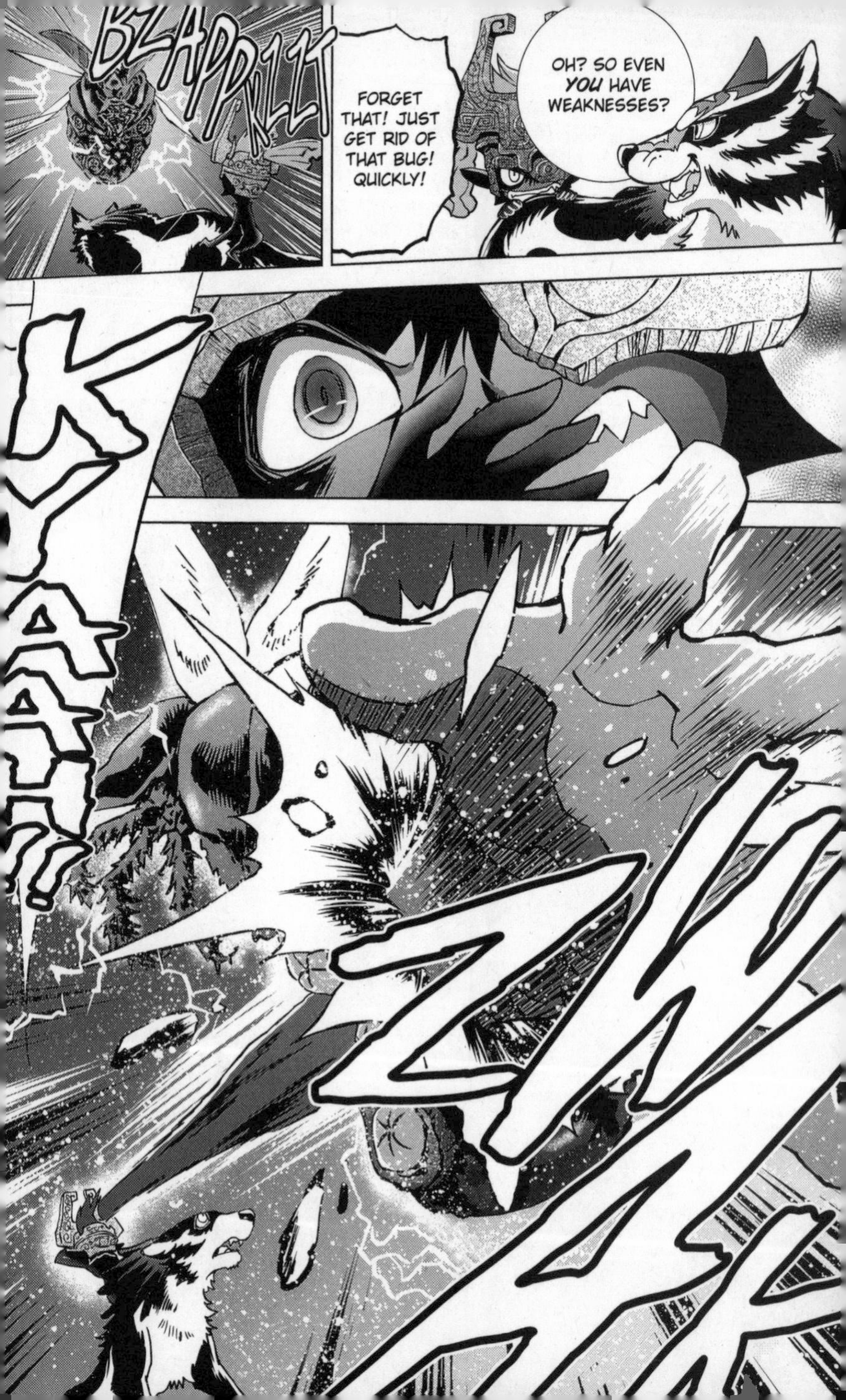
OH? SO EVEN *YOU* HAVE WEAKNESSES?
FORGET THAT! JUST GET RID OF THAT BUG! QUICKLY!
BZAPPKZZT
KYAA!!

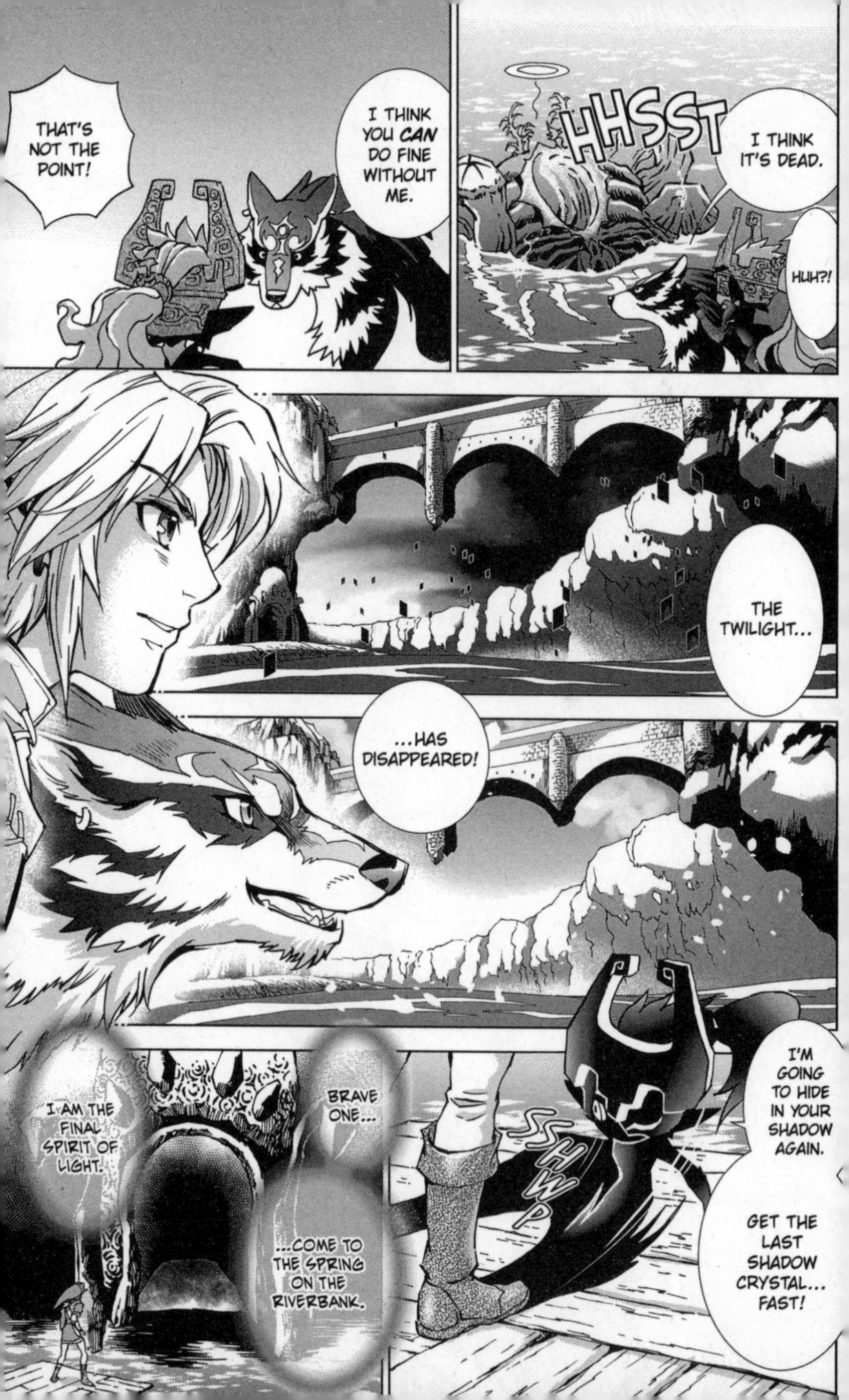
HHSST
I THINK IT'S DEAD.
HUH?!
I THINK YOU CAN DO FINE WITHOUT ME.
THAT'S NOT THE POINT!
THE TWILIGHT...
...HAS DISAPPEARED!
I'M GOING TO HIDE IN YOUR SHADOW AGAIN.
SSHWP
GET THE LAST SHADOW CRYSTAL... FAST!
BRAVE ONE...
I AM THE FINAL SPIRIT OF LIGHT.
...COME TO THE SPRING ON THE RIVERBANK.

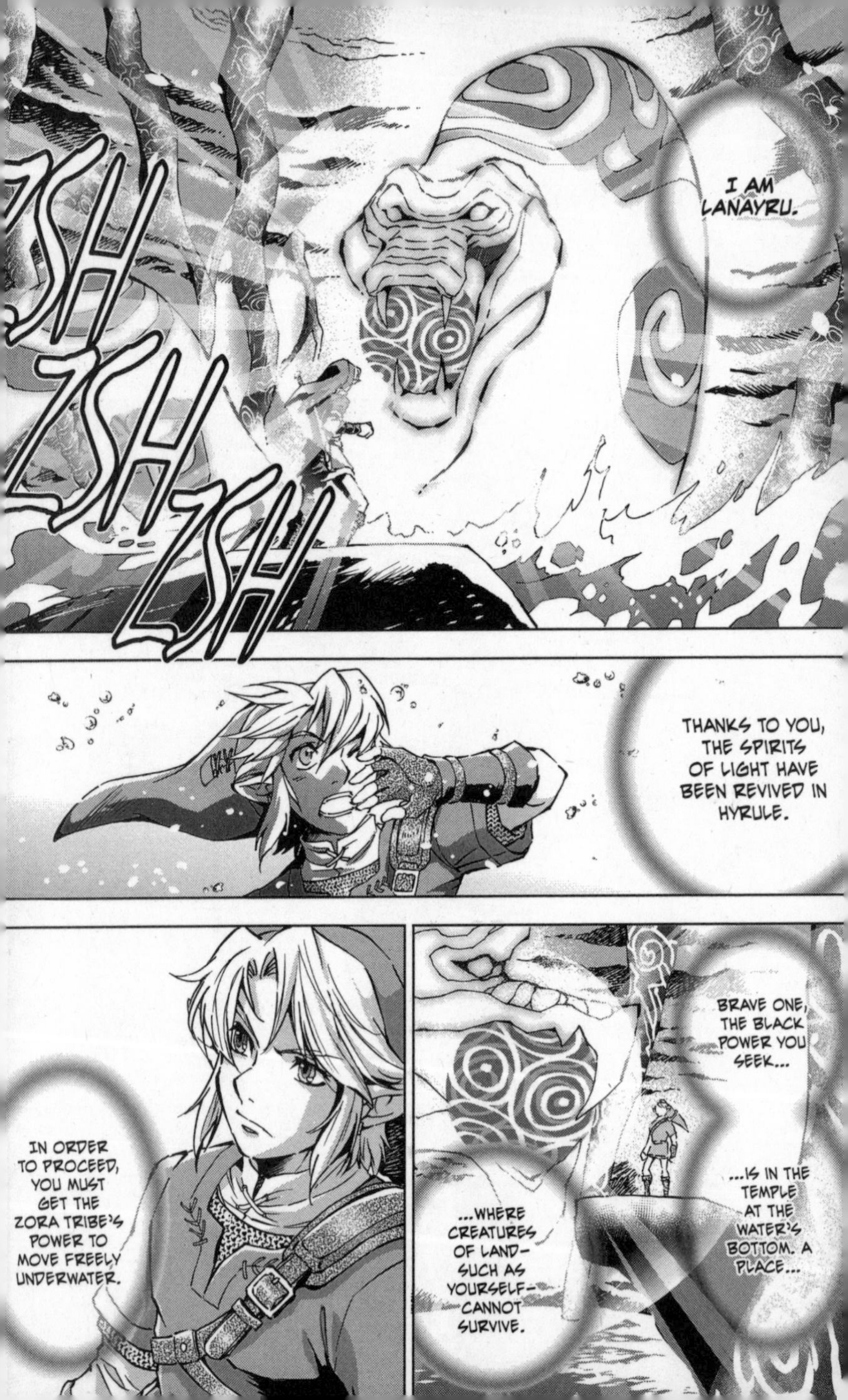
I AM LANAYRU.
ZSH ZSH ZSH
THANKS TO YOU, THE SPIRITS OF LIGHT HAVE BEEN REVIVED IN HYRULE.
BRAVE ONE, THE BLACK POWER YOU SEEK...
...IS IN THE TEMPLE AT THE WATER'S BOTTOM. A PLACE...
...WHERE CREATURES OF LAND—SUCH AS YOURSELF—CANNOT SURVIVE.
IN ORDER TO PROCEED, YOU MUST GET THE ZORA TRIBE'S POWER TO MOVE FREELY UNDERWATER.

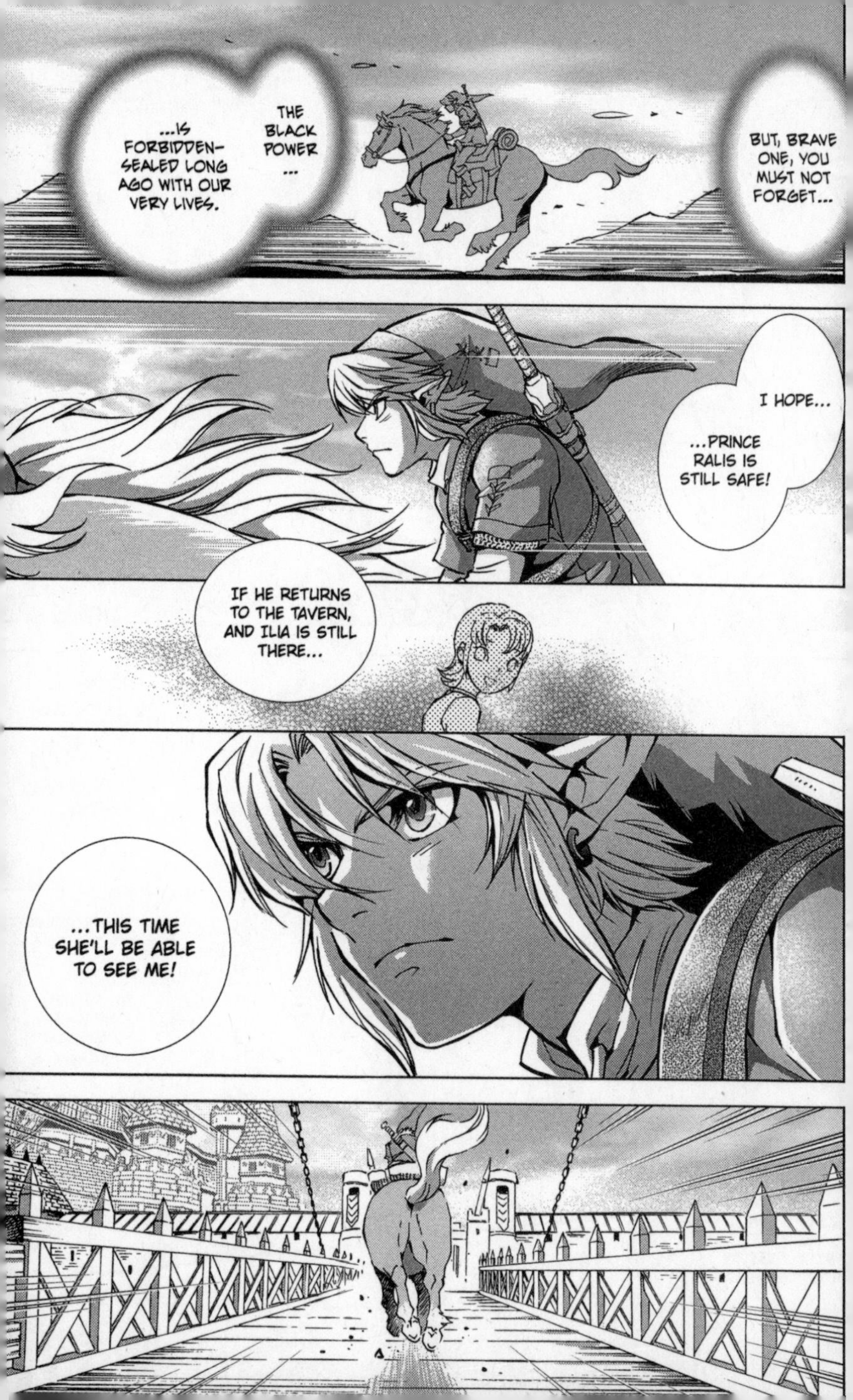
BUT, BRAVE ONE, YOU MUST NOT FORGET...
THE BLACK POWER ...
...IS FORBIDDEN-SEALED LONG AGO WITH OUR VERY LIVES.
I HOPE...
...PRINCE RALIS IS STILL SAFE!
IF HE RETURNS TO THE TAVERN, AND ILIA IS STILL THERE...
...THIS TIME SHE'LL BE ABLE TO SEE ME!

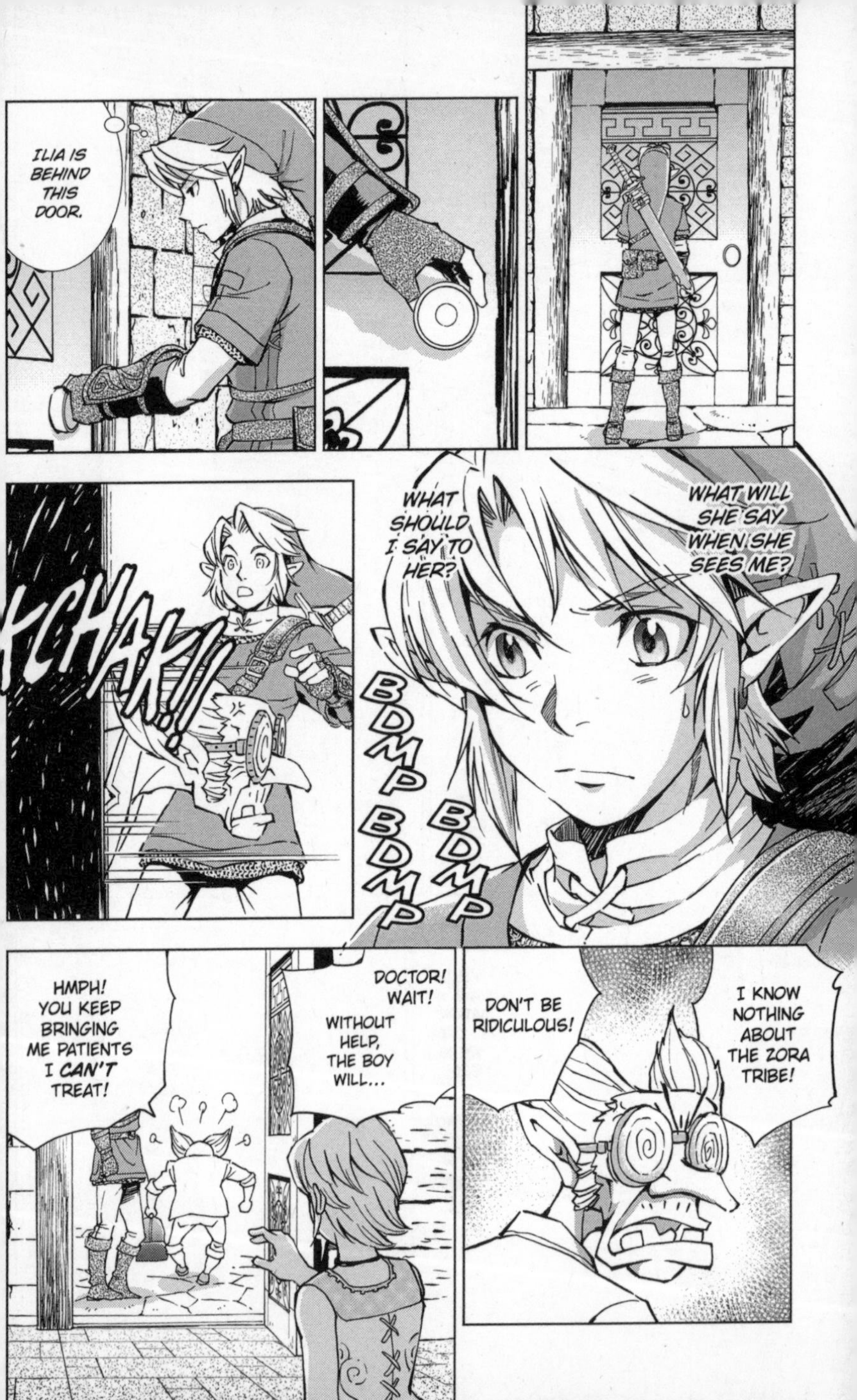
ILIA IS BEHIND THIS DOOR.
WHAT WILL SHE SAY WHEN SHE SEES ME?
WHAT SHOULD I SAY TO HER?
BDMP BDMP
BDMP BDMP
CHAK!!
I KNOW NOTHING ABOUT THE ZORA TRIBE!
DON'T BE RIDICULOUS!
DOCTOR! WAIT!
WITHOUT HELP, THE BOY WILL...
HMPH! YOU KEEP BRINGING ME PATIENTS I **CAN'T** TREAT!

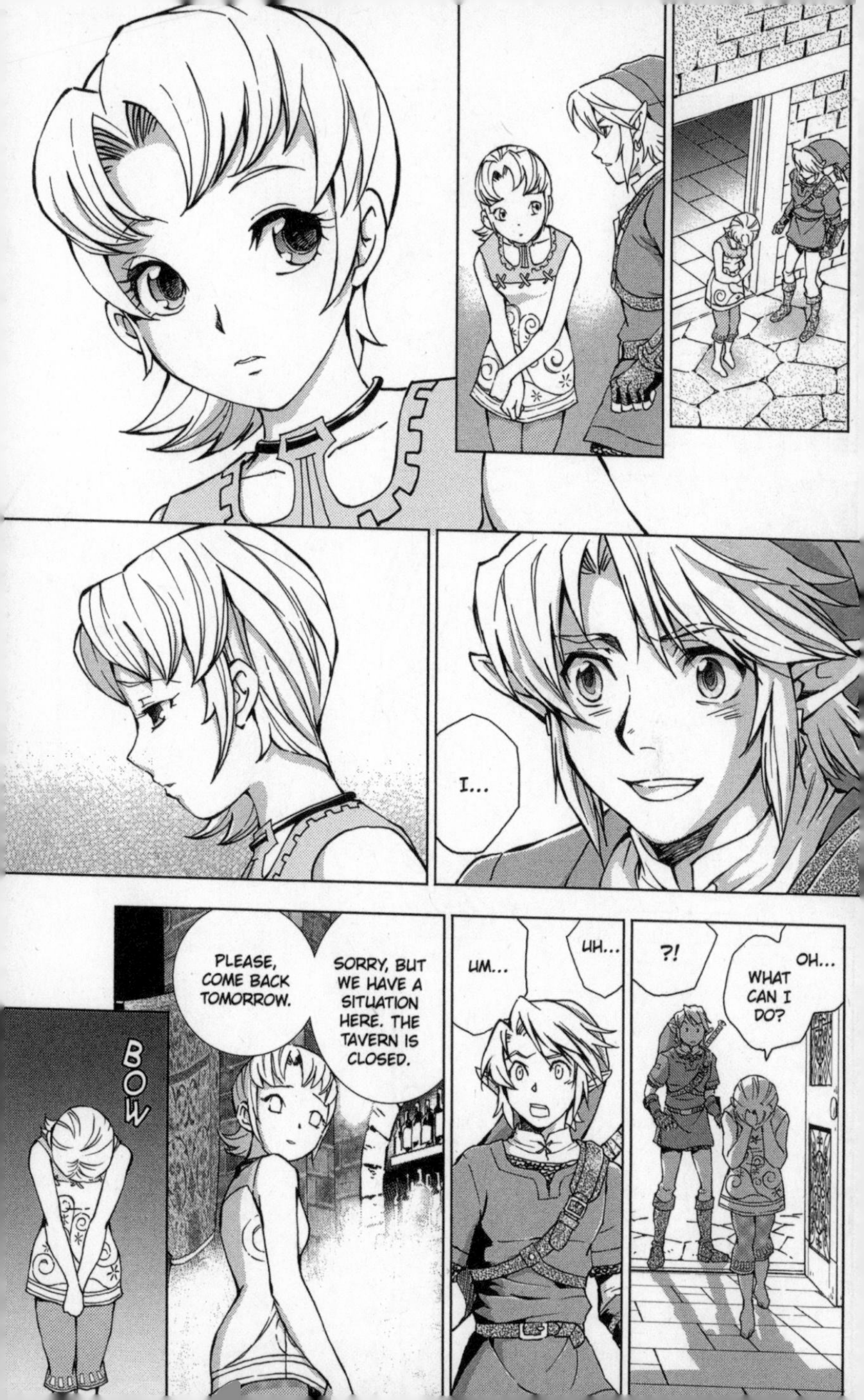

I...
OH... WHAT CAN I DO?
?!
UH...
UM...
SORRY, BUT WE HAVE A SITUATION HERE. THE TAVERN IS CLOSED.
PLEASE, COME BACK TOMORROW.
BOW

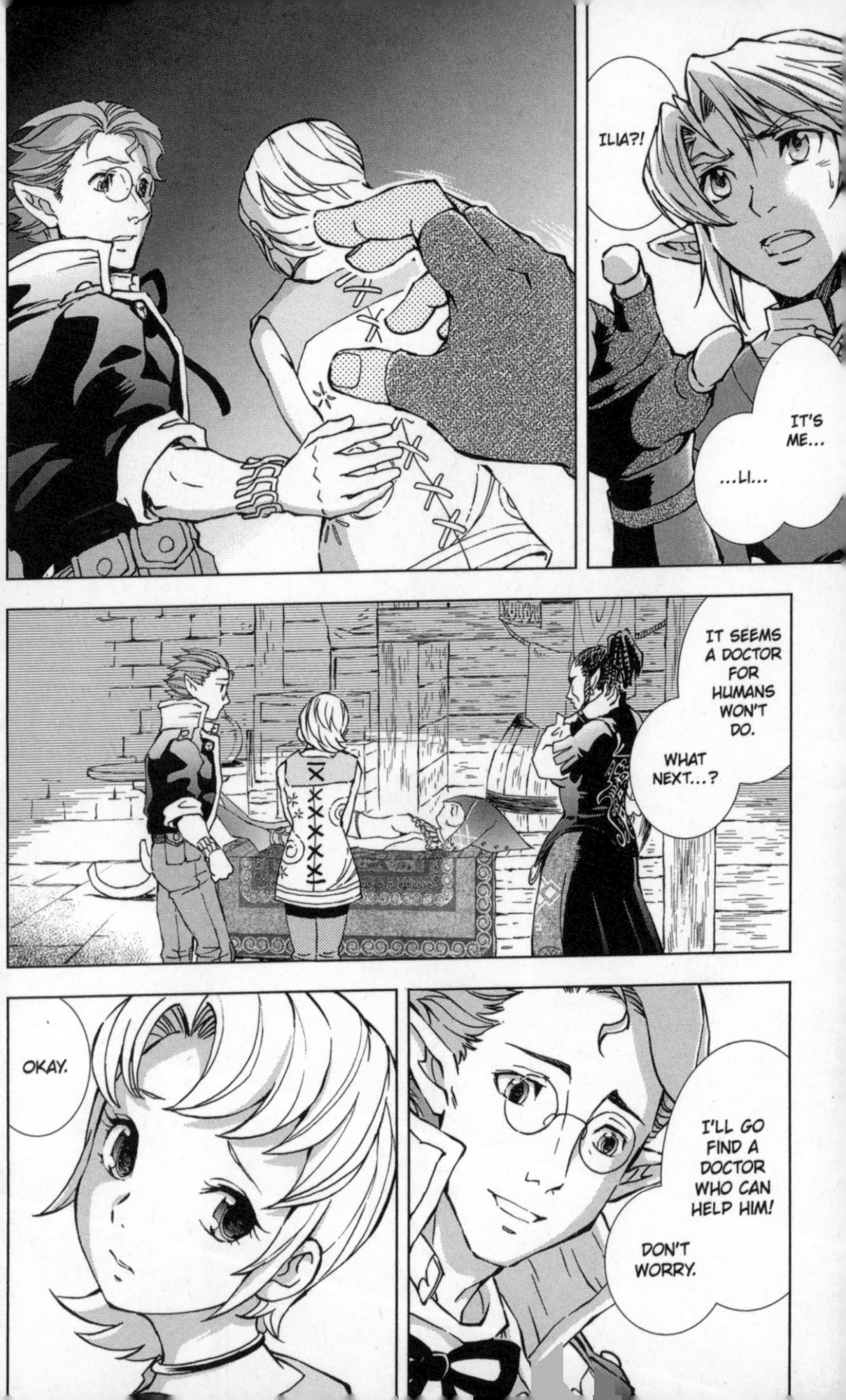
ILIA?!
IT'S ME...
...LI...
IT SEEMS A DOCTOR FOR HUMANS WON'T DO.
WHAT NEXT...?
I'LL GO FIND A DOCTOR WHO CAN HELP HIM!
DON'T WORRY.
OKAY.

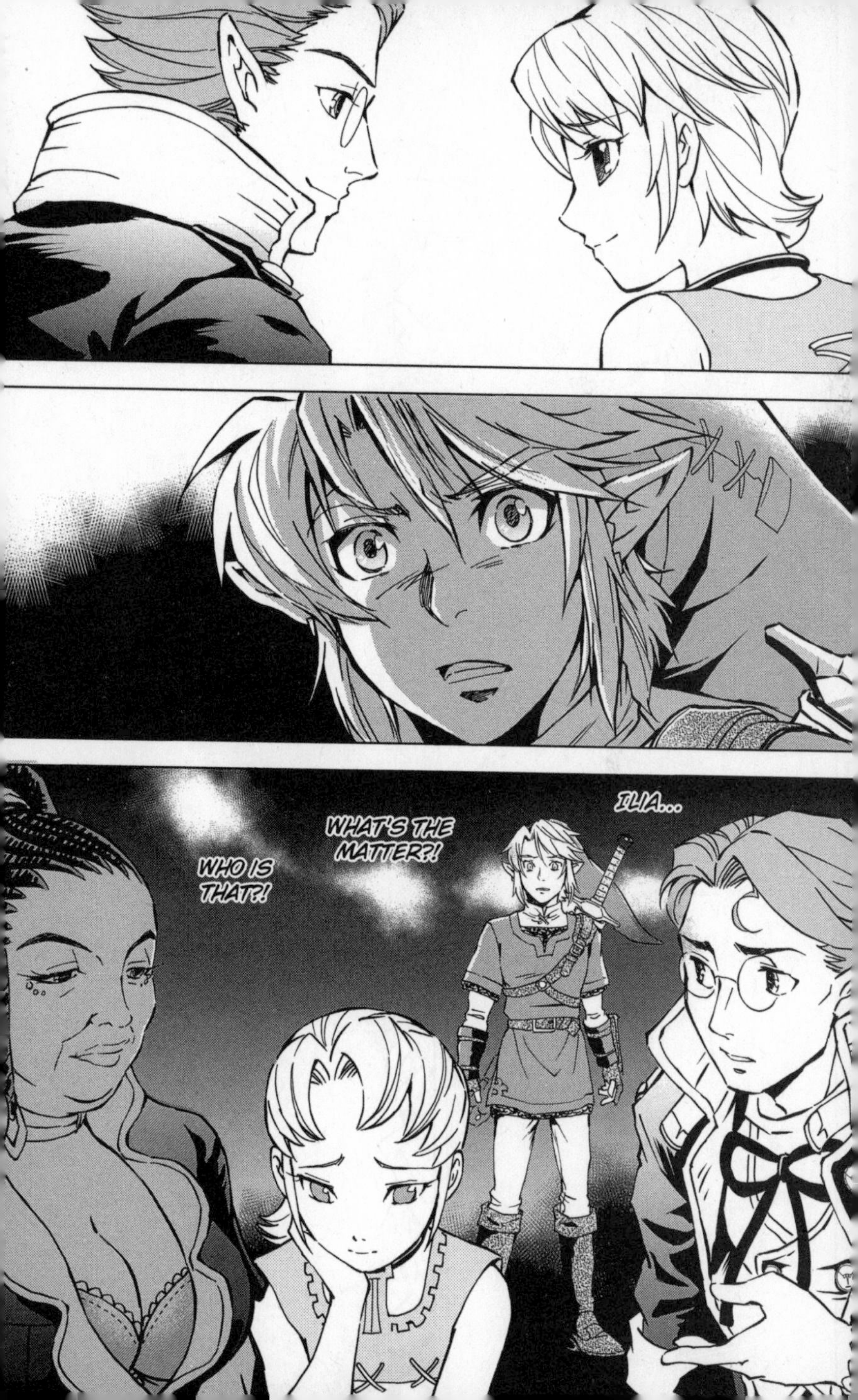
ILIA...
WHAT'S THE MATTER?!
WHO IS THAT?!

#29. MEMORY TRACKS

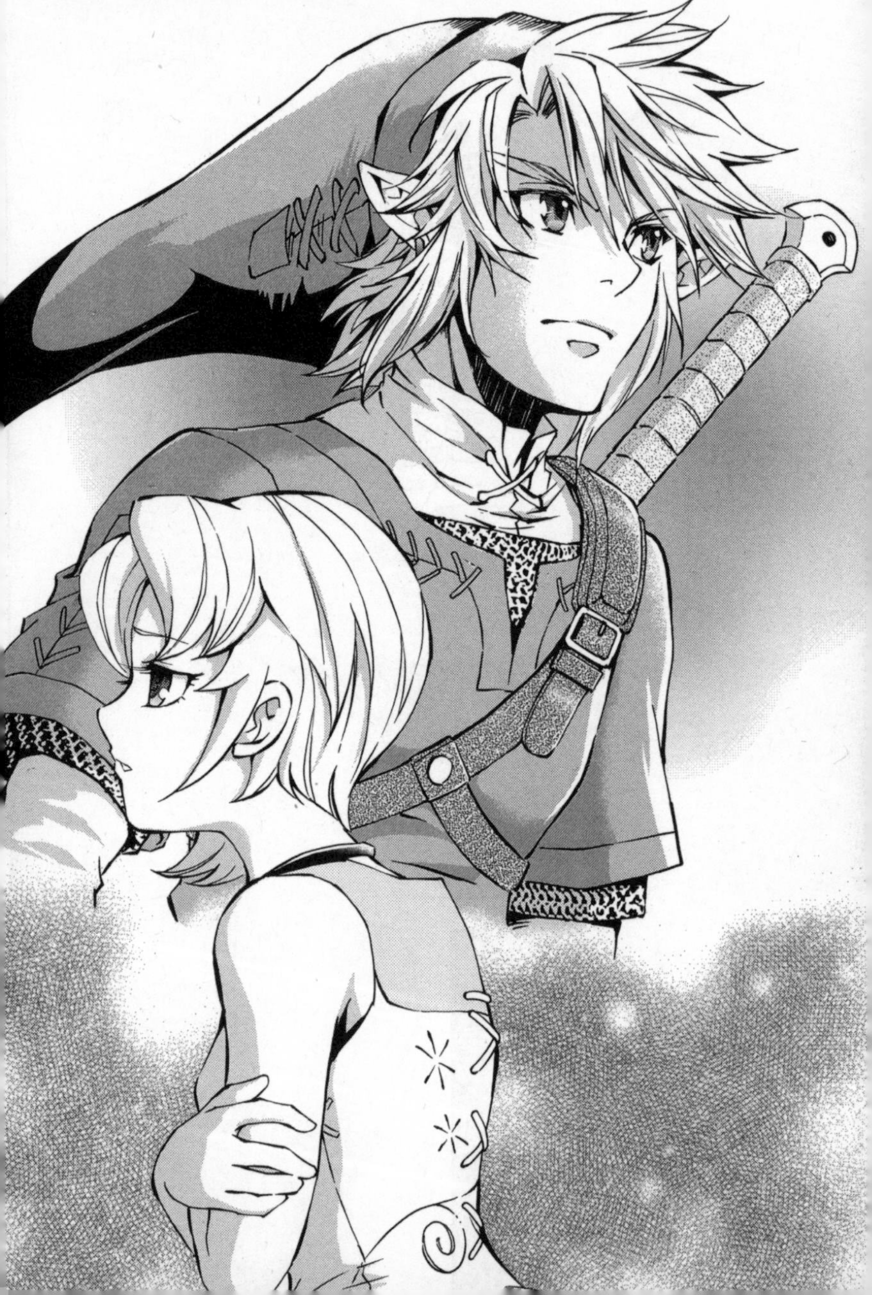

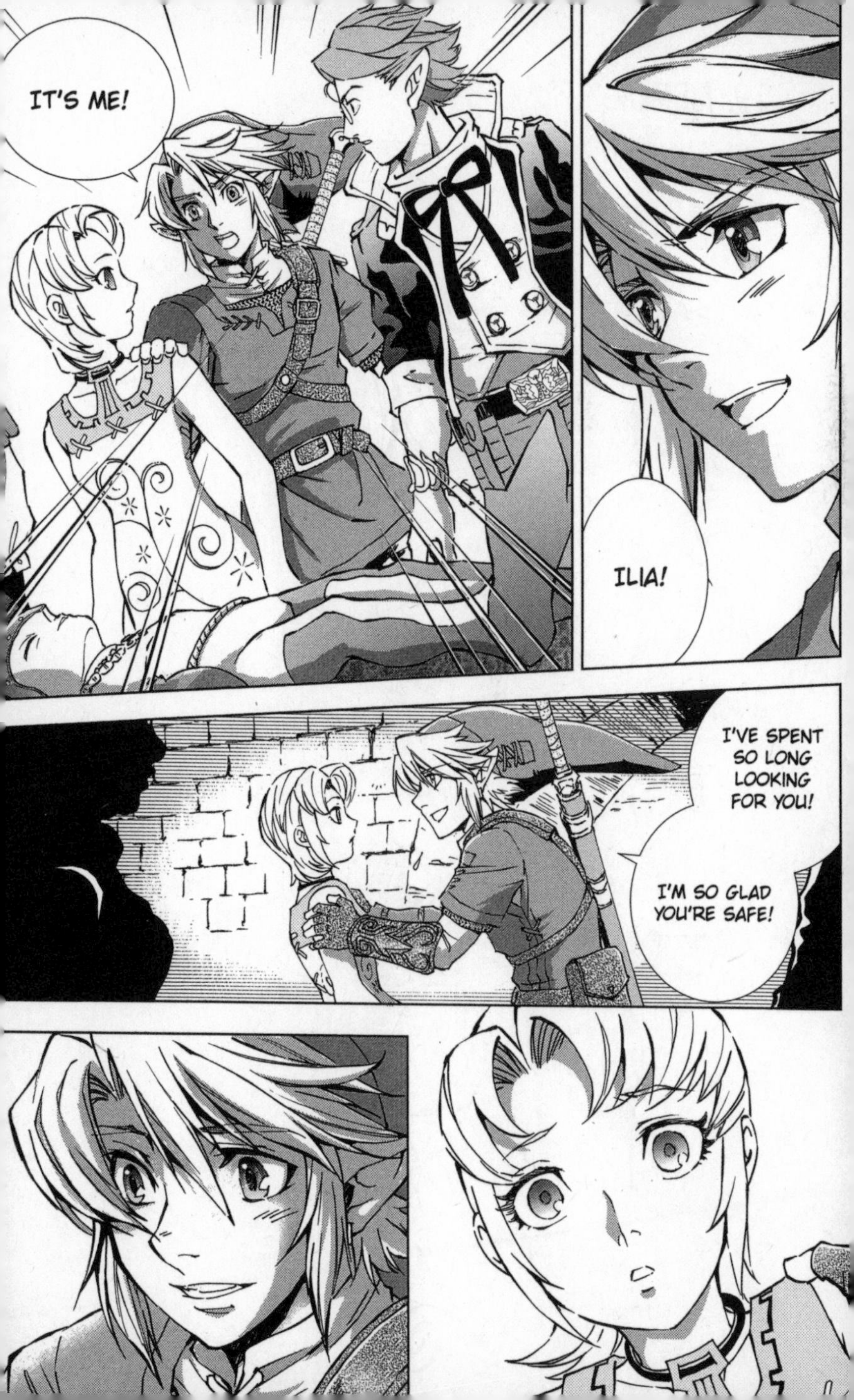
ILIA!
IT'S ME!
I'VE SPENT SO LONG LOOKING FOR YOU!
I'M SO GLAD YOU'RE SAFE!

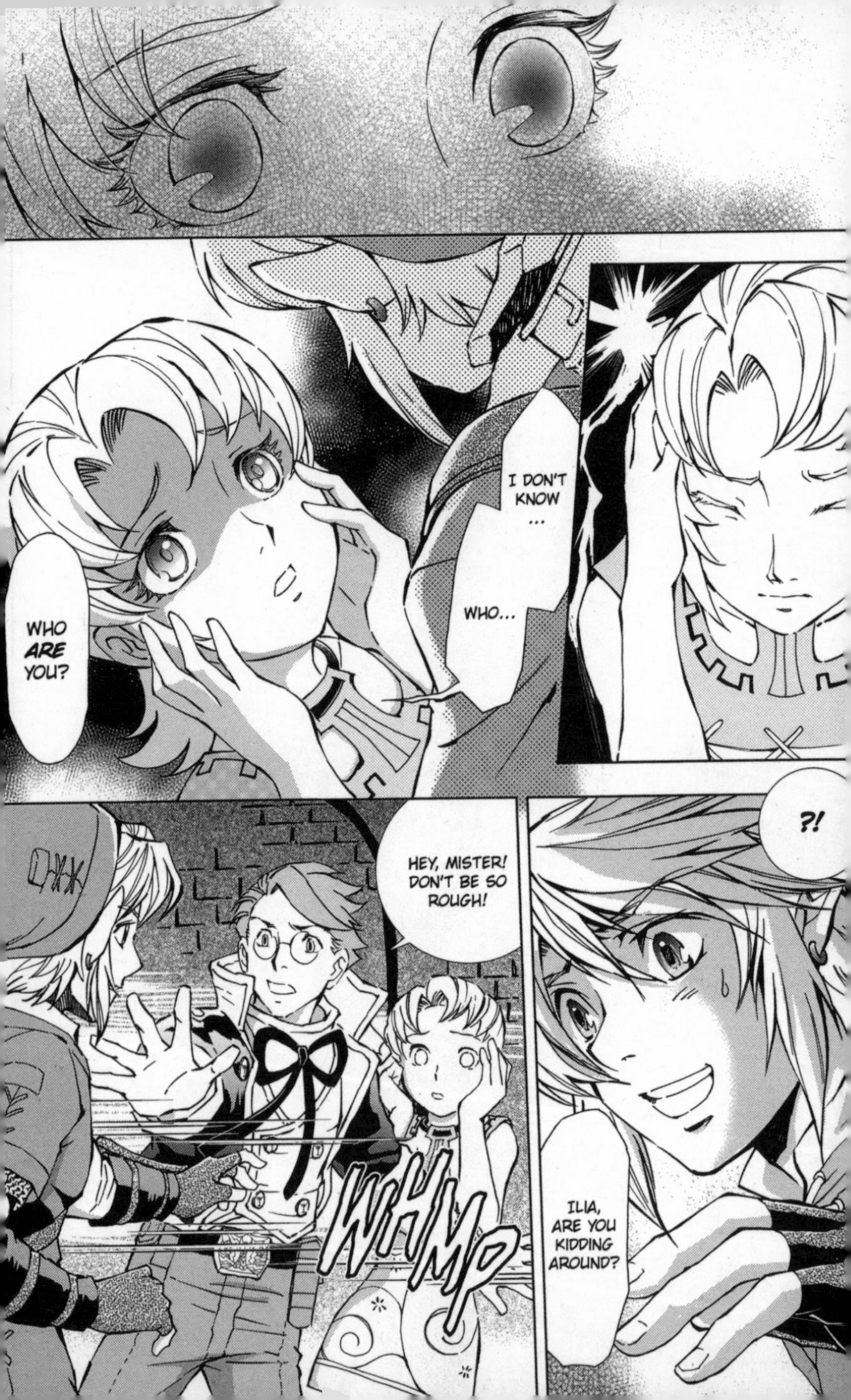
I DON'T KNOW ...
WHO...
WHO ARE YOU?
?!
ILIA, ARE YOU KIDDING AROUND?
HEY, MISTER! DON'T BE SO ROUGH!
WHMP

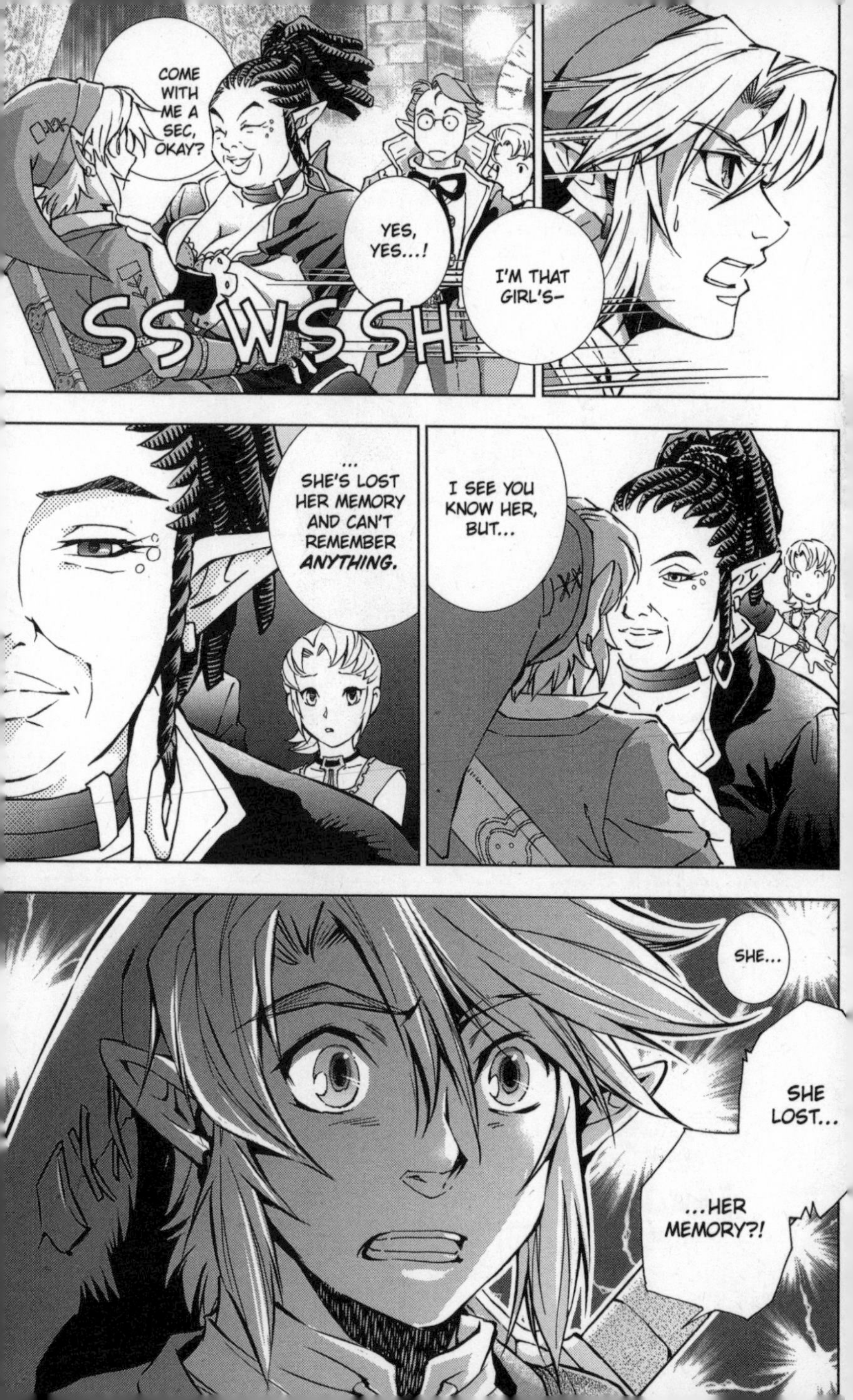
I'M THAT GIRL'S-
COME WITH ME A SEC, OKAY?
YES, YES...!
SSWSSH
I SEE YOU KNOW HER, BUT...
... SHE'S LOST HER MEMORY AND CAN'T REMEMBER *ANYTHING.*
SHE...
SHE LOST...
...HER MEMORY?!

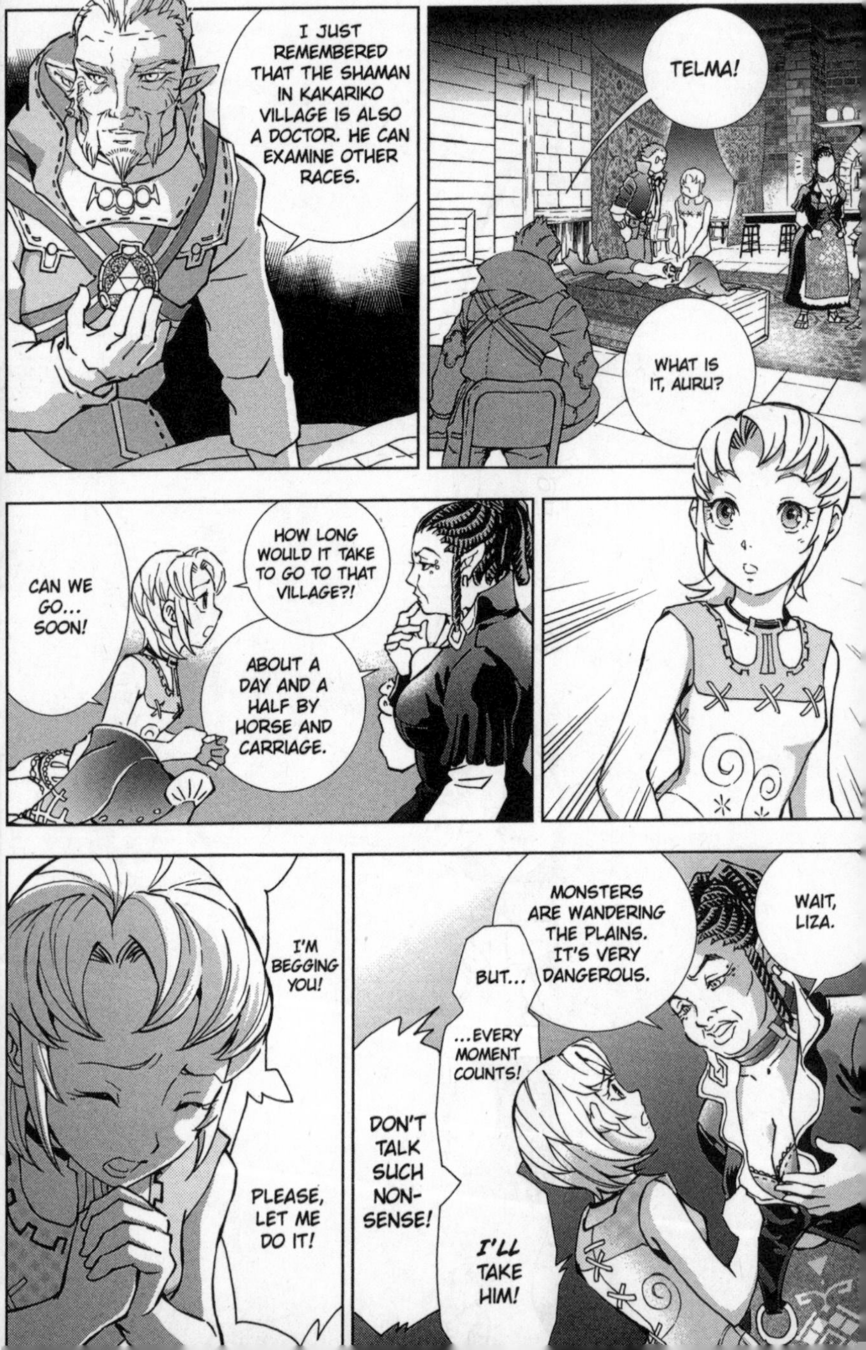
TELMA!
WHAT IS IT, AURU?
I JUST REMEMBERED THAT THE SHAMAN IN KAKARIKO VILLAGE IS ALSO A DOCTOR. HE CAN EXAMINE OTHER RACES.
HOW LONG WOULD IT TAKE TO GO TO THAT VILLAGE?!
ABOUT A DAY AND A HALF BY HORSE AND CARRIAGE.
CAN WE GO... SOON!
WAIT, LIZA.
MONSTERS ARE WANDERING THE PLAINS. IT'S VERY DANGEROUS.
BUT...
...EVERY MOMENT COUNTS!
DON'T TALK SUCH NONSENSE!
I'LL TAKE HIM!
I'M BEGGING YOU!
PLEASE, LET ME DO IT!

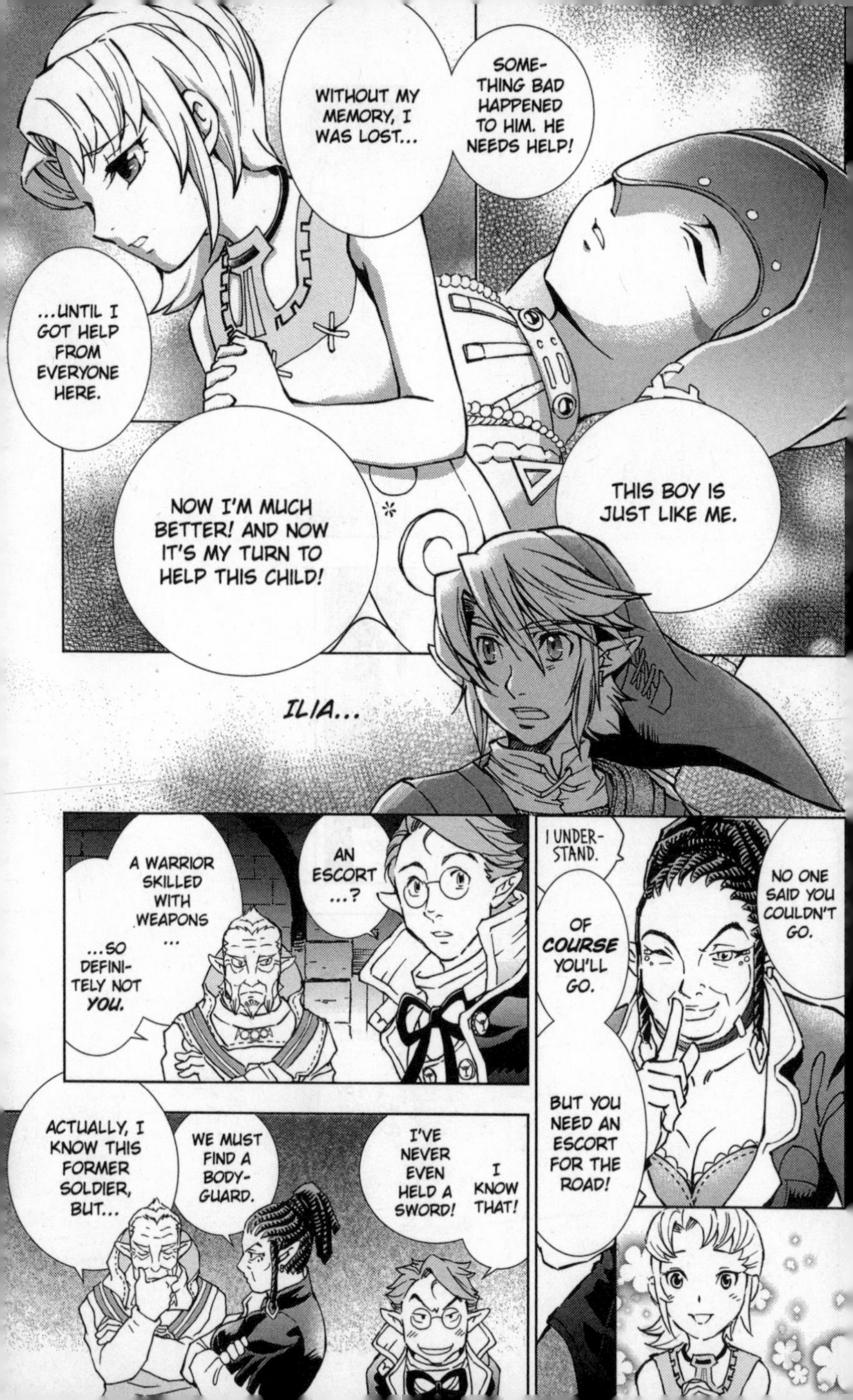
SOME-
THING BAD
HAPPENED
TO HIM. HE
NEEDS HELP!
WITHOUT MY
MEMORY, I
WAS LOST...
...UNTIL I
GOT HELP
FROM
EVERYONE
HERE.
THIS BOY IS
JUST LIKE ME.
NOW I'M MUCH
BETTER! AND NOW
IT'S MY TURN TO
HELP THIS CHILD!
ILIA...
I UNDER-
STAND.
NO ONE
SAID YOU
COULDN'T
GO.
OF
COURSE
YOU'LL
GO.
BUT YOU
NEED AN
ESCORT
FOR THE
ROAD!
AN
ESCORT
...?
A WARRIOR
SKILLED
WITH
WEAPONS
...
...SO
DEFINI-
TELY NOT
YOU.
I
KNOW
THAT!
I'VE
NEVER
EVEN
HELD A
SWORD!
WE MUST
FIND A
BODY-
GUARD.
ACTUALLY, I
KNOW THIS
FORMER
SOLDIER,
BUT...

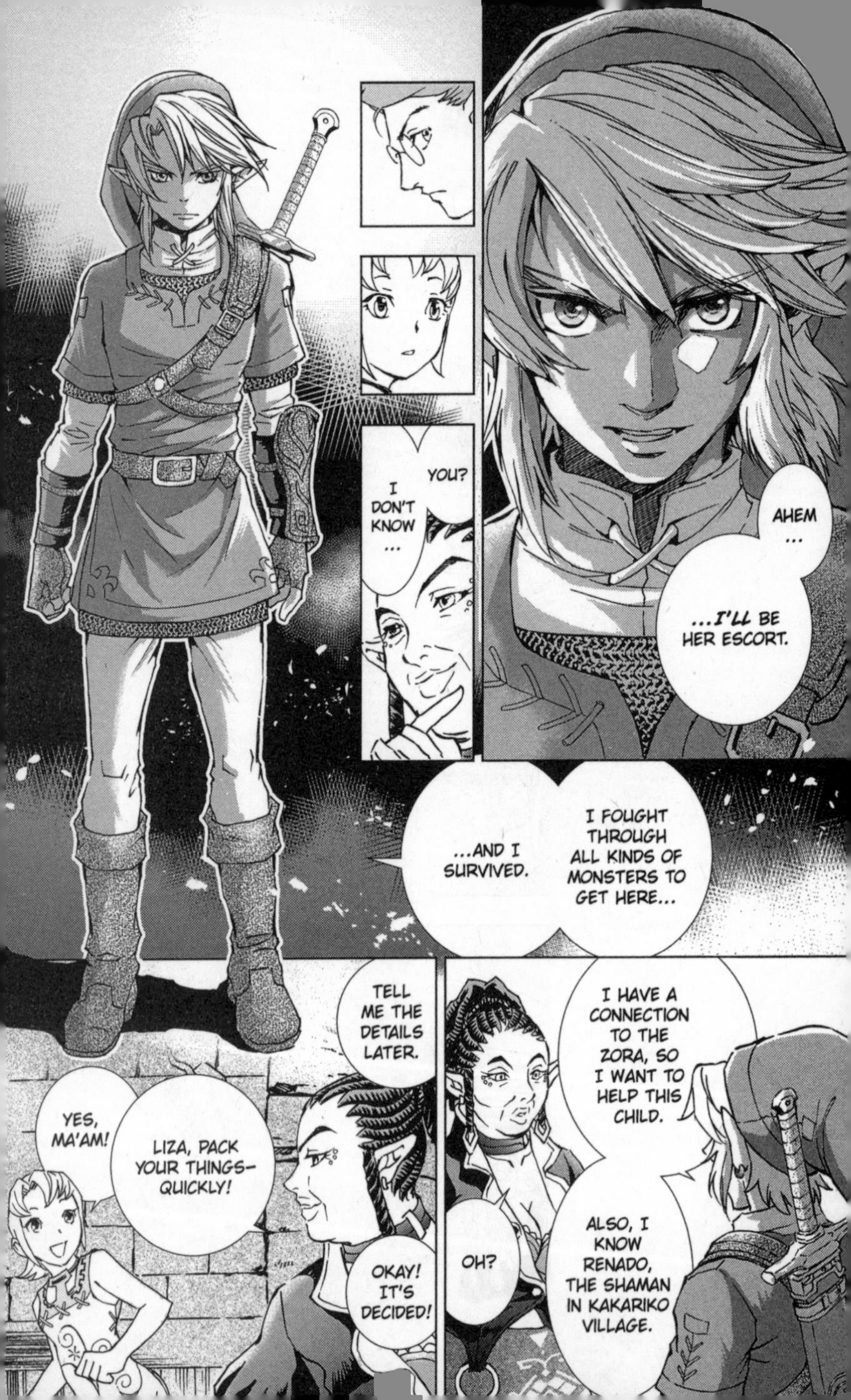
AHEM ...
...I'LL BE HER ESCORT.
YOU?
I DON'T KNOW ...
I FOUGHT THROUGH ALL KINDS OF MONSTERS TO GET HERE...
...AND I SURVIVED.
I HAVE A CONNECTION TO THE ZORA, SO I WANT TO HELP THIS CHILD.
ALSO, I KNOW RENADO, THE SHAMAN IN KAKARIKO VILLAGE.
OH?
OKAY! IT'S DECIDED!
TELL ME THE DETAILS LATER.
LIZA, PACK YOUR THINGS-QUICKLY!
YES, MA'AM!

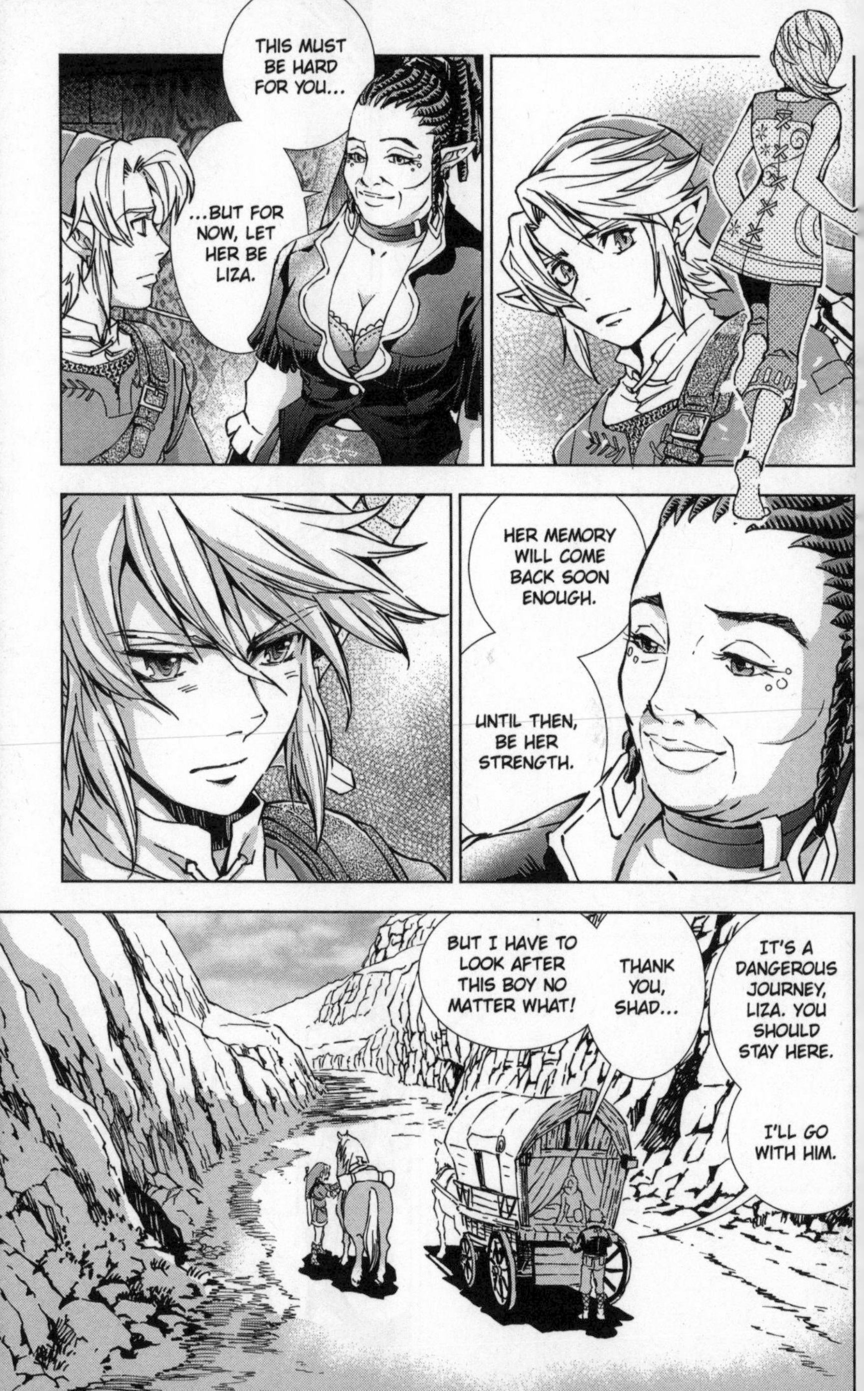
THIS MUST BE HARD FOR YOU...
...BUT FOR NOW, LET HER BE LIZA.
HER MEMORY WILL COME BACK SOON ENOUGH.
UNTIL THEN, BE HER STRENGTH.
IT'S A DANGEROUS JOURNEY, LIZA. YOU SHOULD STAY HERE.
I'LL GO WITH HIM.
THANK YOU, SHAD...
BUT I HAVE TO LOOK AFTER THIS BOY NO MATTER WHAT!

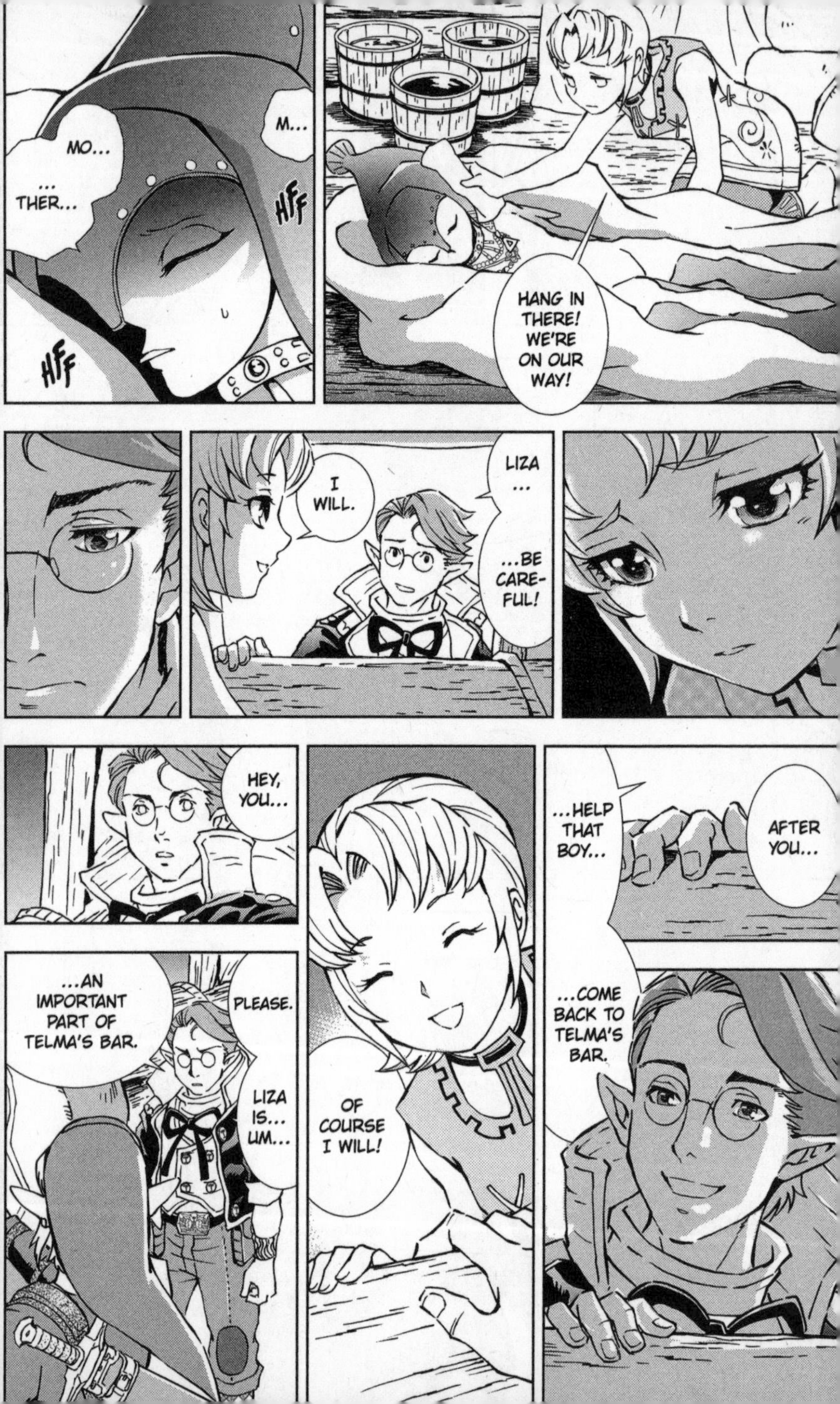
...
HANG IN THERE! WE'RE ON OUR WAY!
M...
HFF
MO... ...THER...
HFF
LIZA ...
...BE CAREFUL!
I WILL.
AFTER YOU...
...HELP THAT BOY...
...COME BACK TO TELMA'S BAR.
OF COURSE I WILL!
HEY, YOU...
LIZA IS... UM...
...AN IMPORTANT PART OF TELMA'S BAR.
PLEASE.

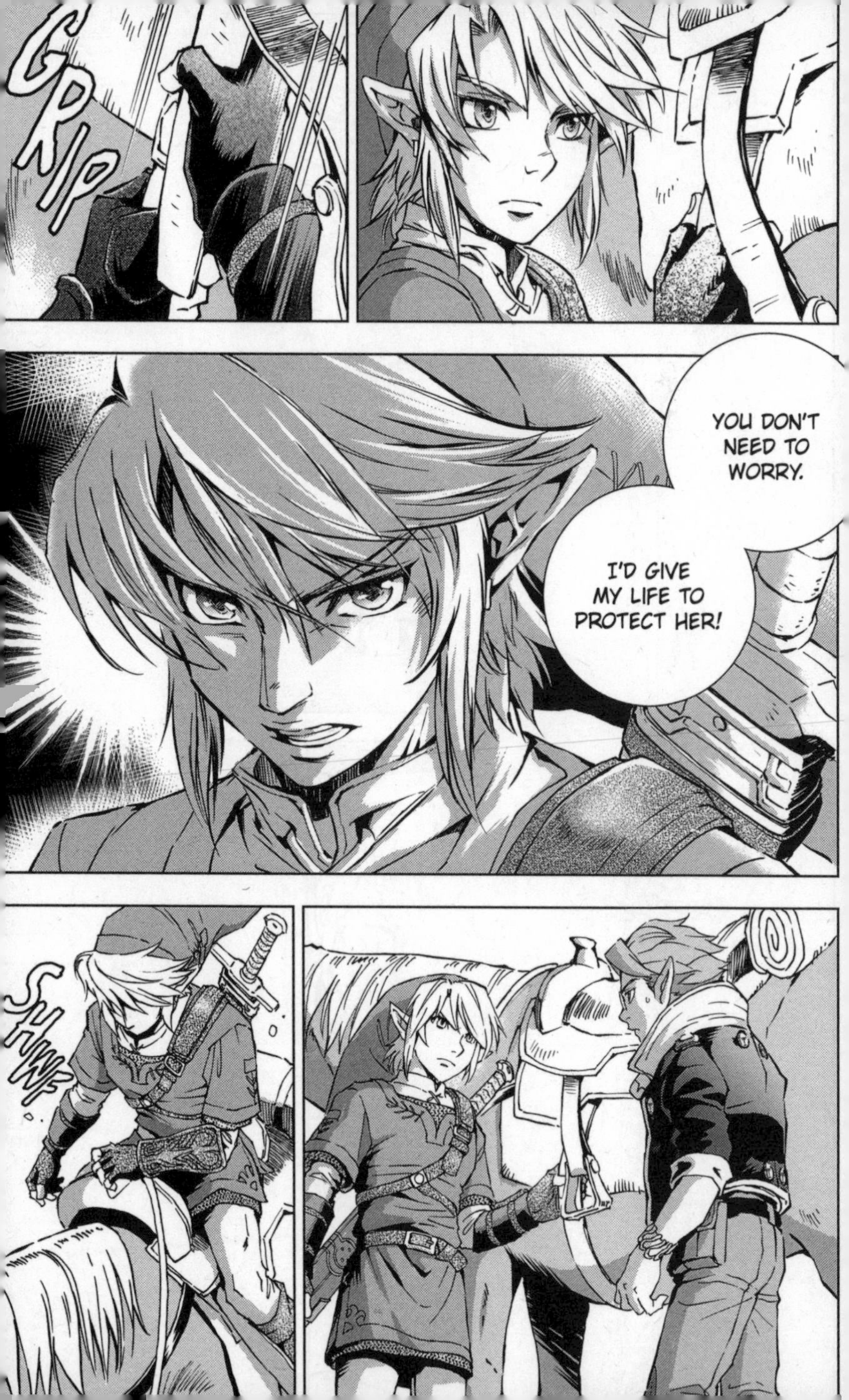
GRIP
YOU DON'T NEED TO WORRY.
I'D GIVE MY LIFE TO PROTECT HER!
SHWF

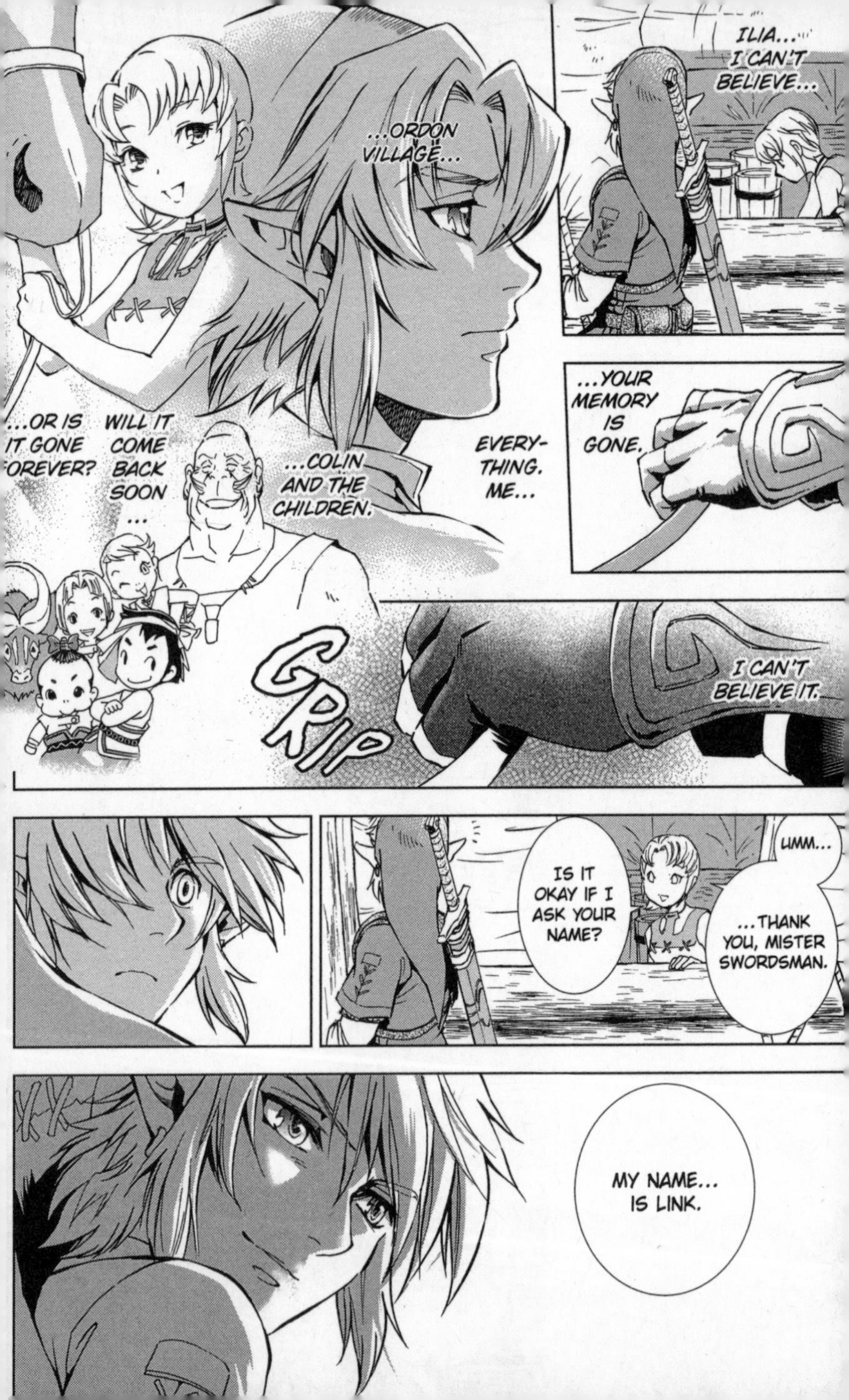
ILIA... I CAN'T BELIEVE...
...YOUR MEMORY IS GONE.
EVERY-THING. ME...
...ORDON VILLAGE...
...COLIN AND THE CHILDREN.
WILL IT COME BACK SOON ...
...OR IS IT GONE FOREVER?
GRIP
I CAN'T BELIEVE IT.
UMM...
...THANK YOU, MISTER SWORDSMAN.
IS IT OKAY IF I ASK YOUR NAME?
MY NAME... IS LINK.

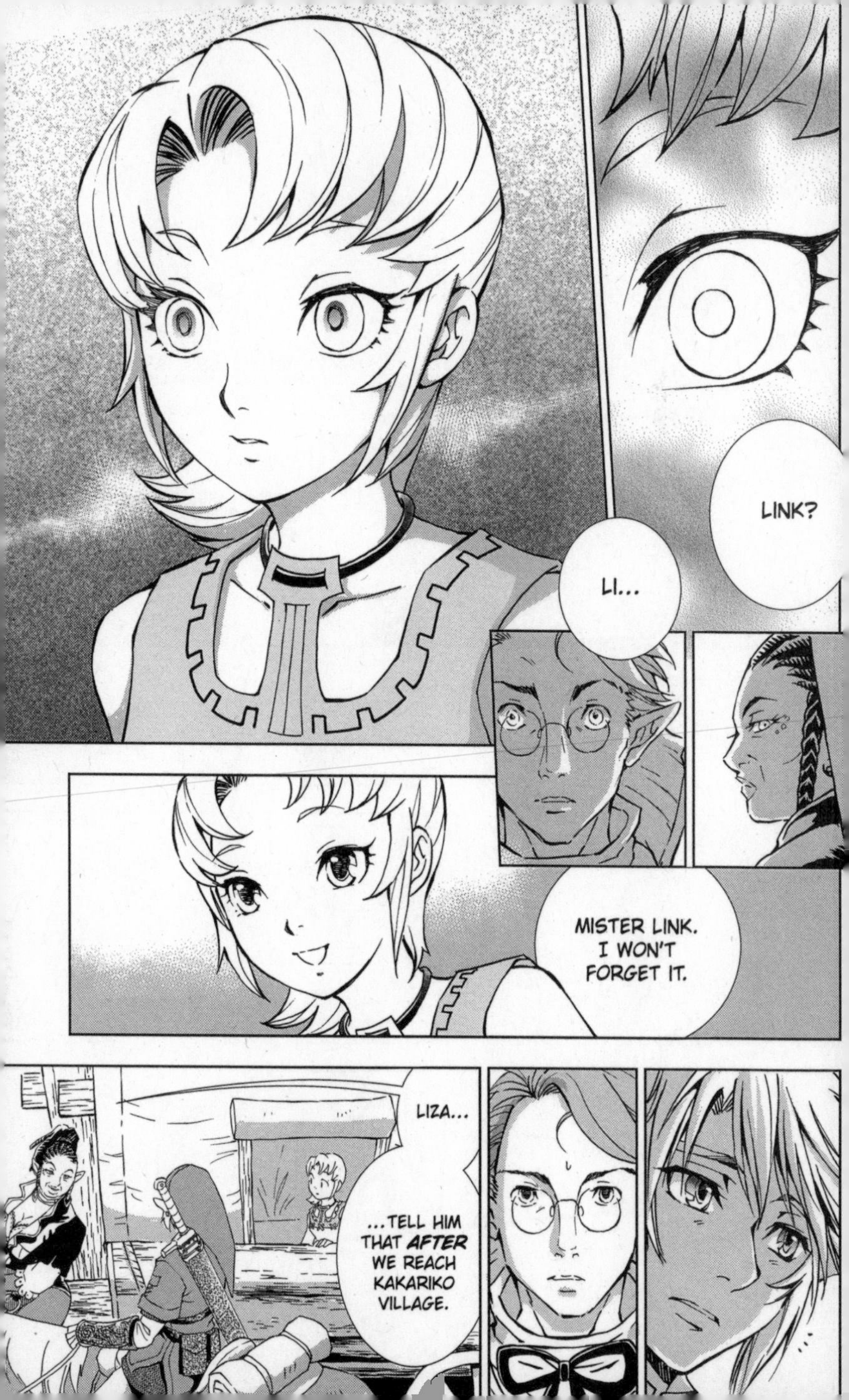
LINK?
LI...
MISTER LINK. I WON'T FORGET IT.
...
LIZA...
...TELL HIM THAT *AFTER* WE REACH KAKARIKO VILLAGE.

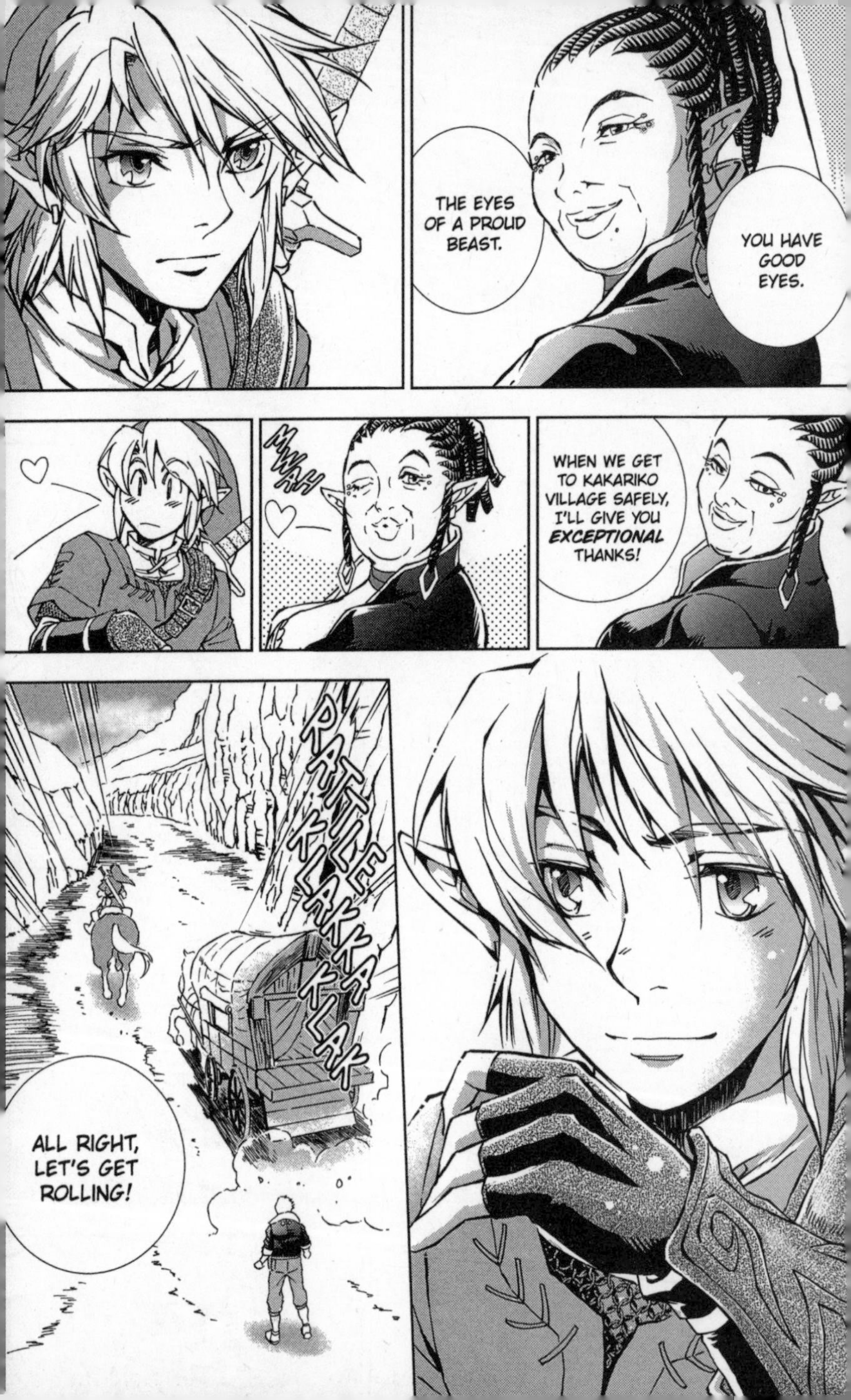
YOU HAVE GOOD EYES.
THE EYES OF A PROUD BEAST.
WHEN WE GET TO KAKARIKO VILLAGE SAFELY, I'LL GIVE YOU *EXCEPTIONAL* THANKS!
MWAH
RATTLE KLAKKA KLAK
ALL RIGHT, LET'S GET ROLLING!

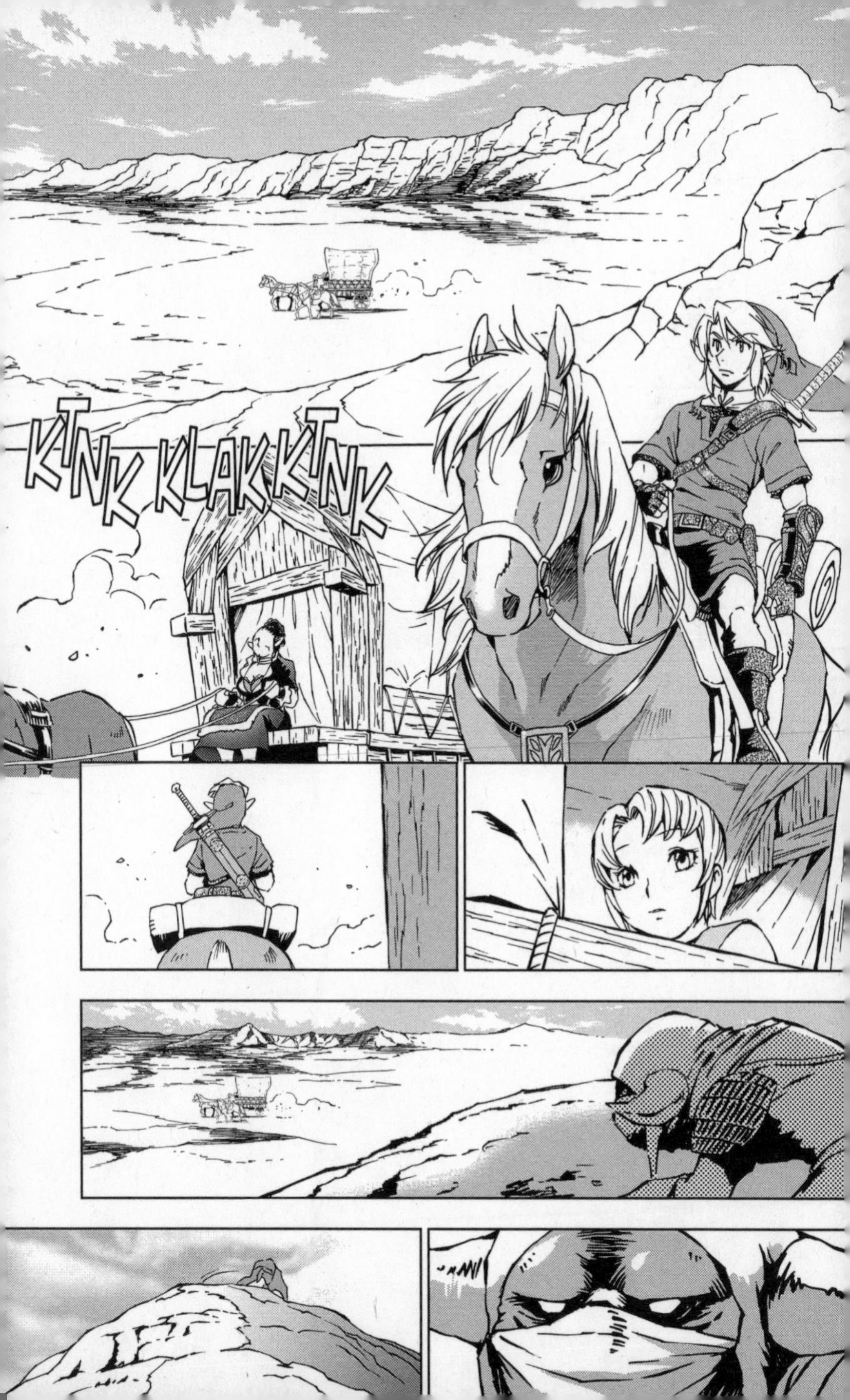
KTINK KLAK KTINK

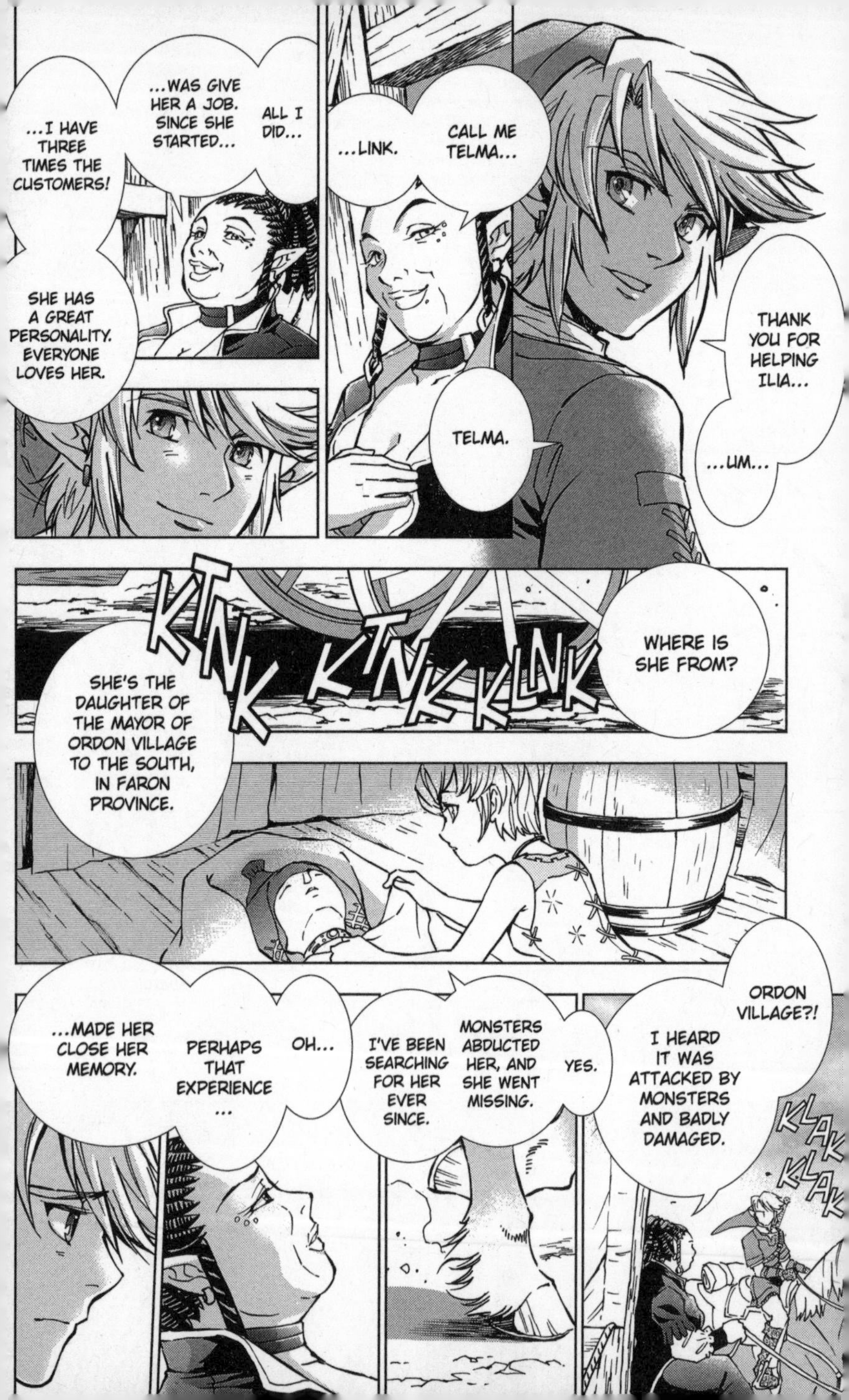
THANK YOU FOR HELPING ILIA...
...UM...
TELMA.
CALL ME TELMA...
...LINK.
ALL I DID...
...WAS GIVE HER A JOB. SINCE SHE STARTED...
...I HAVE THREE TIMES THE CUSTOMERS!
SHE HAS A GREAT PERSONALITY. EVERYONE LOVES HER.
WHERE IS SHE FROM?
KTNK KTNK KLNK
SHE'S THE DAUGHTER OF THE MAYOR OF ORDON VILLAGE TO THE SOUTH, IN FARON PROVINCE.
ORDON VILLAGE?!
I HEARD IT WAS ATTACKED BY MONSTERS AND BADLY DAMAGED.
KLAK KLAK
YES.
MONSTERS ABDUCTED HER, AND SHE WENT MISSING.
I'VE BEEN SEARCHING FOR HER EVER SINCE.
OH...
PERHAPS THAT EXPERIENCE ...
...MADE HER CLOSE HER MEMORY.

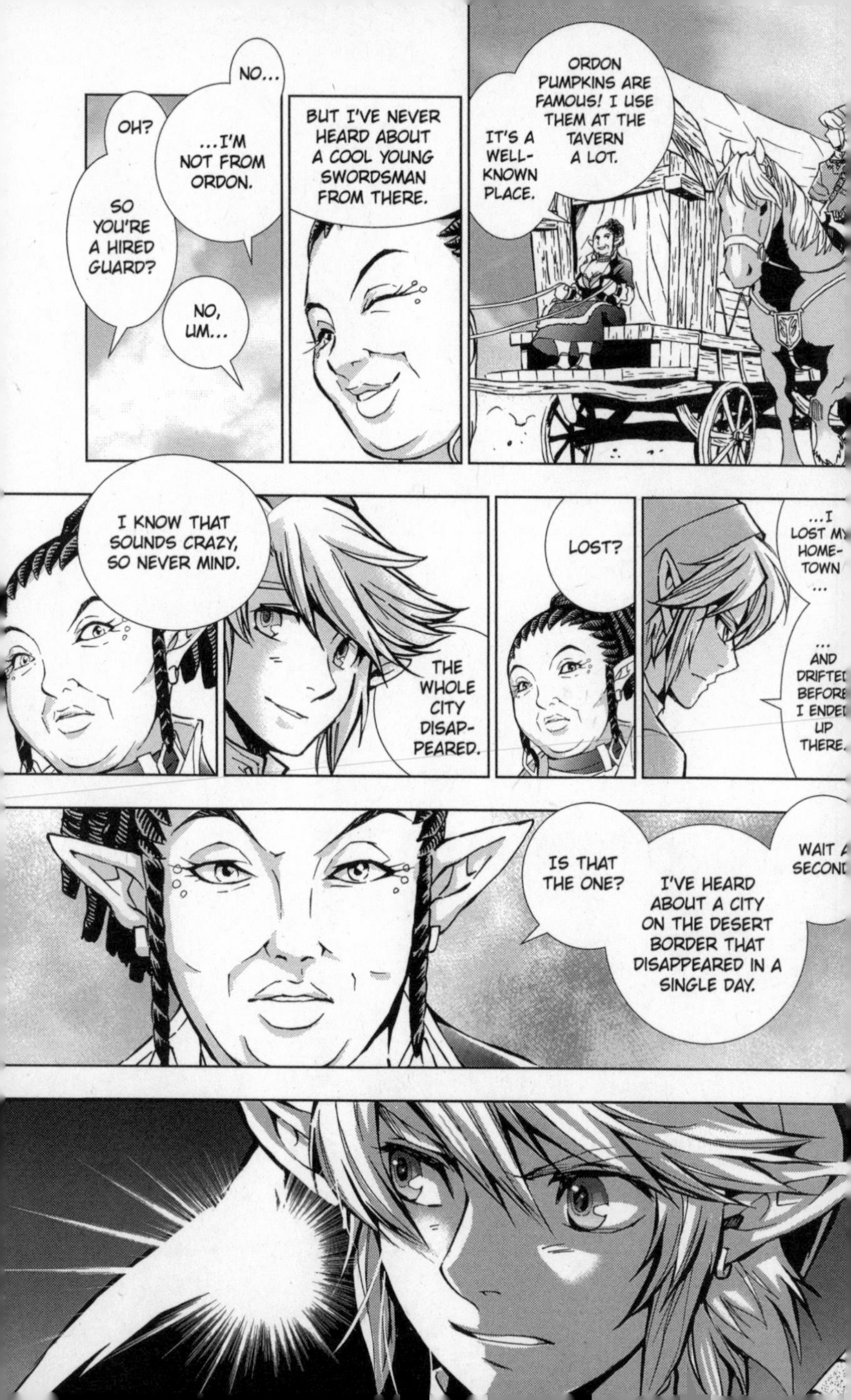
ORDON PUMPKINS ARE FAMOUS! I USE THEM AT THE TAVERN A LOT.
IT'S A WELL-KNOWN PLACE.
BUT I'VE NEVER HEARD ABOUT A COOL YOUNG SWORDSMAN FROM THERE.
NO...
...I'M NOT FROM ORDON.
OH?
SO YOU'RE A HIRED GUARD?
NO, UM...
...I LOST MY HOMETOWN...
...AND DRIFTED BEFORE I ENDED UP THERE.
LOST?
THE WHOLE CITY DISAPPEARED.
I KNOW THAT SOUNDS CRAZY, SO NEVER MIND.
WAIT A SECOND
I'VE HEARD ABOUT A CITY ON THE DESERT BORDER THAT DISAPPEARED IN A SINGLE DAY.
IS THAT THE ONE?

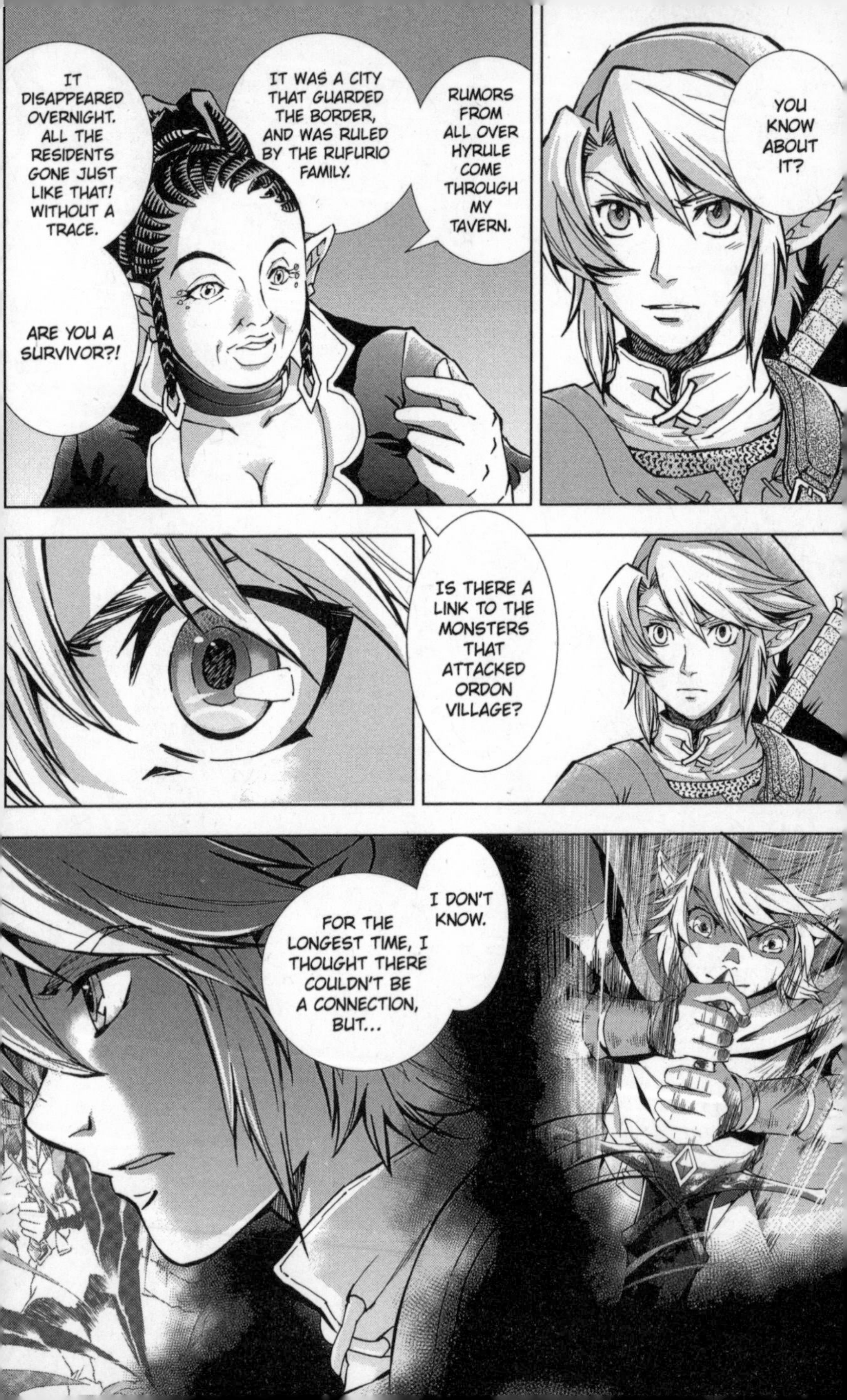
YOU KNOW ABOUT IT?
RUMORS FROM ALL OVER HYRULE COME THROUGH MY TAVERN.
IT WAS A CITY THAT GUARDED THE BORDER, AND WAS RULED BY THE RUFURIO FAMILY.
IT DISAPPEARED OVERNIGHT. ALL THE RESIDENTS GONE JUST LIKE THAT! WITHOUT A TRACE.
ARE YOU A SURVIVOR?!
IS THERE A LINK TO THE MONSTERS THAT ATTACKED ORDON VILLAGE?
I DON'T KNOW.
FOR THE LONGEST TIME, I THOUGHT THERE COULDN'T BE A CONNECTION, BUT...

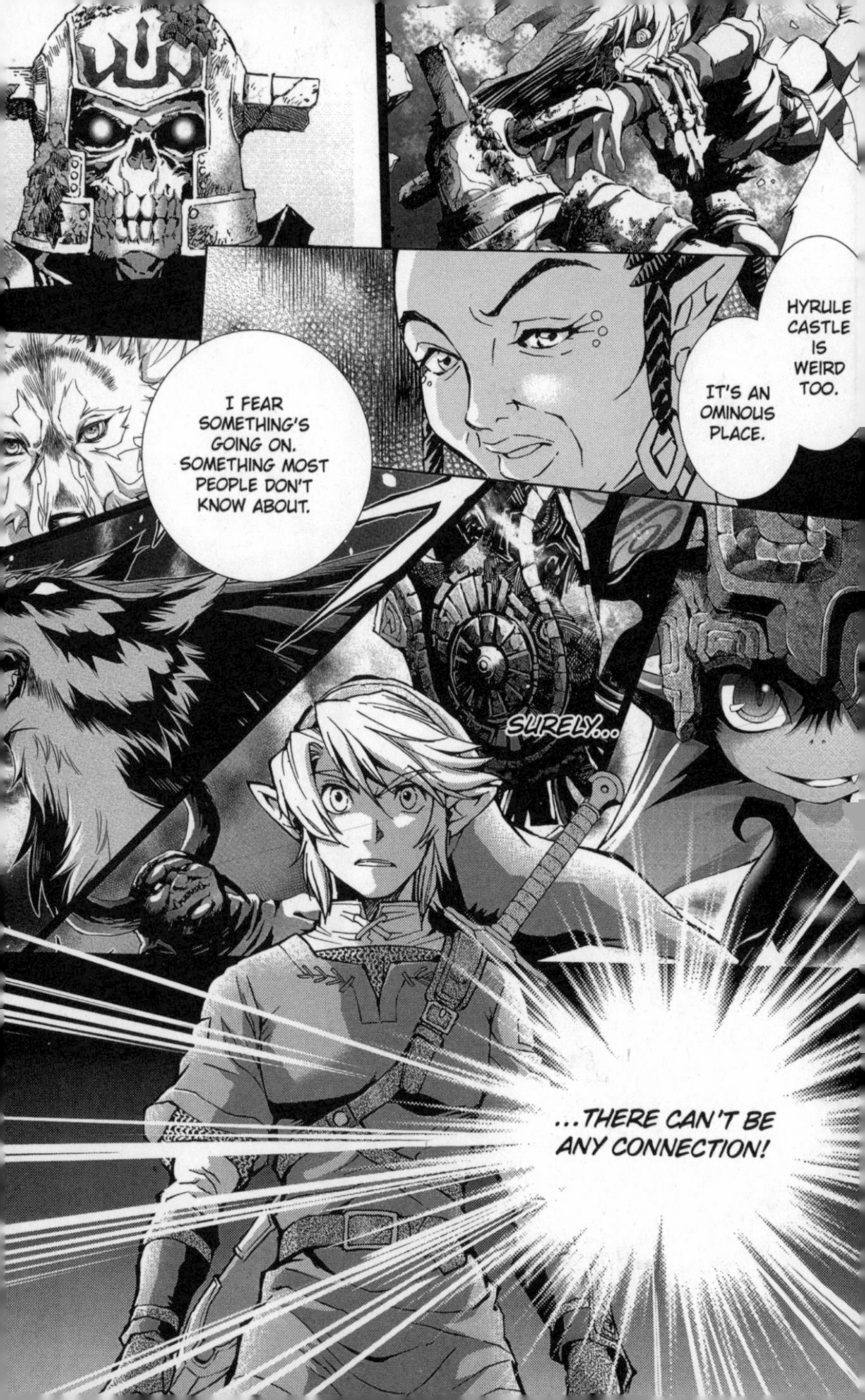
HYRULE CASTLE IS WEIRD TOO.
IT'S AN OMINOUS PLACE.
I FEAR SOMETHING'S GOING ON. SOMETHING MOST PEOPLE DON'T KNOW ABOUT.
SURELY...
...THERE CAN'T BE ANY CONNECTION!

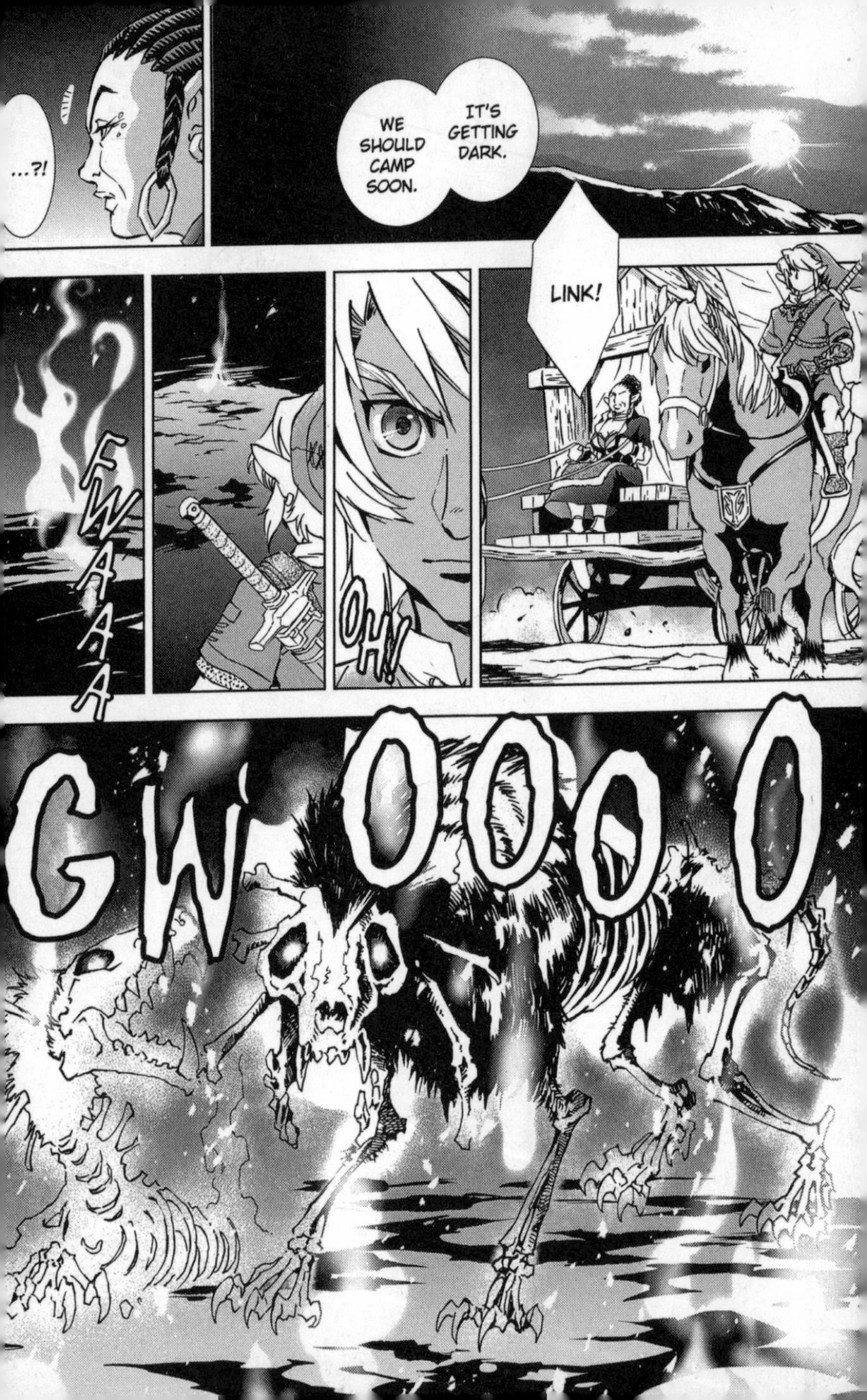
IT'S GETTING DARK.
WE SHOULD CAMP SOON.
...?!
LINK!
OH!
FWAAAAA
GWOOOO

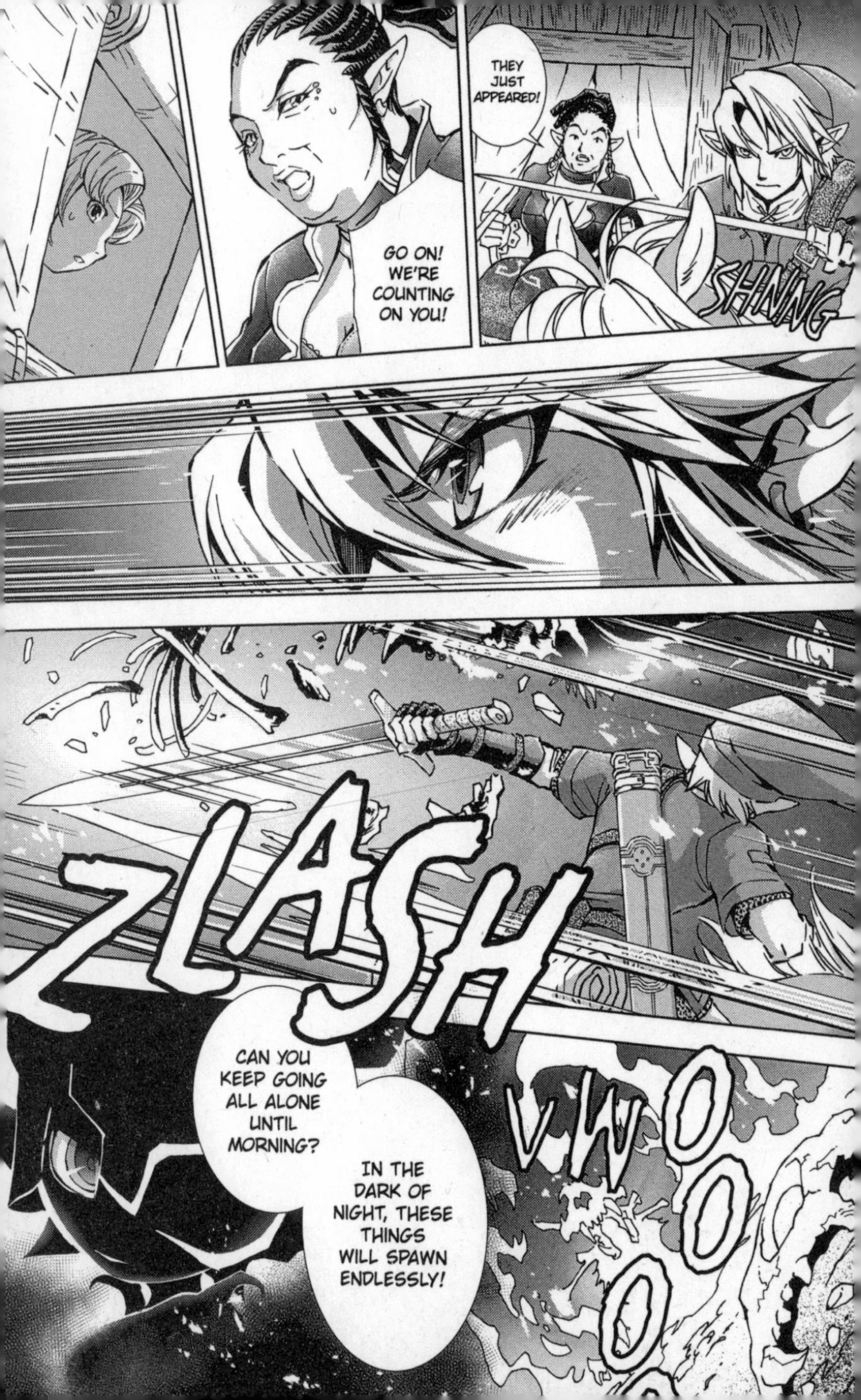
THEY JUST APPEARED!
SHINNG
GO ON! WE'RE COUNTING ON YOU!
ZLASH
VWOOOO
CAN YOU KEEP GOING ALL ALONE UNTIL MORNING?
IN THE DARK OF NIGHT, THESE THINGS WILL SPAWN ENDLESSLY!

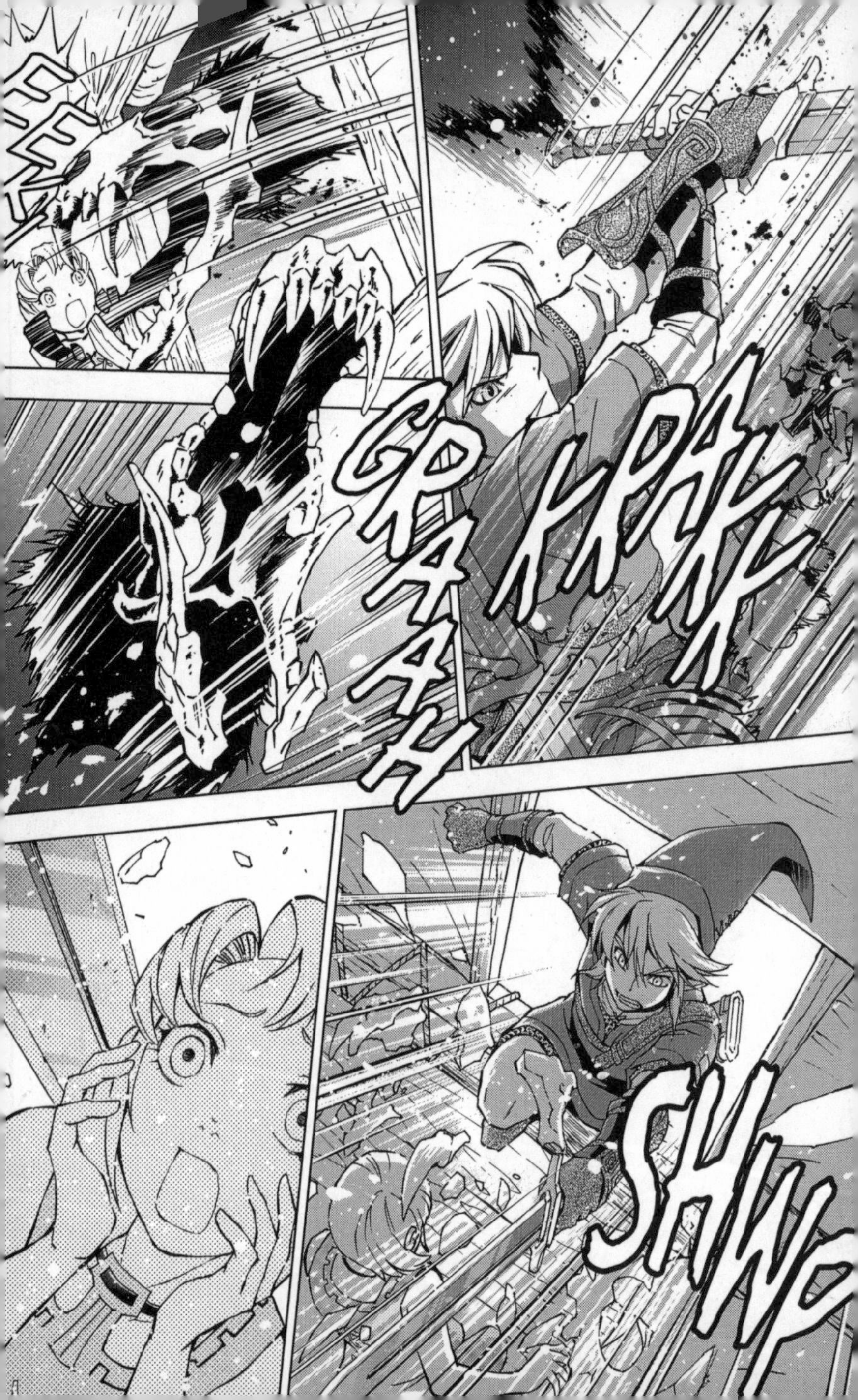
EEE
KRAKK
GRAAH
SHWP

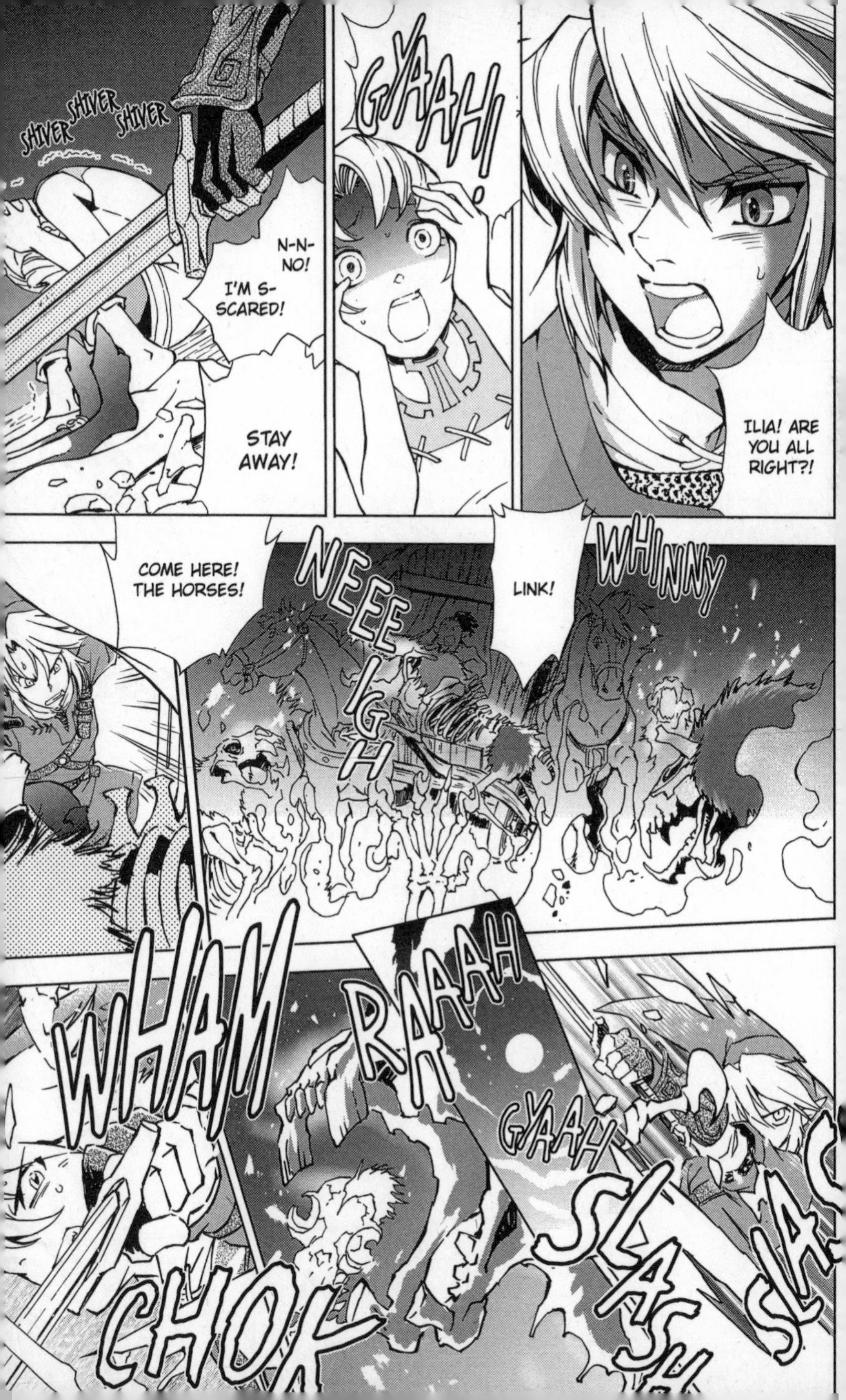
ILIA! ARE YOU ALL RIGHT?!
GYAAH!
N-N-NO! I'M S-SCARED!
STAY AWAY!
SHIVER SHIVER SHIVER
WHINNY
LINK!
NEEEIGH
COME HERE! THE HORSES!
SLASH
SLASH
GYAAH
RAAAAH
WHAM
CHOP

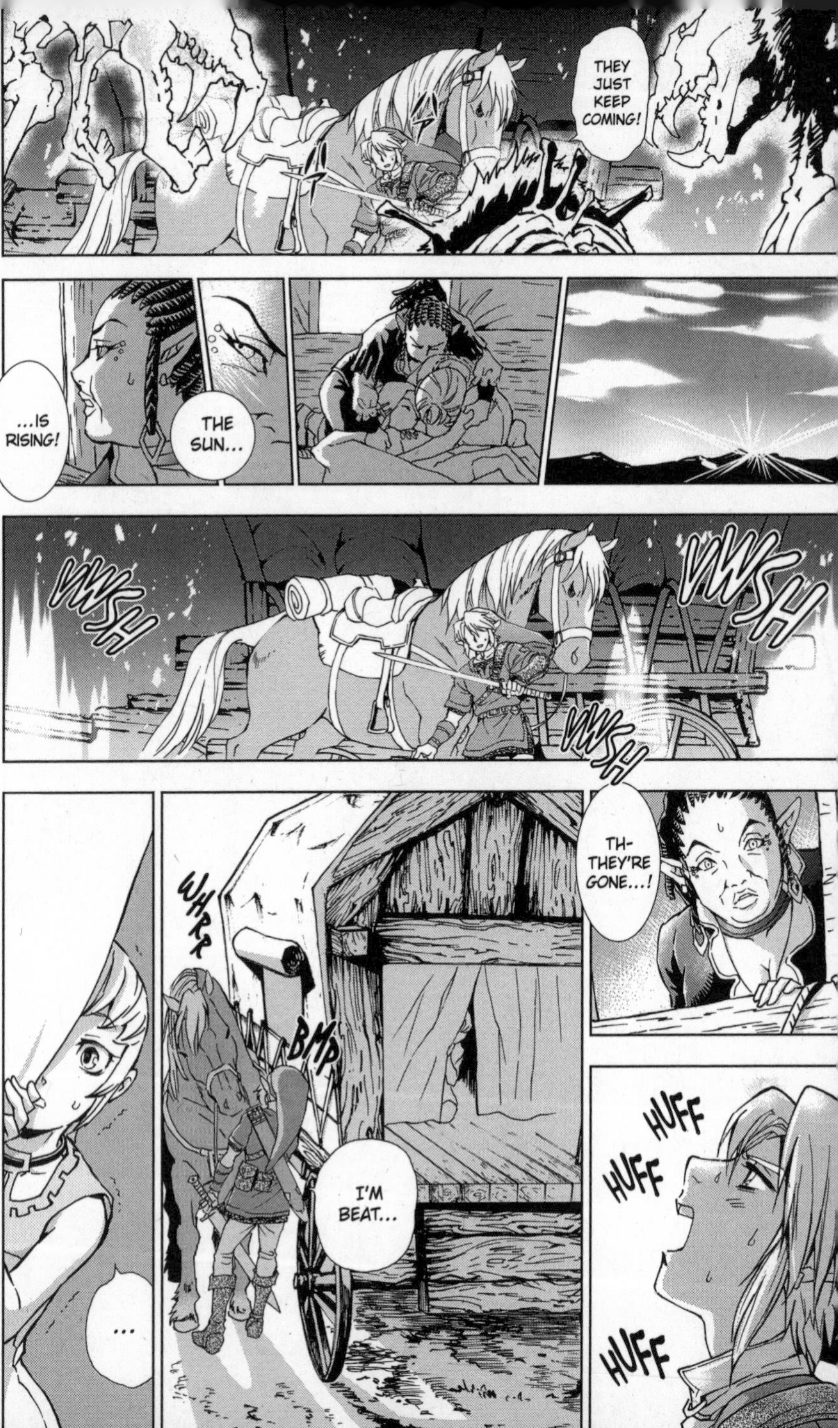
THEY JUST KEEP COMING!
THE SUN...
...IS RISING!
VWSH
VWSH
VWSH
TH- THEY'RE GONE...!
HUFF
HUFF
HUFF
WHRR
BMP
I'M BEAT...
...

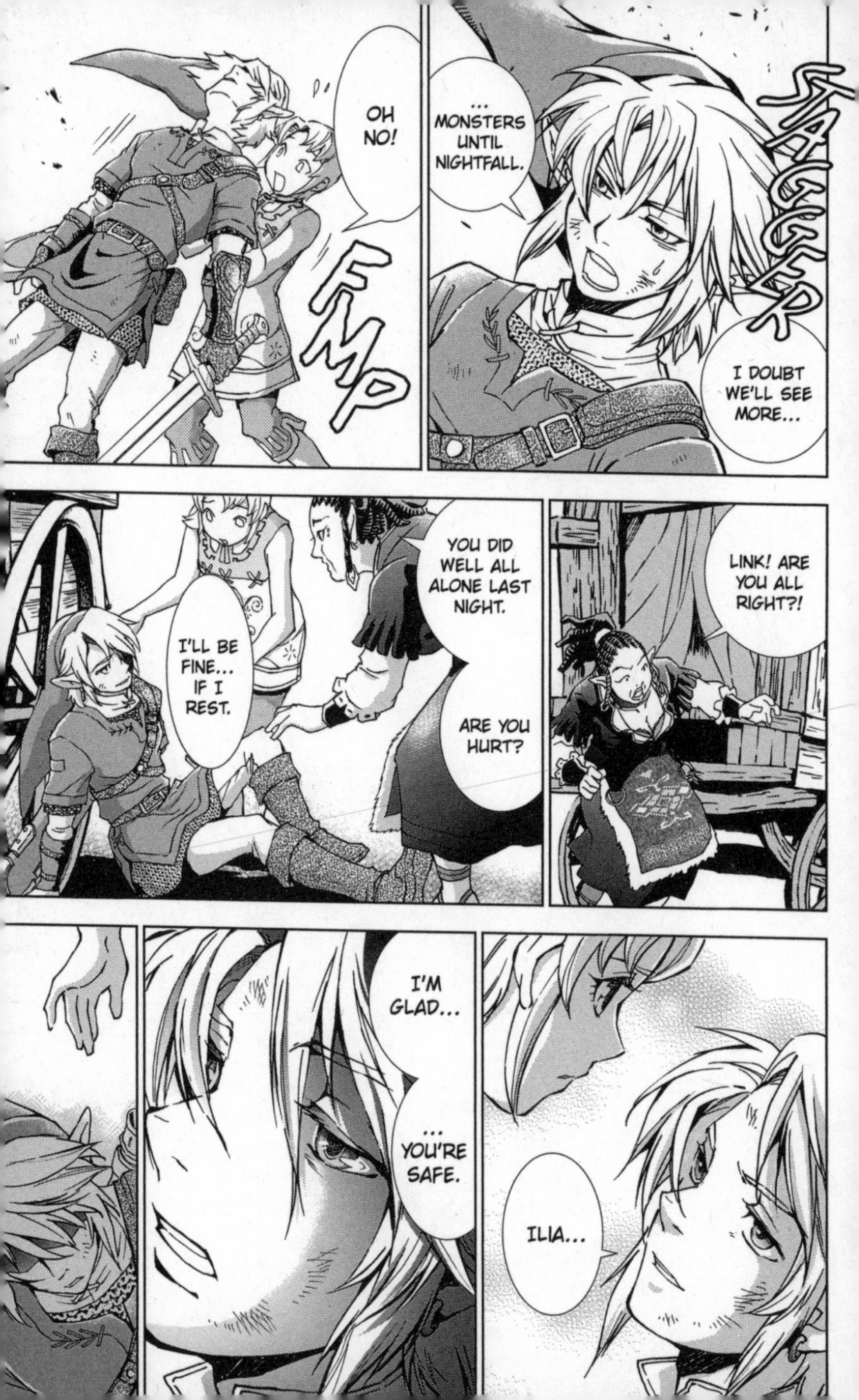
STAGGER
I DOUBT WE'LL SEE MORE...
... MONSTERS UNTIL NIGHTFALL.
OH NO!
FMP
LINK! ARE YOU ALL RIGHT?!
YOU DID WELL ALL ALONE LAST NIGHT.
ARE YOU HURT?
I'LL BE FINE... IF I REST.
ILIA...
I'M GLAD...
... YOU'RE SAFE.

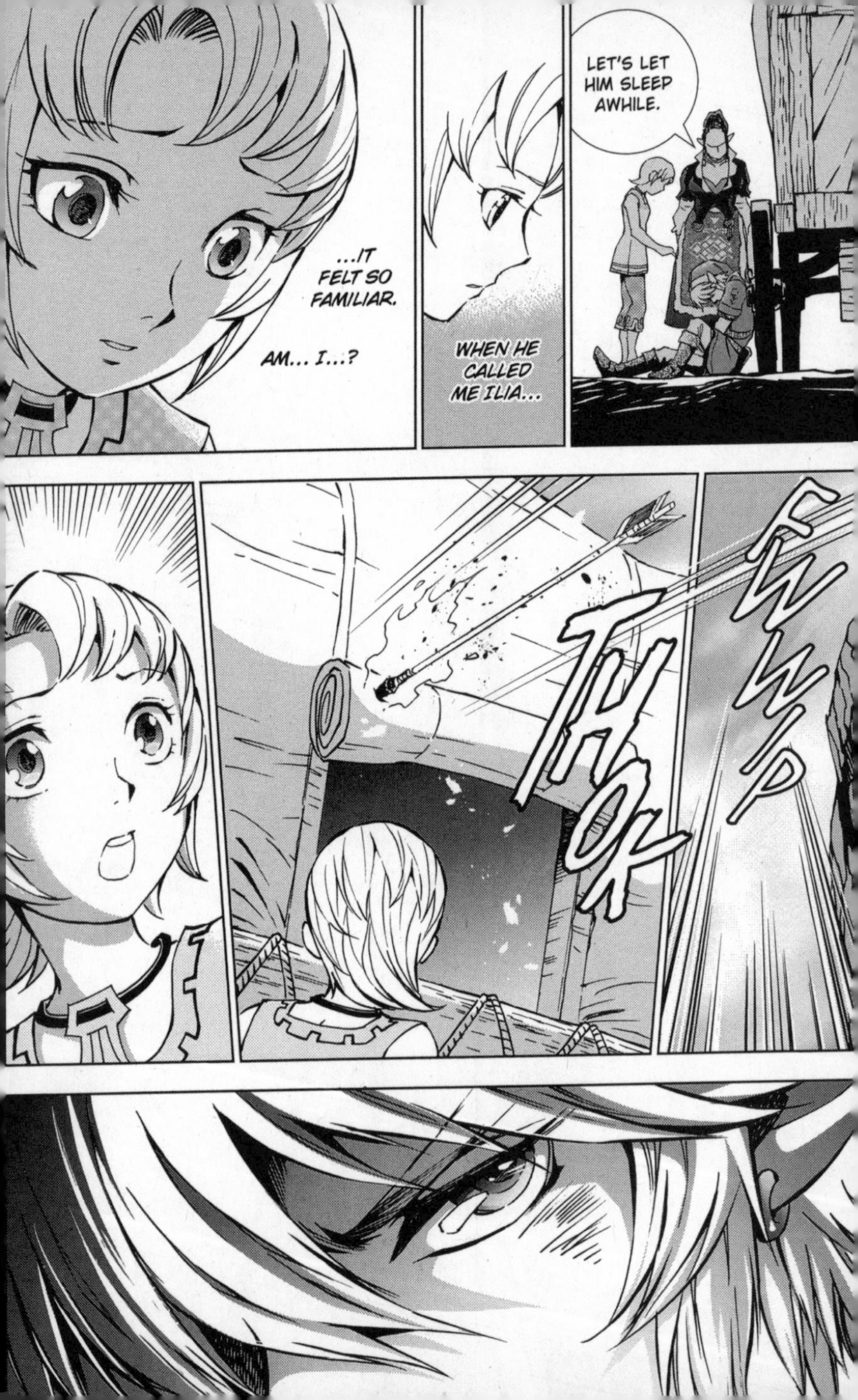
LET'S LET HIM SLEEP AWHILE.
WHEN HE CALLED ME ILIA...
...IT FELT SO FAMILIAR.
AM... I...?
FWIP
THOK

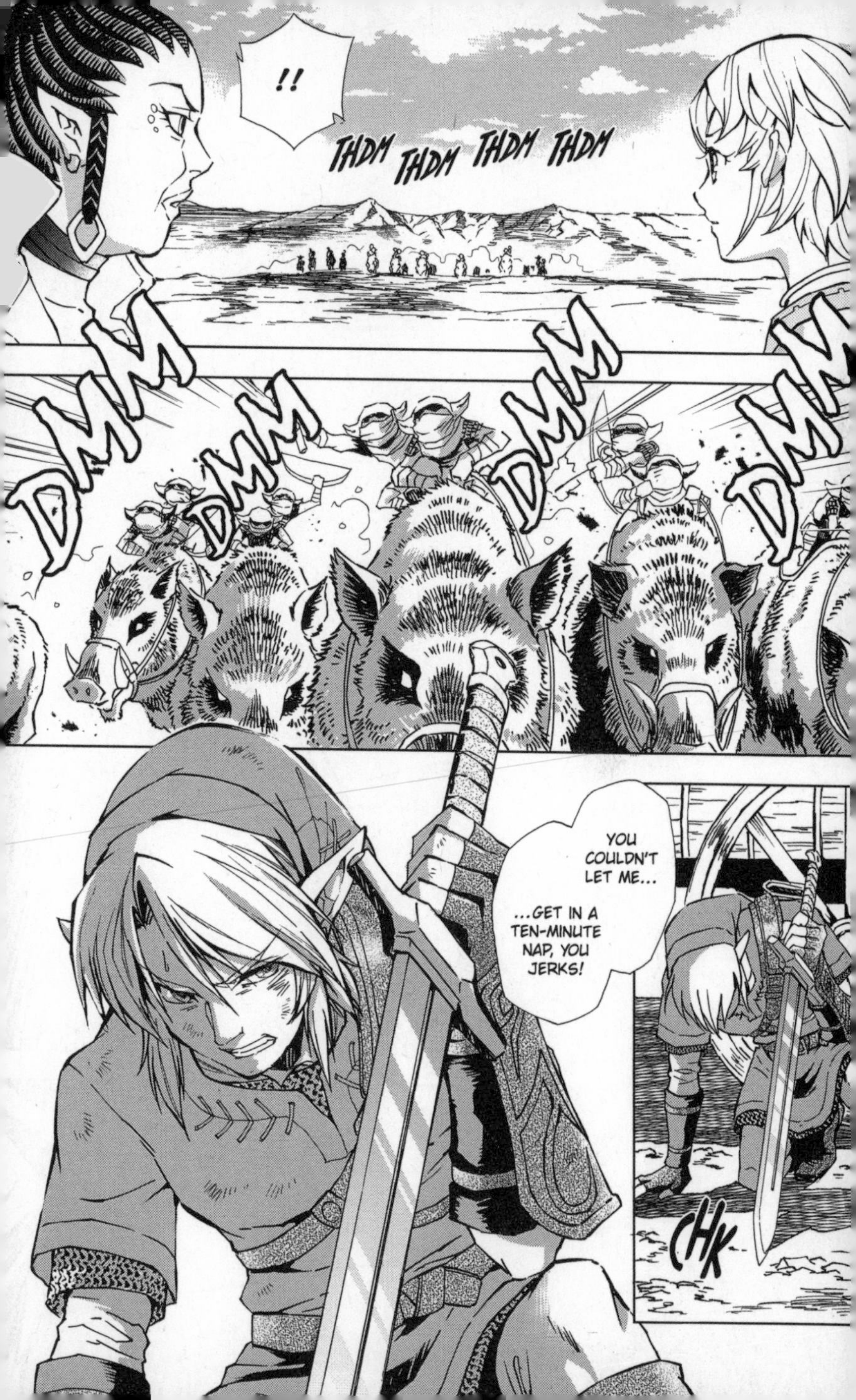
!!
THDM THDM THDM THDM
DMM DMM DMM DMM
YOU COULDN'T LET ME...
...GET IN A TEN-MINUTE NAP, YOU JERKS!
CHK

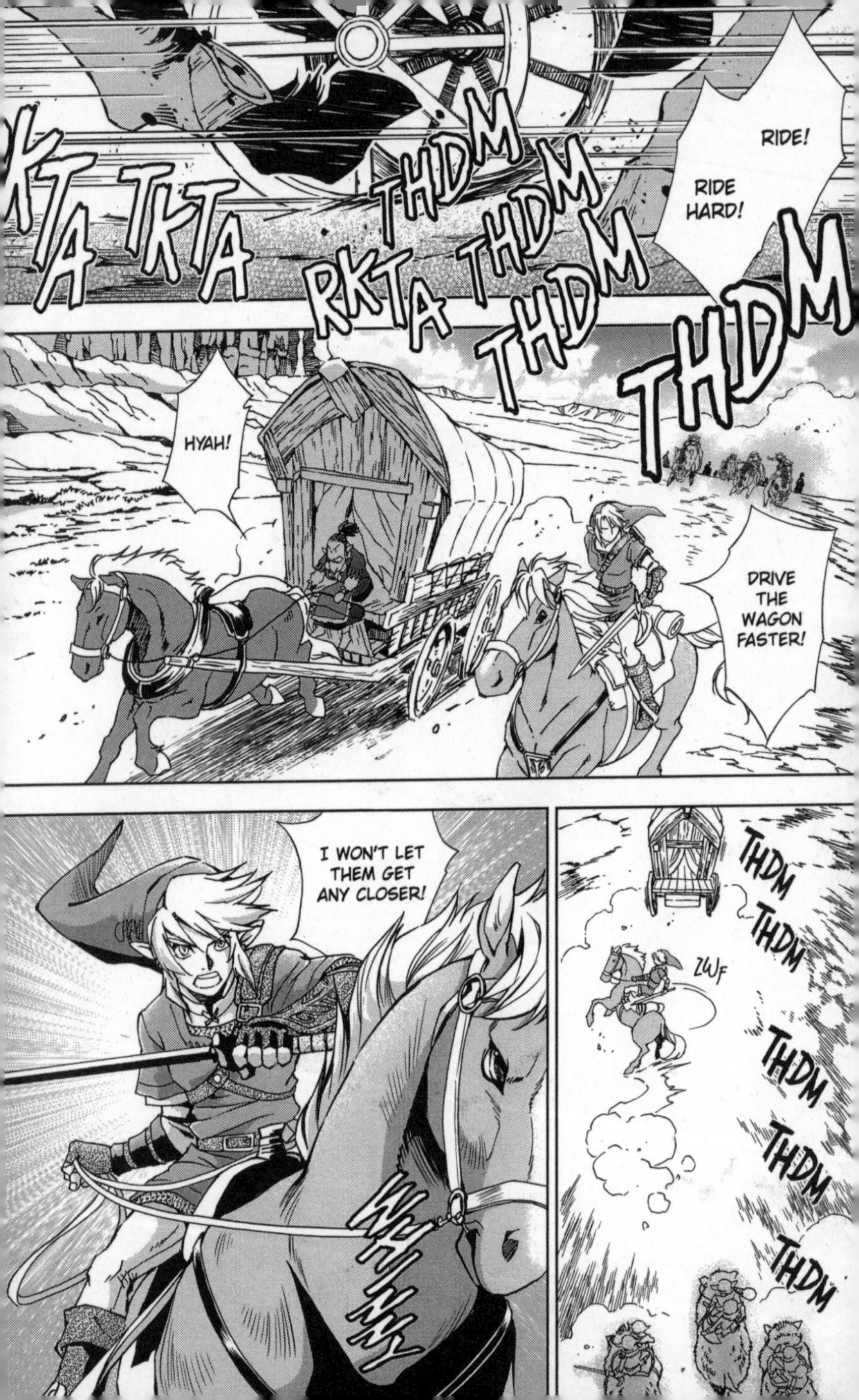
RIDE!
RIDE HARD!
THDM
RKTA THDM
THDM
KTA TKTA
THDM
DRIVE THE WAGON FASTER!
HYAH!
THDM
THDM
ZWF
THDM
THDM
THDM
I WON'T LET THEM GET ANY CLOSER!
WHINNY

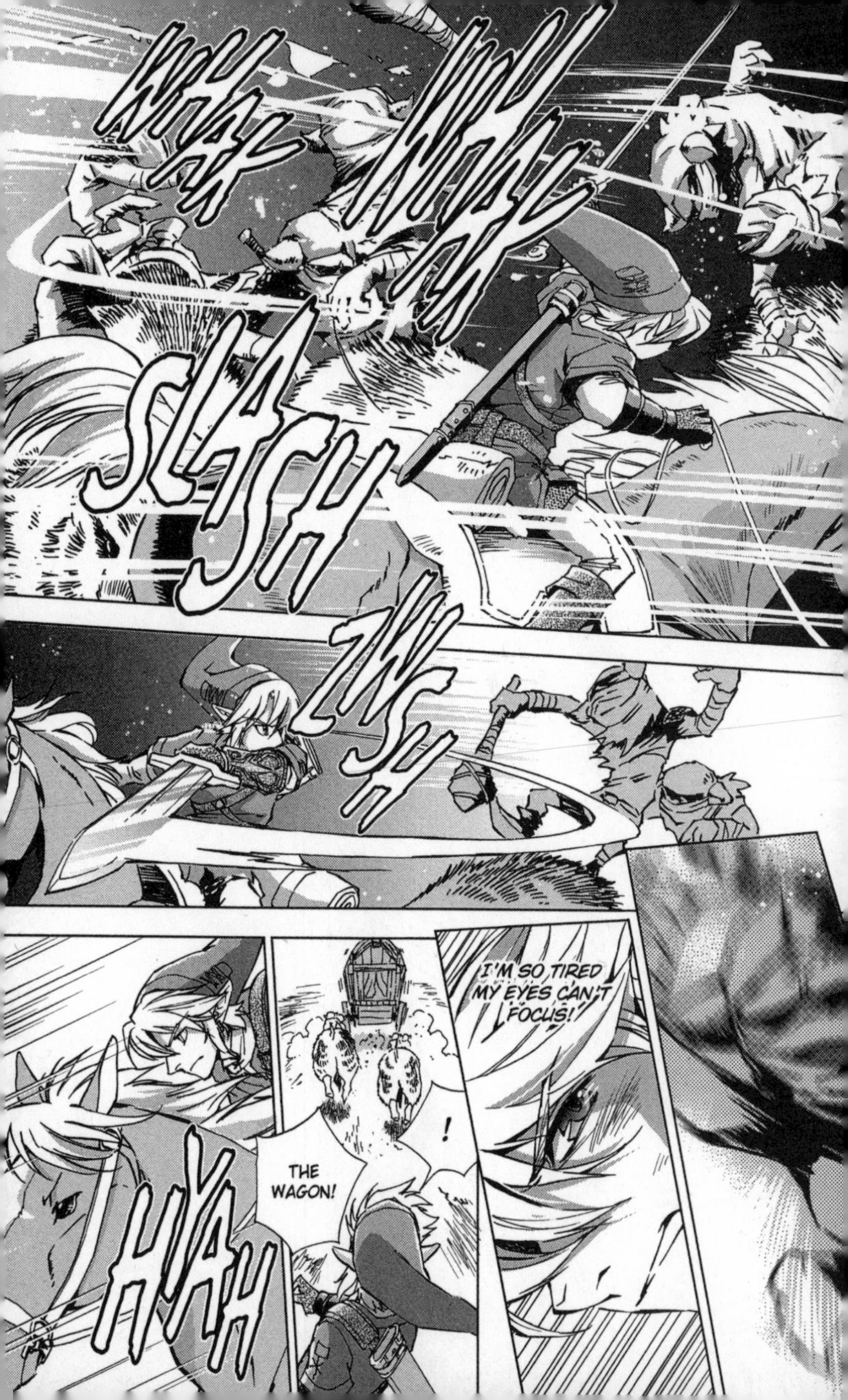
SLASH
I'M SO TIRED MY EYES CAN'T FOCUS!
!
THE WAGON!
HYAH

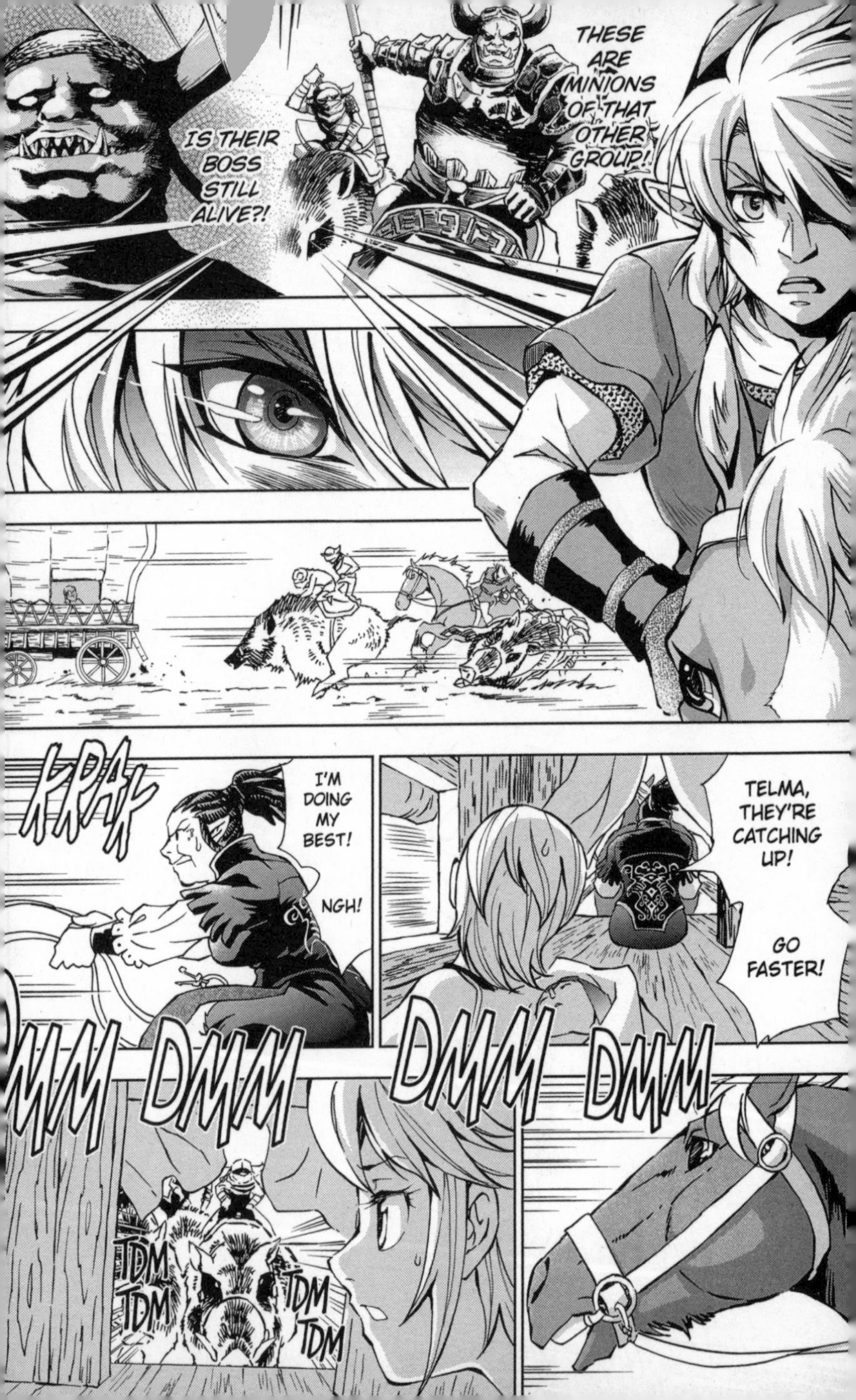
THESE ARE MINIONS OF THAT OTHER GROUP!
IS THEIR BOSS STILL ALIVE?!
TELMA, THEY'RE CATCHING UP!
GO FASTER!
KRAK
I'M DOING MY BEST!
NGH!
DMM DMM
DMM DMM
TDM TDM
TDM TDM

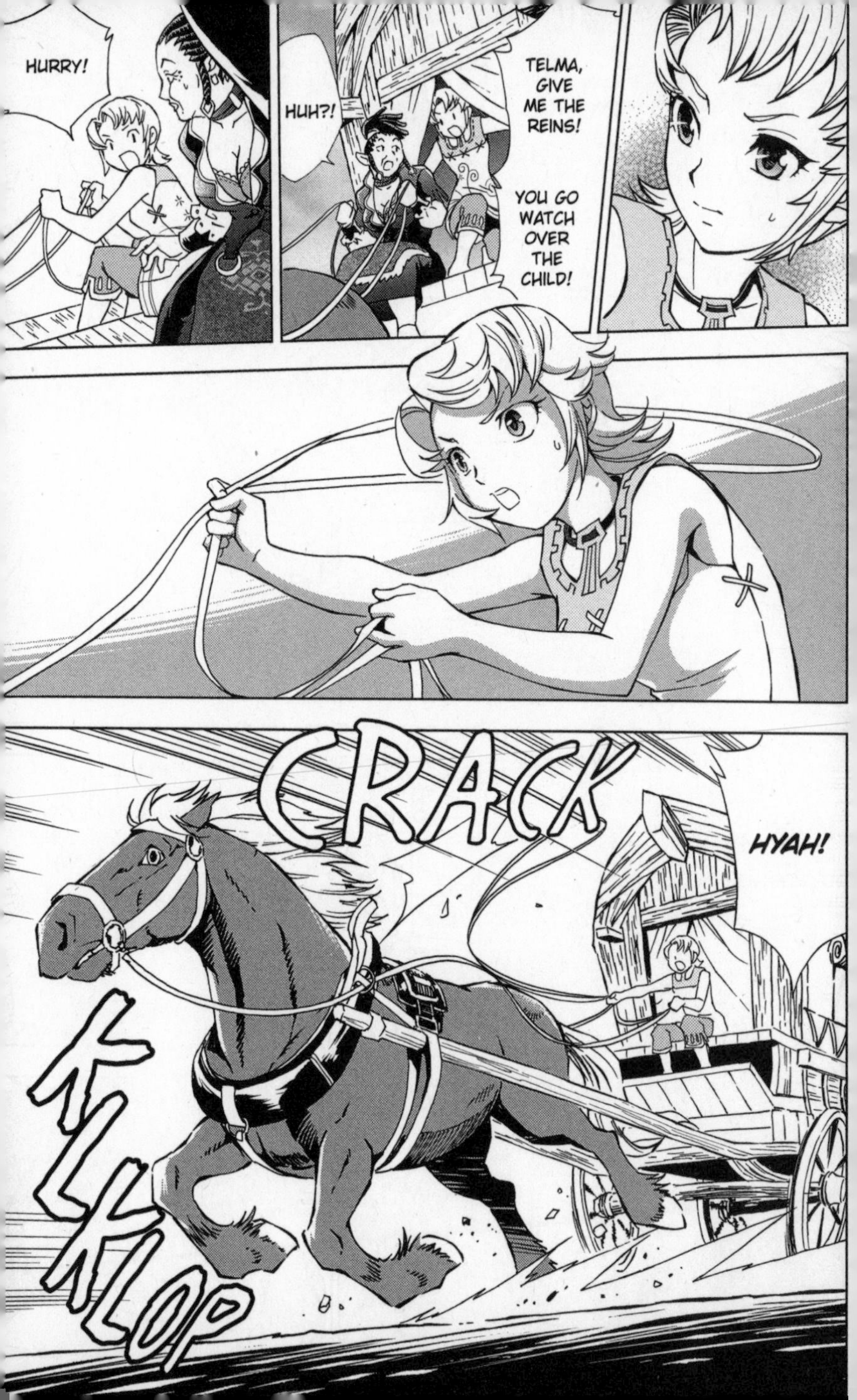
TELMA, GIVE ME THE REINS!
YOU GO WATCH OVER THE CHILD!
HUH?!
HURRY!
HYAH!
CRACK
KLKLOP

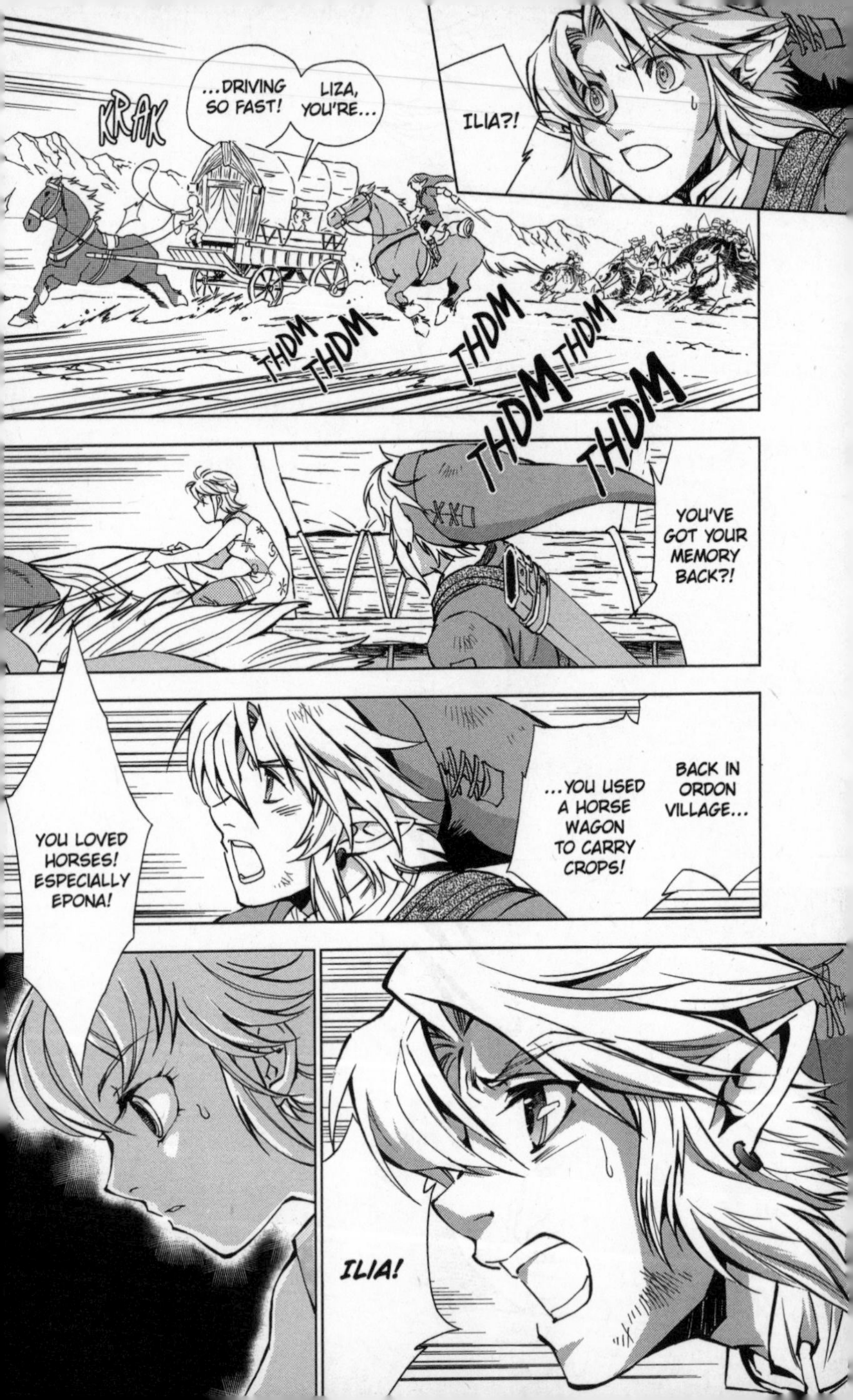
ILIA?!
LIZA, YOU'RE...
...DRIVING SO FAST!
KRAK
THDM THDM THDM THDM THDM THDM
YOU'VE GOT YOUR MEMORY BACK?!
BACK IN ORDON VILLAGE...
...YOU USED A HORSE WAGON TO CARRY CROPS!
YOU LOVED HORSES! ESPECIALLY EPONA!
ILIA!

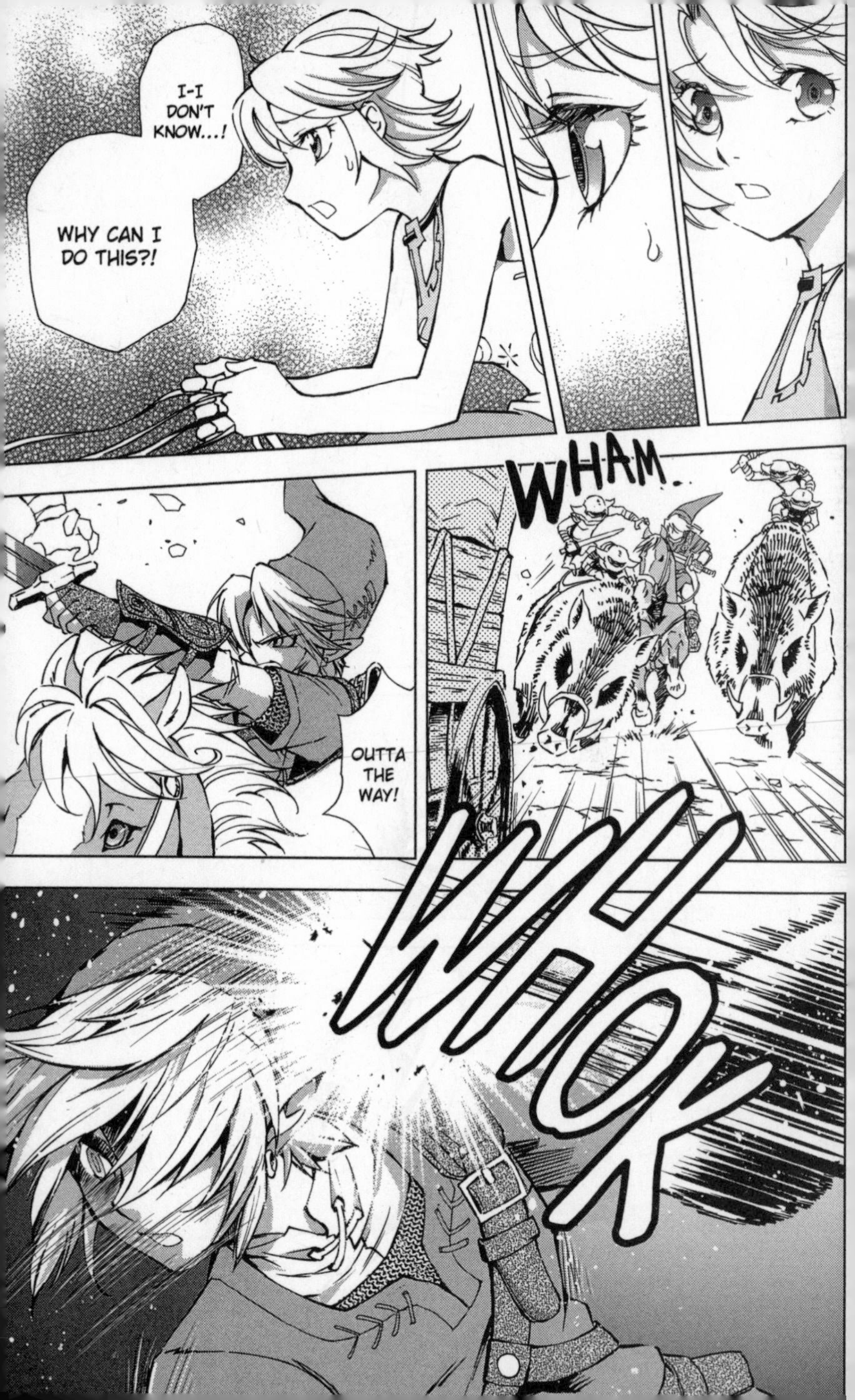
I-I DON'T KNOW...!
WHY CAN I DO THIS?!
WHAM
OUTTA THE WAY!
WHOK

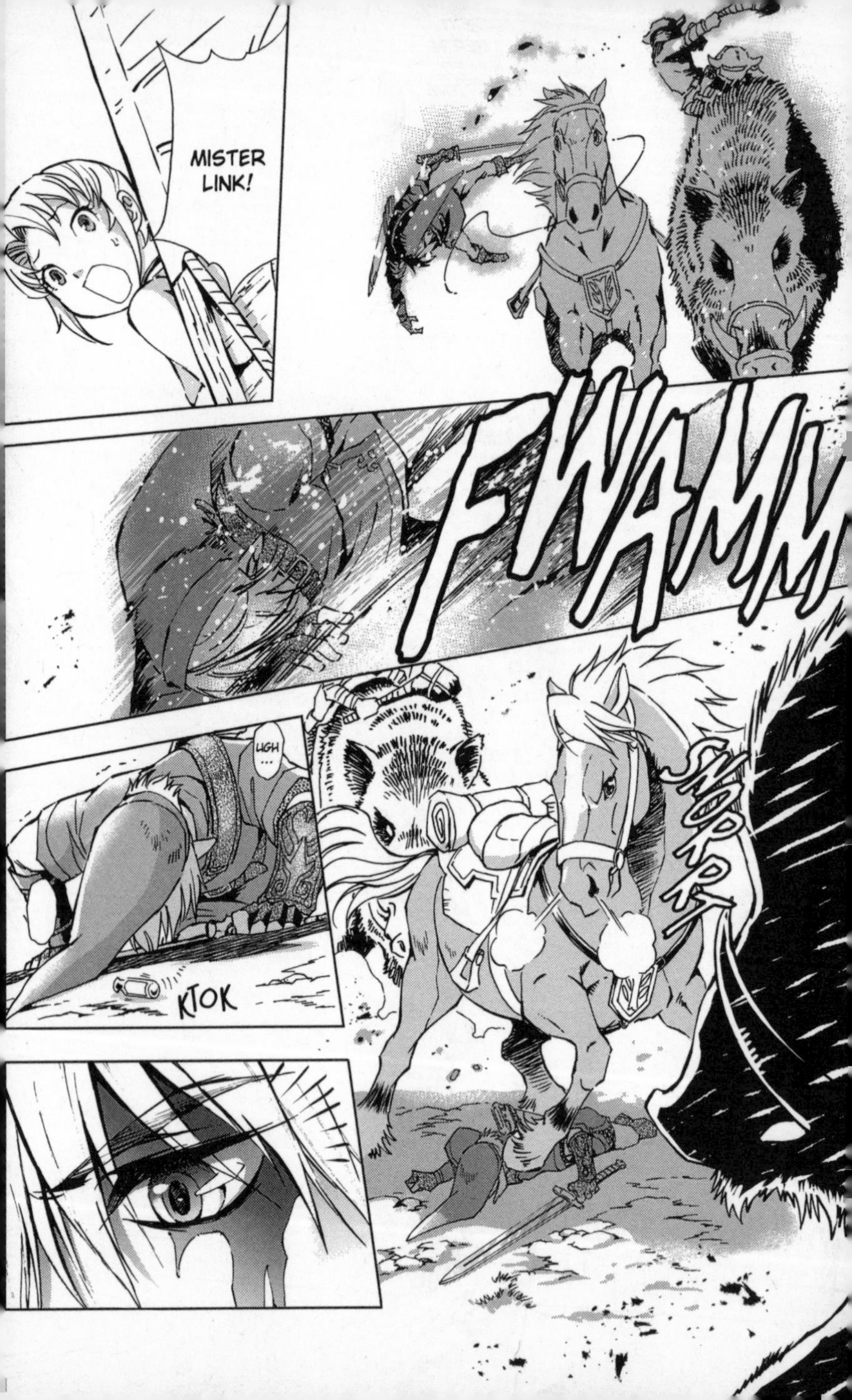
MISTER LINK!
FWAMM
SNORRT
UGH ...
KTOK

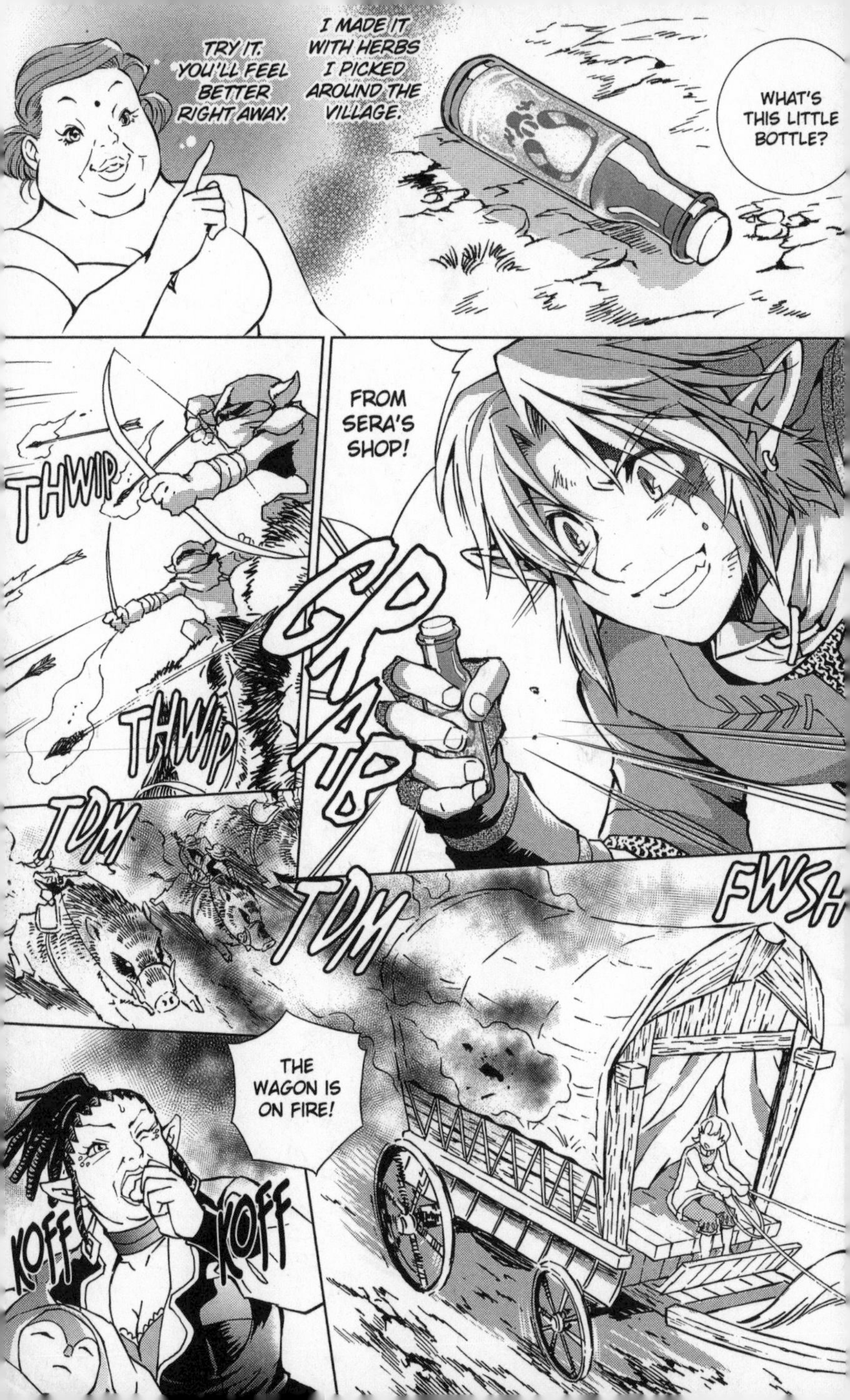
WHAT'S THIS LITTLE BOTTLE?
I MADE IT WITH HERBS I PICKED AROUND THE VILLAGE.
TRY IT. YOU'LL FEEL BETTER RIGHT AWAY.
FROM SERA'S SHOP!
GRAB
THWIP
THWIP
TDM
TDM
FWSH
THE WAGON IS ON FIRE!
KOFF
KOFF

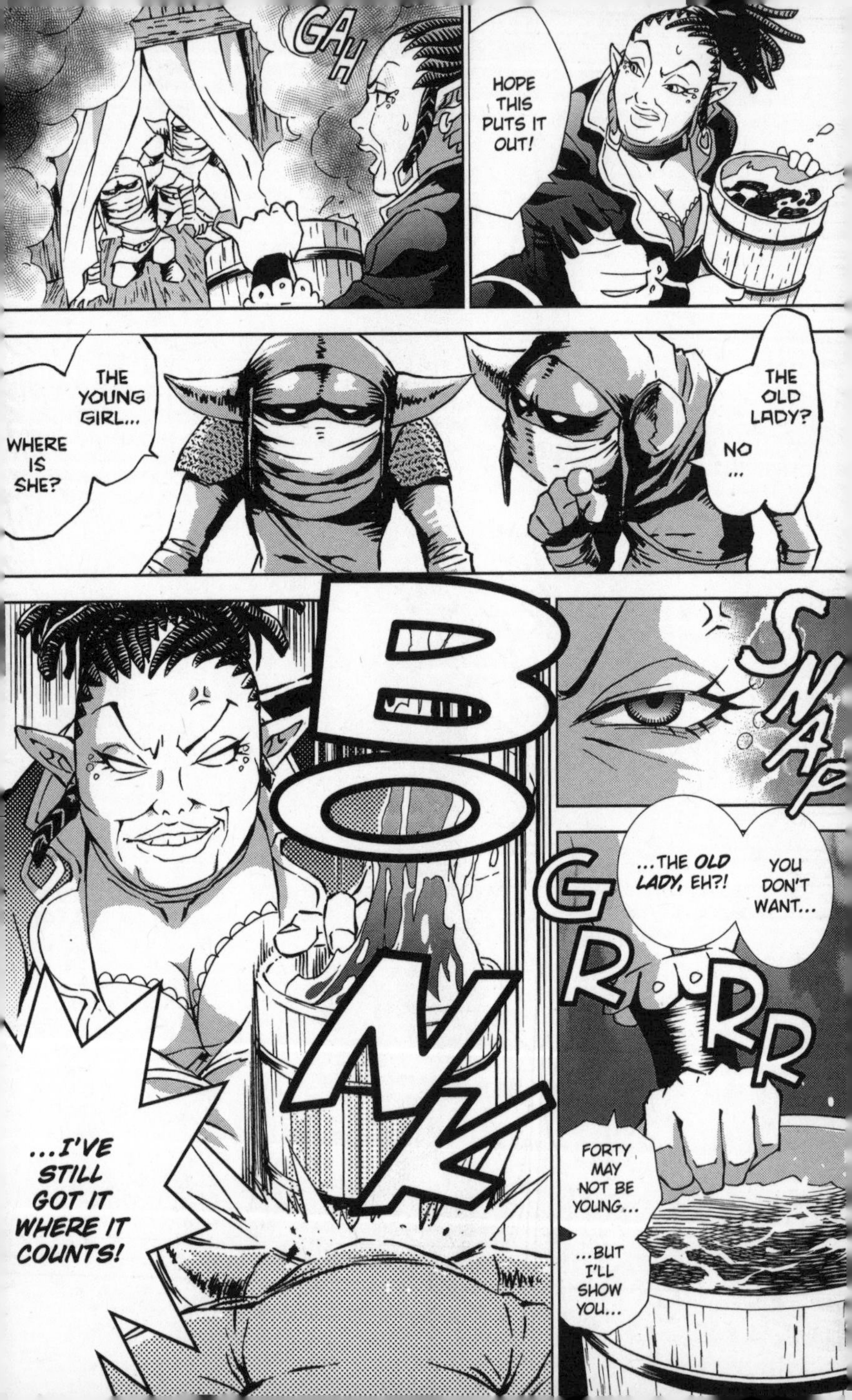
HOPE THIS PUTS IT OUT!
GAH
THE OLD LADY?
NO ...
THE YOUNG GIRL...
WHERE IS SHE?
SNAP
YOU DON'T WANT...
...THE *OLD LADY*, EH?!
GRRRR
FORTY MAY NOT BE YOUNG...
...BUT I'LL SHOW YOU...
BONK
...I'VE STILL GOT IT WHERE IT COUNTS!

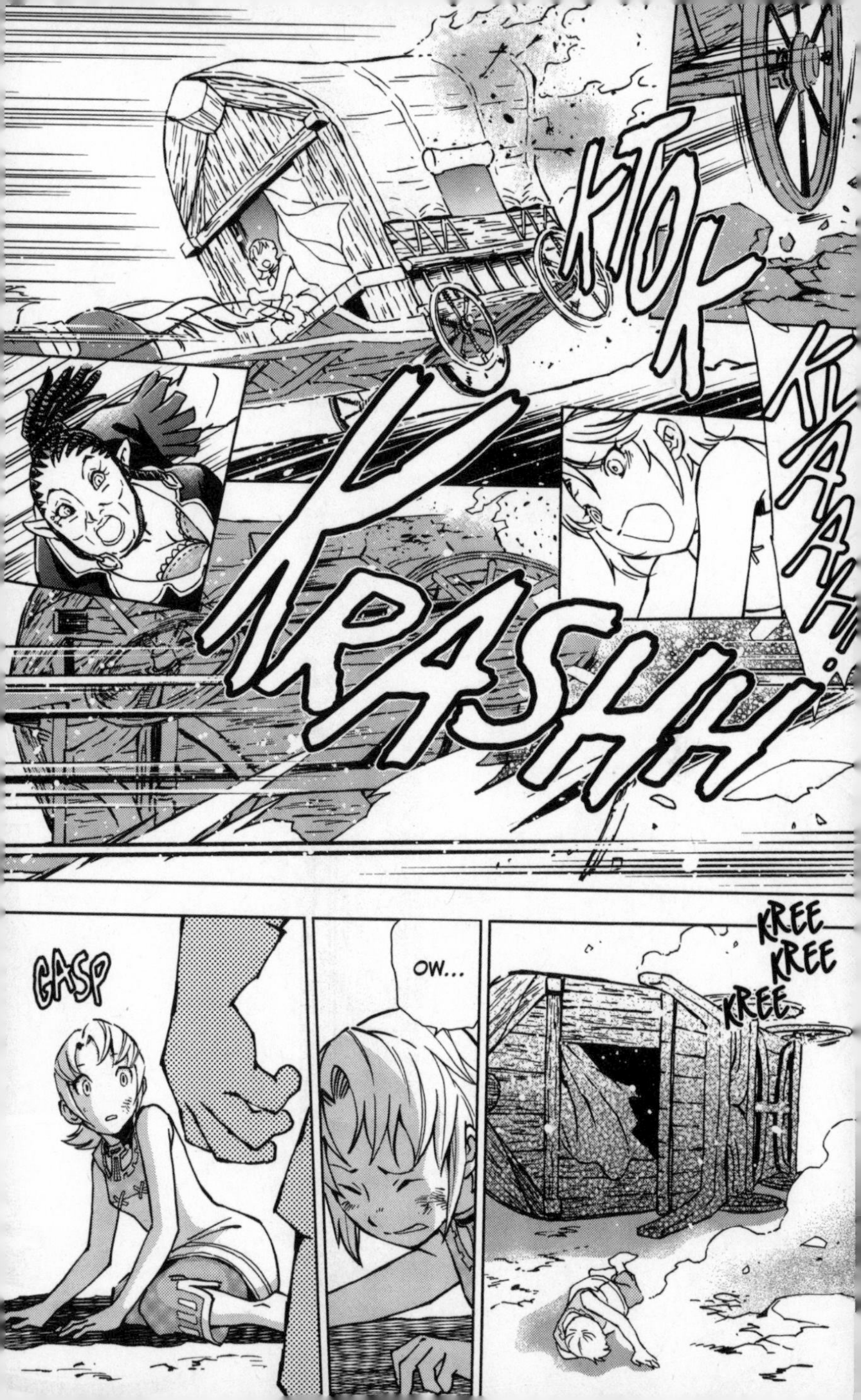
KTOK
KYAAH!
KRASHH
KREE
KREE
KREE
OW...
GASP

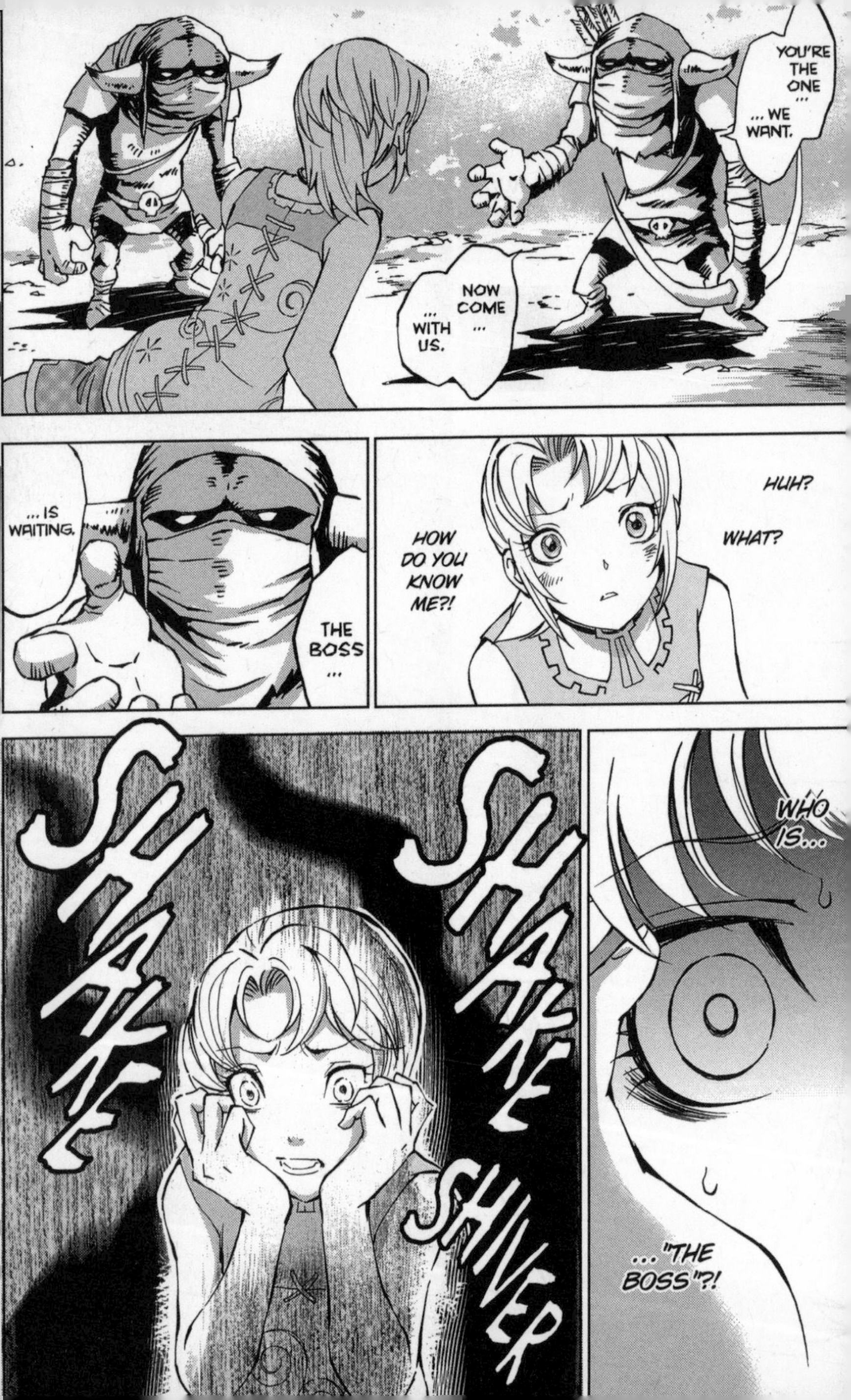
YOU'RE THE ONE... ...WE WANT.
NOW COME... ...WITH US.
HUH? WHAT?
HOW DO YOU KNOW ME?!
THE BOSS...
...IS WAITING.
WHO IS...
..."THE BOSS"?!
SHAKE SHIVER
SHAKE

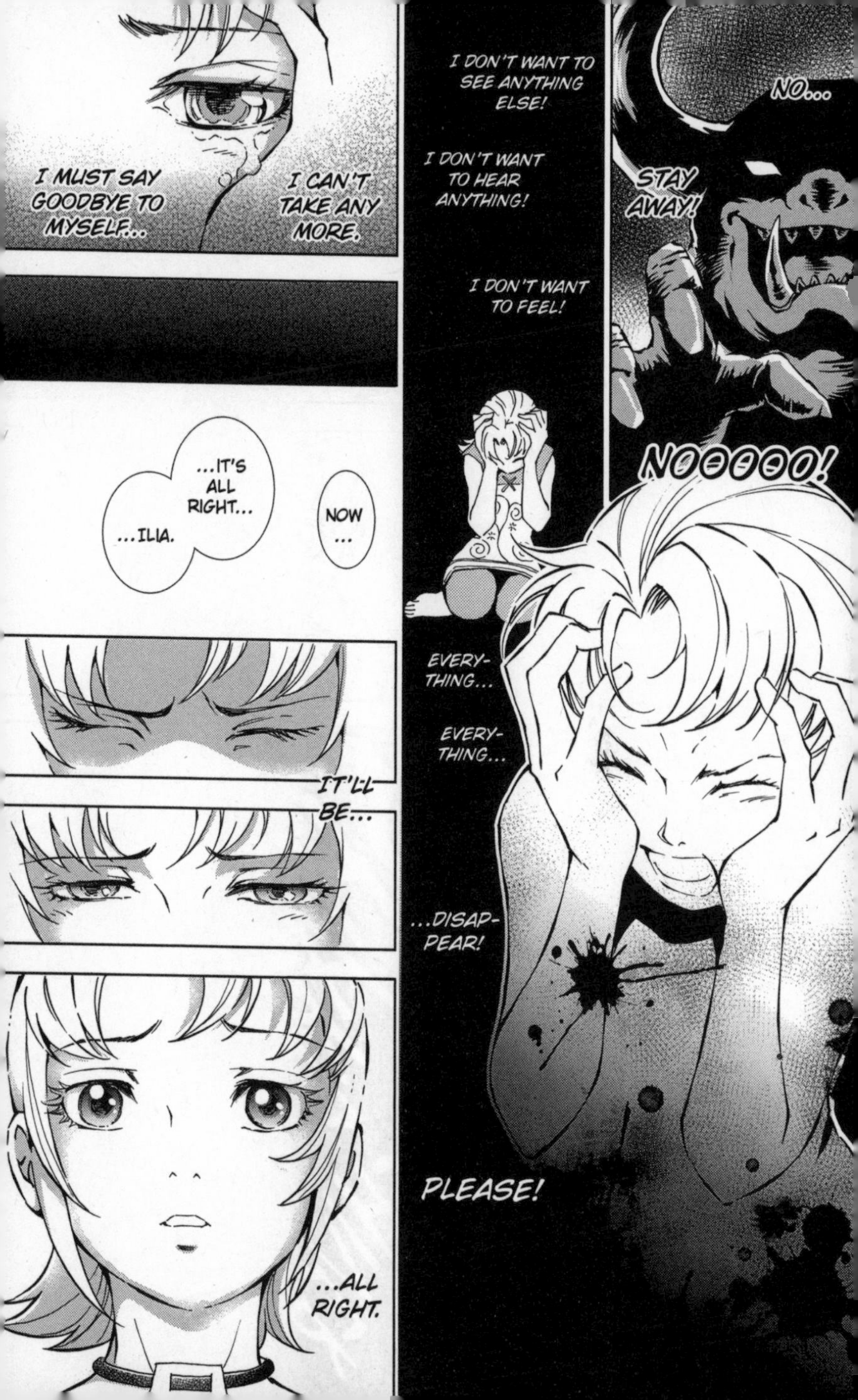
NO...
STAY AWAY!
I DON'T WANT TO SEE ANYTHING ELSE!
I DON'T WANT TO HEAR ANYTHING!
I DON'T WANT TO FEEL!
NOOOOOO!
EVERY-THING...
EVERY-THING...
...DISAP-PEAR!
PLEASE!
I CAN'T TAKE ANY MORE.
I MUST SAY GOODBYE TO MYSELF...
NOW...
...IT'S ALL RIGHT...
...ILIA.
IT'LL BE...
...ALL RIGHT.

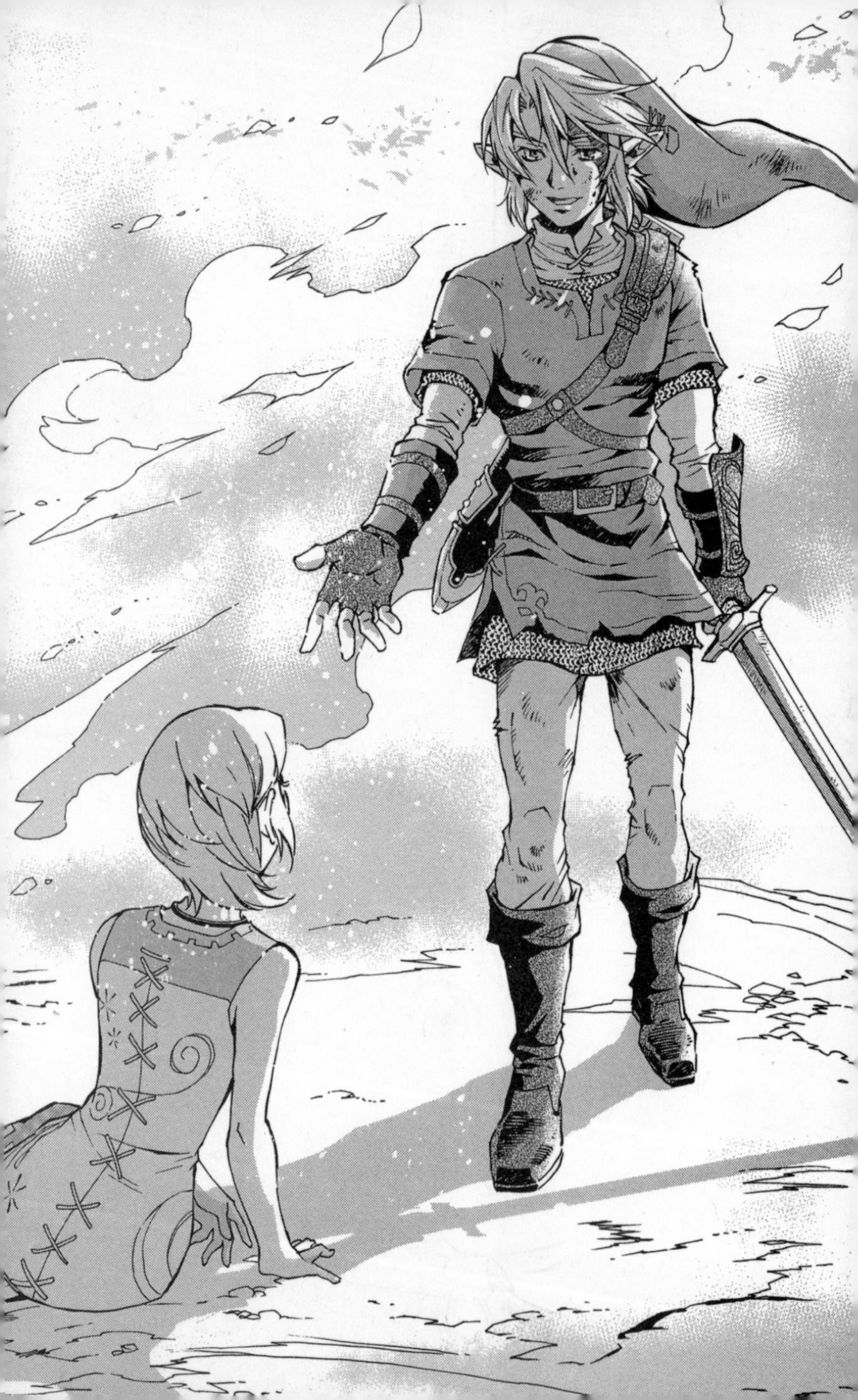

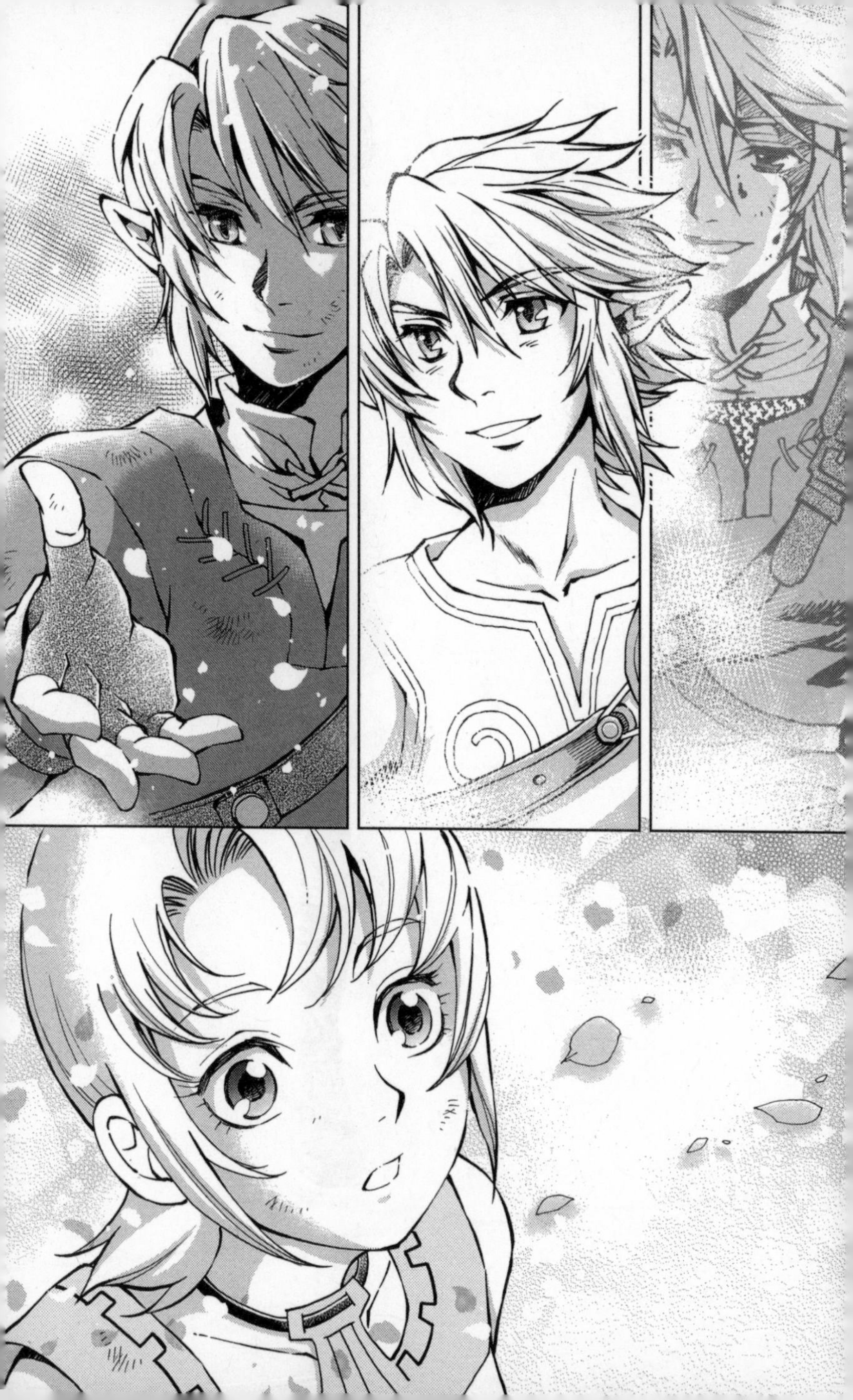

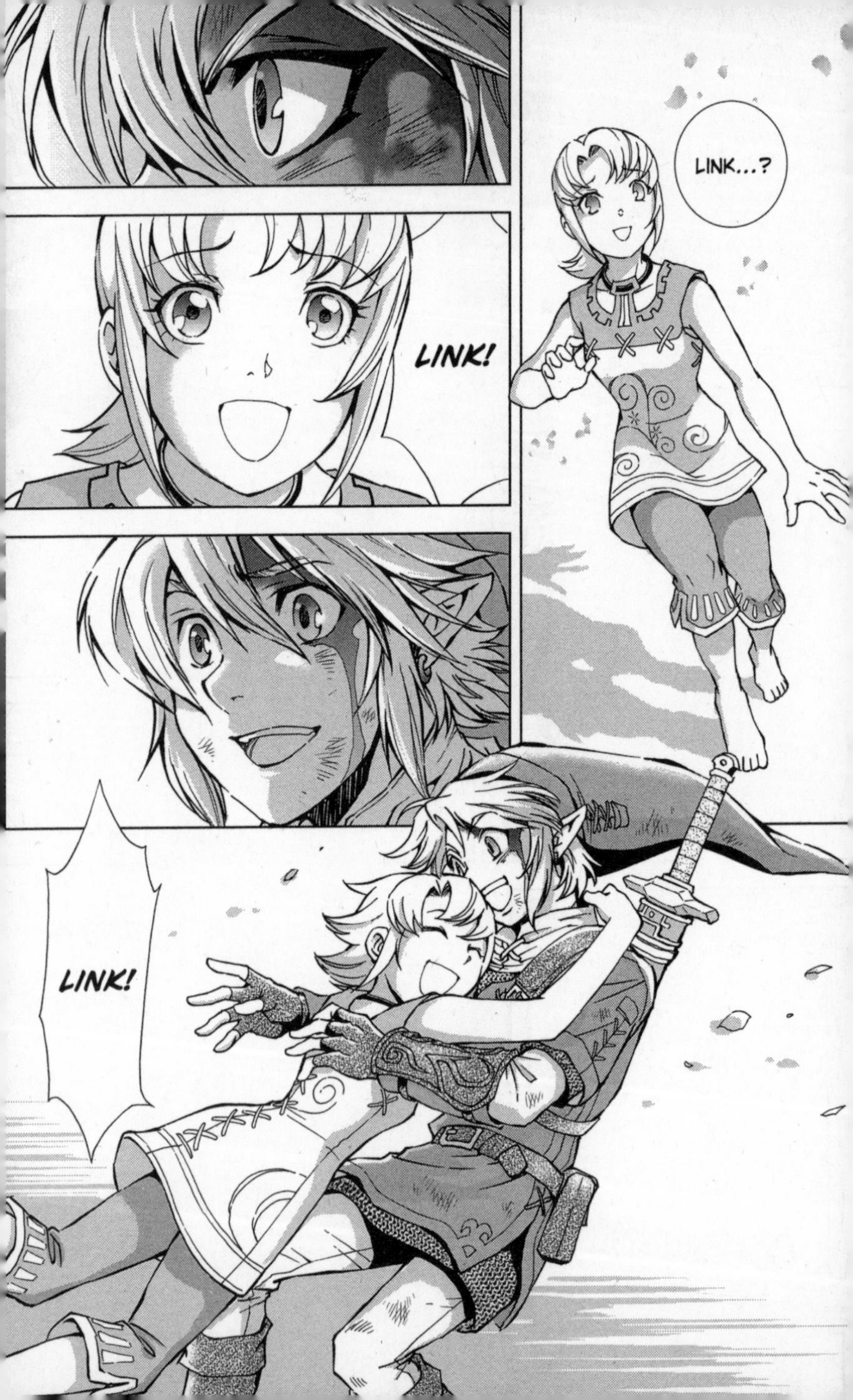
LINK...?
LINK!
LINK!

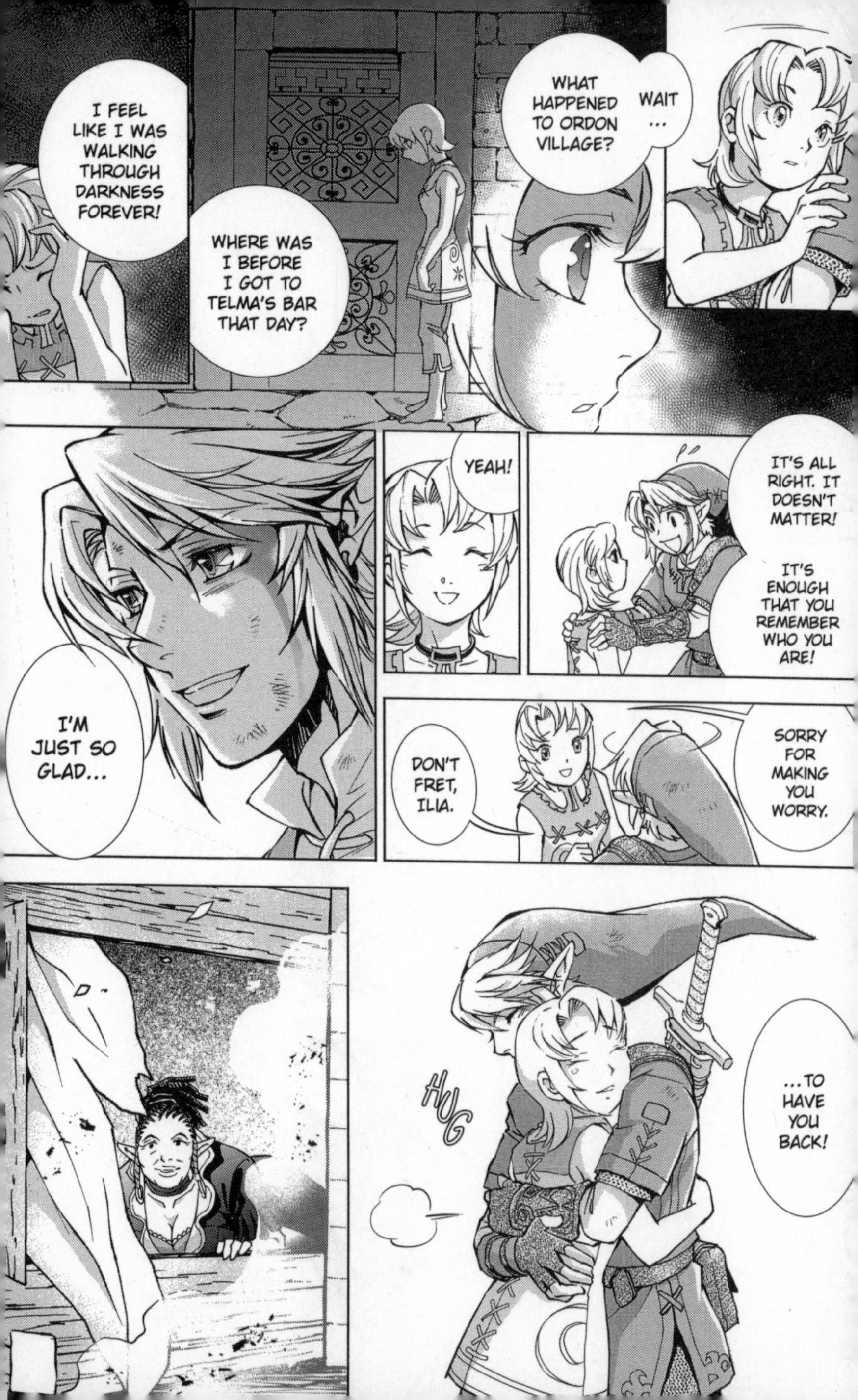
WAIT ...
WHAT HAPPENED TO ORDON VILLAGE?
WHERE WAS I BEFORE I GOT TO TELMA'S BAR THAT DAY?
I FEEL LIKE I WAS WALKING THROUGH DARKNESS FOREVER!
IT'S ALL RIGHT. IT DOESN'T MATTER!
IT'S ENOUGH THAT YOU REMEMBER WHO YOU ARE!
YEAH!
SORRY FOR MAKING YOU WORRY.
DON'T FRET, ILIA.
I'M JUST SO GLAD...
HUG
...TO HAVE YOU BACK!

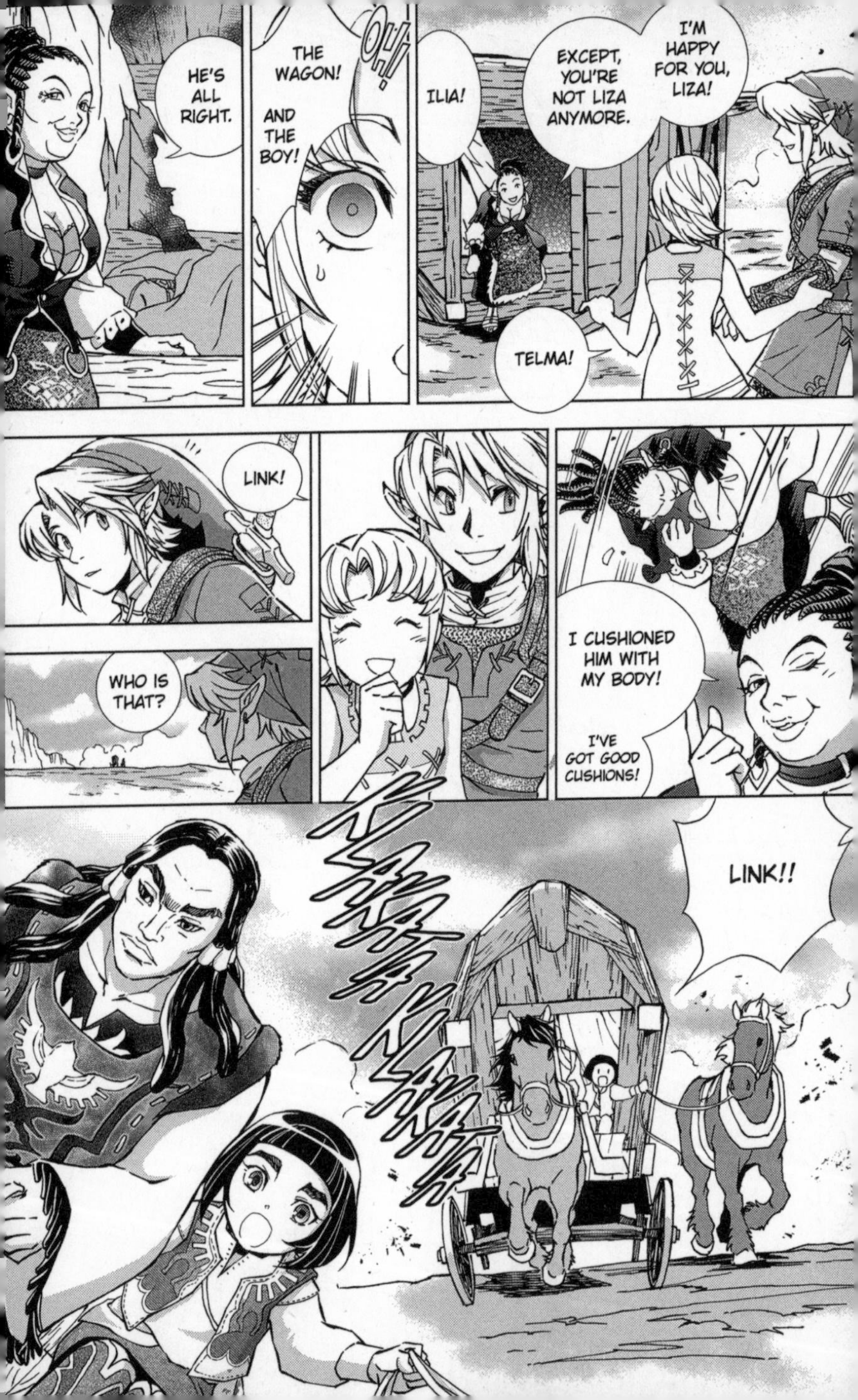
I'M HAPPY FOR YOU, LIZA!
EXCEPT, YOU'RE NOT LIZA ANYMORE.
ILIA!
TELMA!
OH!
THE WAGON!
AND THE BOY!
HE'S ALL RIGHT.
I CUSHIONED HIM WITH MY BODY!
I'VE GOT GOOD CUSHIONS!
LINK!
WHO IS THAT?
LINK!!

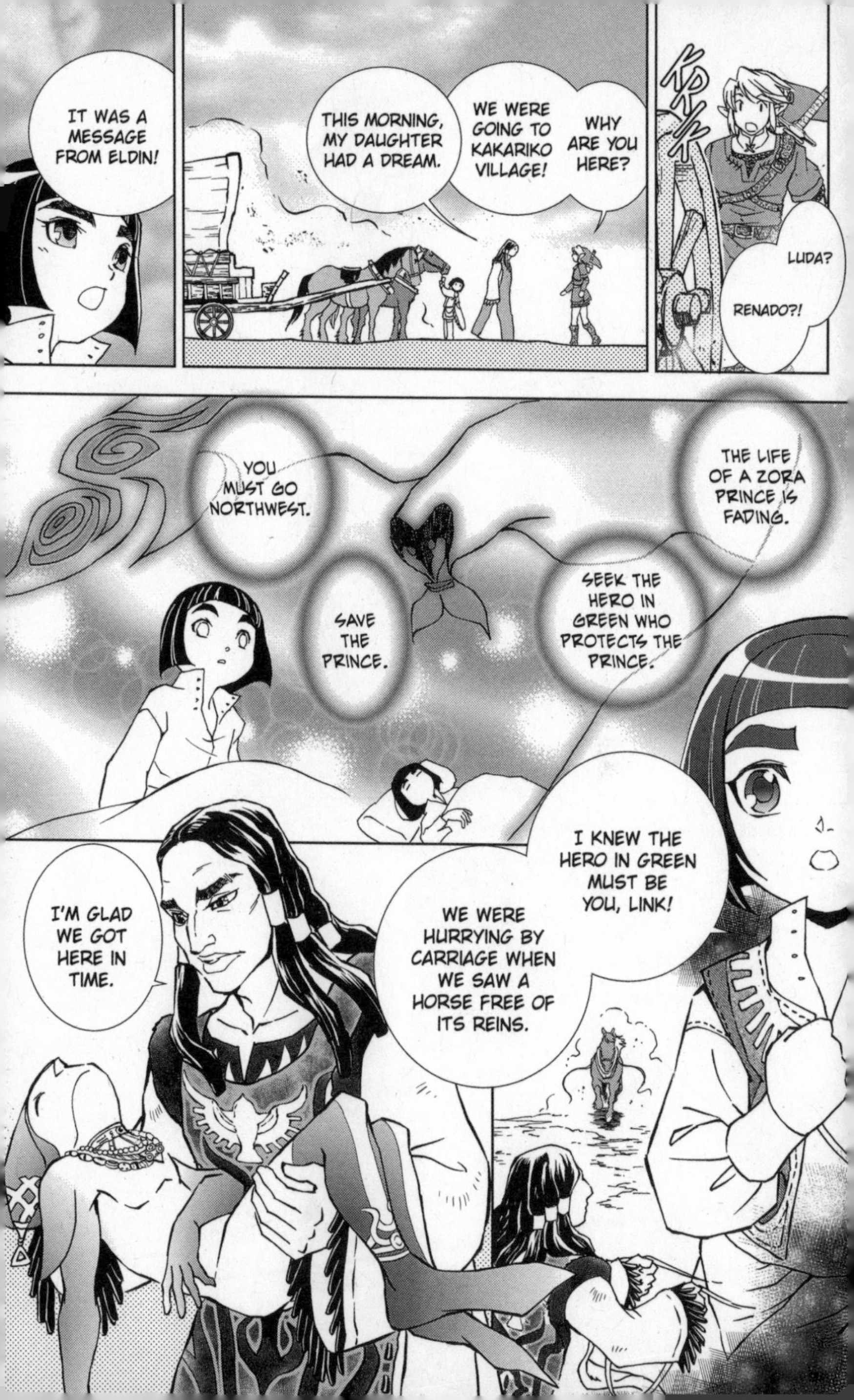
KRK
LUDA?
RENADO?!
WHY ARE YOU HERE?
WE WERE GOING TO KAKARIKO VILLAGE!
THIS MORNING, MY DAUGHTER HAD A DREAM.
IT WAS A MESSAGE FROM ELDIN!
THE LIFE OF A ZORA PRINCE IS FADING.
SEEK THE HERO IN GREEN WHO PROTECTS THE PRINCE.
SAVE THE PRINCE.
YOU MUST GO NORTHWEST.
I KNEW THE HERO IN GREEN MUST BE YOU, LINK!
WE WERE HURRYING BY CARRIAGE WHEN WE SAW A HORSE FREE OF ITS REINS.
I'M GLAD WE GOT HERE IN TIME.

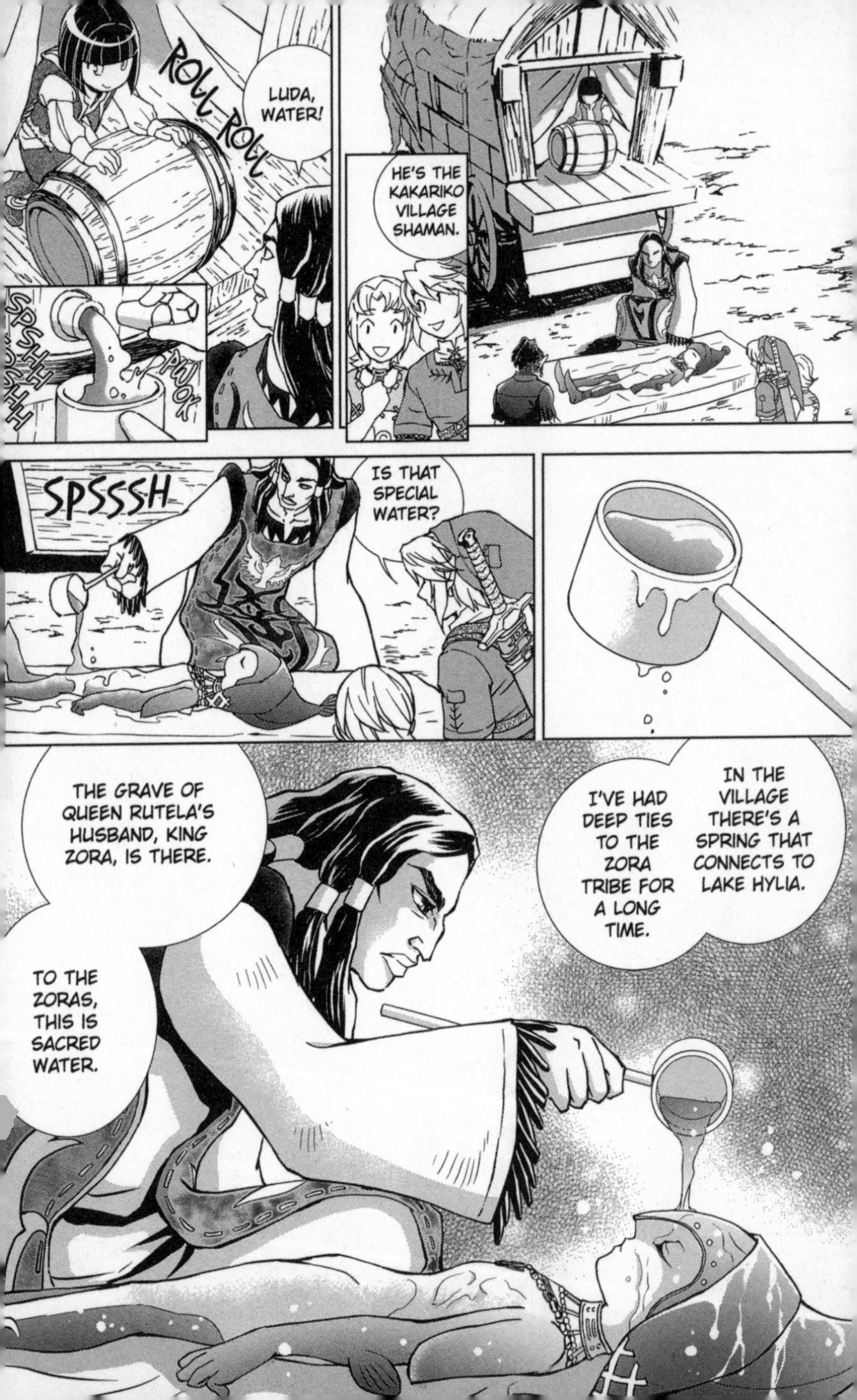
HE'S THE KAKARIKO VILLAGE SHAMAN.
ROLL ROLL
LUDA, WATER!
SPSHH SPSHH
PWOK
IS THAT SPECIAL WATER?
SPSSSH
IN THE VILLAGE THERE'S A SPRING THAT CONNECTS TO LAKE HYLIA.
I'VE HAD DEEP TIES TO THE ZORA TRIBE FOR A LONG TIME.
THE GRAVE OF QUEEN RUTELA'S HUSBAND, KING ZORA, IS THERE.
TO THE ZORAS, THIS IS SACRED WATER.

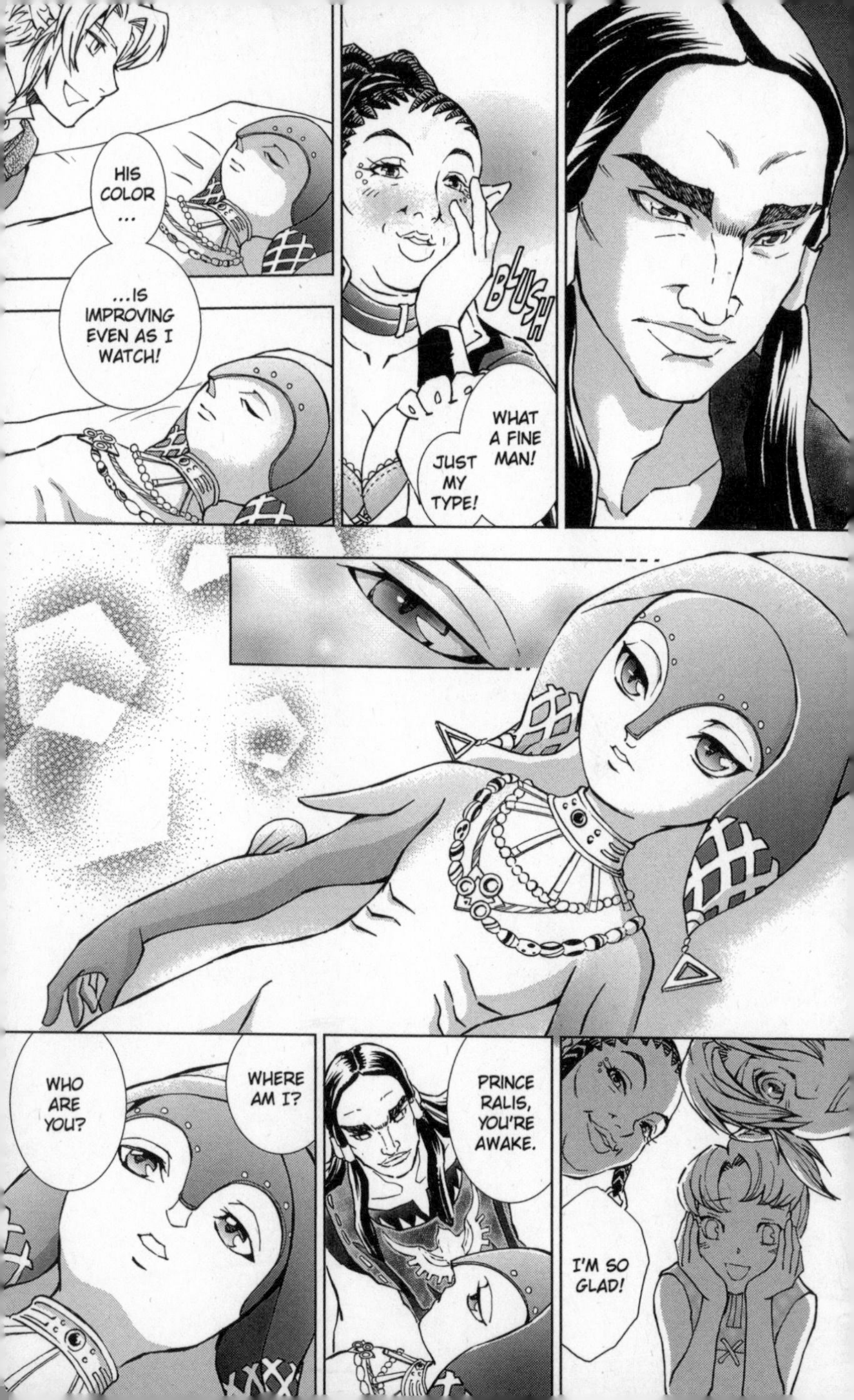
WHAT A FINE MAN!
JUST MY TYPE!
BLUSH
HIS COLOR ...
...IS IMPROVING EVEN AS I WATCH!
I'M SO GLAD!
PRINCE RALIS, YOU'RE AWAKE.
WHERE AM I?
WHO ARE YOU?

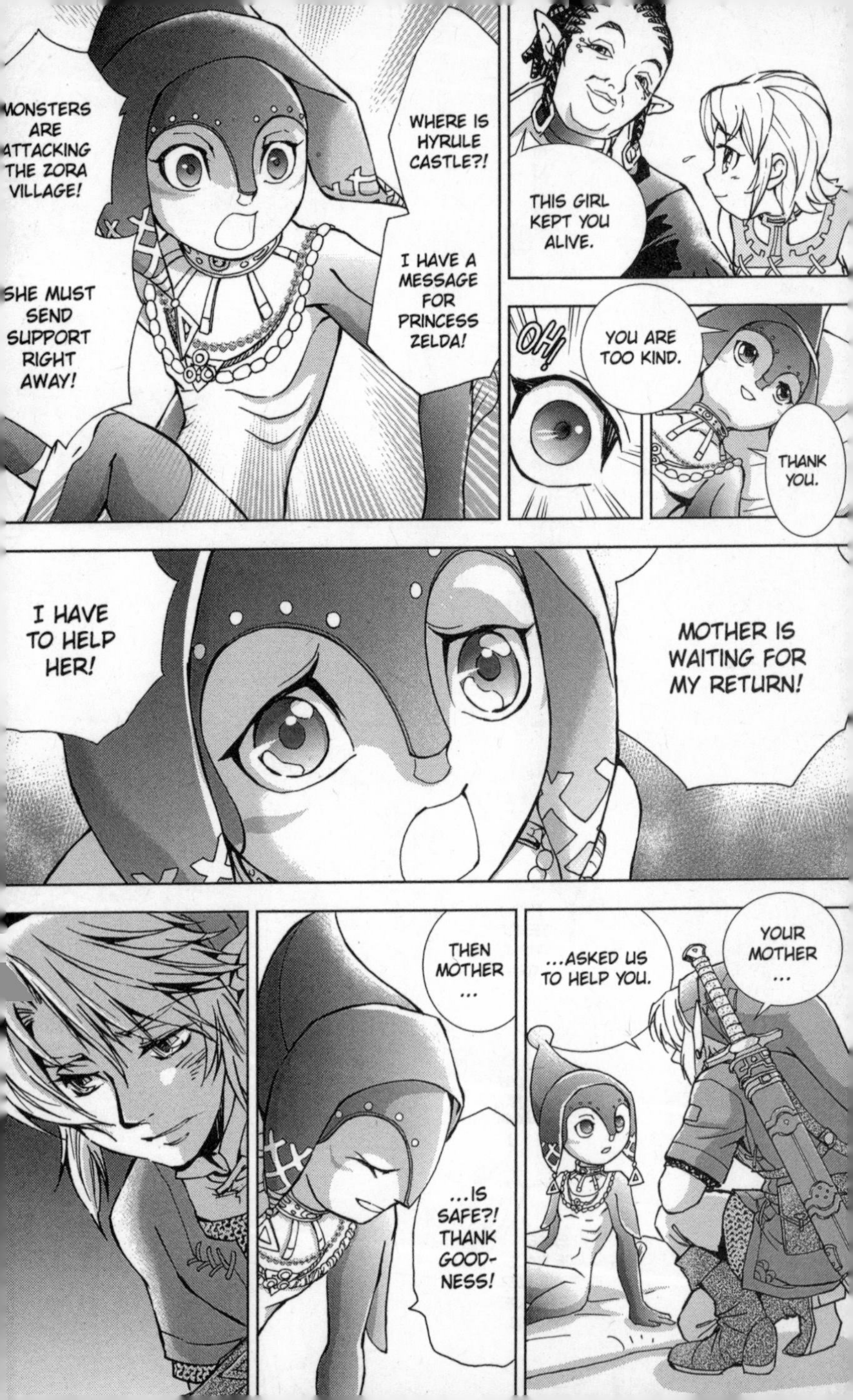
THIS GIRL KEPT YOU ALIVE.
YOU ARE TOO KIND.
OH!
THANK YOU.
WHERE IS HYRULE CASTLE?!
I HAVE A MESSAGE FOR PRINCESS ZELDA!
MONSTERS ARE ATTACKING THE ZORA VILLAGE!
SHE MUST SEND SUPPORT RIGHT AWAY!
MOTHER IS WAITING FOR MY RETURN!
I HAVE TO HELP HER!
YOUR MOTHER ...
...ASKED US TO HELP YOU.
THEN MOTHER ...
...IS SAFE?! THANK GOODNESS!

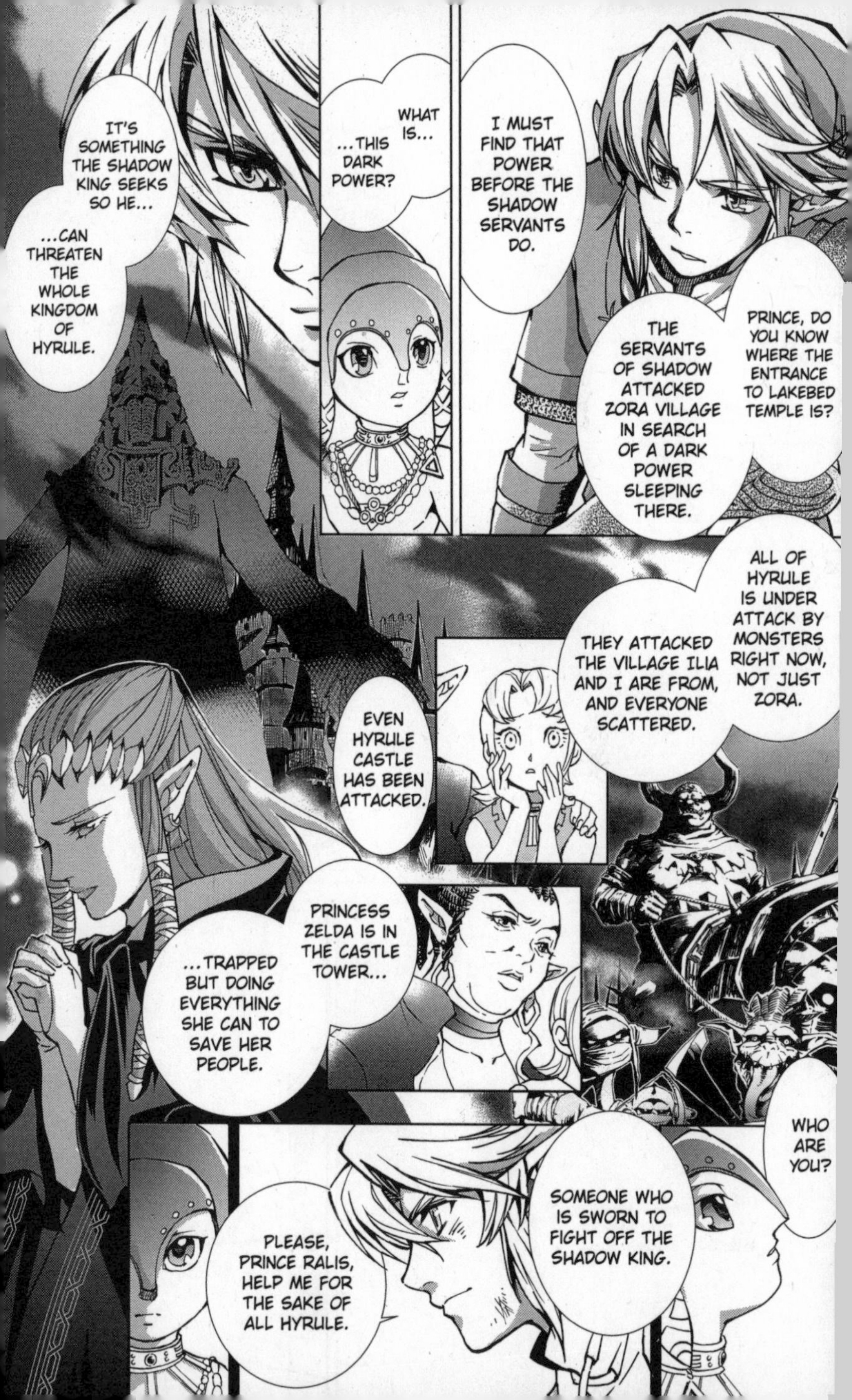
I MUST FIND THAT POWER BEFORE THE SHADOW SERVANTS DO.
PRINCE, DO YOU KNOW WHERE THE ENTRANCE TO LAKEBED TEMPLE IS?
THE SERVANTS OF SHADOW ATTACKED ZORA VILLAGE IN SEARCH OF A DARK POWER SLEEPING THERE.
WHAT IS...
...THIS DARK POWER?
IT'S SOMETHING THE SHADOW KING SEEKS SO HE...
...CAN THREATEN THE WHOLE KINGDOM OF HYRULE.
ALL OF HYRULE IS UNDER ATTACK BY MONSTERS RIGHT NOW, NOT JUST ZORA.
THEY ATTACKED THE VILLAGE ILIA AND I ARE FROM, AND EVERYONE SCATTERED.
EVEN HYRULE CASTLE HAS BEEN ATTACKED.
PRINCESS ZELDA IS IN THE CASTLE TOWER...
...TRAPPED BUT DOING EVERYTHING SHE CAN TO SAVE HER PEOPLE.
WHO ARE YOU?
SOMEONE WHO IS SWORN TO FIGHT OFF THE SHADOW KING.
PLEASE, PRINCE RALIS, HELP ME FOR THE SAKE OF ALL HYRULE.

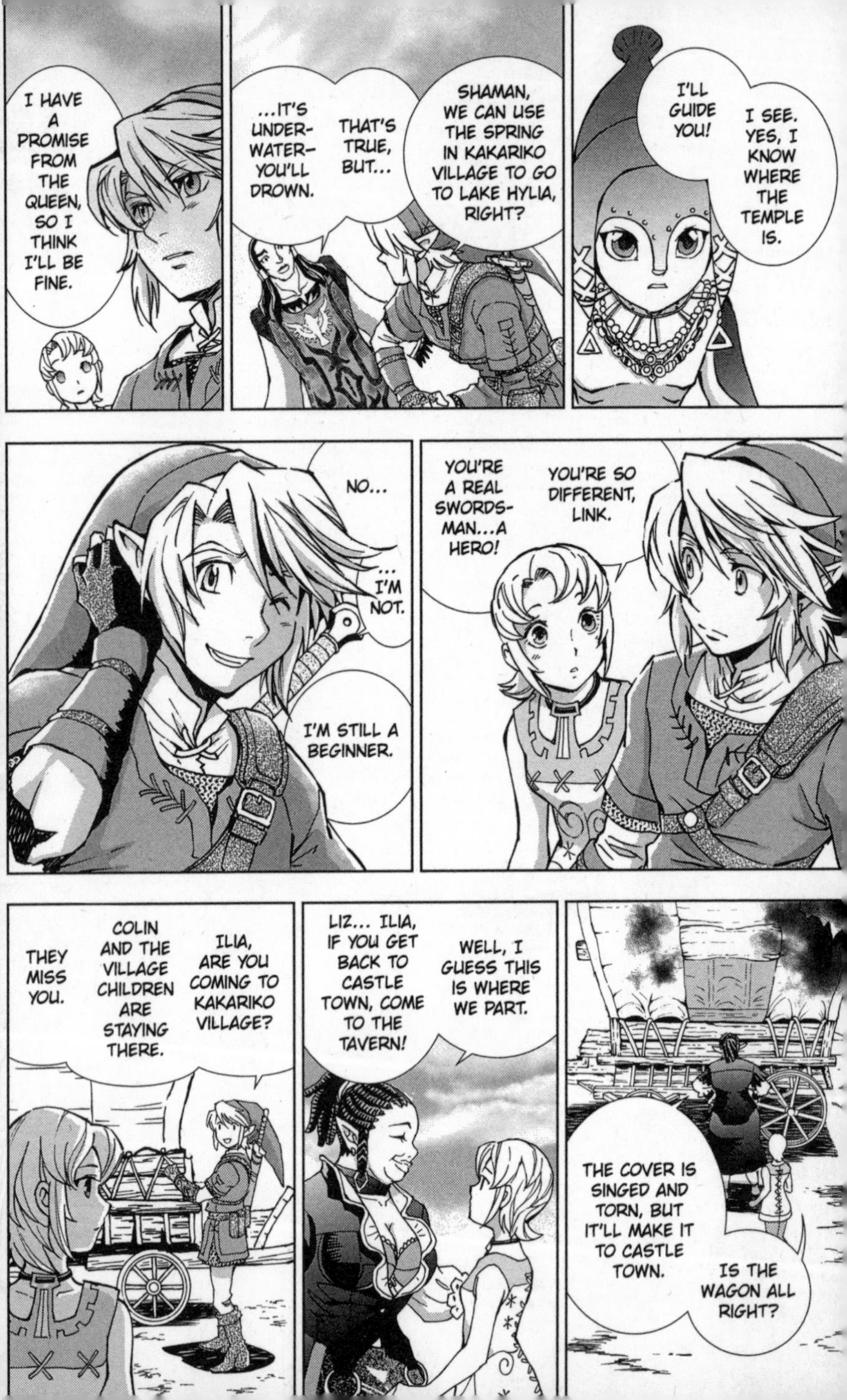
I SEE. YES, I KNOW WHERE THE TEMPLE IS.
I'LL GUIDE YOU!
SHAMAN, WE CAN USE THE SPRING IN KAKARIKO VILLAGE TO GO TO LAKE HYLIA, RIGHT?
THAT'S TRUE, BUT...
...IT'S UNDER-WATER– YOU'LL DROWN.
I HAVE A PROMISE FROM THE QUEEN, SO I THINK I'LL BE FINE.
YOU'RE SO DIFFERENT, LINK.
YOU'RE A REAL SWORDS-MAN...A HERO!
NO...
...I'M NOT.
I'M STILL A BEGINNER.
IS THE WAGON ALL RIGHT?
THE COVER IS SINGED AND TORN, BUT IT'LL MAKE IT TO CASTLE TOWN.
WELL, I GUESS THIS IS WHERE WE PART.
LIZ... ILIA, IF YOU GET BACK TO CASTLE TOWN, COME TO THE TAVERN!
ILIA, ARE YOU COMING TO KAKARIKO VILLAGE?
COLIN AND THE VILLAGE CHILDREN ARE STAYING THERE.
THEY MISS YOU.

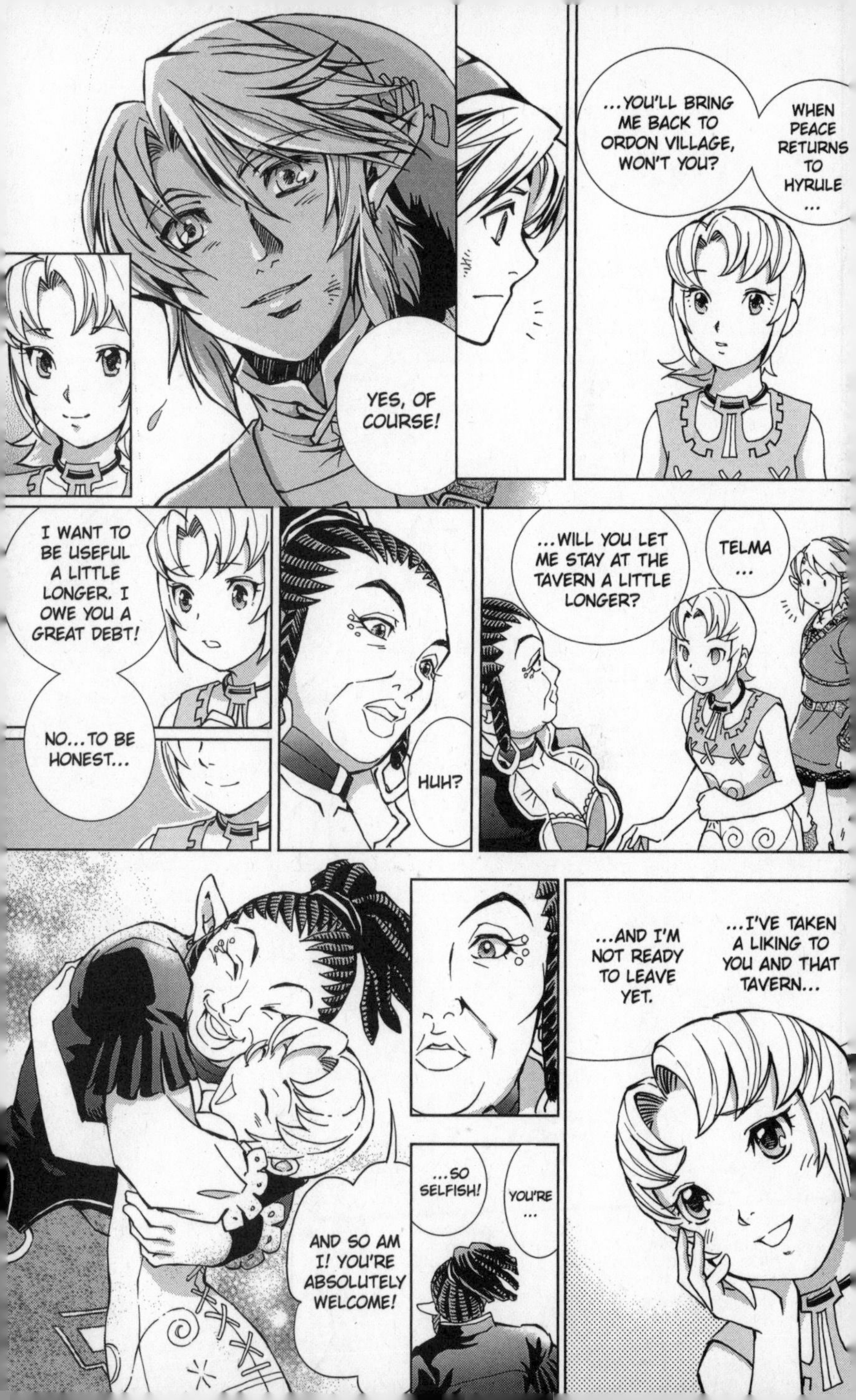
WHEN PEACE RETURNS TO HYRULE...
...YOU'LL BRING ME BACK TO ORDON VILLAGE, WON'T YOU?
YES, OF COURSE!
TELMA...
...WILL YOU LET ME STAY AT THE TAVERN A LITTLE LONGER?
HUH?
I WANT TO BE USEFUL A LITTLE LONGER. I OWE YOU A GREAT DEBT!
NO...TO BE HONEST...
...I'VE TAKEN A LIKING TO YOU AND THAT TAVERN...
...AND I'M NOT READY TO LEAVE YET.
YOU'RE...
...SO SELFISH!
AND SO AM I! YOU'RE ABSOLUTELY WELCOME!

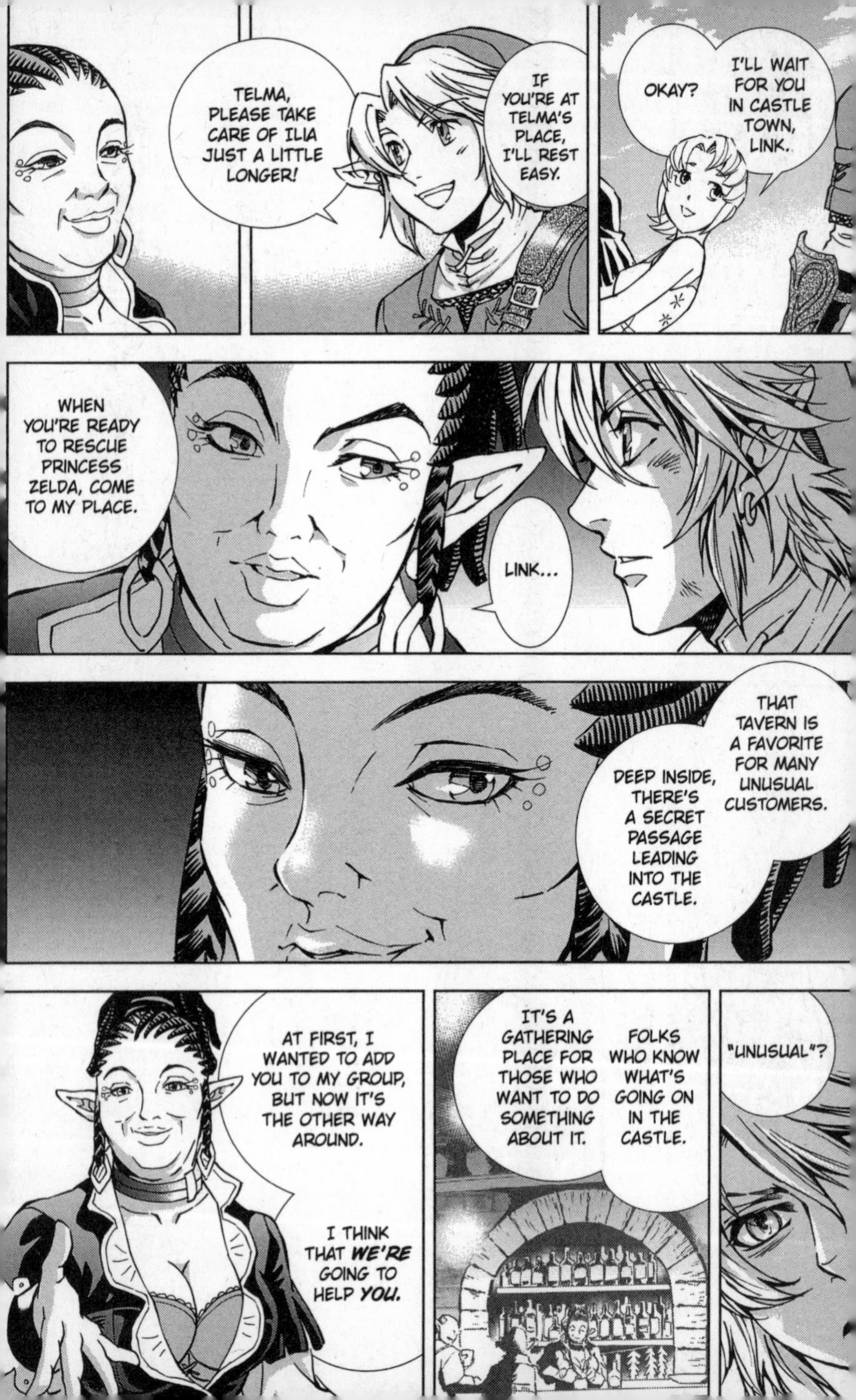
I'LL WAIT FOR YOU IN CASTLE TOWN, LINK.
OKAY?
IF YOU'RE AT TELMA'S PLACE, I'LL REST EASY.
TELMA, PLEASE TAKE CARE OF ILIA JUST A LITTLE LONGER!
LINK...
WHEN YOU'RE READY TO RESCUE PRINCESS ZELDA, COME TO MY PLACE.
THAT TAVERN IS A FAVORITE FOR MANY UNUSUAL CUSTOMERS.
DEEP INSIDE, THERE'S A SECRET PASSAGE LEADING INTO THE CASTLE.
"UNUSUAL"?
FOLKS WHO KNOW WHAT'S GOING ON IN THE CASTLE.
IT'S A GATHERING PLACE FOR THOSE WHO WANT TO DO SOMETHING ABOUT IT.
AT FIRST, I WANTED TO ADD YOU TO MY GROUP, BUT NOW IT'S THE OTHER WAY AROUND.
I THINK THAT ***WE'RE*** GOING TO HELP ***YOU.***

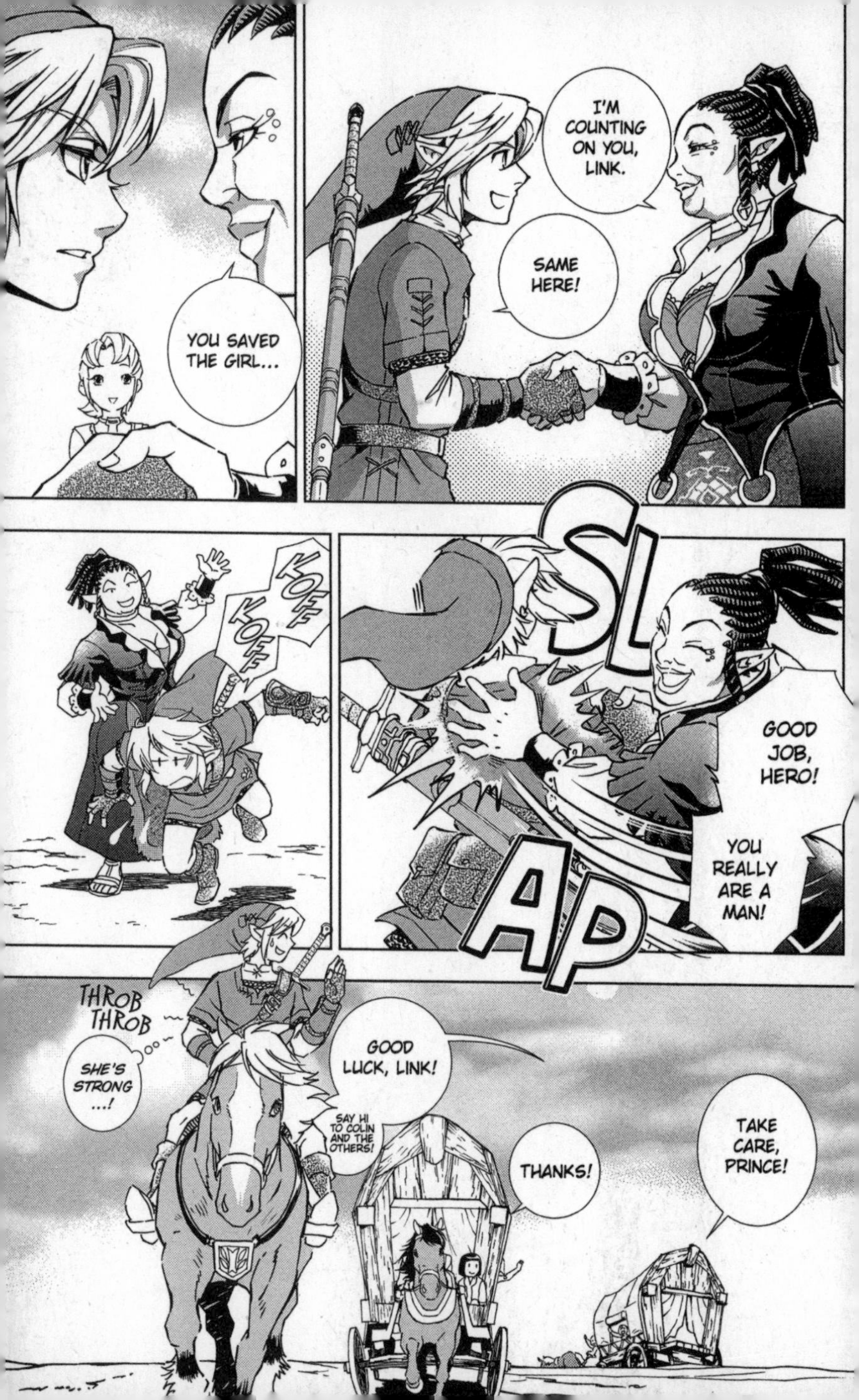
I'M COUNTING ON YOU, LINK.
SAME HERE!
YOU SAVED THE GIRL...
SLAP
GOOD JOB, HERO!
YOU REALLY ARE A MAN!
KOFF KOFF
TAKE CARE, PRINCE!
THANKS!
GOOD LUCK, LINK!
SAY HI TO COLIN AND THE OTHERS!
THROB THROB
SHE'S STRONG ...!

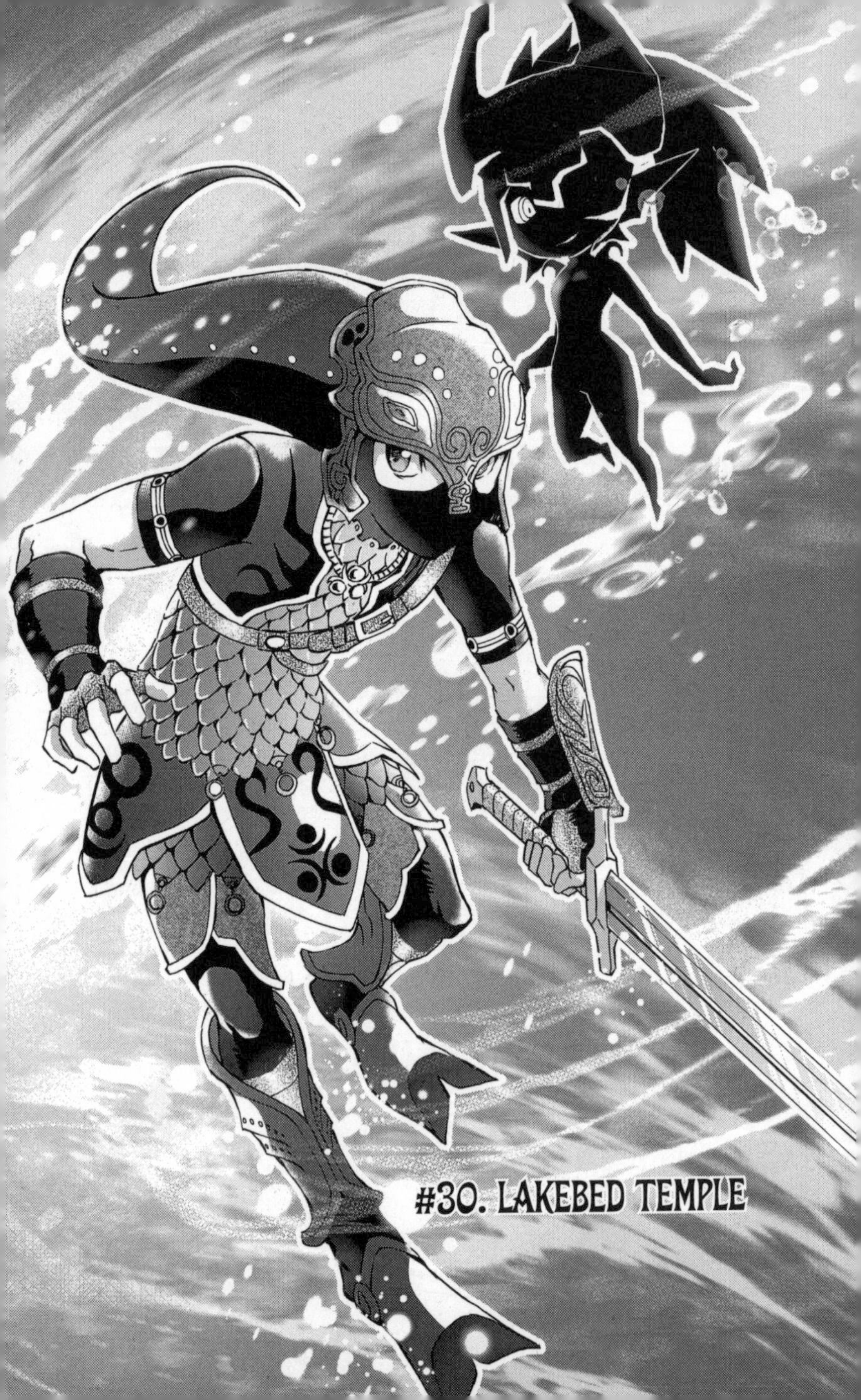
#30. LAKEBED TEMPLE

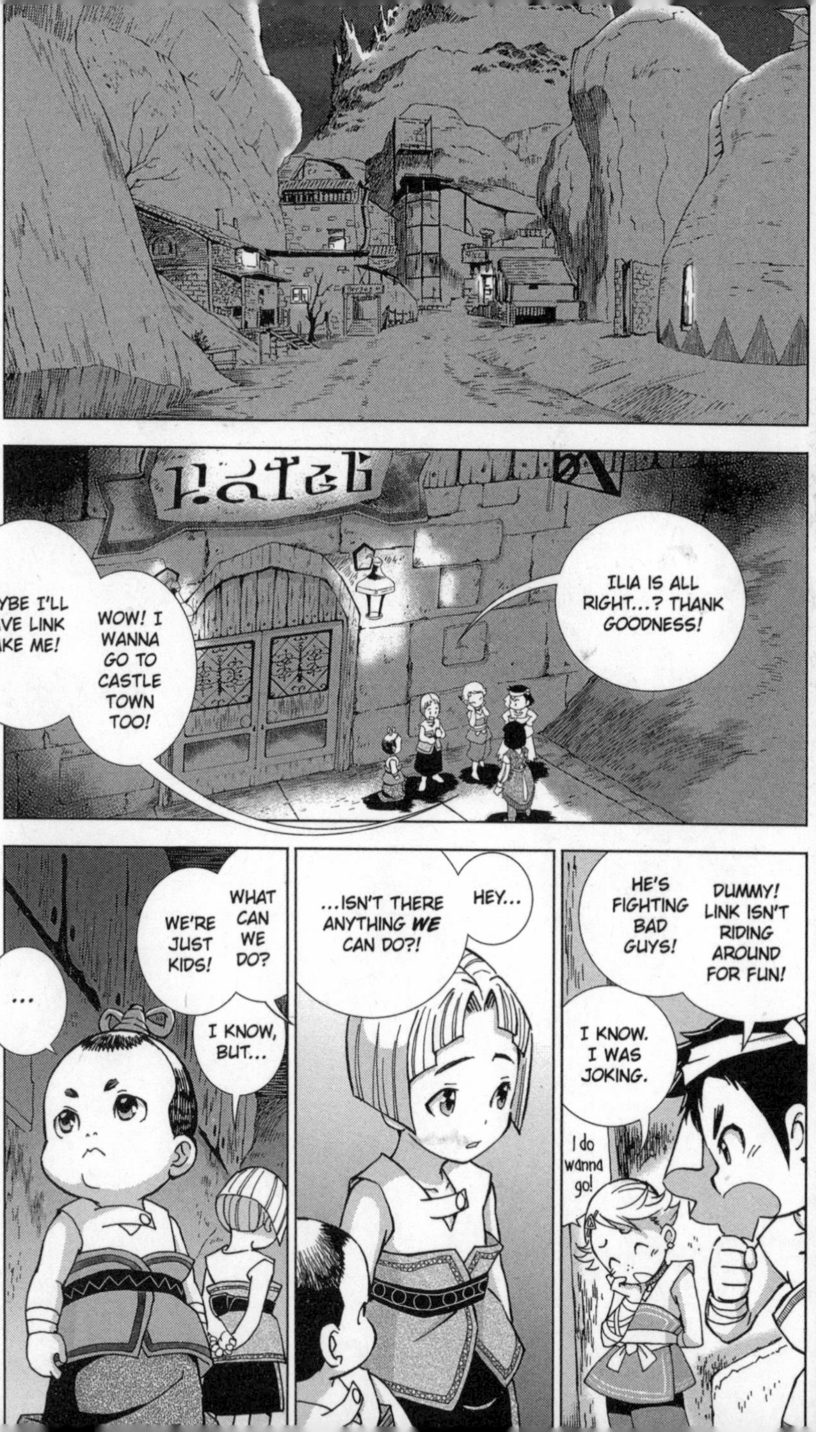
ILIA IS ALL RIGHT...? THANK GOODNESS!
WOW! I WANNA GO TO CASTLE TOWN TOO!
MAYBE I'LL HAVE LINK TAKE ME!
DUMMY! LINK ISN'T RIDING AROUND FOR FUN!
HE'S FIGHTING BAD GUYS!
I KNOW. I WAS JOKING.
I do wanna go!
HEY...
...ISN'T THERE ANYTHING *WE* CAN DO?!
WHAT CAN WE DO?
WE'RE JUST KIDS!
I KNOW, BUT...
...

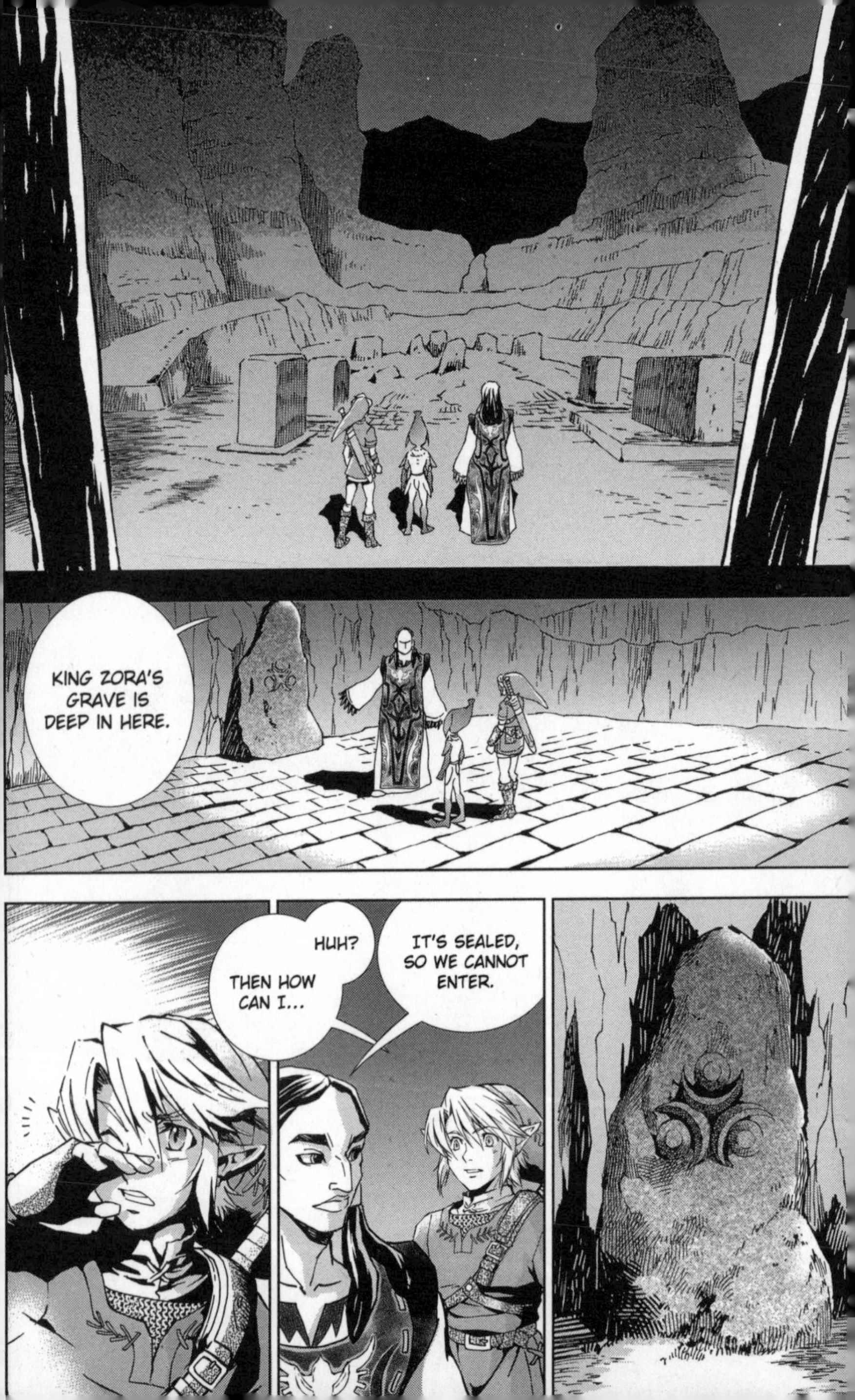
KING ZORA'S GRAVE IS DEEP IN HERE.
IT'S SEALED, SO WE CANNOT ENTER.
HUH?
THEN HOW CAN I...

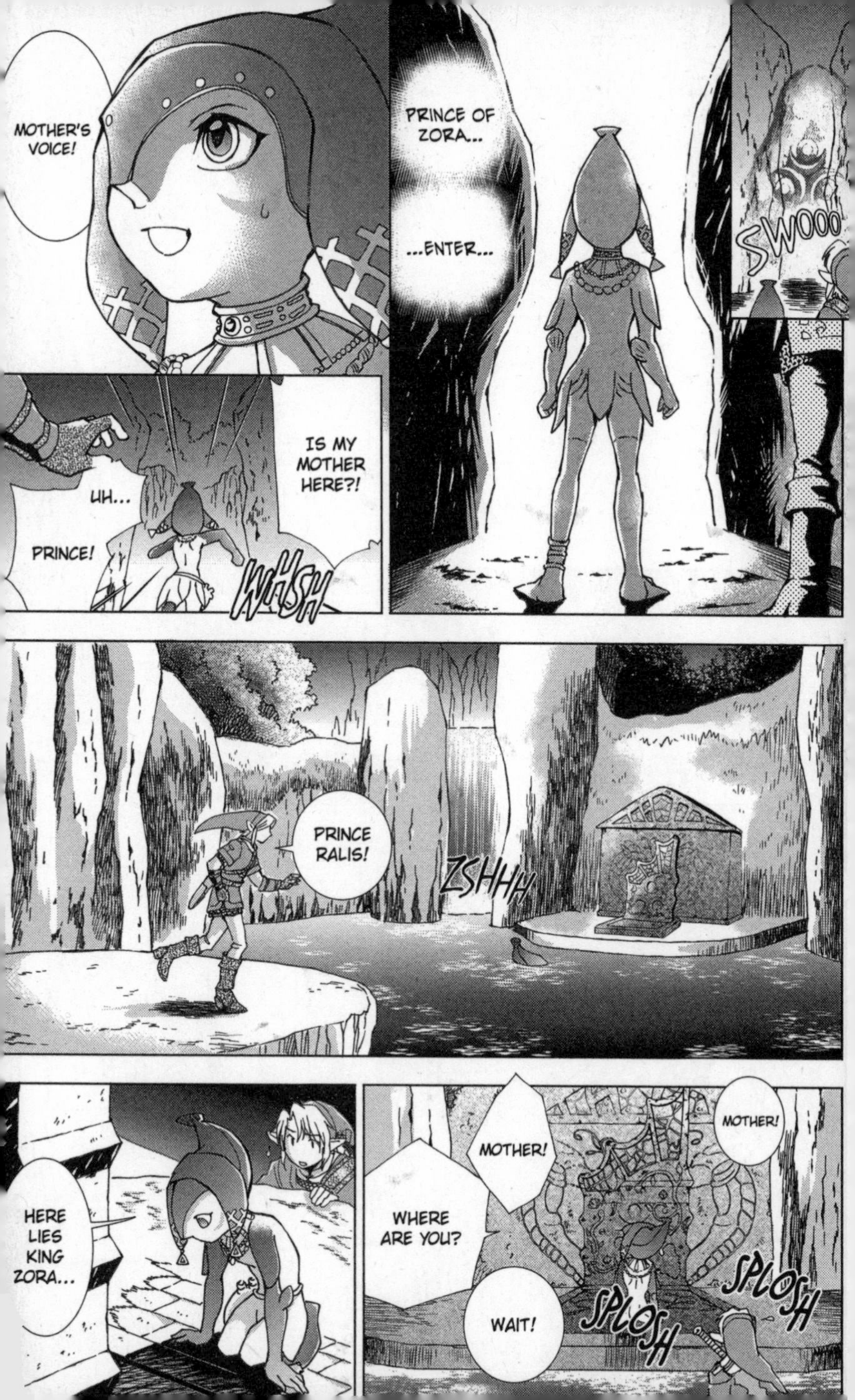
SWOOO
PRINCE OF ZORA...
...ENTER...
MOTHER'S VOICE!
IS MY MOTHER HERE?!
UH...
PRINCE!
WHSH
ZSHHH
PRINCE RALIS!
MOTHER!
MOTHER!
WHERE ARE YOU?
SPLOSH
SPLOSH
WAIT!
HERE LIES KING ZORA...

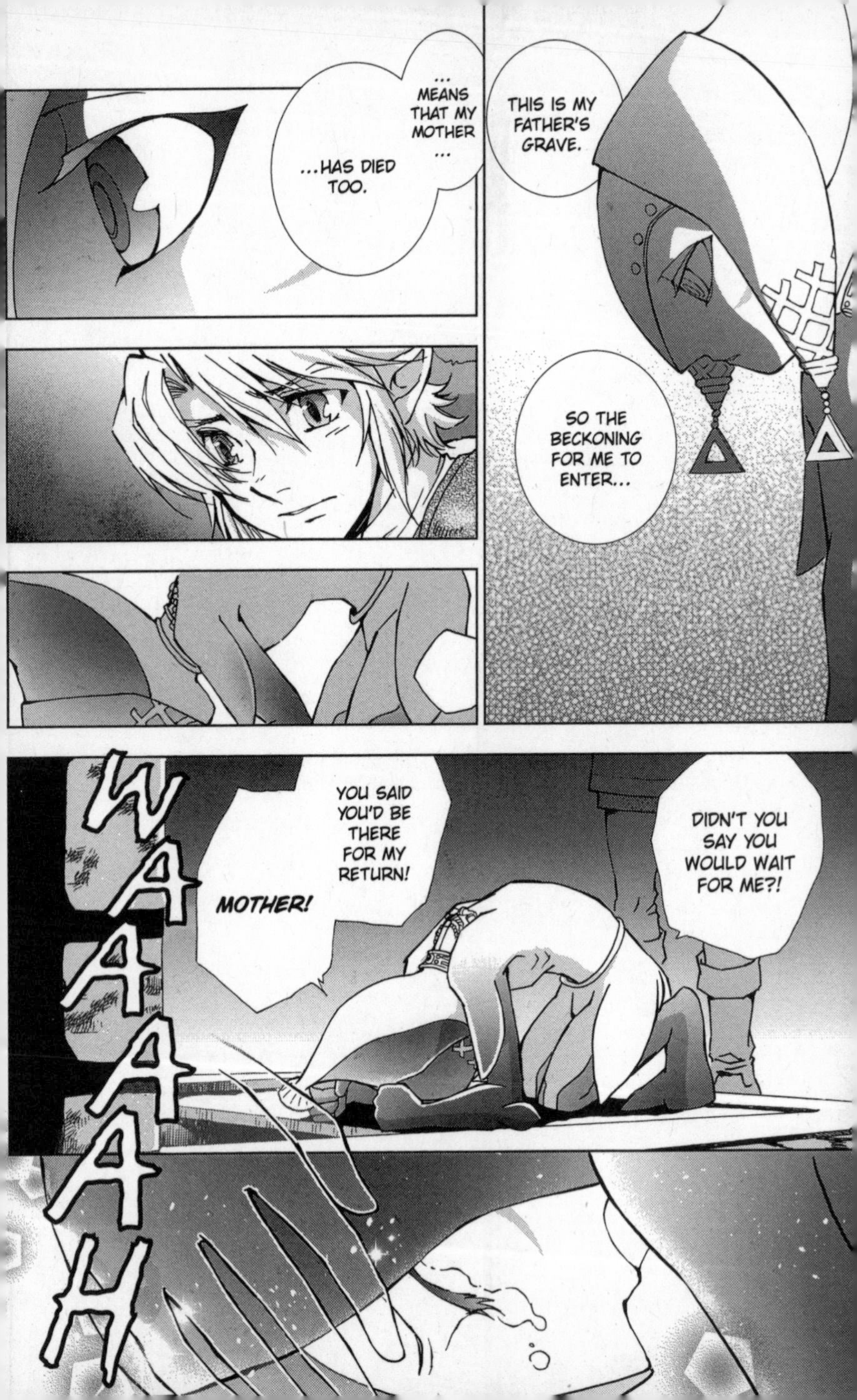
THIS IS MY FATHER'S GRAVE.
SO THE BECKONING FOR ME TO ENTER...
... MEANS THAT MY MOTHER ...
...HAS DIED TOO.
DIDN'T YOU SAY YOU WOULD WAIT FOR ME?!
YOU SAID YOU'D BE THERE FOR MY RETURN!
MOTHER!
WAAAAAH

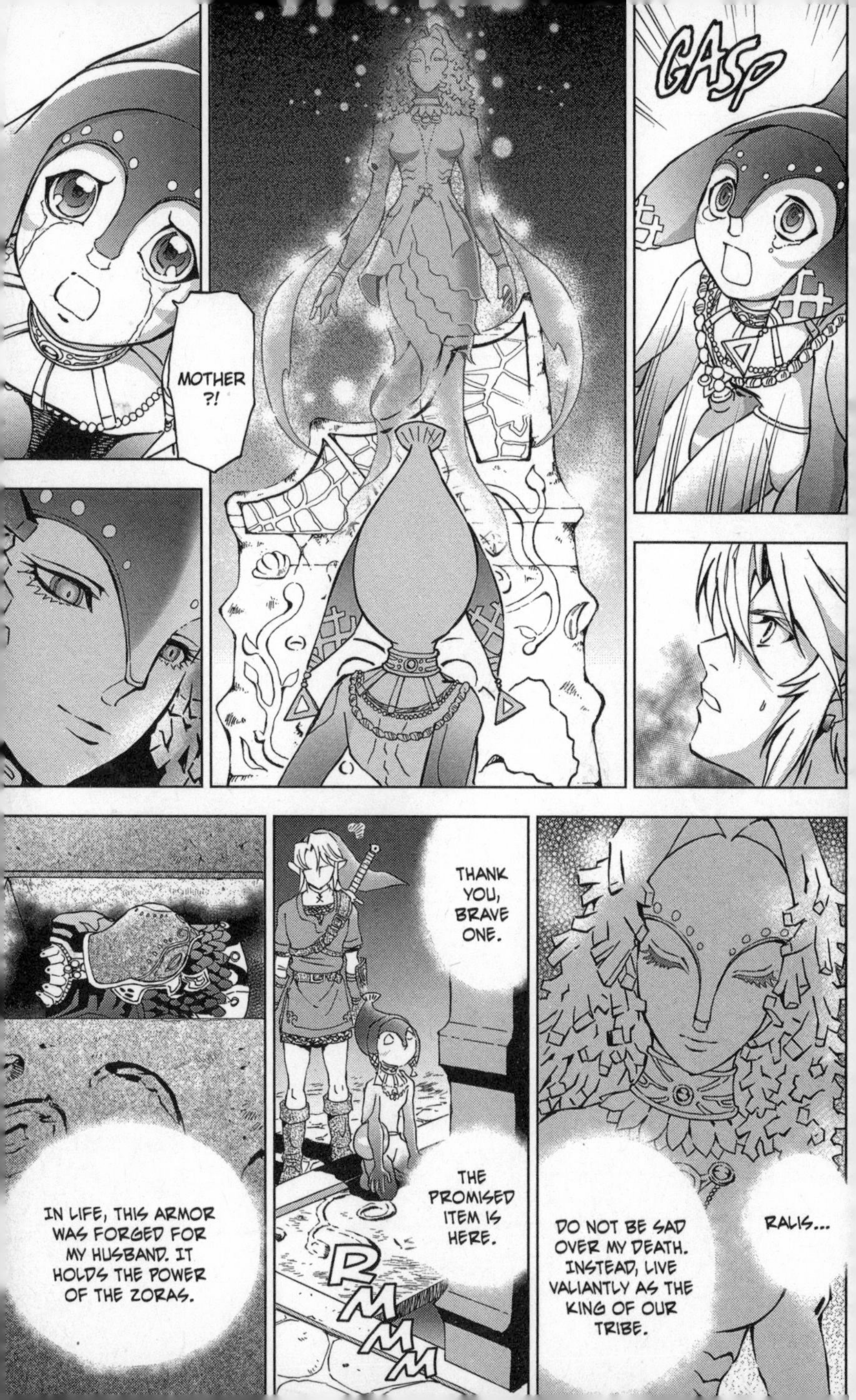
GASP
MOTHER ?!
RALIS...
DO NOT BE SAD OVER MY DEATH. INSTEAD, LIVE VALIANTLY AS THE KING OF OUR TRIBE.
THANK YOU, BRAVE ONE.
THE PROMISED ITEM IS HERE.
RMMM
IN LIFE, THIS ARMOR WAS FORGED FOR MY HUSBAND. IT HOLDS THE POWER OF THE ZORAS.

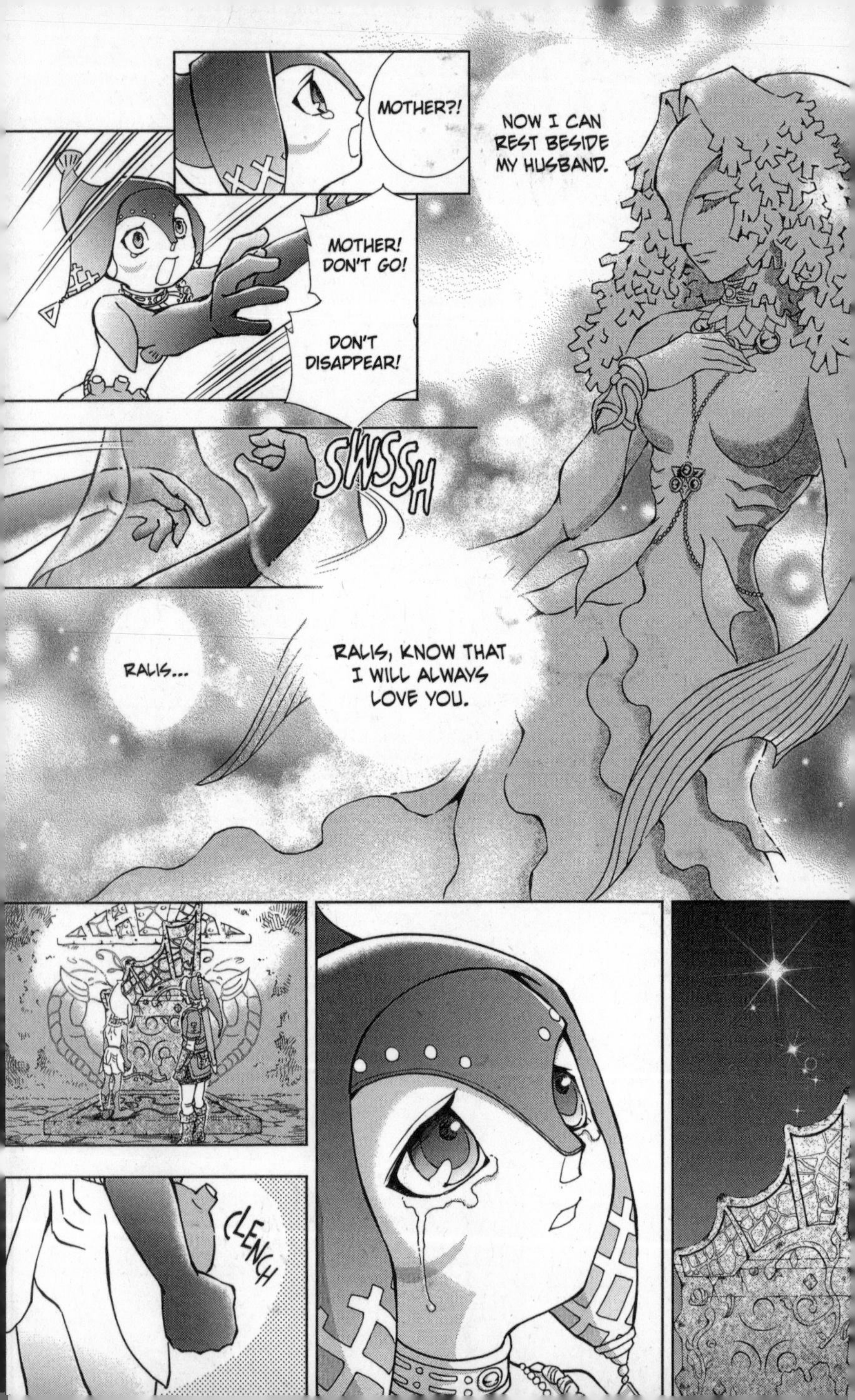
NOW I CAN REST BESIDE MY HUSBAND.
MOTHER?!
MOTHER! DON'T GO!
DON'T DISAPPEAR!
SWSSH
RALIS, KNOW THAT I WILL ALWAYS LOVE YOU.
RALIS...
CLENCH

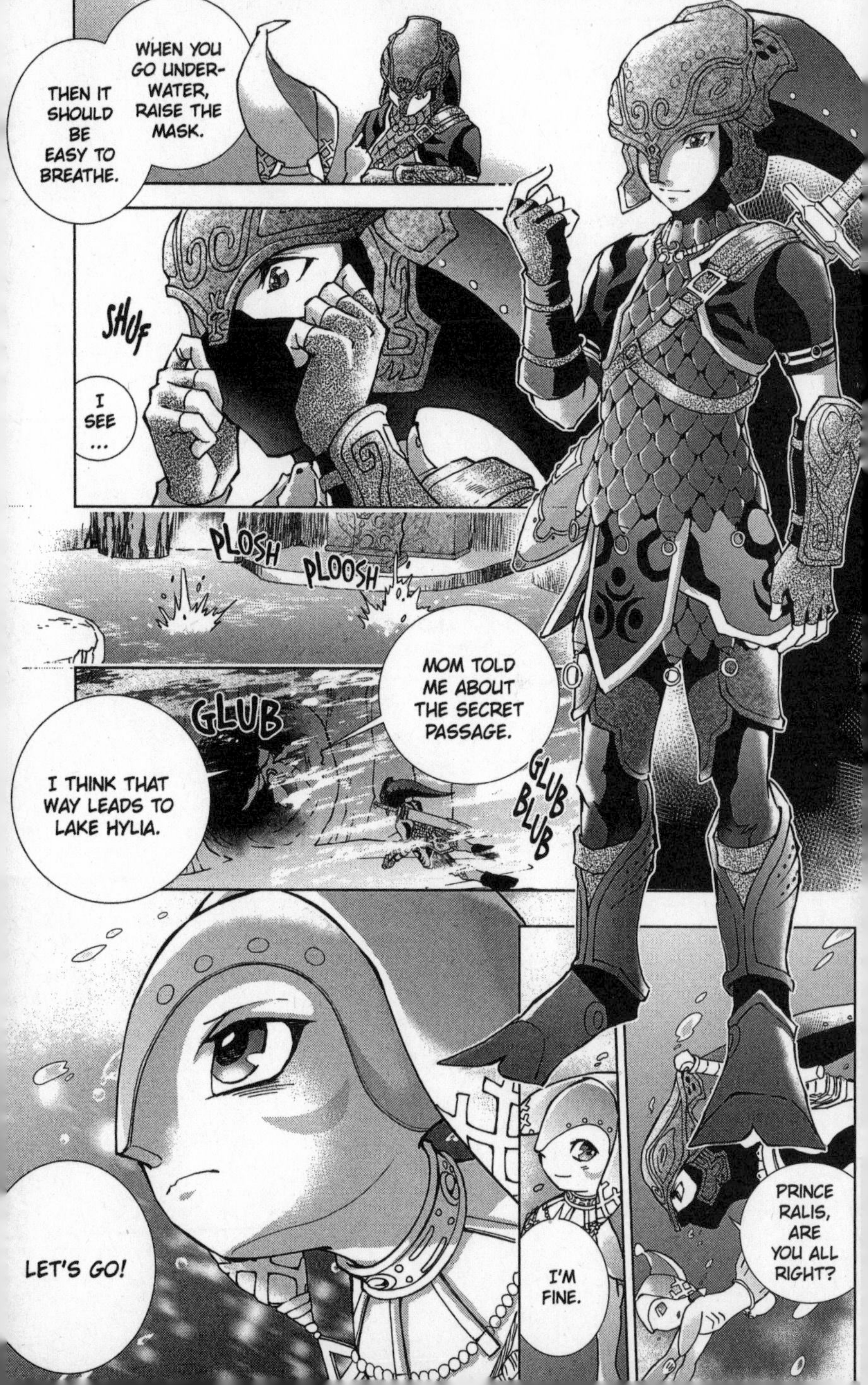
WHEN YOU GO UNDER-WATER, RAISE THE MASK.
THEN IT SHOULD BE EASY TO BREATHE.
SHUF
I SEE ...
PLOSH
PLOOSH
MOM TOLD ME ABOUT THE SECRET PASSAGE.
GLUB
GLUB BLUB
I THINK THAT WAY LEADS TO LAKE HYLIA.
PRINCE RALIS, ARE YOU ALL RIGHT?
I'M FINE.
LET'S GO!

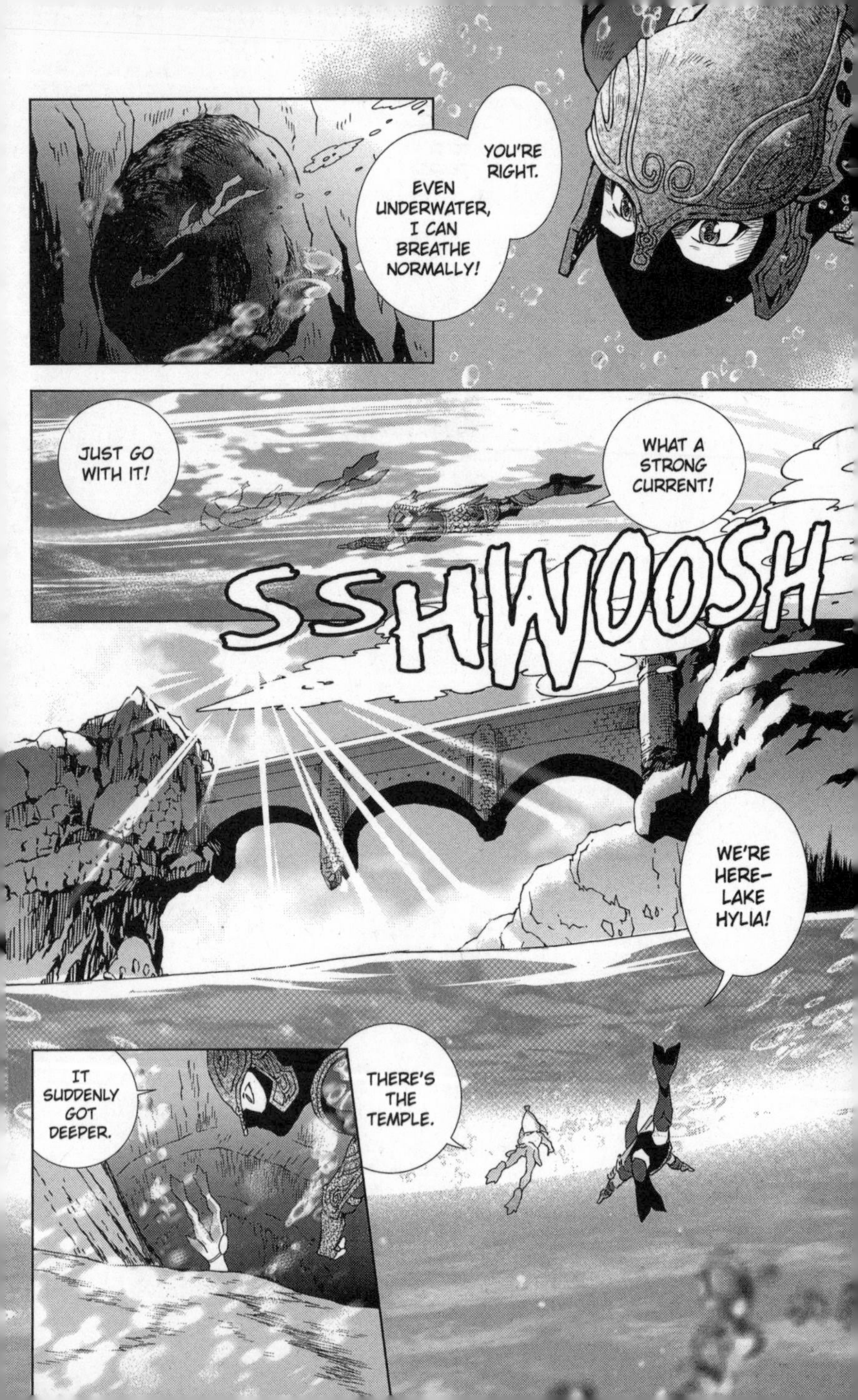
YOU'RE RIGHT.
EVEN UNDERWATER, I CAN BREATHE NORMALLY!
WHAT A STRONG CURRENT!
JUST GO WITH IT!
SSHWOOSH
WE'RE HERE—LAKE HYLIA!
THERE'S THE TEMPLE.
IT SUDDENLY GOT DEEPER.

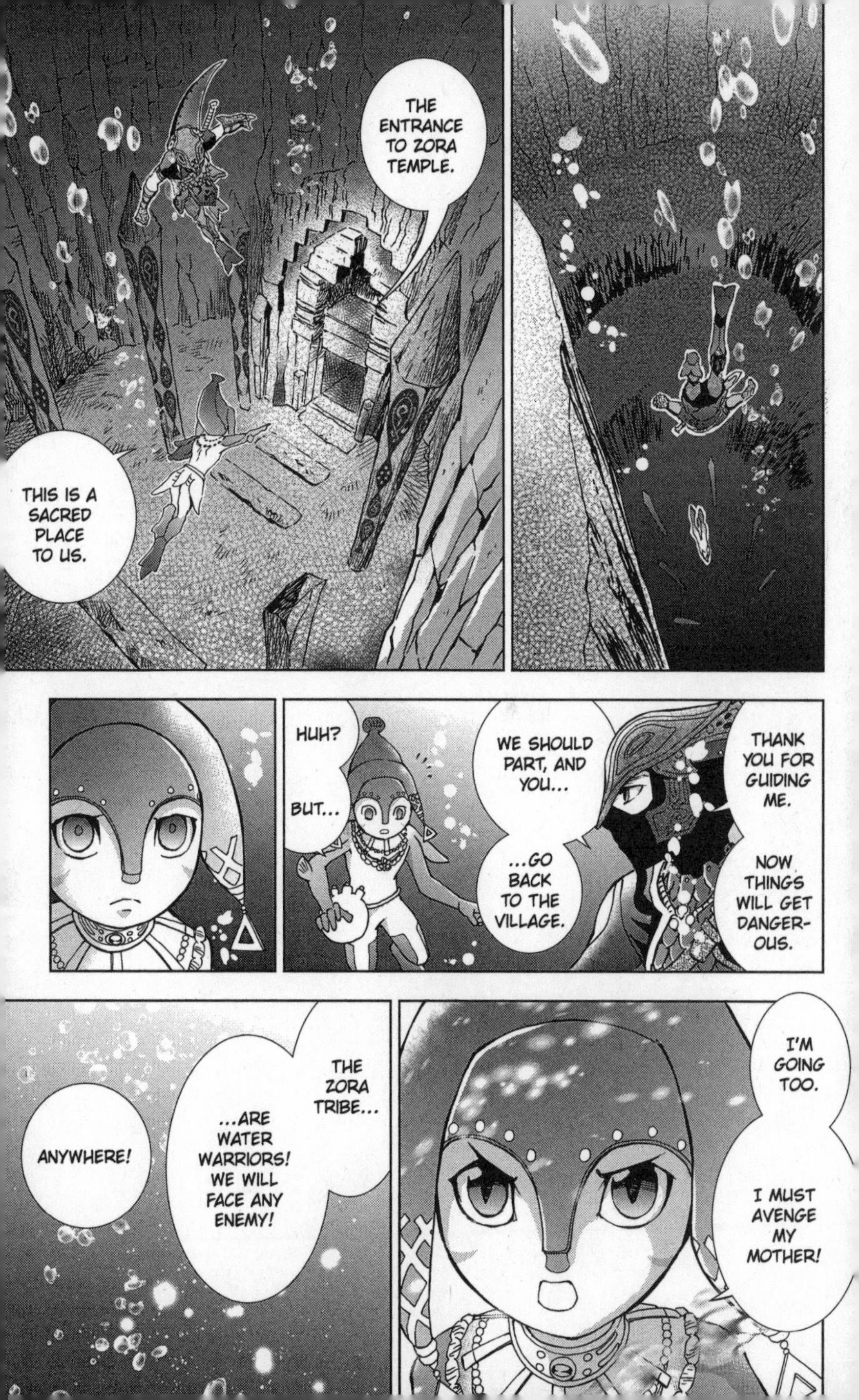
THE ENTRANCE TO ZORA TEMPLE.
THIS IS A SACRED PLACE TO US.
THANK YOU FOR GUIDING ME.
NOW THINGS WILL GET DANGER-OUS.
WE SHOULD PART, AND YOU...
...GO BACK TO THE VILLAGE.
HUH?
BUT...
I'M GOING TOO.
I MUST AVENGE MY MOTHER!
THE ZORA TRIBE...
...ARE WATER WARRIORS! WE WILL FACE ANY ENEMY!
ANYWHERE!

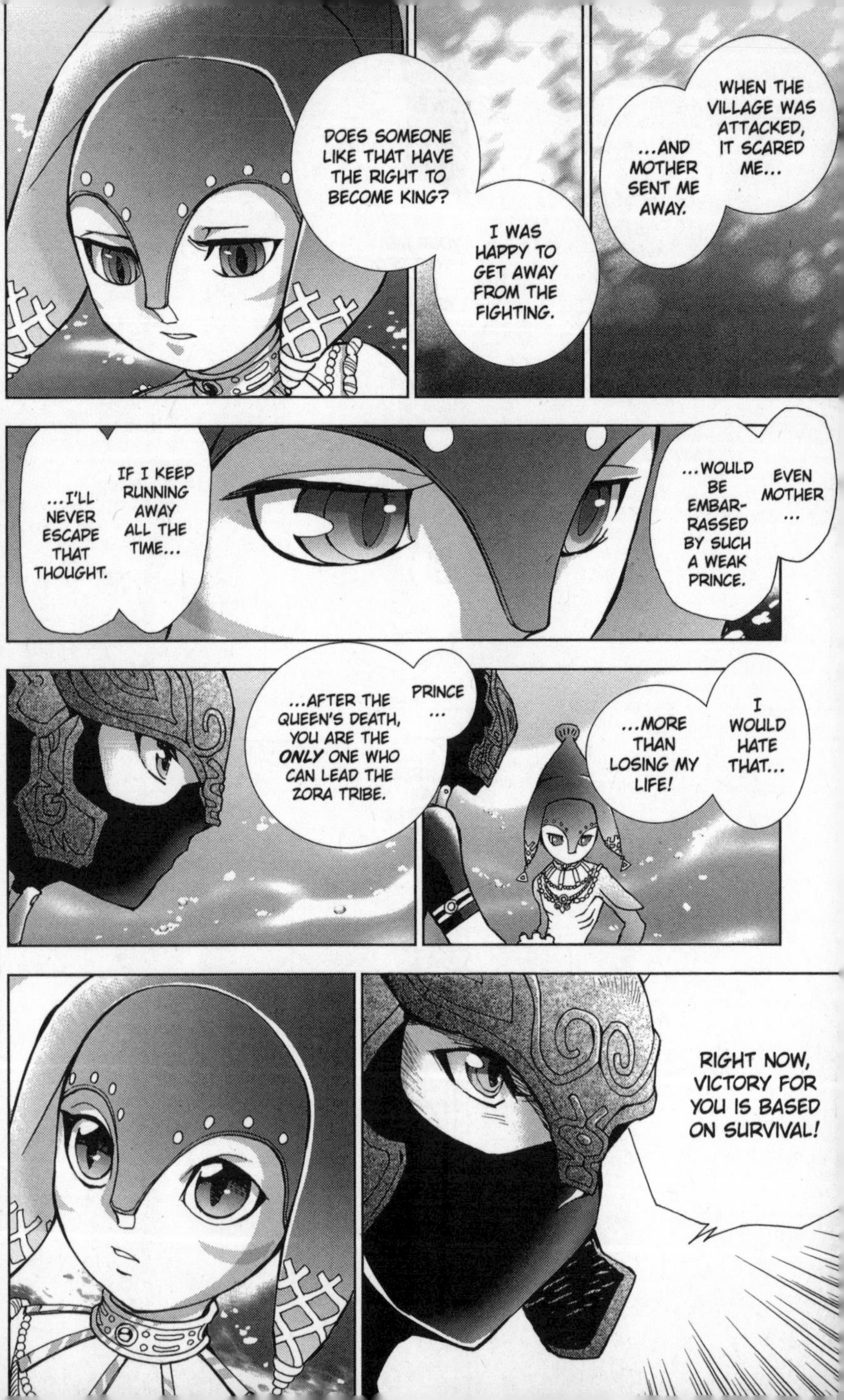
WHEN THE VILLAGE WAS ATTACKED, IT SCARED ME...
...AND MOTHER SENT ME AWAY.
I WAS HAPPY TO GET AWAY FROM THE FIGHTING.
DOES SOMEONE LIKE THAT HAVE THE RIGHT TO BECOME KING?
EVEN MOTHER...
...WOULD BE EMBAR-RASSED BY SUCH A WEAK PRINCE.
IF I KEEP RUNNING AWAY ALL THE TIME...
...I'LL NEVER ESCAPE THAT THOUGHT.
I WOULD HATE THAT...
...MORE THAN LOSING MY LIFE!
PRINCE...
...AFTER THE QUEEN'S DEATH, YOU ARE THE *ONLY* ONE WHO CAN LEAD THE ZORA TRIBE.
RIGHT NOW, VICTORY FOR YOU IS BASED ON SURVIVAL!

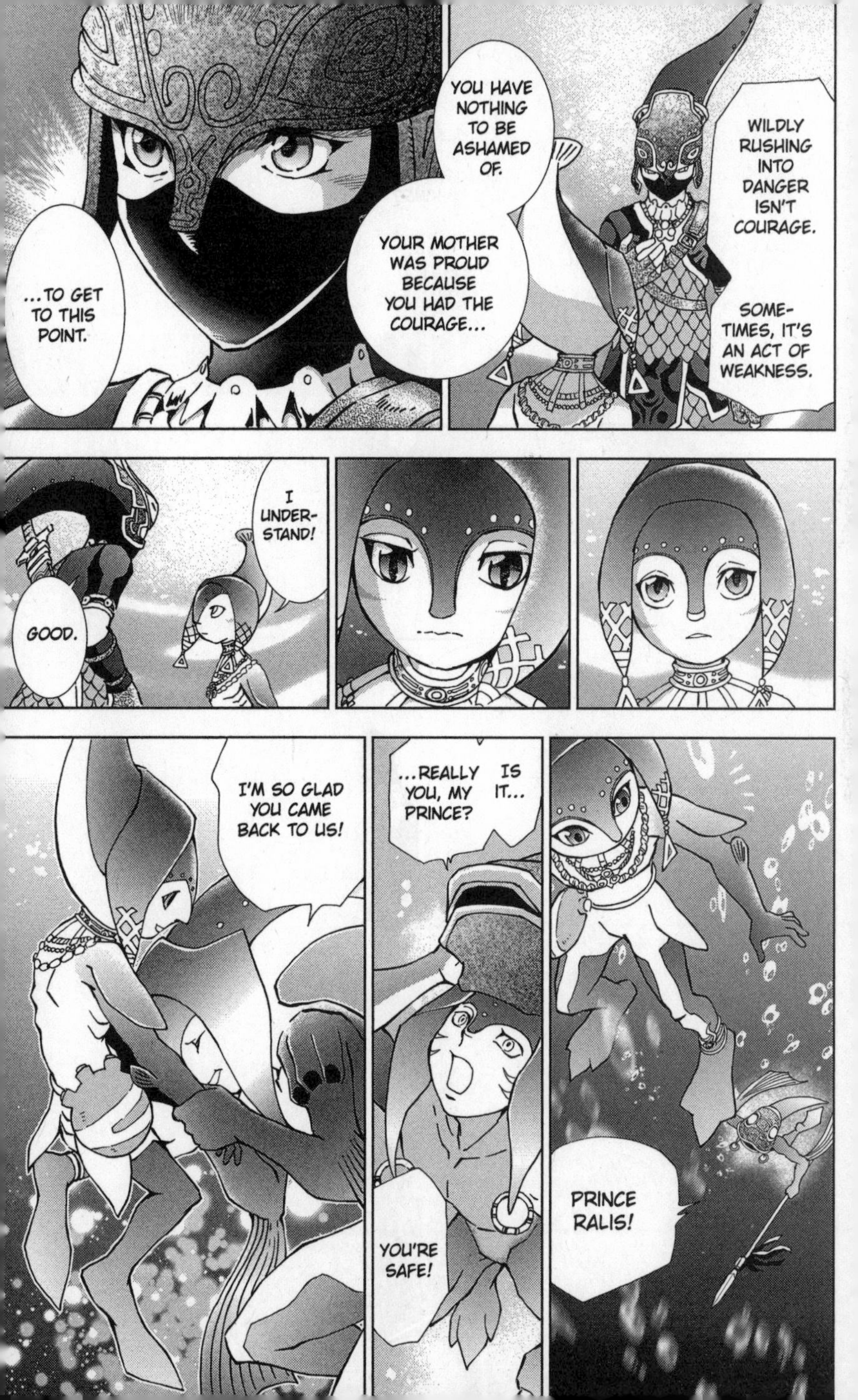
WILDLY RUSHING INTO DANGER ISN'T COURAGE.
SOMETIMES, IT'S AN ACT OF WEAKNESS.
YOU HAVE NOTHING TO BE ASHAMED OF.
YOUR MOTHER WAS PROUD BECAUSE YOU HAD THE COURAGE...
...TO GET TO THIS POINT.
I UNDERSTAND!
GOOD.
PRINCE RALIS!
IS IT...
...REALLY YOU, MY PRINCE?
YOU'RE SAFE!
I'M SO GLAD YOU CAME BACK TO US!

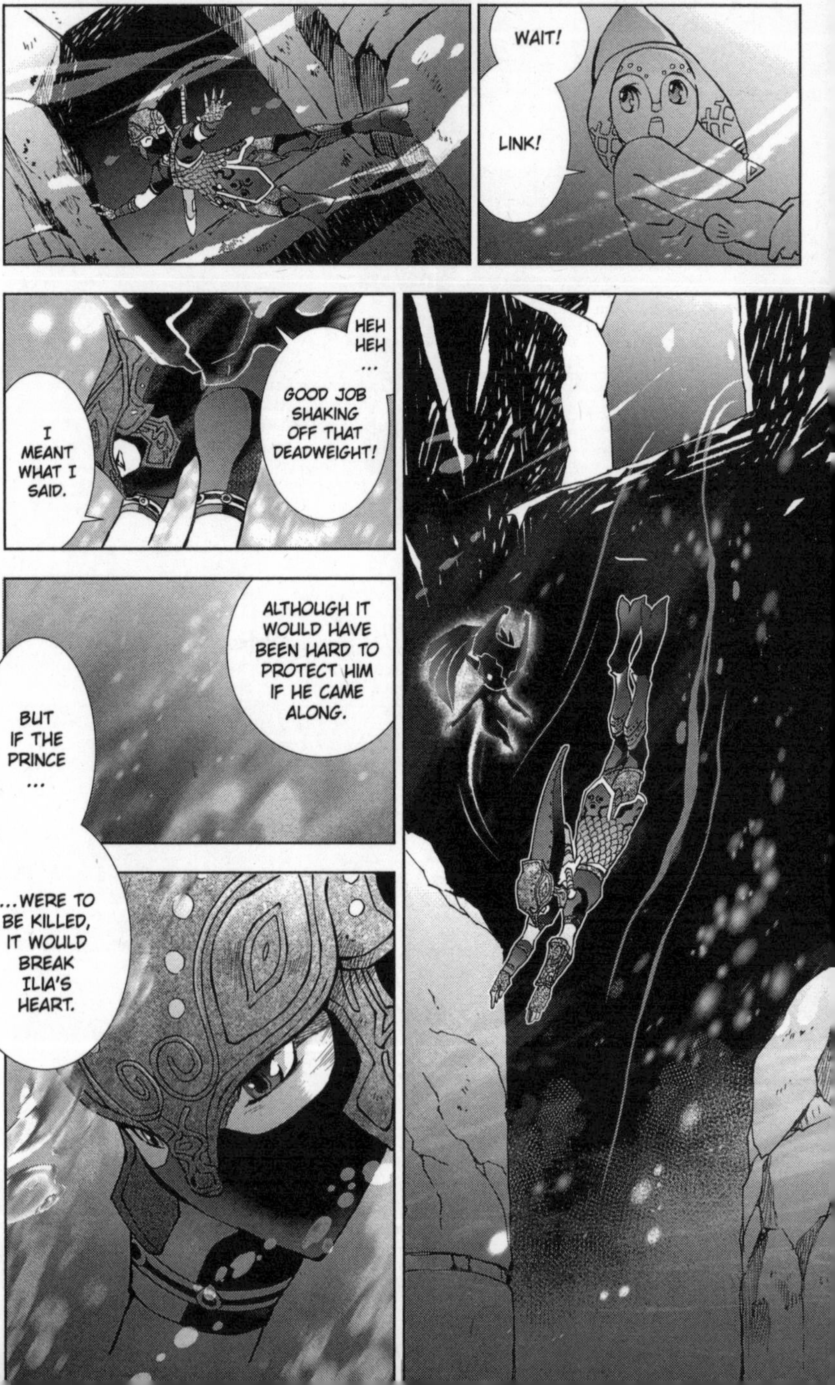
WAIT!
LINK!
HEH HEH ...
GOOD JOB SHAKING OFF THAT DEADWEIGHT!
I MEANT WHAT I SAID.
ALTHOUGH IT WOULD HAVE BEEN HARD TO PROTECT HIM IF HE CAME ALONG.
BUT IF THE PRINCE ...
...WERE TO BE KILLED, IT WOULD BREAK ILIA'S HEART.

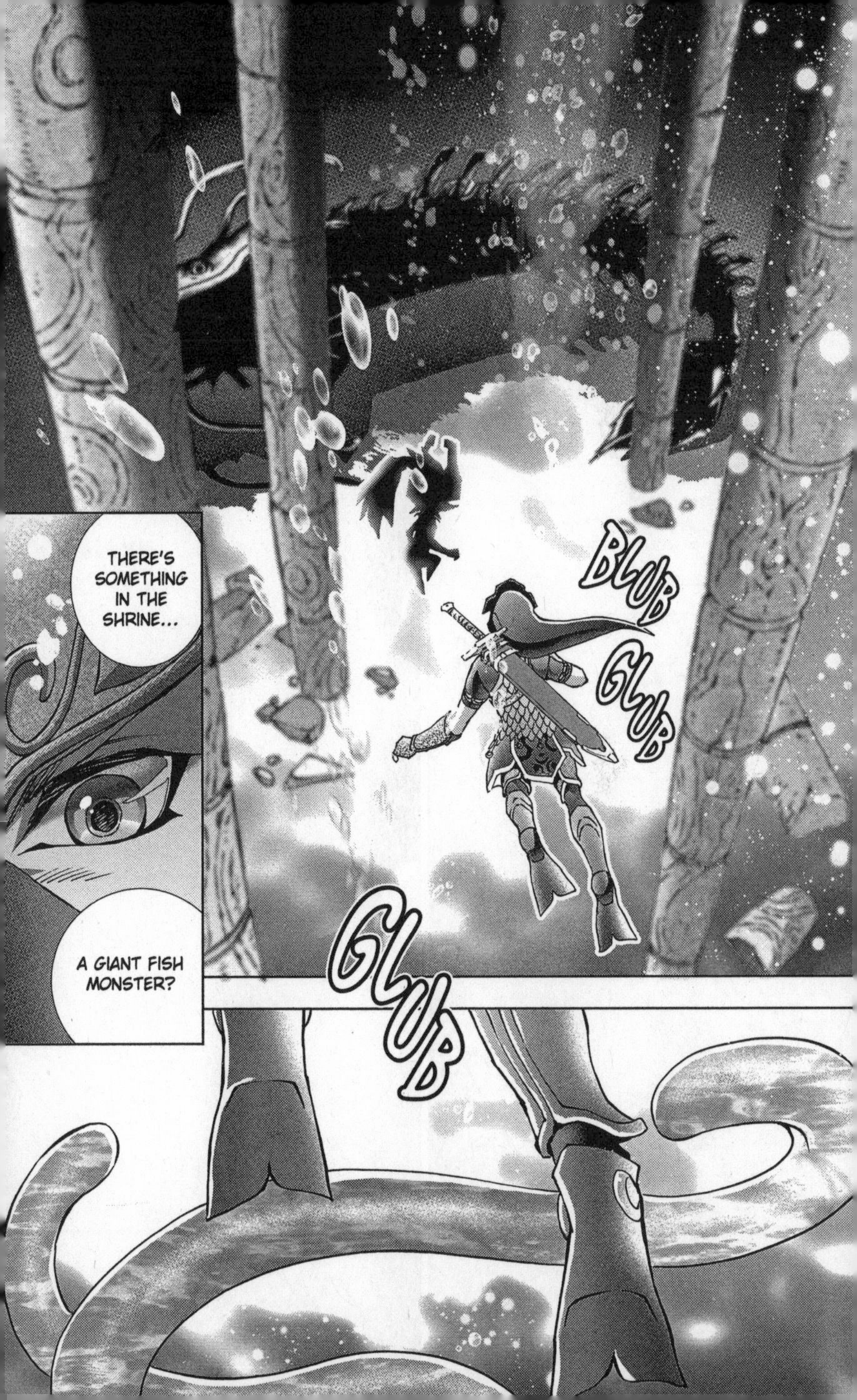
BLUB
GLUB
GLUB
THERE'S SOMETHING IN THE SHRINE...
A GIANT FISH MONSTER?

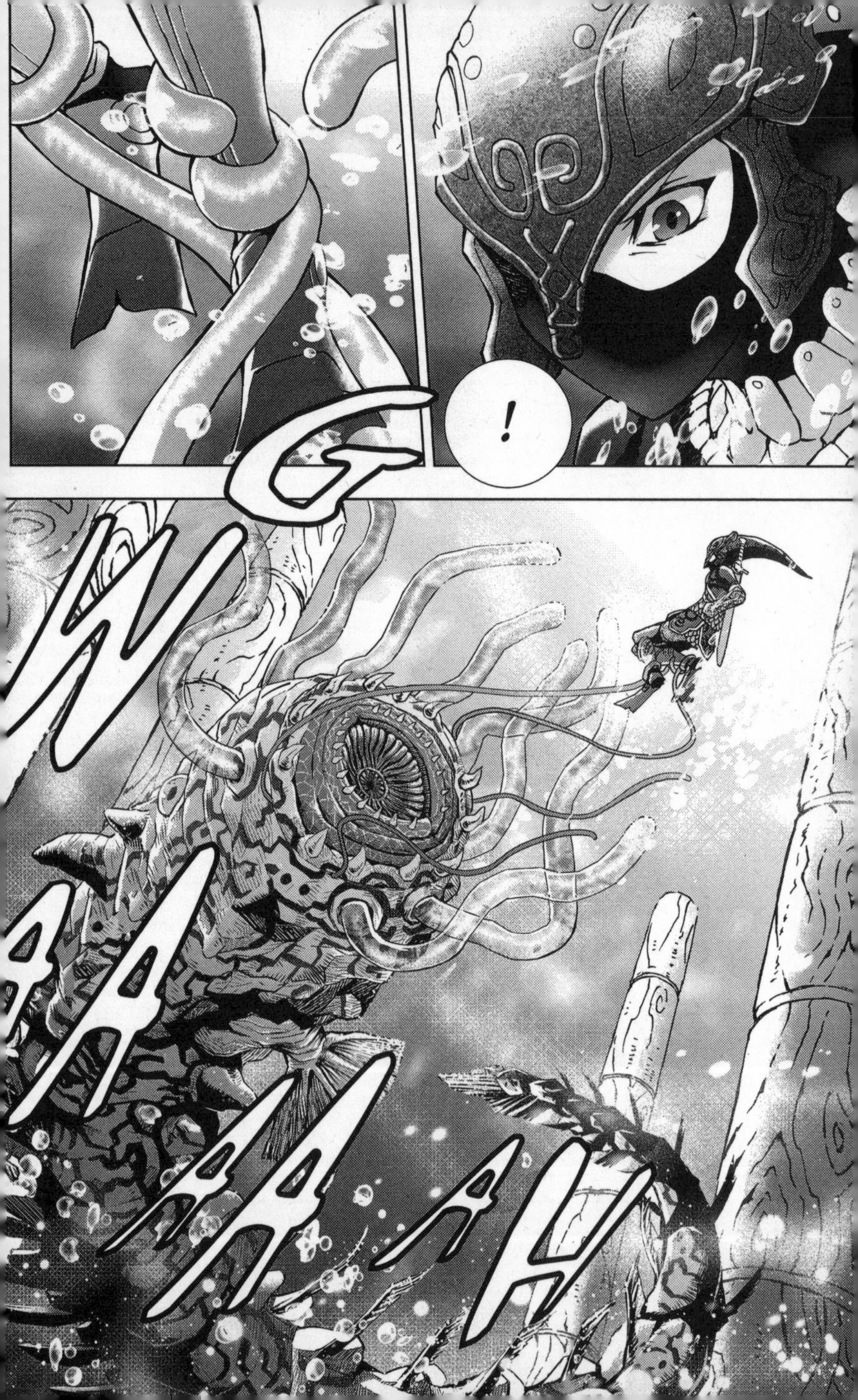
!
GWAAAAH

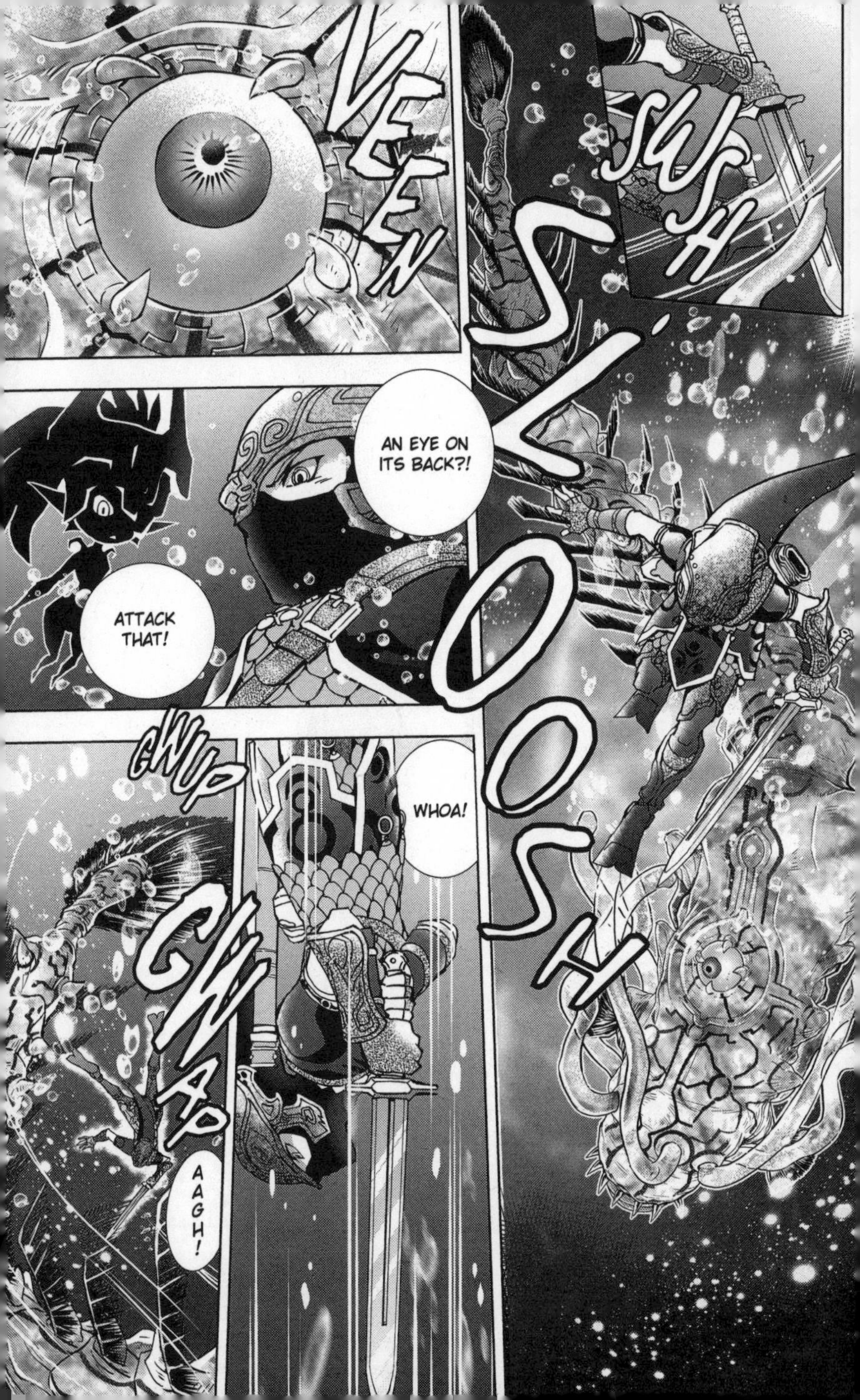
SLISH
VEEN
SWOOSH
AN EYE ON ITS BACK?!
ATTACK THAT!
WHOA!
GWUP
CHAP
AAGH!

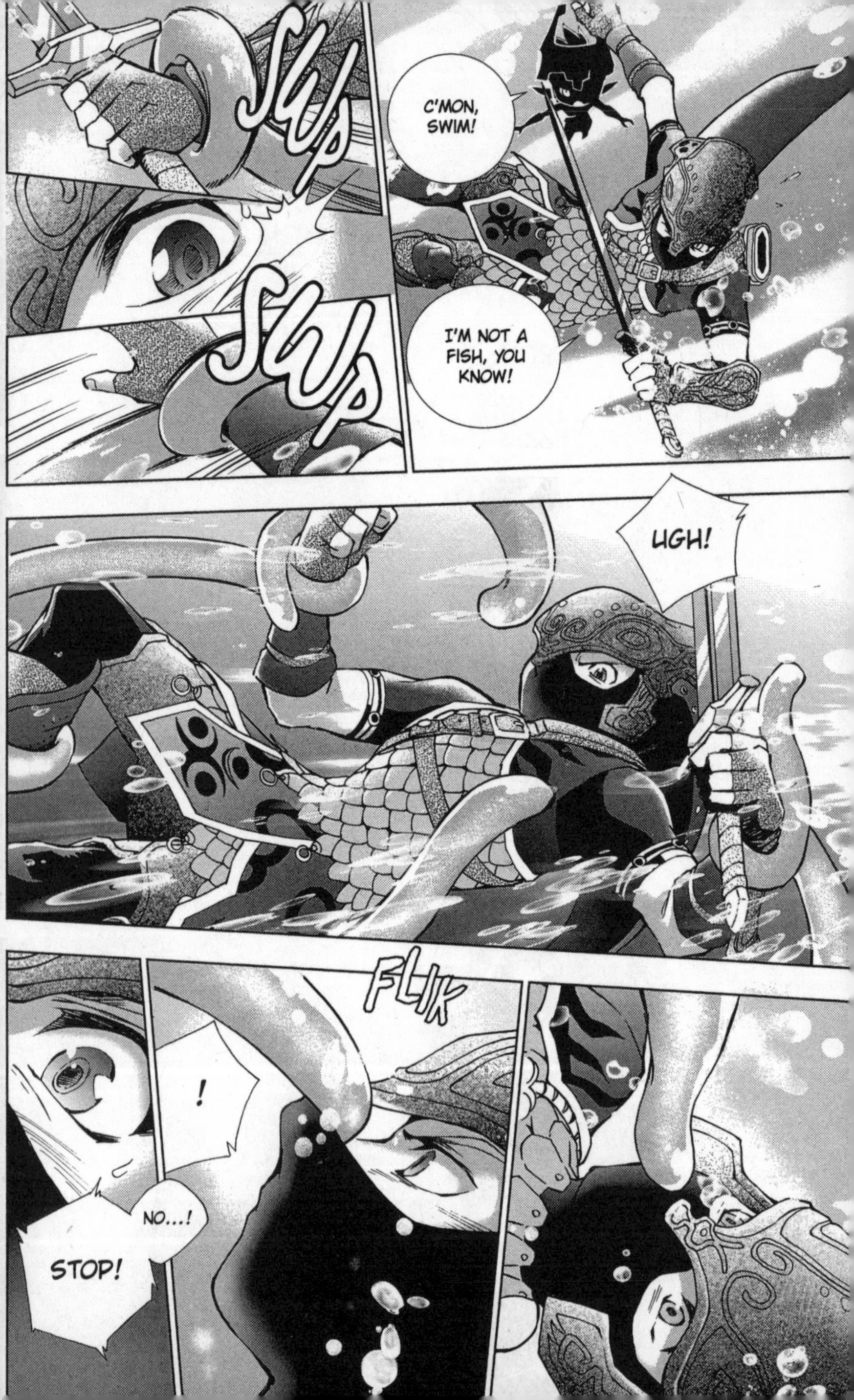
C'MON, SWIM!
I'M NOT A FISH, YOU KNOW!
SLIP
SLIP
UGH!
FLIK
!
NO...!
STOP!

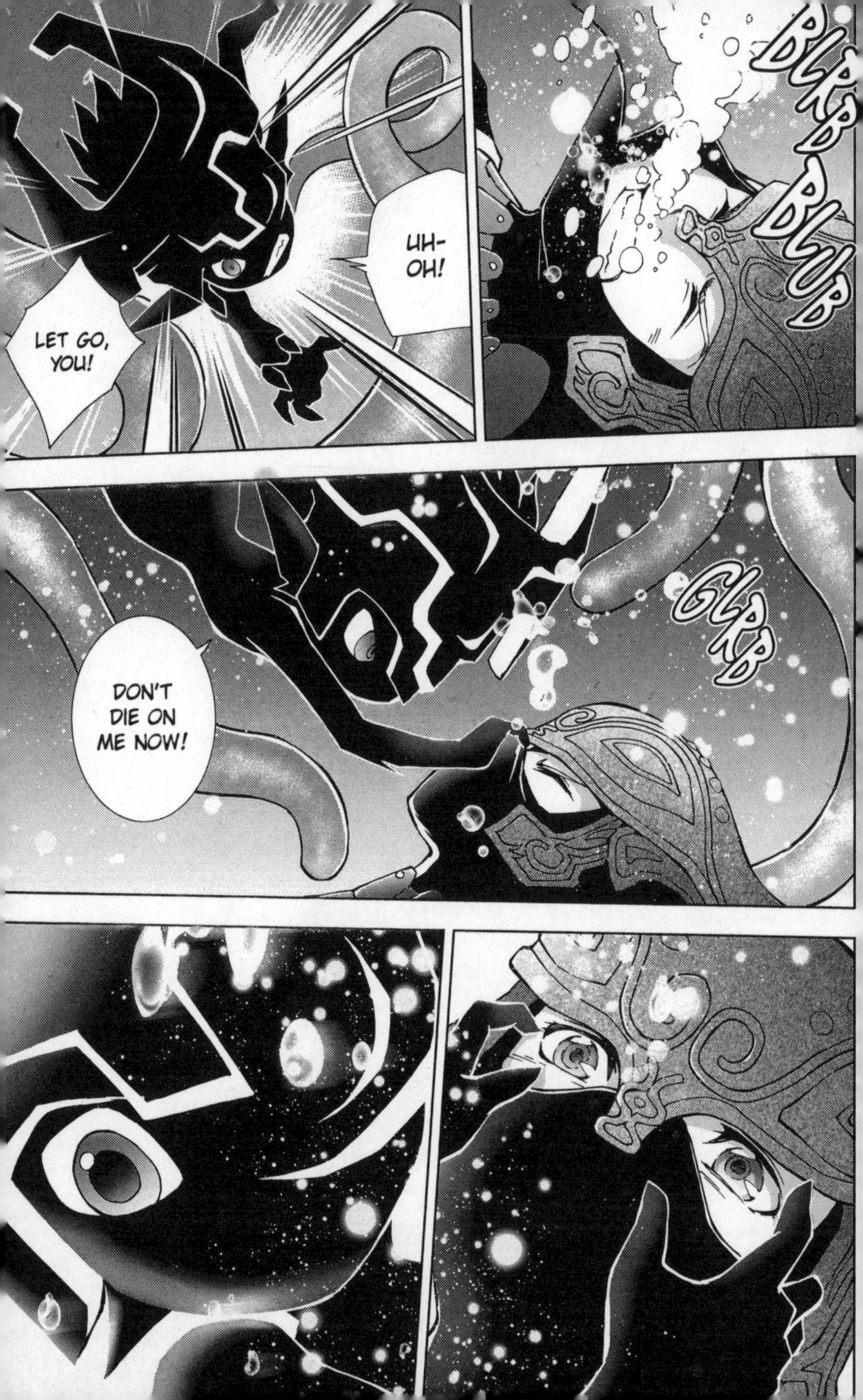
BLRB BLUB
UH-OH!
LET GO, YOU!
GLRB
DON'T DIE ON ME NOW!

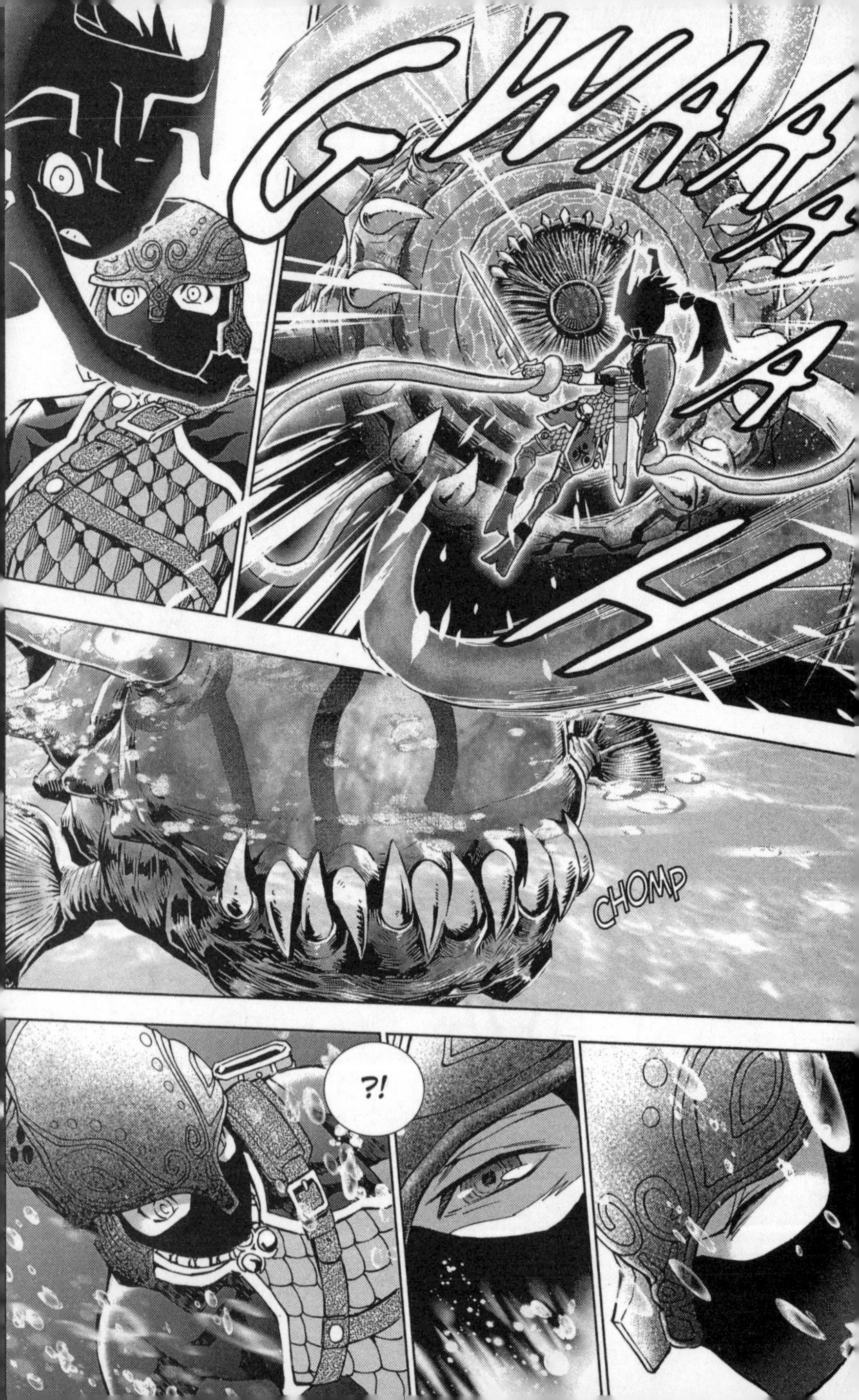
GWAAAAH
CHOMP
?!

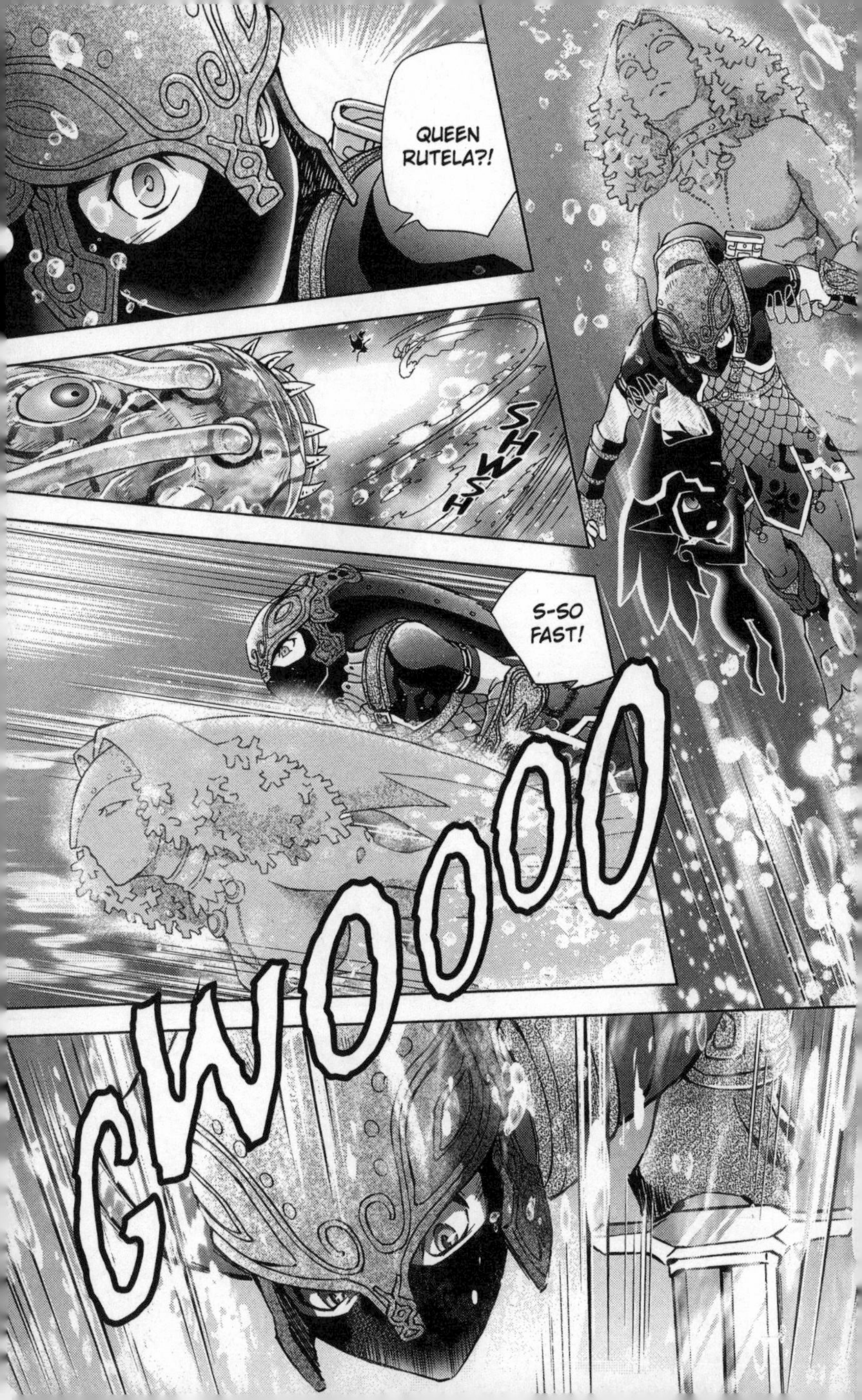
QUEEN RUTELA?!
SHWSH
S-SO FAST!
GWOOOOOO

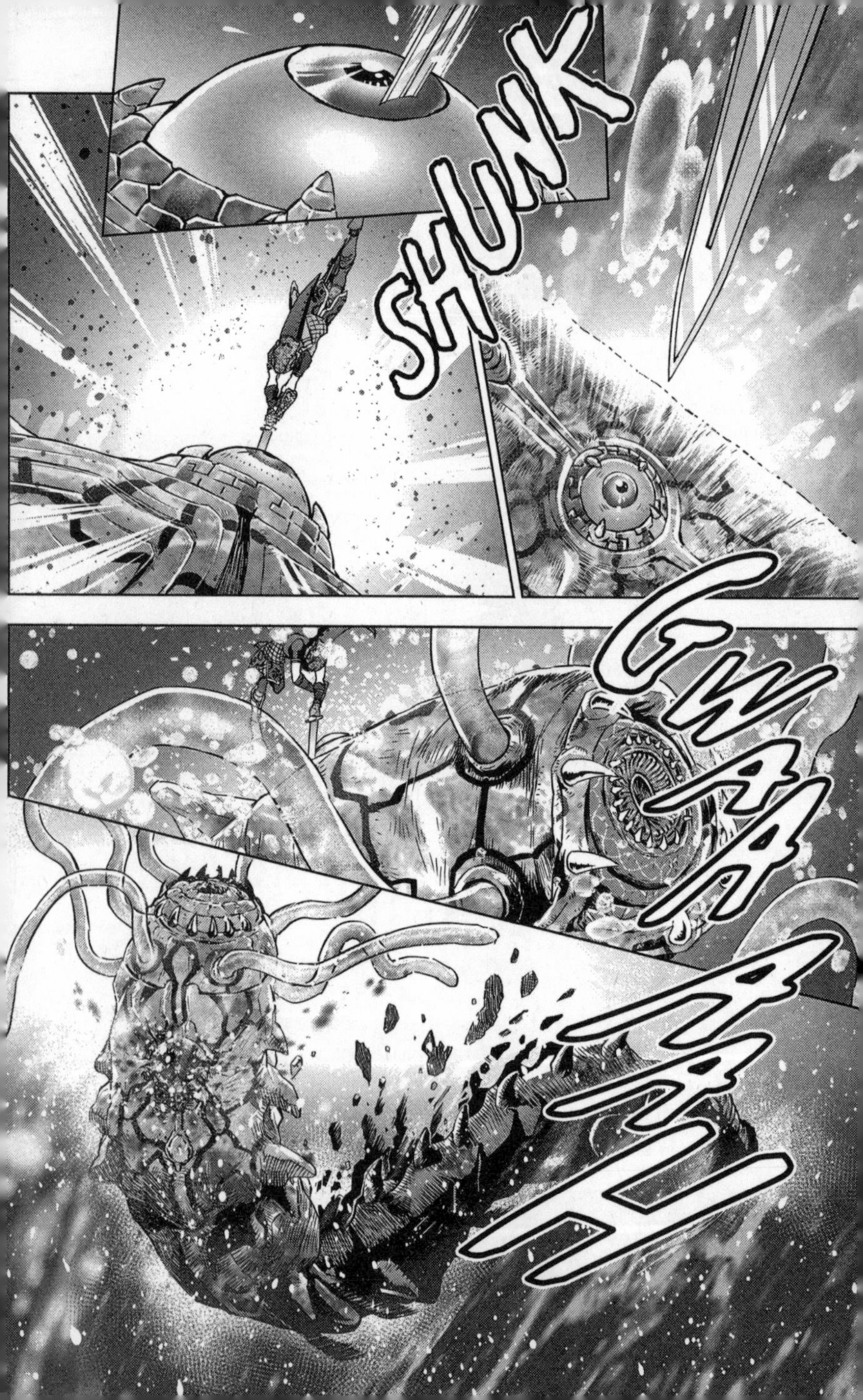
SHUNK
GWAAAAAAAH

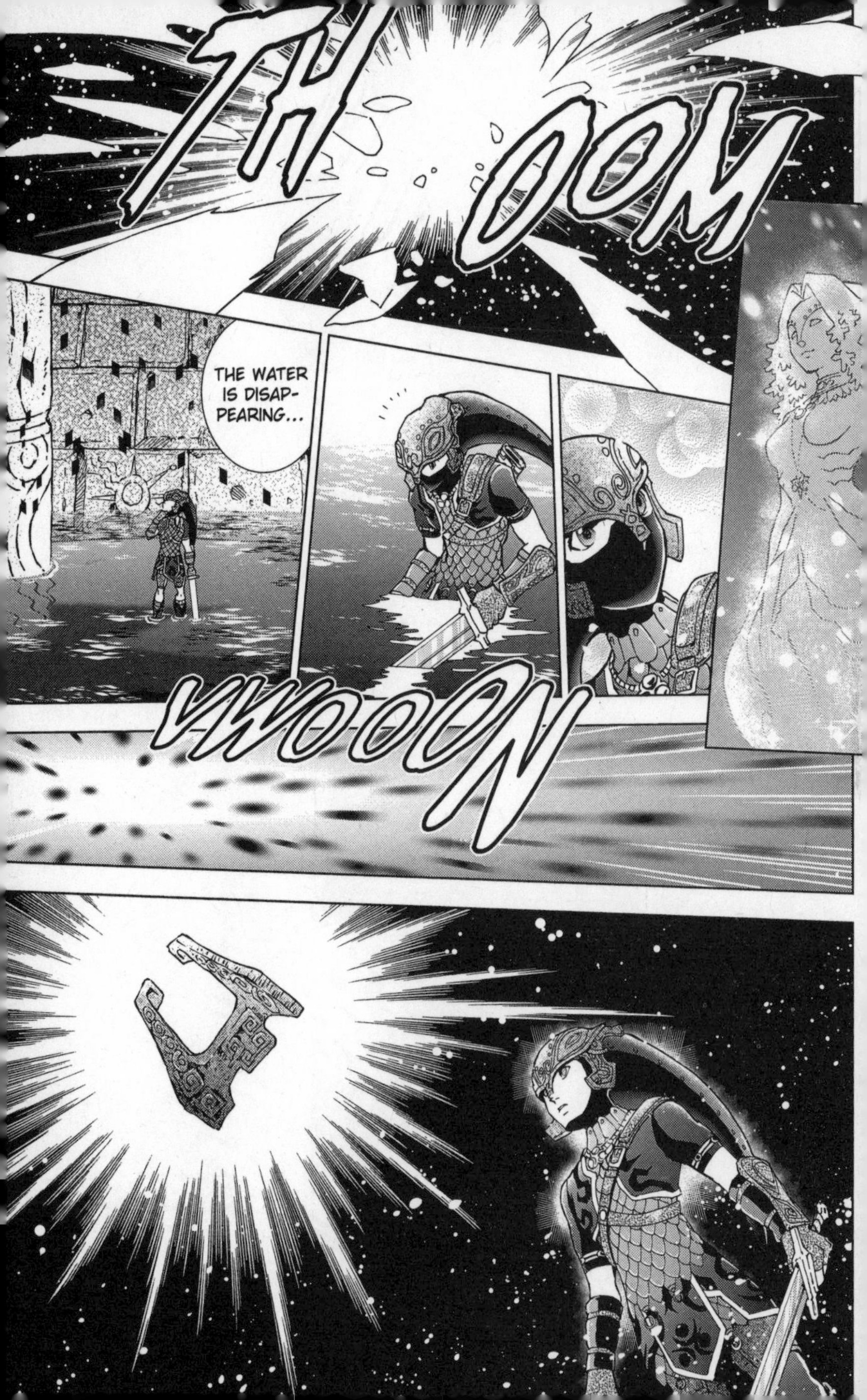
THOOM
THE WATER IS DISAP-PEARING...
VWOOON

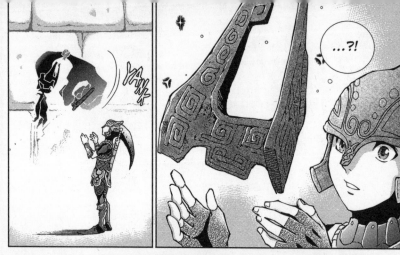

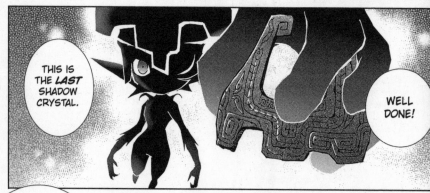

...?!
YANK
WELL DONE!
THIS IS THE *LAST* SHADOW CRYSTAL.
MIDNA, IT'S...
...THE SAME SHAPE AS YOUR CROWN.
SWIP
NEVER MIND THAT.
WHAT DO YOU MEAN, "NEVER MIND"?

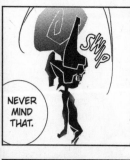

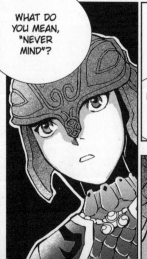

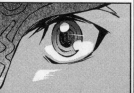

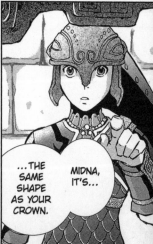

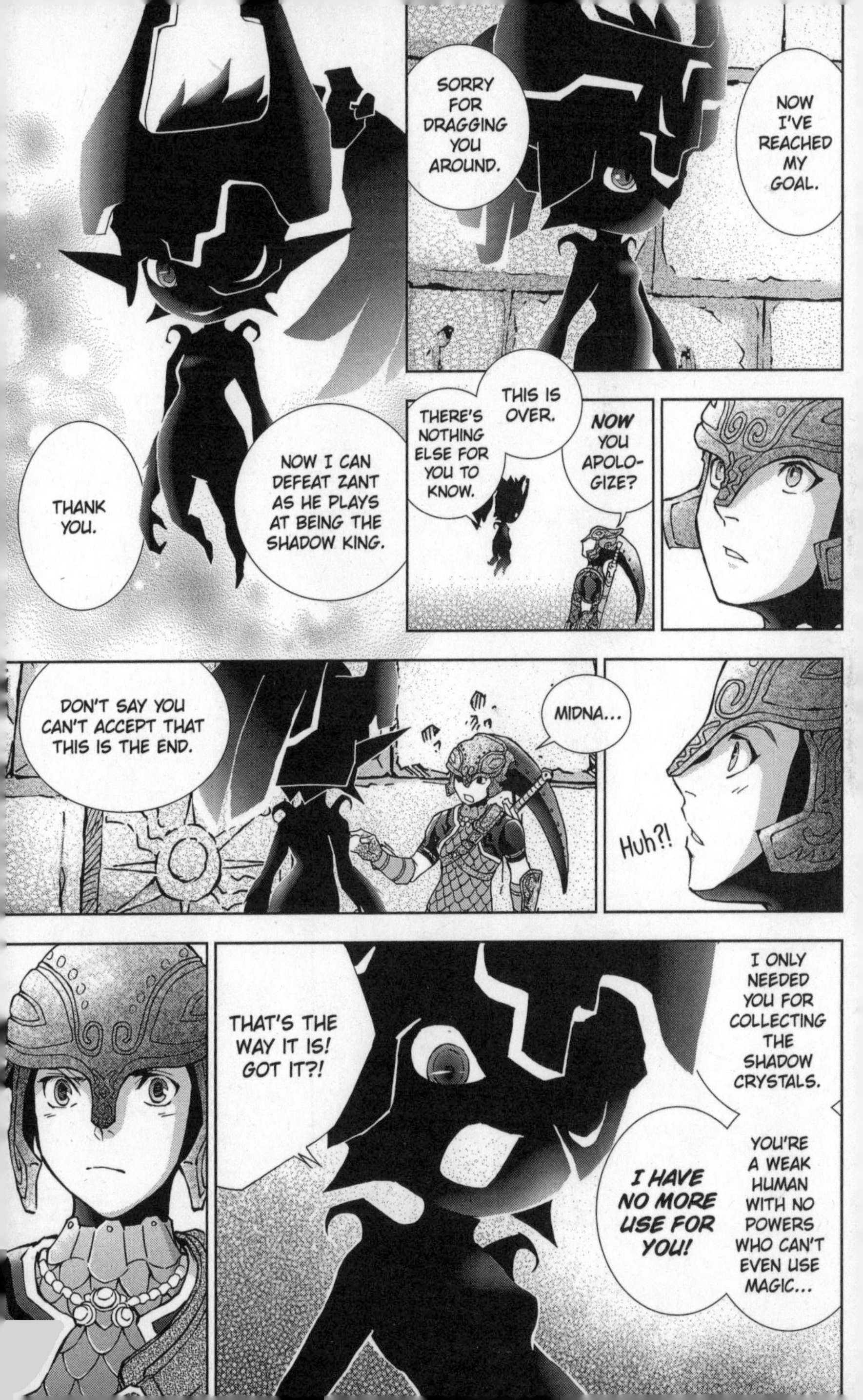
NOW I'VE REACHED MY GOAL.
SORRY FOR DRAGGING YOU AROUND.
NOW YOU APOLOGIZE?
THIS IS OVER.
THERE'S NOTHING ELSE FOR YOU TO KNOW.
NOW I CAN DEFEAT ZANT AS HE PLAYS AT BEING THE SHADOW KING.
THANK YOU.
Huh?!
MIDNA...
DON'T SAY YOU CAN'T ACCEPT THAT THIS IS THE END.
I ONLY NEEDED YOU FOR COLLECTING THE SHADOW CRYSTALS.
YOU'RE A WEAK HUMAN WITH NO POWERS WHO CAN'T EVEN USE MAGIC...
I HAVE NO MORE USE FOR YOU!
THAT'S THE WAY IT IS! GOT IT?!

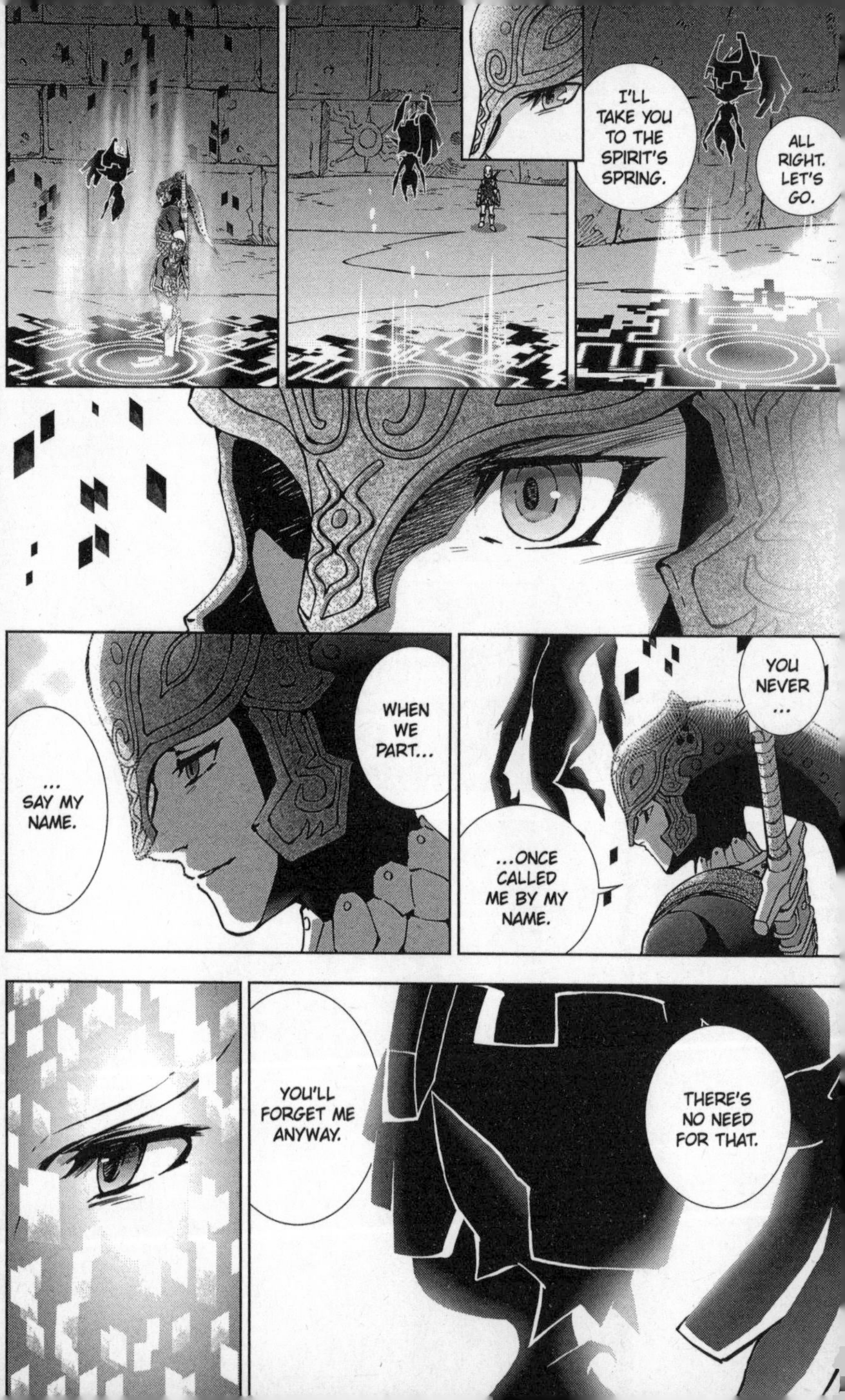
I'LL TAKE YOU TO THE SPIRIT'S SPRING.
ALL RIGHT. LET'S GO.
YOU NEVER ...
...ONCE CALLED ME BY MY NAME.
WHEN WE PART...
... SAY MY NAME.
THERE'S NO NEED FOR THAT.
YOU'LL FORGET ME ANYWAY.

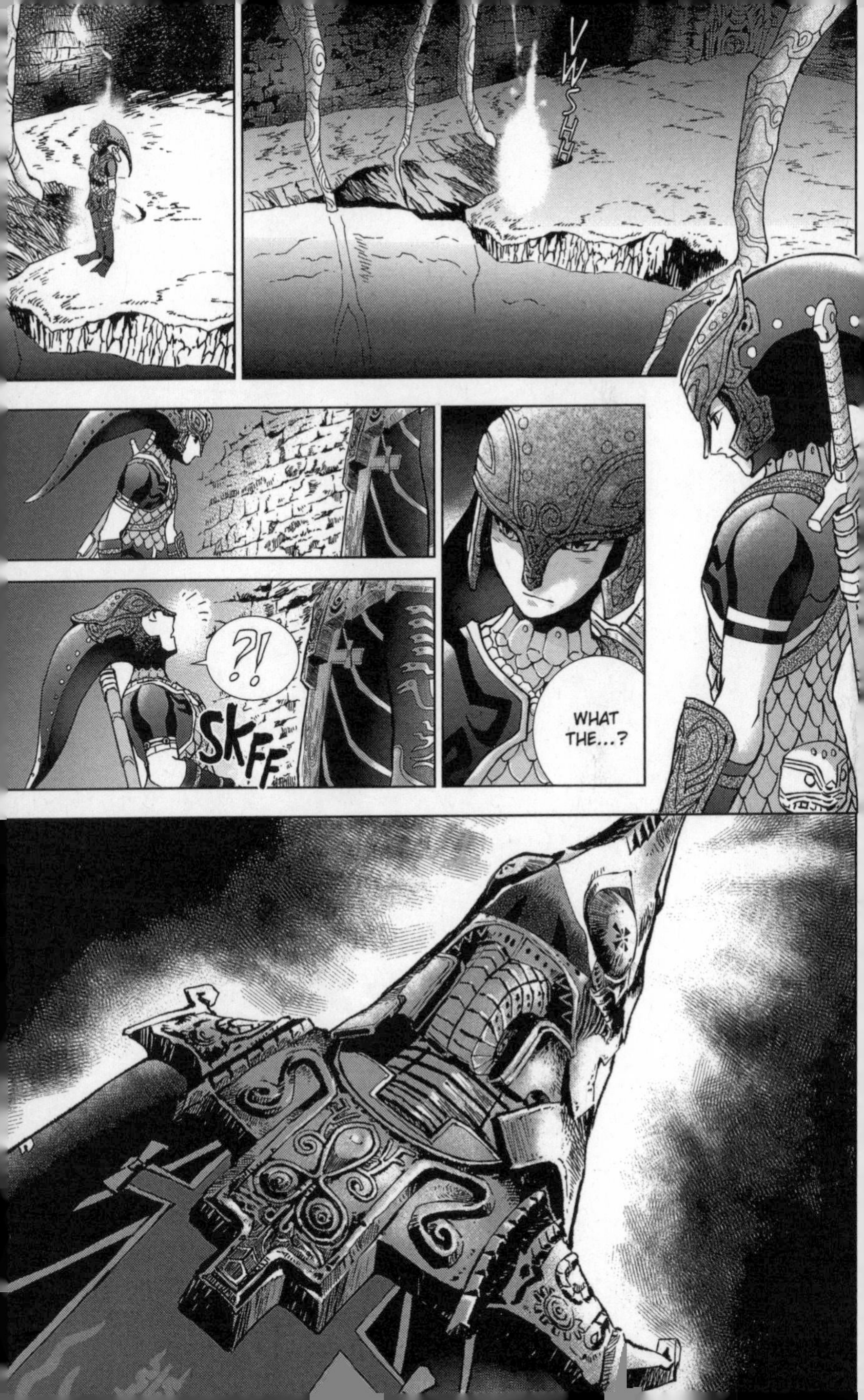
VWSHH
WHAT THE...?
?!
SKFF

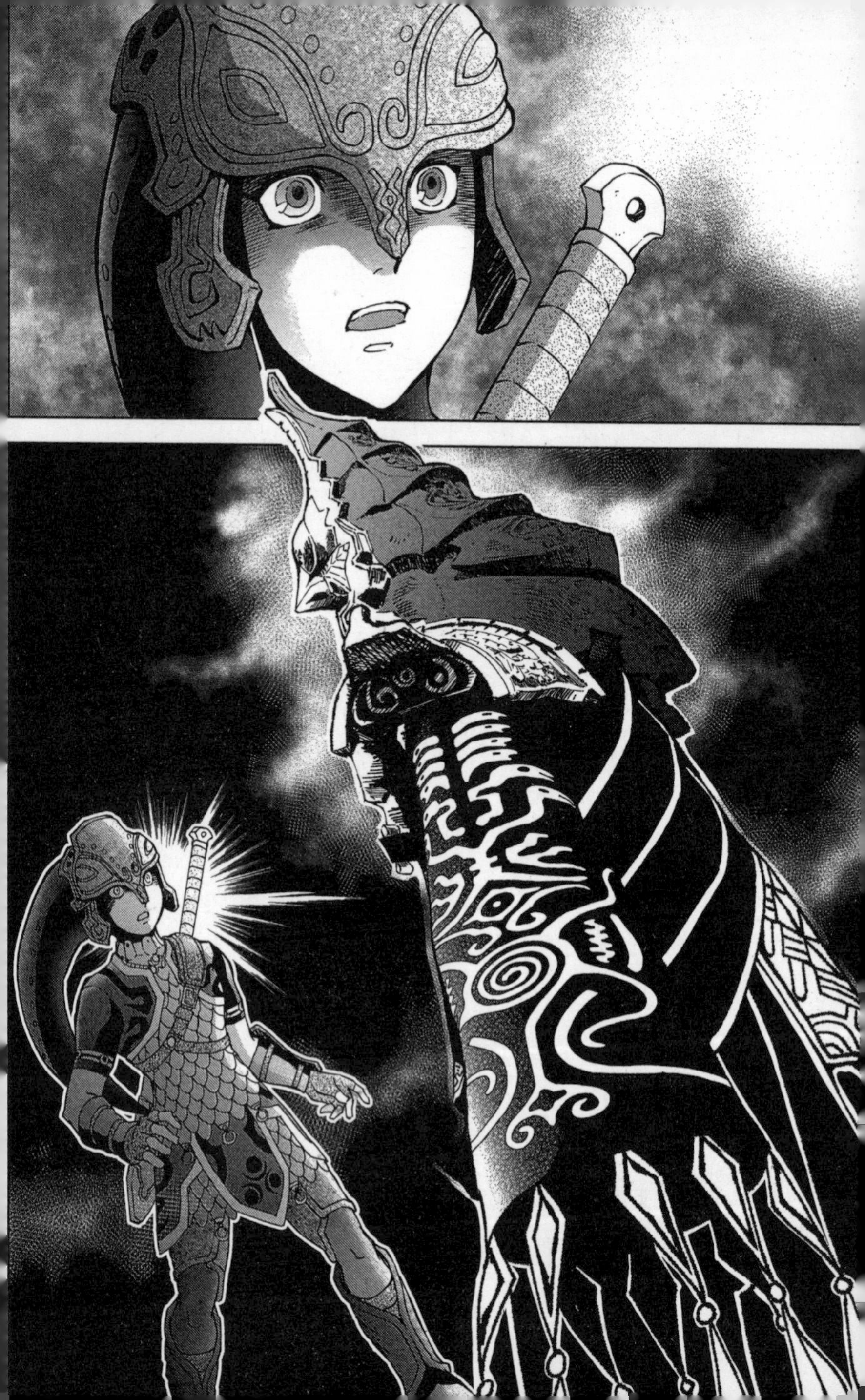

AUTHOR'S NOTE

In 2017 we were invited to be guests at fan events—one in Germany and two in the U.S.—where we signed autographs and met with fans. We were moved all over again at how appreciation of manga is the same all over the world, across cultures and customs. We hope that the manga will continue to reach as many people as possible from now on as well!

Akira Himekawa is the collaboration of two women, A. Honda and S. Nagano. Together they have created ten manga adventures featuring Link and the popular video game world of *The Legend of Zelda*™. Their most recent work, *The Legend of Zelda*™: *Twilight Princess*, is serialized digitally on Shogakukan's MangaONE app in Japan.

Hey! You're Reading in the Wrong Direction!

This is the **end** of this graphic novel!

To properly enjoy this VIZ graphic novel, please turn it around and begin reading from **right to left**. Unlike English, Japanese is read right to left, so Japanese comics are read in reverse order from the way English comics are typically read.

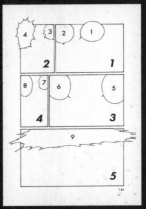

Follow the action this way

This book has been printed in the original Japanese format in order to preserve the orientation of the original artwork. Have fun with it!

THE LEGEND OF ZELDA™

•TWILIGHT PRINCESS•

Volume 4—VIZ Media Edition

story and art by
Akira Himekawa

translation John Werry
english adaptation Stan!
touch-up art & lettering Evan Waldinger
designer Shawn Carrico
editor Mike Montesa

Original design by Kazutada YOKOYAMA

The stories, characters and incidents mentioned in this publication are entirely fictional.

Printed in the U.S.A.

Published by VIZ Media, LLC
P.O. Box 77010
San Francisco, CA 94107

10 9 8 7 6 5 4 3 2 1
First printing, September 2018

VIZ MEDIA
viz.com

ratings.viz.com RATED T TEEN

PARENTAL ADVISORY
THE LEGEND OF ZELDA is rated T for Teen and is recommended for ages 13 and up. This volume contains fantasy violence.